LONGMAN SOCIAL POLICY IN MODERN BRITAIN

Series Editor:
Jo Campling

LONGMAN SOCIAL POLICY IN BRITAIN SERIES

Older People in Modern Society

Anthea Tinker

4th Edition

LONGMAN

London and New York

Addison Wesley Longman Limited,
Edinburgh Gate, Harlow,
Essex CM20 2JE, England
and Associated Companies throughout the world.

*Published in the United States of America
by Addison Wesley Longman Publishing Company, New York*

First published 1981
Second edition 1984
Third edition 1992
Fourth edition 1997

ISBN 0 582 29488 6

British Library Cataloguing-in-Publication Data

A catalogue record for this book is
available from the British Library

Library of Congress Cataloging-in-Publication Data
Tinker, Anthea
    Older people in modern society / Anthea Tinker. – 4th ed.
        p.   cm. – (Longman social policy in Britain series)
    Rev. ed. of: Elderly people in modern society. 3rd ed. 1992.
    Includes bibliographical references and index.
    ISBN 0–582–29488–6 (pbk.)
    1. Old age assistance–Great Britain.   2. Aged–Services for–
Great Britain.   I. Tinker, Anthea. Elderly people in modern
society.   II. Title.   III. Series
HV1481.G72T55   1997
362.6'0941–dc21   96-37684
                                                                              CIP

Set in 10/11pt Times by 33
Produced through Longman Malaysia, PP

To the beloved memory of my father and my grandparents

CONTENTS

EDITOR'S PREFACE

This series, written by practising teachers in universities, is produced for students who are required to study social policy and administration, either as social science undergraduates or on the various professional courses. The books provide studies focusing on essential topics in social policy and include new areas of discussion and research, to give students the opportunity to explore ideas and act as a basis of seminar work and further study. Each book combines an analysis of the selected theme, a critical narrative of the main developments and an assessment putting the topic into perspective as defined in the title. The supporting documents and comprehensive bibliography are an important aspect of the series, and the reader is clearly referred to the corresponding items in the section of documents which follows the main text.

In *Older People in Modern Society*, Anthea Tinker has brought together for the first time the literature and research evidence from many sources about this important group of people. Viewing the topic in the widest perspective, it provides basic information on the development of the services together with a more theoretical approach, redefining concepts like community care in relation to older people and their needs, and identifying likely issues for the future. It will be invaluable for students and indeed professionals in a variety of disciplines.

AUTHOR'S PREFACE TO THE FOURTH EDITION

In 1980 I wrote the first edition of this book and updated it in 1983 and 1992. In this new edition I again update the material and include the important new developments in policy, research and practice. But, as before, I have deliberately left in references to early studies because it is salutary to realise that many findings, for example about community care, are depressingly similar to those of the 1950s. It is not without significance that I have changed the title of the book from *Elderly People in Modern Society* to *Older People in Modern Society*. This is because of growing recognition that the term 'elderly people' gives the impression of a clearly defined group.

It is hoped that this book will not only be of general interest but will also be helpful to students and others who wish to follow up particular topics in essays, dissertations and theses. The references in this edition have been substantially increased because there has been an explosion of writing on gerontology.

As in previous editions I owe a great deal to others. My main debt is to my husband, without whose unfailing support none of these editions would have been written. On a personal level the death of my father and the birth of my grandchildren have enhanced my understanding of ageing. Many of the ideas have been discussed with former colleagues at City University and the Department of the Environment as well as with students on the many courses in which I have been involved. I am particularly grateful to colleagues at King's College London and to members of staff of Age Concern England and to others who have supplied information or commented on drafts. These include Janet Askham, Andy Brittan, Justin Davis Smith, Emily Grundy, Ruth Hancock, Claire Jarvis, Evelyn McEwen, Claudine McCreadie, Barbara Meredith, Jane Minter, Cathy Pharoah, Sally Redfern, Louise Russell, Sally West, Raphael Wittenberg and Fay Wright. Laura Lock's assistance in producing the manuscript is much appreciated. I alone, of course, am responsible for any errors and for the views expressed.

Anthea Tinker
August 1996

ACKNOWLEDGEMENTS

We are grateful to the following for permission to reproduce copyright material:

Ace Books for a figure from *Black and Asian Older People in Britain* by J. Barker (Age Concern England, 1984); Blackwell Publishers for an extract from *Family Obligations and Social Change* by J. Finch (Polity Press, 1989); the Controller of Her Majesty's Stationery Office for Crown copyright material; NHS Executive for the figure 'Structure of the NHS 1996'; Laing & Buisson for a table and a figure from *Care of Elderly People: Market Survey 1996* (Laing & Buisson, 1996); Joseph Rowntree Foundation for an extract from a Table from *Coming to Terms with Change?* by K. Young and N. Rao (LGC Communications, 1994).

LIST OF ABBREVIATIONS

AARP	American Association of Retired Persons
ACE	Age Concern England
ACIOG	Age Concern Institute of Gerontology (King's College London)
AIDS	Acquired Immune Deficiency Syndrome
AIMS	Advice Information and Mediation Service for Retirement Housing
ARHM	Association of Retirement Housing Managers
BASW	British Association of Social Workers
BMA	British Medical Association
CAB	Citizens Advice Bureau
CCETSW	Central Council for Education and Training in Social Work
CIPFA	Chartered Institute of Public Finance and Accountancy
COI	Central Office of Information
CPA	Centre for Policy on Ageing
CSO	Central Statistical Office
DFLE	Disability Free Life Expectancy
DHA	District Health Authority
DHSS	Department of Health and Social Security
DoE	Department of the Environment
DoH	Department of Health
DSS	Department of Social Security
DTI	Department of Trade and Industry
EC	European Community
EOC	Equal Opportunities Commission
FES	*Family Expenditure Survey*
FHSA	Family Health Services Authority
GB	Great Britain
GHS	*General Household Survey* (a continuous annual survey in GB)
GP	General Practitioner
HA	Housing Association
HALE	Healthy Active Life Expectancy
HAS	Health Advisory Service
HASS	Home Accident Surveillance System

HBF	Housebuilders Federation
HIP	Housing Investment Programme
HMSO	Her Majesty's Stationery Office
ICA	Invalid Care Allowance
JRF	Joseph Rowntree Foundation
LA	Local Authority
MHLG	Ministry of Housing and Local Government
MoH	Ministry of Health
MORI	Market and Opinion Research International
MPNI	Ministry of Pensions and National Insurance
MRC	Medical Research Council
NAB	National Assistance Board
NAHA	National Association of Health Authorities
NAO	National Audit Office
NCC	National Consumer Council
NCCOP	National Corporation for the Care of Old People
NCSS	National Council of Social Service
NCVO	National Council of Voluntary Organisations
NFHA	National Federation of Housing Associations
NHBC	National House Building Council
NHS	National Health Service
NHTPC	National Housing and Town Planning Council
NISW	National Institute of Social Work
NOPWC	National Old People's Welfare Council
OECD	Organisation for Economic Co-operation and Development
OPCS	Office of Population, Censuses and Surveys
OT	Occupational Therapy
PSSRU	Personal Social Services Research Unit (University of Kent)
QALY	Quality Adjusted Life Years
RAWP	Resource Allocation Working Party
RICA	Research Institute for Consumer Affairs
SBC	Supplementary Benefits Commission
SCPR	Social and Community Planning Research
Sec. of St.	Secretary(ies) of State
SERPS	State Earnings Related Pension Scheme
SPRU	Social Policy Research Unit (University of York)
SSI	Social Services Inspectorate
STG	Special Transitional Grant
STICERD	Suntory-Toyota International Centre for Economics and Related Disciplines, London School of Economics
UK	United Kingdom
UN	United Nations
USA	United States of America
WHO	World Health Organisation
WO	Welsh Office

PART ONE

The Background

CHAPTER 1

Introduction

This book is intended for students of social policy and administration (now usually referred to by the generic term social policy) and gerontology and for all who are concerned about older people. It is hoped that students on gerontology, social science, medical and nursing courses will find it a useful textbook. Professionals such as social workers, town planners, the medical and allied professions, together with those working for voluntary bodies all share an interest in this relatively new subject.

Social policy is a hybrid subject which owes its origins to the other social sciences. Because it is a synthesis – an interdisciplinary way of studying certain social institutions, problems and processes in society – it can draw on the theory of other disciplines, such as economics, politics and sociology. This brings advantages in looking at a subject from different perspectives. The corollary, however, is the need continually to decide in what depth to consider each aspect. In this book, for example, decisions had continually to be made about how far to explore such issues as the social implications of the family, the medical aspects of health, the architectural aspects of design and the political theories of decision making. Bringing together these aspects, even though not always in great depth, and relating them is the function and the fascination of social policy.

This book also reflects the current state of social policy in another way. The study of the subject has gone on in parallel with the growth of the welfare state, through the expansion and extension of the statutory and voluntary social services. Probably as a result of this, social policy has tended to concentrate on two major facets: a study of social pathology, and an evaluation of provision by the statutory and voluntary services. Until relatively recently policy makers and researchers have paid much less attention to alternative systems of providing care. However, not only does the market (e.g. private health care insurance) have a considerable role to play, but the involvement of family and neighbourly help was, until recently, largely ignored. In the last 25 years more attention has been given to examining the wider possibilities of the supply of social services. Researchers have looked beyond the conventional suppliers of services (statutory and voluntary bodies) to the more ill-defined area of what is provided by family, friends and neighbours.

Like social policy, gerontology – the study of ageing – is a relatively new academic discipline. It is less developed in this country than in the United States, but is beginning to expand. This is partly because there are now more older people in the population than in the middle of the century. Among other reasons are the interest of the commercial sector in the growing number of older people with substantial assets, the involvement of old people themselves and media interest (Tinker 1990). Professionals are increasingly finding that older people form one of the main client groups. Within gerontology, geriatric medicine is well established but has tended to concentrate, as does most medical practice, on the problems which older people have. Research in both the clinical and biological aspects of ageing is more advanced than social gerontology. The latter is described as 'the study of the ways in which social and cultural factors enter into the ageing process' (Hendricks and Hendricks 1986: 15). Although social gerontology has been slower to develop, social policy analysts, sociologists, demographers, psychologists, geographers, economists and other social scientists are now displaying more interest and undertaking research.

Older people are particularly interesting to study. Not only are they one of the largest of what are labelled 'special groups', but they are also the group to which in due course most of us will belong. Unlike deviant groups such as offenders, older people represent a cross-section of ordinary people whose sole common denominator is their age. Because they are such a large group, and because most people will in time reach old age, it is a matter of self-interest to consider their role in, and contribution to, society as well as their problems and needs.

This book attempts to present some of the evidence about older people in society, neither assuming that they necessarily have the same characteristics as younger age groups, nor assuming that they present no problems. There are widely contrasting images of this group. 'Senior citizen' or 'silly old woman'? Consumers of large amounts of social services, or the proud minority who prefer to suffer cold or poverty and not ask for help? A golden age, or one which is 'sans everything'? This book is intended to bring together existing evidence about older people and how they live. It is not written from a particular political or other stance and its aim is to give the facts and summarise both research and the views of others. For those who have extended essays or a thesis to prepare it gives ample references and points to other sources of information.

The outline of the book is as follows. Part one provides background material. First a picture is presented of older people giving basic data about who they are. This brings out some of the reasons why they represent one of the most important challenges to social policy. Alongside this demographic background there is a discussion about how society sees ageing. Then follows a review of the literature which shows that what has been written falls into a number of different categories.

Part two seeks to outline the major general developments in policy, first with a broad brush and then in detail for individual services, with a concentration on statutory provision. This is followed by evidence about informal networks of care.

In Part three an assessment is made of the position and status of older people in society. First there is a discussion about the contribution of older people both to their own welfare and to that of others. Then there is an examination of some of the general problems. These include different views of need, variations in services, the evaluation of services, the meaning of community care, economic constraints and issues to do with a mixed economy of welfare. Finally, the topic is considered in perspective. Similarities and differences with other groups, priority for resources, the stresses and compensations for older people in modern society and the implications for professionals are discussed.

Part four comprises the documents which relate to the text.

CHAPTER 2

A profile of older people

Introduction

One of the concerns of social policy is with particular groups. It is important, therefore, that they should be defined with some accuracy. Levels of disability can be measured. Offenders can be categorised by type of crime and by kind of sentence. Ethnic minorities can be divided into groups by country of birth, country of parents' birth and by the colour of their skin.

In contrast, older people are the whole of a generation who have survived to a certain age. *Our Future Selves* is the apt title of one book (Roberts 1970). They are not a deviant group or one small special section of the population. They are ordinary people who happen to have reached a particular age. This cannot be emphasised too much, particularly to professionals who are, as a result of their training and experience at work, concerned primarily with the abnormal.

Problems of definition

One definition is those over retirement age, which is usually measured by the age at which a person is eligible for a state pension. In the United Kingdom (UK) this is currently 65 for a man and 60 for a woman; but under recent legislation for equalisation between men and women it will become 65 for both (see also Chapter 5). The European Commission (EC) uses 60 and the United States of America (USA) Bureau of the Census 55. On terminology, a survey of the over-60s across Europe revealed that one third like to be called 'older people' and one third 'senior citizens' (Walker 1993). A survey of the over-55s in Great Britain (GB) showed that similar proportions would like to be called 'retired' and 'senior citizens' (Midwinter 1991). The term 'older people' is increasingly being used, for example, an OPCS study *Trends in Dependency Among Older People in England* states that in 1991 there were over 7.5 million 'elderly (or older) people aged 65 or more in England' (Bone 1996: 1). (Note that in general the term 'older people' is used in this book except where other research, publications or demographic data have used another term.)

The lack of a generally agreed definition creates difficulties for those who wish to compare research data. What is particularly interesting is the distinction which was increasingly being made in the 1970s in medical and social studies between young and old older people. For example, Hodkinson stated that it is older people over the age of 75 with whom the geriatrician is mostly concerned (Hodkinson 1975). Two studies which came out in 1978, *The Elderly at Home* (Hunt 1978) and *Beyond Three Score and Ten* (Abrams 1978, 1980), made comparisons between older people under the age of 75 and those above that age. It is significant that 80 and over replaced 75 and over as a category in *Social Trends* from 1990 (Central Statistical Office 1990). Interest is also now being focused on the over-90s (e.g. Bury and Holme 1991) and on centenarians (e.g. OPCS and Government Actuary's Department 1994).

The 'third age' has also become a focus of increasing attention. Peter Laslett traces the origin of this interest to the founding of the Universities of the Third Age in France in the 1970s. In his book, *A Fresh Map of Life* (1989), Laslett describes the life course as: 'First comes an era of dependence, socialisation, immaturity and education; second an era of independence, maturity and responsibility, of earning and saving; third an era of personal fulfilment; and fourth an era of final dependence' (1989: 4). The third age formed the basis for an inquiry which reported in 1993 (Carnegie Inquiry into the Third Age 1993).

If older people are so varied, why are they then labelled as one group? One main reason is that retirement, which is a relatively recent phenomenon (Hannah 1986), marks a watershed. In pre-industrial societies and for women not in the labour market or for the self-employed, the definition may be less satisfactory. People may go on working for as long as they are physically capable and, if they continue in their job, their status remains that of a worker. But for most people now retirement brings an end to that particular role.

The folly of generalising

Few people would attribute the same characteristics to a 30-year-old as they would to a 60-year-old. Why then should those in their sixties and in their nineties be classed together as one group? It is very easy to assume that all older people want this or feel that. It might be more realistic to generalise if people were divided according to how old they appeared in behaviour, attitudes and thought. 'As old as you feel' is one approach, and if to act old is to be set in one's ways, to lack flexibility of thought and to look generally old-fashioned, then there are many people in their twenties and thirties who would qualify.

Social class, family support, physical and mental disability, religion and work patterns vary among older people as much as they do among the rest of the population. A growing number of writers are pointing to the wide differences between various groups of older people such as between men and women and between the white population and black and minority ethnic groups. It is therefore only reasonable to expect that the demands of this group on society, their expectations of it and their contributions to it will be as varied as those of the rest of the population.

David Hobman, the former Director of Age Concern England (ACE), once rightly rounded on a speaker at a conference who described this group rather patronisingly as 'old dears'. He pointed out that some might well be the exact opposite of 'old dears'. There is a tendency for *all* age groups to generalise on occasion about other age groups, for example, 'immature young', 'wet behind the ears', 'middle-aged fixed in their ways', and so on. It seems unlikely that someone who is awkward and finds difficulty in making friends will suddenly become the life and soul of the bingo sessions on reaching the magic age of retirement. And why the association between bingo and old age? Just as some teenagers enjoy chess while others opt for pop music, so the leisure pursuits of older people are likely to be just as varied.

How society sees ageing

It is difficult to make comparisons with attitudes in past years since so little is known except what is recorded in fiction. Was there a time when old people in this country were looked on as founts of all knowledge and repositories of great wisdom? Even if there was, there are several reasons why this should not be so now. Children were much less likely to have had a grandparent alive in the last century and so the latter had scarcity value. Older people were also likely to have had comparatively greater skills and knowledge, since these changed little from generation to generation. Today the rapid increase in knowledge and changes in technology may make it difficult for one generation to keep up with the next. This is particularly so in specialist subjects.

Shakespeare painted a depressing picture of old age in *As You Like It* and one commentator on social policy took the final two words of one speech 'sans everything' as the title for her book (Robb 1967). The physical changes that come with age are varied and do not necessarily develop at the same time in each older person. It is useful to have some understanding of these physical and mental changes, and to know what is normal and what is abnormal. Keddie, a consultant psychiatrist, argues that: 'Positive thinking is needed here. Unfortunately many of the public still feel that little can be done for an elderly man or woman who is ill – it is assumed that the old person's condition is simply due to his age. In fact, most old people are suffering from a treatable disease of one sort or another' (1978:

64). Hodkinson, a geriatrician, has taken a similar view (1975: 19). Freer, writing about health and health care of older people, claims that much discussion is inappropriately negative, pessimistic and too often couched in crisis terms (1988: 13). A similarly optimistic conclusion was taken from the research on health in the third age (Evans *et al.* 1992).

In what way, then, does society view this ageing process, and what bearing has this on social policy? There is little doubt that in a society that seems geared to youth there is great emphasis on remaining young. Advice on appearance, particularly hair and skin, is not confined to women. And when people are old the terms used to describe them, such as members of 'evergreen' clubs, seem to deny the process of ageing. This may be reinforced by the nostalgia of some older people for their youth.

Growing importance is being attached to the effect of images of ageing and steps are being suggested to counteract poor images. Featherstone and Hepworth (1993, see also Featherstone and Wernick 1995), who have written extensively on images and ageing, comment:

Human society is a process and it is dangerous to assume that attitudes towards elderly people and images of old age which currently exist enjoyed the same currency in the past or necessarily will do so in the future. Hence for all the talk about our youth dominated society we should be aware that while the qualities associated with youthfulness have been valued in history, this valuation must be related to the balance of power between the generations, which undergoes periodic fluctuations.

(1993: 332)

Note also the jealousy of some older people for what they see as the delights and privileges of the young.

Will more attention now be focused on older people since their numbers have increased so rapidly? A distinguished social scientist claimed in 1975 that although the fortunes of teenagers had been the focus of discussion and research since the 1960s, elderly people were about to come into their own (Abrams 1975) [Document 1]. Yet society does not always find it easy to come to terms with this group. As Hobman has noted, there are a great many myths about ageing [Document 2]. Comfort (1977) has argued that ageism – discrimination against old people on the grounds of their being old – is part of the prejudice against older people (see also Bytheway 1995). Its impact on employment policies is explored in Chapter 5.

The sociological concept of disengagement must also be noted (see also Chapter 12). This is the theory that the individual, recognising the inevitability of death, starts a process of advance adjustment to it. But this view is now strongly challenged as neither necessarily happening, nor being desirable. Older people themselves are recording their anger at being put into a ghetto at 60 or 65. For example, one wrote about the experiences of her generation under the title of *The Alienated* (Elder 1977). Other authors recording the views of older people entitled their book, *I Don't Feel Old: The Experience of Later Life* (Thompson *et al.* 1990). In the 1980s and 1990s many newspapers and journals have gone almost to the extreme in giving a positive picture of the accomplishments of active older people.

It is important to raise these questions about how society sees ageing because it has implications for social policy. The assumptions that 'the elderly' are a social problem or even a burden, that they have similar aspirations and that they all need certain services are all questionable.

Numbers

When considering the provision of services it is important to try to get as accurate an estimate as possible of how many recipients there will be. As with any kind of crystal gazing, the future is not always easy to predict. Some elements, however, are relatively certain. If, for example, there are 4 million young people aged 16–18 about to leave school and go on to higher education or work, it is probable that in 10 years' time something like that number will be needing services appropriate to people in their late twenties. But forecasting further ahead assumes no major alteration in circumstances. War can wipe out almost a complete generation and migration can have an effect. Illnesses, such as AIDS, or an increase in unhealthy habits such as smoking or drug-taking can cause premature death or turn a healthy person into one who is physically disabled. On the other hand, medical advances, such as the early diagnosis of illnesses or cures for what seemed terminal illnesses, can prolong life.

One striking feature has been the increase in the number of elderly people since the beginning of the twentieth century. While the total population in the UK has grown, it has been at a much slower rate than that which has occurred among elderly people. Table 2.1 summarises this growth. From this table it can be seen that projections show that both the total population and that of people of pensionable age will increase. The projected rise in numbers of the latter from 1994 to 2001 is only 100,000 and from 1994 to 2011 1.3 million. The more dramatic increase is later when the 10.6 million in 1994 is projected to rise to 14.8 million in 2025 (Table 2.1 and Figure 2.1). Fluctuating numbers are largely due to past changes in the number of birth (births are a function of the fertility rate and numbers of women of child-bearing age). The low birth rate during the First World War, the post-war bulge, the trough of births in 1940–42, the post-Second World War bulge, the baby boom of the 1960s and the 'baby bust' of the 1970s, all affect numbers of elderly people in subsequent years [Document 3]. These changes in the number of births are one of the reasons why demographic forecasting has proved to be fraught with problems. The ageing of the population

Table 2.1 **Population figures United Kingdom 1901–2025**

	Total population (millions)	Percentage increase	Elderly* (millions)	Percentage increase
1901[1†]	38.2	–	2.4	–
1951[1]	50.5	32.2	6.9	188
1981[1]	56.4	11.5	10.0	44.9
1991[2]	57.8	2.6	10.6	5.6
1994[3]	58.4	1.0	10.6	0.3
2001[3]	59.5	1.8	10.7	0.7
2011[3]	60.5	1.7	11.9	10.7
2025[3]	61.1	1.0	14.8	24.6

* Males 65 and over, females 60 and over.
† UK as then constituted.
[1] Estimated figures derived from CSO, *Social Trends*, (No. 13), 1983, Table 1.2, p. 12.
[2] Projected figures from Government Actuary's Department, Population Projections 1991–2061, provided on disk.
[3] Projected figures from Government Actuary's Department, Population Projections 1994–2064, provided on disk (note that women's right to draw the state pension at 65 rather than 60 is being phased in between 2010 and 2020).

is also due to 'the rapid decline in premature mortality in the first half of this century, and to a more recent, and projected future, reduction in mortality at older ages' (Bone 1996: 1, see also Grundy 1995b: 4).

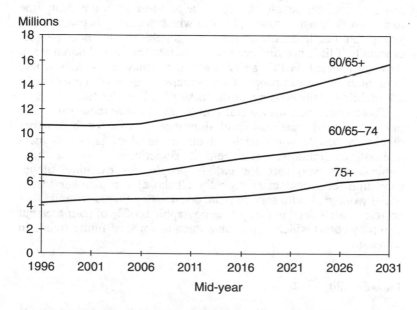

Figure 2.1 **Projected size of the elderly population, United Kingdom**
Source: Gerontology Data Service at Age Concern Institute of Gerontology, King's College London. Based on Government Actuary's 1994 projections.

Regional and local variations

It has already been stated that generalisations about older people are dangerous. It is equally unwise to assume that overall figures, such as the percentage of elderly people in the population, will be the same for every part of the country. There are considerable regional variations.

Twenty-one per cent of all residents in GB in the 1991 Census were aged 60 or over (OPCS *Topic Monitor* July 1993). (Note that the Census covers the whole population but the *General Household Surveys* only cover people living in private households.) In some areas, such as some Inner London boroughs and the South Midlands it was under 18 per cent. Reasons for a low proportion may include an above average number of young families from non-white ethnic groups (Grundy 1996a). The highest proportion of people over the age of 60 was mainly in coastal retirement areas such as the district of Christchurch in Dorset and Rother in East Sussex, both of which had 37 per cent. The region with the highest proportion was the South West (24 per cent) and the lowest the South East (20 per cent). The reasons for these differences are various. An above-average number of older people can be the result of people finding an attractive area to retire to or younger people may have moved out – say from an inner-city area into the suburbs. Or there can be a bulge of people reaching retirement age at the same time, as a consequence of a large group of younger people having in the past moved at the same time to new work or a new town. The area which suddenly became full of young families becomes in due time largely one of older people, especially if little housing becomes available for their children when they get married. Within an area too, there may be pockets where large numbers of old people live, perhaps because of the nature or affordability of the housing, or the lack of facilities for families.

Those concerned with social policy have to take these variations into account. At a national level allowance is made for the number of elderly people when deciding on the level of grants to local authorities. Similarly, extra help is sometimes given to those professionals who care for elderly people, for example, higher capitation fees for doctors. Locally, all those who plan services – social workers, health service planners, housing managers and other professionals – need not only a demographic profile of their area but also projections which will enable them to forecast future trends in demand.

The very old

It has already been seen that the total number of elderly people will not rise appreciably in the near future. What is most significant now is the decline in the number of young elderly and the rise in the number of old elderly. Table 2.2 demonstrates that the projected drop of about 400,000 in numbers of the under-75s is matched by a rise of the same number of the over-75s by the beginning of the next century. The percentage of people of pensionable age who are over 75 has risen from 21 per cent in 1901 to 37 per cent in 1994. It is then projected to rise to 41 per cent in 2001 and fluctuates after that (Table 2.2). Looking at the over-80s in the UK there were estimated to be 0.7 million in 1951 and 2.4 million in 1996. Numbers are projected to increase to 2.6 million in 2006 and 3.2 million in 2025 [Document 4].

As already mentioned, part of the reason for this increase in the numbers and proportions of very old people is the bulge in the number of births in previous years. But there is another process involved, a rise in survivorship. Not only has expectation of life at birth increased but so has that at later ages. Expectation of life in the UK at birth in 1901 for a male was 45.5 years and for a female 49 years. In 1961 this had risen to 67.8 and 73.6 years respectively. In 1996 it was 74.4 years for a male and 79.7 for a female (CSO 1996: 130). Life expectancy at 60 increased by 2.4 years for men (from 15.3 years to 17.7 years) and 2.1 years for women (from 19.8 years to 21.9 years) between 1971 and 1991 (Grundy 1996a).

The significance of the growing number of very old people is that this group makes the highest demands on health and social services (Chapter 6). Disability rises rapidly with age and those who are over 75 years make greater demands than those between 65 and 75, and those over 85 years make even heavier demands (OPCS, 1996). In

Table 2.2 The very old as a percentage of elderly people in the United Kingdom 1901–2025

	All elderly people* (millions)	Elderly people* under 75 (millions)	The very old – 75 and over (millions)	Percentage of all elderly people who are very old
1901[1†]	2.4	1.9	0.5	21
1951[1]	6.9	5.1	1.8	26
1981[1]	10.0	6.8	3.3	33
1991[2]	10.6	6.6	4.0	38
1994[3]	10.6	6.7	4.0	37
2001[3]	10.7	6.3	4.4	41
2011[3]	11.9	7.3	4.5	38
2025[3]	14.8	8.9	5.9	40

* Males 65 and over, females 60 and over.
† UK as then constituted.
[1] Estimated figures derived from CSO, *Social Trends*, (No. 13), 1983, Table 1.2, p. 12.
[2] Projected figures from Government Actuary's Department, Population Projections 1991–2061, provided on disk.
[3] Projected figures from Government Actuary's Department, Population Projections 1994–2064, provided on disk.

the 1991 Census 24 per cent of all women and 14 per cent of men aged 85 and over in GB were in a residential institution (OPCS *Topic Monitor* December 1993a). However, one should beware of generalisations. A study of the over-90s concluded that the depiction of very old age as constituting major levels of dependence needs to be qualified (Bury and Holme 1991).

Proportions of elderly people in the population and dependency rates

Elderly people have formed an increasingly large section of the population since the beginning of the century, but the percentage of pensionable age is projected to remain at 18 per cent until 2011 when it becomes 20 per cent rising to 24 per cent in 2025 (Table 2.3).

In relation to publicly provided services which have to be paid for largely by people of working age, and other goods and services which are produced, the percentage of the population which is dependent is significant. Two groups are usually regarded as dependent, children under school-leaving age and people over the age of retirement. The latter are not considered to be of working age, although some do work or are productive as volunteers, carers, and so on. It is also assumed that all those of working age do work, and if at any time any large number are unemployed or otherwise not in the workforce (and therefore dependent), this could upset calculations.

Interestingly, dependency rates, that is the number of dependants related to those of working age, have altered little throughout this

Table 2.3 Elderly people* as a percentage of the population of the United Kingdom 1901–2025

	Total population (millions)	Elderly people* (millions)	Elderly people as percentage of total
1901[1][†]	38.2	2.4	6
1951[1]	50.5	6.9	14
1981[1]	56.4	10.0	18
1991[2]	57.8	10.6	18
1994[3]	58.4	10.6	18
2001[3]	59.5	10.7	18
2011[3]	60.5	11.9	20
2025[3]	61.1	14.8	24

* Males 65 and over, females 60 and over.
[†] UK as then constituted.
[1] Estimated figures derived from CSO, *Social Trends*, (No. 13), 1983, Table 1.2, p. 12.
[2] Projected figures from Government Actuary's Department, Population Projections 1991–2061, provided on disk.
[3] Projected figures from Government Actuary's Department, Population Projections 1994–2064, provided on disk.

Table 2.4 **Percentage of the population who are 'dependants' United Kingdom 1901–2025**

	Total population (millions)	Elderly people* (millions)	Children under 16 (millions)	Percentage who are 'dependent'*
1901[1][†]	38.2	2.4	13.2	41
1951[1]	50.5	6.9	12.0	37
1981[1]	56.4	10.0	12.5	40
1991[2]	57.8	10.6	11.7	39
1994[3]	58.4	10.6	12.1	39
2001[3]	59.5	10.7	12.1	38
2011[3]	60.5	11.9	11.1	38
2025[3]	61.1	14.8	10.7	42

* Elderly people: males 65 and over, females 60 and over; Dependants: children under 16 (15 for 1901–51) plus elderly people.
[†] UK as then constituted.
[1] Estimated figures derived from CSO, *Social Trends*, (No. 13), 1983, Table 1.2, p. 12.
[2] Projected figures from Government Actuary's Department, Population Projections 1991–2061, provided on disk.
[3] Projected figures from Government Actuary's Department, Population Projections 1994–2064, provided on disk.

century (Table 2.4). The reason there has been so little change during a period of rapidly increasing numbers of elderly people is that there has been a simultaneous decline in the total fertility rate (the average number of children that would be born to each woman if the current age-specific birth rates persisted throughout her child-bearing life).

Not until the second decade of the next century does the ratio of dependants increase much above today's level, from 39 per cent in 1994 to 42 per cent in 2025 (Table 2.4 and Figure 2.2). The percentage of people of working age, that is, 16–64 (but note that many of those aged 16–19 will be dependent) will drop from 64 per cent in 1994 to 58 per cent in 2031 (calculated from CSO 1996: 39, note that this is not a straight fall but there are fluctuations). As the number of workers per pensioner decreases there will be pressure on pension provision (Chapter 14). Some suggest that the effects of the so-called 'demographic time bomb', the fall in numbers of young people joining the labour market, have been exaggerated (National Economic Development Office 1989). In *The Future of Welfare* it is shown that the numbers of people of working age for each elderly person is falling, but less rapidly in Great Britain than elsewhere (Hills 1993).

The balance of the sexes

In general there tend to be more women than men among older people, especially among the very old, because women, on average,

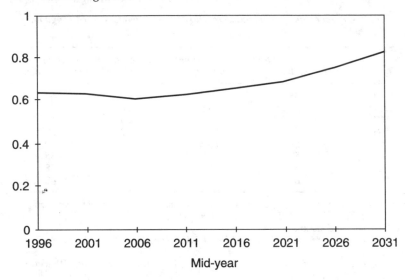

Figure 2.2 Projected dependency rates[1] 1996–2029

[1]The dependency ratio is the under-16s and elderly people of pensionable age (i.e. men at 65 and women at 60) and over as a proportion of the working population.
Source: Gerontology Data Service at Age Concern Institute of Gerontology, King's College London. Based on Government Actuary's 1994 projections.

live longer. Whether this will continue in the long term is a matter for debate. In the 1970s there was already evidence that women were drinking and smoking more and becoming more involved in stressful occupations (Department of Health and Social Security (DHSS) 1976c: 38–9). More women are also becoming drivers with the subsequent dangers of death and accidents. Another factor that can alter the balance is if large numbers of either sex emigrate or are killed (e.g. World War 1).

In the foreseeable future women are expected to continue to outnumber men heavily in the upper age groups in the U.K:

in 1995 there were 3.0 million men and 3.8 million women aged 65–79 and 0.7 million men and 1.6 million women aged over 80.

It is projected that:

in 2030 there will be 4.8 million men and 5.3 million women aged 65–79 and 1.5 million men and 2.3 million women aged over 80. (Government Actuaries Department mid-1994 based population projections provided on disk, 1996).

Part of the reason for the excess of females is the greater improvement in female mortality. They are, however, more likely to be physically disabled (see Chapter 6).

With whom elderly people live

Ninety-five per cent of people aged 65 and over in GB lived in private households in 1991 and only 5 per cent in communal establishments (institutions) (OPCS *Topic Monitor* December 1993a derived from Table 2 and OPCS 1993). A striking feature of recent years has been the growing proportion of elderly people living alone. In 1961, 7 per cent of households in GB were made up of one person over pensionable age, while in 1994/5 this had risen to 15 per cent (CSO 1996: 51). What is particularly significant is the link between growing older and living alone. The *GHS* in 1994 showed that in Great Britain 50 per cent (40 per cent in 1973) of the over-75s (33 per cent of men and 59 per cent of women) lived alone. The figures for those aged 65–74 were 29 per cent (18 per cent for men and 39 per cent for women) (OPCS 1996: 38).

The trend towards smaller households seems likely to continue, not only because of an increase in numbers of elderly people but also because of the increase in numbers of young people, especially men, living alone and also because of divorce. However, older people are expected to form a declining proportion of one-person households. The largest proportion of people living alone in 1994 were women of pensionable age or over (12 per cent) but this is projected to remain the same in 2011 (CSO 1996: 50–1). The largest increase recently has been of people under pensionable age, and by 2011 it is predicted that men will form the largest group of one-person households (13 per cent compared with 8 per cent in 1994) (CSO 1996: 50–1).

In 1994 in the *GHS* in GB for people over the age of 65:

- 62 per cent of men and 35 per cent of women lived with their spouse only;
- 24 per cent of men and 49 per cent of women lived alone;
- 9 per cent of men and 4 per cent of women lived with a spouse and others;
- 2 per cent of men and 7 per cent of women lived with a son or daughter;
- 3 per cent of men and 4 per cent of women lived in another type of household.

(OPCS 1996: 138)

Overall co-residence rates between adult children and their older parents or parents-in-law are low in England and Wales, but vary considerably with socio-demographic characteristics (Grundy 1992).

The number of elderly people living alone could be hailed as an advance in that they are not being forced to live either with relatives or in residential care. There is indeed a good deal of evidence that this is what they want. But there are implications for services. For example, an old person living alone may find it difficult to summon help in an emergency.

Marital status

Widows comprise the largest group of elderly people. In the 1991 Census in Great Britain 43 per cent of women of pensionable age were widowed compared with 18 per cent of men (OPCS *Topic Monitor* February 1993). The 1994 *GHS* showed that nearly two thirds (65 per cent) of women aged 75 or over were widowed, whereas a similar proportion (63 per cent) of men in this age group were still married (CSO 1996: 42). This reflects the fact that on average women live longer than men and also tend to marry men older than themselves. Few elderly people are divorced (3.7 per cent of those aged 60 and over in 1991 compared with 2.1 per cent in 1981) but this is likely to increase as divorced younger people move into old age (OPCS *Topic Monitor* July 1993).

Elderly people from black and minority ethnic groups

In 1995 there were 3.2 million people (6 per cent of the population in GB) from black and minority ethnic groups compared with 52.8 million from the white population (CSO 1996: 40). But whereas 21 per cent of the white population were aged 60 or over, only 6 per cent of the black and minority ethnic groups were. There are other differences such as the larger proportion of white people of pensionable age who live alone. In the 1991 Census 16 per cent of white households comprised a lone pensioner compared with 4 per cent of black and 2 per cent of Indian, Pakistani and Bangladeshi households (OPCS *Topic Monitor* December 1993b). There is also danger in generalising about ethnic minorities. For example, Indian, Pakistani and Bangladeshi populations are more likely to live within extended families than white, West Indian, Chinese, African and Arab populations (Haskey 1989, see also Chapter 9).

International comparisons

One of the important demographic contrasts in the world today is the variation in the proportion of elderly people which occurs when there is a shift from high mortality/high fertility to low mortality/low fertility. In industrialised countries people over the age of 65 were on average 13 per cent of the population in 1995 while in developing countries they averaged only 4.5 per cent (Kinsella 1996: 33).

Conclusion

Numbers of elderly people have quadrupled since the beginning of the century. While in 1901 in the UK people over pensionable age represented 6 per cent of the population, in 1994 this figure had grown to 18 per cent. Future projections suggest that there will be little rise in numbers or proportions of people of pensionable age until the beginning of the next century. There is, therefore, a short period of relative stability. By 2025 numbers of women over the age of 60 and men over the age of 65 in the United Kingdom will have risen by 4.2 million compared with 1994, and the proportion will rise from 18 per cent to 24 per cent. Elderly women outnumber elderly men in all age groups.

The differences that have been commented upon in relation to gender, living arrangements and where people live make it clear that any generalisations are unwise.

There are still many unanswered questions. For example it is difficult to forecast what medical advances there may be which will enable people to live longer or help them to be less disabled. On the other hand, there may be a swing in public opinion against positive medical intervention to help keep them alive.

CHAPTER 3

General review of the literature

Introduction

It is remarkable that although numbers of elderly people more than doubled between 1901 and 1945 very little information was gathered in these years on either elderly people at home or in residential care. 'A dearth of published information and, apparently, of interest too' is how Townsend and Wedderburn (1965: 10) described the situation [Document 5].

To obtain a picture of what has been written one must search a number of different sources. The medical profession, sociologists, psychologists, geographers, social workers and many others have looked at this group from their own different viewpoints. Similarly, research has been undertaken by a variety of bodies: central government, local authorities, voluntary societies and political parties, as well as by individuals. In this chapter reference is made to some literature which was written some years ago either because it is important to see a thread, such as the development of a multidisciplinary approach, in what has been written or because it is still relevant.

Social surveys

One of the first large-scale social surveys was undertaken in 1944–6 for the Rowntree Committee on the *Problems of Ageing and the Care of Old People* and published in 1947. As this was a pioneering study the terms of reference to the report are given [Document 6]. Most surveys carried out in the 1940s and early 1950s were concerned with medical aspects of ageing, although some, such as those by Walker (1952) and Sheldon (1948), while starting from a medical viewpoint, went on to consider further issues. Others were restricted in geographical scope.

The social surveys of the late 1950s, the 1960s and 1970s concentrated mainly on the frail, sick and needy. They were primarily concerned with the relationship between need and provision, and second with the importance of taking into account informal networks (particularly the family) as well as statutory provision. Some of the government surveys had a specific focus. Among the early ones were the Phillips Report on *The Economic and Financial Problems of the Provision for Old Age* (Chancellor of the Exchequer 1954) and the Boucher Report on *Survey of Services Available to the Chronic Sick and Elderly 1954–55* (MoH 1957).

At the same time sociological studies were throwing new light on the place of older people in the family. One of the earliest and most important was Townsend's study of *The Family Life of Old People* (Townsend 1957). Although there were certain factors peculiar to Bethnal Green, where the research took place, the findings about the close links between the generations surprised a good many people. Willmott and Young's subsequent study of Woodford, *Family and Class in a London Suburb*, was an attempt to compare middle-class families with the working-class ones of Bethnal Green (Willmott and Young 1960). They found that the ties between relatives were much looser, but none the less still quite considerable.

All the research relating to social provision showed that this was not as effective as many had supposed. One of the first studies was Townsend and Wedderburn's *The Aged in the Welfare State*, which was part of a cross-national survey to find out how effective social services were in meeting the needs of old people (Townsend and Wedderburn 1965). The authors set out in particular to discover whether certain functions formerly performed by the family had been taken over by the social services. Their findings did not support this view. The cross-national survey, *Old People in Three Industrial Societies*, clarified and substantiated certain concepts related to the family and to isolation among old people (Shanas *et al.* 1968). The researchers found, for example, that there was flexibility in the patterns of relationships which existed in families between the generations. Even when families were small, they noted, old people would adapt and substitute and could often turn to their siblings or the children of siblings for support.

The Government Social Survey's *Social Welfare for the Elderly* questioned whether planning was being based on the needs of elderly people or on what the local authorities thought they could afford (Harris 1968). The 1960s also brought some useful studies of specific topics including that by Ministry of Pensions and National Insurance (MPNI), *Financial and Other Circumstances of Retirement Pensioners* (MPNI 1966), and that by the Government Social Survey, *Handicapped and Impaired in Great Britain* (Harris 1971).

Tunstall's *Old and Alone* was another part of the cross-national survey (Tunstall 1966). As well as his conclusion that social policy must do more to help old people remain independent, his findings and subsequent discussion about living alone, social isolation and loneliness are as relevant now as when they were published. In the 1970s both academic and the more popular literature turned to the particular problems of very old people. Two major social surveys were published in 1978 which made some comparisons. Abrams in *Beyond Three Score and Ten* surveyed 1,646 old people to discover more about their needs, conditions and resources (Abrams 1978, 1980). The other study which has proved to be an important benchmark was *The Elderly at Home* (Hunt 1978). This was a survey of 2,622 elderly people living in private households and was designed to provide information on their social circumstances as a base for social policy. One of the issues which this study brought out was the differences between young and old elderly people.

In the 1980s there were very few national surveys. One of the main sources of information came from the 1980 *General Household Survey (GHS)* (OPCS 1982) which contained an extensive series of questions to people aged 65 and over which were repeated with some minor changes in 1985 (OPCS 1989) and again in 1991 (OPCS 1994a) and 1994 (OPCS 1996). These surveys have been a rich source of data for secondary analysis. Another survey which yielded a great deal of data was that on disability, undertaken by OPCS. Of particular interest are *The Prevalence of Disability Among Adults* (Martin *et al.* 1988), *The Financial Circumstances of Disabled Adults Living in Private Households* (Martin and White 1988) and *Disabled Adults: Services, Transport and Employment* (Martin *et al.* 1989). These surveys confirmed that the overall rate of disability rises with age, slowly at first then accelerating after 50 and rising very steeply after about 70.

After the earlier bursts of work on the general circumstances of elderly people and their health and use of various social services it is interesting that housing is coming to the fore. Two large national surveys were carried out in the 1980s by the Department of the Environment (DoE) in conjunction with the DHSS. The first was a study of innovatory ways of enabling older people to stay in their own homes, *Staying at Home: Helping Elderly People* (Tinker 1984) and the second *An Evaluation of Very Sheltered Housing* (Tinker 1989b). A later large study was of the housing needs of, and provision for, elderly people (McCafferty 1994).

Other surveys included one by OPCS of 3,500 people aged 55–69 in 1988–9 on retirement and retirement plans which yielded much data on jobs, pensions and support given and received (Bone *et al.* 1992). The British Gas Report on *Attitudes to Ageing 1991* was based on interviews with 764 people over the age of 55 and provided useful information on this topic (Midwinter 1991). *Life After Ninety*, a national survey of 222 people in 1986, was a pioneering study of this age group (Bury and Holme 1991).

The 1981 and 1991 Censuses have yielded crucial data on elderly people, as have various general surveys such as the annual *Health Surveys for England, British Social Attitudes Surveys*, and *British Household Panel Surveys* as well as continuous surveys such as the *Family Resources Survey* and *Family Expenditure Survey.*

What is missing from research has been any longitudinal studies (i.e. following a group of people over a period of time), which would greatly help an understanding of ageing.

Medical and psychological aspects

It is interesting to note that medical aspects still continue to take a central place in the literature. Some classics, such as *The Social Needs of the Over Eighties* (Brockington and Lempert 1966) and *Survival of the Unfittest* (Isaacs *et al.* 1972) were primarily concerned with a medical perspective but were also highly relevant to other professions. Others, such as *Geriatric Medicine* (Anderson and Judge 1974) and *Health Care of the Elderly* (Arie 1981), had chapters which were concerned with other aspects of care of elderly people. There is now a growing tendency for medical books (e.g. *Epidemiology in Old Age* by Ebrahim and Kalache 1996) and those on geriatric medicine to contain chapters which are written by social scientists (e.g. Pathy 1991 and update in press, Bennett and Ebrahim 1992, Evans 1993a, Brocklehurst *et al.* 1992 and update in press).

This growing appreciation of the value of a multidisciplinary approach can also be seen in textbooks on nursing elderly people (e.g. Norman and Redfern 1997) but the separation of 'health' from 'social' care makes it difficult to achieve this.

A particular medical problem revealed in this growing collection of written material is that of elderly mentally disordered people. Robb's *Sans Everything* painted a bleak picture of conditions in psychiatric hospitals (Robb 1967). It attracted a lot of publicity although many of the allegations were found not proved by an official investigation. *Taken for a Ride* was also a description of institutions for mentally infirm elderly people (Meacher 1972). The discipline of psychogeriatrics has developed rapidly and some of the books, such as *Psychiatry in the Elderly* (Jacoby and Oppenheimer 1991), *Recent Advances in Psychogeriatrics 2* (Arie 1992) and *Ageing and Dementia* (Burns 1993) combine medical and non-medical content as do the *International Journal of Geriatric Psychiatry* and *Reviews in Clinical Gerontology*.

A welcome addition to the literature has been a growing number of publications on preventive care and promotion of good health, much of which is summarised in Allsop (1995: Ch. 11). More specifically *Promoting Health among Elderly People* offers pointers derived from practice and research (Kalache *et al.* 1988) as does subsequent work by Kalache (1996). Another welcome addition is interest in medical ethics, and books like *Medical Ethics and Elderly People* (Elford 1987), which resulted from collaboration between medical specialists and moral philosophers, demonstrate a valuable approach.

Much more attention is being paid to the psychological aspects of ageing (Birren and Schaie 1990, Bromley 1990, Stuart-Hamilton 1991, Stokes 1992, Pratt and Norris 1994). Psychologists are concerned with 'the effects of ageing upon learning, memory, intelligence, skills, personality, motivations and emotions' (Harris 1990: 11).

The development of gerontology

Gerontology, the scientific study of ageing, is still in its infancy in the UK. In the USA services are less developed, but the scale of research and publications and the number of gerontology courses and institutes are more developed than anywhere else in the world (Warnes 1989). An illuminating account of the development of gerontology in the United States is in *Crossing Frontiers* (Achenbaum 1995). Perhaps the most encouraging development is the growth of multidisciplinary research and teaching in gerontology. Bringing together the psychological, social and cultural study of ageing with biomédical knowledge and clinical application should enable a far greater understanding of its processes and problems (Tinker 1990). *Human Ageing and Later Life* edited by Warnes (1989) is an example which brings in a number of disciplines.

Advances have also been made in the field of social gerontology, where the focus is on the social aspects of ageing. The British Society of Gerontology, whose membership has increased rapidly since its creation in 1973, has published a series of books based on its annual conferences which have been helpful in bringing together a number of papers (Jerrome 1983, Bromley 1984, Butler 1985, Phillipson *et al.* 1986, di Gregorio 1987, Bytheway and Johnson 1990, Laczko and Victor 1992, Morgan 1992, Arber and Evandrou 1993). They have also sponsored two books which have helped those with an interest in ageing and particularly those who teach gerontology. *Ageing in Society* (Bond *et al.* 1993) is an introduction to social gerontology and covers a wide range of topics to explain ageing within the perspective of the whole life span. *Researching Social Gerontology* (Peace 1990) offers an introduction to key concepts, methods and issues in research. American textbooks such as *Handbook of Aging and the Social Sciences* (Binstock and George 1990) and *Aging: An Introduction to Gerontology* (Aiken 1995) are widely used.

In specific areas of social gerontology a growing number of British academics are beginning to write books in particular disciplines. In social policy the first edition of *The Elderly in Modern Society* (Tinker 1980a) was followed by *Ageing and Social Policy: A Critical Assessment* (Phillipson and Walker 1986) and *Old Age in Modern Society* (Victor 1987, second edition 1994). *The Sociology of Old Age* has also been a helpful addition to the literature (Fennell *et al.* 1988). Sociology has been defined as 'the scientific study of human interaction' (Harris 1990: 11). A relatively new area of study is educational gerontology. In 1986 the editorial in the first issue of the *Journal of Educational Gerontology* (April 1986) distinguished between educational gerontology (the education and learning of older people) and gerontological education (education about ageing and teaching gerontology). In the latter area the pioneering courses put on at the Age Concern Institute of Gerontology (ACIOG), King's College London; the Centre for Extra

Mural Studies, Birkbeck College, University of London and the University of Keele should be noted and they have now been followed by others. Other disciplines where there has been a growth of interest have included geography, economics, demography, law and anthropology.

In geography the pioneering work of Warnes has particularly focused on migration (see Warnes 1982, Warnes 1987, Warnes and Ford 1995). Warnes has pointed out that, while studies of the geographical aspects of older people's social and environmental circumstances have been numerous and diverse, only a few geographers have made successive contributions (Warnes 1990).

Economic aspects of ageing, especially the costings of alternative types of provision, have been noticeably sparse. Wager in 1972 produced an innovatory exercise in cost benefits, *Care of the Elderly*, (Wager 1972) and Davies has also done much work in this area (e.g. Davies and Challis 1986). Other work on costing alternative patterns of care have been done by academics (Wright *et al.* 1981) and by DoE (Tinker 1984, 1989b, McCafferty 1994). Most of the Audit Commission's work has involved costings. Johnson and Falkingham's *Ageing and Economic Welfare* (1992) and Netten and Beecham's *Costing Community Care: Theory and Practice* (1993) have added to knowledge.

Demographers are another group who are increasingly turning their attention to ageing especially to the implications of an ageing population (see especially publications by Grundy 1983, 1987, 1989, 1991a, 1991b, 1992, 1995a, 1995b, 1996a, 1996b, Joshi 1989, 1995, Ermisch 1990, Falkingham (e.g. with Victor 1991), Clarke 1995).

Possible changes in law and practice which might help to represent and protect the interests of this group of older people were considered in *The Law and Vulnerable Elderly People* (ACE 1986). *The Law and Elderly People* covers most of the services which older people may need and states the legal position (Griffiths *et al.* 1990). Bridging law and medicine, studies of ethical issues are beginning to come to the fore. *The Living Will*, about consent to treatment at the end of life (Kennedy 1988), and *Medical Ethics and Elderly People* (Elford 1987) open up discussion about the inability of certain groups of older people to speak on their own behalf in certain circumstances. Both these books are examples of collaboration between groups of professionals such as medical specialists, lawyers and moral philosophers. In the field of anthropology, notable contributions have been made by researchers such as Jerrome, Wenger and Kellaher.

Another feature of the recent literature has been attention given to differences in old age such as those between men and women (e.g. Bernard and Meade 1993, Arber and Ginn 1991, 1995), people of different ethnic backgrounds (e.g. Askham, Henshaw and Tarpey 1995a, Blakemore and Boneham 1994), and of different ages (e.g. Carnegie Inquiry into the Third Age 1993).

Individual services

There is an increasing amount of specialist literature on particular services. Much of this is referred to in the appropriate chapters. Particularly fruitful areas for study in the 1980s and 1990s have been community care, financial circumstances, housing and carers. Especially influential have been reports from House of Commons' Select Committees (notably Health and Social Services).

Local studies

Local studies provide a rich source of data on ageing. An early example of research undertaken by an academic was Shenfield's *Social Policies for Old Age* (1957). More recently Wenger's study of areas in North Wales, *The Supportive Network*, has provided useful evidence about informal patterns of care (Wenger 1984, see also 1992) as has that in Sheffield by Qureshi and Walker (1989). Probably the best known example of a local study was the community care project in Kent, which has now been replicated in a number of other areas (Challis and Davies 1986, Davies and Challis 1986). The model of the Kent community care project has also been instrumental in moulding central government's policies.

Practical advice

Another noticeable feature of the literature of the last 25 years has been the growing number of books offering practical advice either to older people or to their relatives and friends. There has also been a steady stream of popular books about retirement as well as on a wide range of topics from incontinence to loneliness (Age Concern has detailed lists of references).

The views of political and voluntary bodies

Some interesting studies, which probably reached a wider audience than some of the more weighty academic books, were produced in the late 1960s and early 1970s by the Fabian Society, the Bow Group and the Conservative Political Centre. Four of the major ones concerned with older people were *Old People in Britain* (Weston and Ashworth 1963), *Old People: Cash and Care* (Bellairs 1968), *The Care of the Old* (Agate and Meacher 1969) and *New Deal for the Elderly* (Bosanquet 1975). These attracted a good deal of publicity. Less has been produced in the 1980s and 1990s from the political parties and it is interesting that there was very little mention of older people in the party manifestos in the elections of 1983, 1987 and 1992.

Research has always been one of the main contributions of the voluntary sector to social policy (but see subsequent chapters for their growing contribution to the provision of services). The Manifesto series in 1974 by Age Concern England comprised excellent accounts by experts on specific problems. Particularly interesting when considering the kinds of policies likely to find favour with older people was a study of the attitudes of 2,700 pensioners (ACE 1974) and the subsequent Manifesto (ACE 1975). Age Concern England marked its golden jubilee in 1990 by publishing a major review of the vital issues which affect older people (ACE 1990b). The research papers to be produced for their Millennium Debate of the Age in 1997 will be helpful as has the survey carried out to put ageing higher on the political agenda (ACE 1996).

In 1986 Age Concern England moved their research unit to King's College London where it became the Age Concern Institute of Gerontology. Apart from the usual publications of an academic group a series of research publications have also been produced. The implications of research for policy and practice have also been publicised in a series of *Ageing Updates* (e.g. Morton 1989a, 1989b, 1989c, 1990a, 1990b, 1991, McCreadie 1994).

The Centre for Policy on Ageing (CPA) have produced an impressive list of publications in the 1970s, 1980s and 1990s (referred to in individual chapters) as well as their widely acclaimed periodical *New Literature on Old Age*. Help the Aged have also produced helpful publications and sometimes sponsored research, as has Counsel and Care.

The views of older people

What older people themselves wish, and their own views, should be a main strand in the literature, but there is a remarkable lack of this. Elder in *The Alienated* explains very vividly why many members of her generation feel as they do (Elder 1977). Stott (1981) has described her feelings on growing older as has Kroll in *Growing Older* (Kroll 1988). Two Committees described the influence which the views of older people themselves had on their findings. The Wagner Committee on residential care appealed for people to write to them (Wagner 1988a, 1988b). While they had some reassuring letters, they also had some of which they said: 'none of us who read those letters could remain unmoved by the depth of unhappiness and despair revealed by the writers' (Wagner 1988a: 2). The Working Party set up by the Board for Social Responsibility of the Church of England to look at ageing had the same experience. In their report *Ageing* they say: 'A distressing number of respondents had felt patronised or scorned on the grounds of their age' (Board for Social Responsibility 1990: 9). But there are ways in which older people can be involved in research (Thornton and Tozer 1994).

International studies

It is beyond the scope of this book to do more than make brief mention of studies made abroad. Those who want to pursue comparative studies will find that comparative social policy is beginning to emerge as a special interest. Jones's *Patterns of Social Policy* (Jones 1985) is an introduction to comparative analysis which describes and compares policies. However, many books are of limited value because they comprise collections of papers by different authors in various countries with no attempt to compare and contrast.

For comparative information publications of the United Nations (UN) and the Organisation for Economic Co-operation and Development (OECD) are among the most helpful (e.g. OECD 1988, 1994). CPA's *World Directory of Old Age* contains much basic data (1989, updated on AgeInfo CD Rom four times a year). Work sponsored by the European Commission can be helpful when trying to compare policies and services. Some examples are *Social Developments Affecting Elderly People in the EC Member States* (Drury 1990), a study of the financial position of older women in Europe (Harrop 1990), *Contrasting European Policies for the Care of Older People* (Jamieson and Illsley 1990) and CPA's *The European Directory of Older Age* (Crosby 1993). A survey of older people across the EC, *Age and Attitudes* (Walker 1993) was part of the European Year of Older People and Solidarity Between Generations.

In Europe research undertaken by the European Foundation for the Improvement of Living and Working Conditions specifically on ageing has been useful (e.g. Fogarty 1987, Salvage 1995). Overviews of research across Europe such as that done on carers (McGlone and Cronin 1994, Salvage 1995) and general polices and services such as *The Coming of Age in Europe* (ACE 1992) and *Ageing and the Care of Older People in Europe* (Hugman 1994) are useful but also show the problems involved in making comparisons.

PART TWO

Needs and How They Are Met

CHAPTER 4

A critical narrative of the main developments in services for older people

It is easy to rationalise when looking back at provision for any group of people and to see a pattern in what has happened. In practice the directions taken by social policy are often in response to all kinds of events and people. A crisis, war, the action of a pressure group or the influence of a dominant person may all change policy, as will the overall political philosophy of a political party.

Policies for older people, as for other groups, have evolved as a result of many different factors. Some of these directions will be explored briefly in this chapter to provide a framework for a more detailed account of individual services later. (Note that Acts of Parliament and Circulars are referred to in the text but not in the bibliography.)

The growth in services

Greater concern

The needs of older people in this country have traditionally been the concern both of central and local government and of voluntary agencies. All of these have paid increasing attention to how appropriate policies and administrative structures may be developed.

Setting up a Royal Commission or a committee to investigate a topic is one conventional way of showing concern. It is interesting that one of the first, which reported in 1895, was the Royal Commission on the Aged Poor. This provided evidence about the poor conditions in which many old people existed. In 1909 both the majority and the minority reports of the Royal Commission on the Poor Laws painted a bleak picture of life for this group. Townsend has commented: 'Both reports recommended improvements in institutional conditions and an extension of separate provision for the old, but little was done for many years to carry out these recommendations' (Townsend 1964: 16). He went on to argue that as far as 'the infirm aged and chronic sick' were concerned, far less information was made available to the public between 1910 and 1946 than was available between 1834 and 1909. No official inquiries were instituted and hardly any books or pamphlets were published which contained more than a few fleeting references to their circumstances or their needs. He believed that the reason for this was the low priority that the welfare of old people had in British society.

Since 1945 many important Commissions and Committees have paid particular attention to older people. Three notable early reports were the Guillebaud Report on the cost of the National Health Service (NHS) (MoH 1956), the Cullingworth Report on council housing (MHLG 1969) and the Seebohm Report on personal and allied social services (Home Office *et al.* 1968).

In 1978 the Labour government produced a discussion document, *A Happier Old Age* (DHSS 1978a), which looked at services for older people. In 1979 the Conservatives came to power and the new administration's White Paper *Growing Older* in 1981 was noticeably less optimistic (DHSS 1981d). Few major changes in policy were outlined but the emphasis was rather on what could be achieved within existing resources. There was stress on the contribution of the private and voluntary sectors – an important theme of the last few years. *The Guardian* in a leader (6.3.1981) criticised the White Paper, saying it: 'makes no attempt even to identify the nature and scale of the problem. Its message is plain: the Government has no intention of spending any more money at all to cope with the extra demand. It is all up to the community'. Similar criticisms came from organisations representing older people. Most of the disappointment centred on the absence of any concrete proposals. The main aim of government policy in relation to elderly people as expressed in *Ageing in the United Kingdom*, produced in 1982 for the World Assembly on Ageing, was 'to enable them to lead full and independent lives in the community to the greatest possible extent' (DHSS 1982a: 1). This is almost identical to the words of the 1981 White Paper, which said policies were: 'to enable elderly people to live independent lives in their own homes wherever possible – which reflects what the majority themselves want' (DHSS 1981d: 6). Similar policies continued with the Conservative victories in the 1983, 1987 and 1992 elections although it is doubtful if the other parties would have adopted a different stance.

In 1988 the Church of England set up a Working Party to consider the major issues of ageing, to offer a Christian contribution to the debate and to evaluate the Church's ministry in this field. Their report in 1990 *Ageing* received widespread media coverage (Board for Social Responsibility 1990). The report challenged negative attitudes to ageing and produced detailed recommendations aimed at the nation and the Church.

In 1990 the Carnegie Inquiry into the Third Age was set up. The Third Age was defined as the active independent stage in life after people have finished their main career or job, or bringing up children, or both. The Inquiry covered issues affecting the life, work and livelihood of people in this age, and reported in 1993 (Carnegie Inquiry into the Third Age 1993).

The last 50 years have also seen the birth of major voluntary organisations. The National Old People's Welfare Council (NOPWC) started in 1940 and became Age Concern in 1971. The National Corporation for the Care of Old People (NCCOP) started in 1947 and subsequently became the Centre for Policy on Ageing. Help the Aged started in 1962. As well as acting as pressure groups these organisations undertake research and policy analysis and are regularly consulted by official bodies.

The development of research

In the review of the literature (Chapter 3) it was noted that increasing attention has been paid to finding out the facts about older people. This has usually taken the form of social surveys, medical enquiries and sociological studies which have often attempted to measure need and provision. This book draws extensively on this research.

Widening scope and changes in organisation

The development of the welfare state: At the beginning of the century there was little provision for older people apart from the Poor Law, charities and almshouses. These services were largely looked on as being for second class citizens. But even before the First World War, social services were beginning to be regarded not as a form of charity, but rather as one of the rights available to citizens, as were services for defence, justice, law and order. During the Second World War the feeling grew that society was not automatically divided into the rich and poor or givers and receivers. A neat summary of the effects of the war is given in DHSS *Collaboration in Community Care*: 'The effects of the war were threefold. First, a degree of physical fitness was required in the entire population. Second, the war had an equalising effect on all classes of society which made selective provision of services less acceptable. Third, the cause of social problems, such as unemployment or handicap, was no longer seen to be the individual's fault but to lie in the social context' (DHSS 1978b: 4).

The term 'welfare state' has been defined as a 'state which has a policy of collective responsibility for individual well-being' (Clegg 1971). The foundations were laid during the Second World War where a landmark was Beveridge's 1942 report *Social Insurance and Allied Services* (Beveridge 1942). As Thane has noted: 'More than any other wartime blueprint for post-war social reconstruction the Beveridge report caught the popular imagination and came to symbolise the widespread hopes for a different, more just, world. These hopes were embodied in the term which, although not quite new, came into wide currency after the publication of the Report' (Thane 1982: 253). It should be noted, incidentally, that Beveridge preferred the term 'social service state'. Again to quote Thane: 'The term welfare state expressed the desire for a more socially just, more materially equal, more truly democratic society, in short, everything that pre-war society had not been' (Thane 1982: 253).

The state has never been the sole provider of welfare in the UK as voluntary bodies, and to a less extent private provision such as in health, have played a role. What has come to the fore since the 1970s, and especially after the Conservatives came to power in 1979, has been the questioning of the role of the state. State provision is particularly important to older people as over half of expenditure on social security, health and personal social services is spent on them. The so-called Thatcher years from 1979 to 1990 have been ones where the emphasis has changed to more reliance on the private and voluntary sectors and on the private individual. The term 'mixed economy of welfare' or 'welfare pluralism' is commonly used to describe provision by different agencies. This is a form of provision which lies between the extremes of a *laissez-faire* model, with minimal government and maximum market forces, and the Marxist model, with an absolute commitment to state-controlled provision (Pinker 1992).

The late 1980s saw major changes away from state provision and towards the contracting out of services by local and health authorities and the encouragement of the private sector through legislation and tax incentives. The compulsory selling off of council houses to tenants and tax incentives to encourage the purchase of private health care are examples. The vision was that an enterprise culture and property-owning democracy would replace the welfare society and dependency. The challenge is not just over the provision of services but about state regulation of private activities and giving more freedom to individuals.

Part of the reason for the questioning of the growing role of the state has been the cost, but there has also been the view that personal responsibility must be encouraged. 'We believe the well-being of individuals is best protected and promoted when they are helped to be independent, to use their talents to take care of themselves and their families and to achieve things on their own' declared John Moore, the Secretary of State for Social Services in a speech to the Conservative Political Centre in 1987. There is also the view that state provision is too bureaucratic (Day and Klein 1987). However, despite the questioning of its role, a large study of the welfare state has concluded that 'the welfare state has been surprisingly robust in the period since 1974. Government welfare spending has *not* fallen in recent years as a share of national income; indeed it reached a peak in 1992/93' (Hills *et al.* 1993: 1). As the authors also point out there has, however, been a change of direction. This has been away from spending on housing and education and towards social security and the National Health Service.

There are three main models of the welfare state:

- a collectivist one where provision by the state is the norm;
- a reluctant collectivist or liberal one where the state takes responsibility for some aspects of provision but in such a way as to encourage individuals to help themselves;
- a residual model where the state provides minimal services.

However, as Glennerster has pointed out, a crucial distinction is between finance and provision (Glennerster 1992). A service may be:

- publicly provided and publicly funded (e.g. NHS hospitals, though even here there may be some voluntary and private input);
- publicly provided and privately funded (e.g. private pay beds in NHS hospitals);
- publicly provided and partly funded publicly and partly privately (e.g. local authority old people's homes which charge fees);
- privately provided and privately funded (e.g. private sheltered housing);
- privately provided and publicly funded (e.g. day care by voluntary bodies);
- privately provided and partly funded publicly and partly privately (e.g. private old people's homes when some residents receive public support and others pay themselves).

Another feature of the welfare state in recent years has been changes in organisation to decentralise services. Smaller organisations such as hospital trusts and fund-holding general practitioner (GP) practices are examples.

Discussions about the welfare state must necessarily take into account that the position is a complicated one and naive assumptions should be avoided. Among recent books which give different perspectives on the welfare state are Williams (1989), Glennerster (1992), Hill (1993), Gould (1993) and the report of the Commission on Social Justice (1994).

At a national level: Looking back on provision in the twentieth century there are some notable landmarks. In terms of central services one of the most important Acts was the 1908 Old Age Pension Act. This was an attempt to make some provision for old people outside the Poor Law. It gave people over 70 a small non-contributory pension but applicants had to undergo a means test and, to begin with, provide evidence that they were of good character. Better provision was made in 1925 under the Widows, Orphans and

Old Age Contributory Pensions Act. During the Second World War the Unemployment Assistance Board took over the Poor Law responsibility for outdoor relief of old people. The Beveridge Report in 1942 recommended [Document 7] that elderly people, and other groups, should be covered by an insurance scheme while an assistance board should provide for those who were not covered. However, after the war pensions were provided on a universal scale (with certain exceptions) out of general taxation, but amounts were not high enough to prevent many having to apply for extra means-tested assistance. Since 1945 a series of Acts have extended pensions to nearly all people of pensionable age. In 1961 graduated pensions were introduced and in 1975 pensions became earnings-related. These measures have enabled older people to be financially independent and, in particular, not to be dependent on their children. However, large numbers have had to have their pensions augmented by the state through income support (formerly called supplementary pension) (see Chapter 5 for details of later legislation).

Under the National Health Service Act 1946 a comprehensive health service was set up for everyone, regardless of means. The object was to promote the establishment of a comprehensive health service designed to secure improvements in the physical and mental health of people and the prevention, diagnosis and treatment of illness, and for that purpose, to provide or secure the effective provision of services. This service has been largely free of charge for those in medical need, and even where charges have been made (e.g. prescriptions) some groups, including pensioners, have been exempt. It has enabled elderly people to be spared the kind of indignities remembered by Elder where 'doctors bills had to be avoided' (Elder 1977: 62). There were three main divisions after 1946: the hospital and specialist services administered through regional hospital boards; the general practitioner services administered by local executive councils; and the domiciliary services (such as home nursing and domestic help) administered by the major local authorities (LA).

The NHS was reorganised in 1974 with the intention that expertise in health care should be concentrated in the NHS (e.g. home nursing was transferred from LAs) and expertise in social work in social services departments (e.g. medical social work was transferred from the NHS). Under the DHSS were 14 Regional Health Authorities, then 90 Area Health Authorities and then District Health Authorities. In April 1982 the Area Health Authorities were abolished, largely on the grounds that there was one tier too many. In the NHS and Community Care Act 1990 major changes took place in organisation, hospital management and finance and family practitioner services and in 1996 a further reorganisation was set in motion (see Chapter 6).

At a local level: For local services the Local Government Act 1929 was a milestone because it transferred the powers and duties of the

Poor Law Guardians to the county councils and county boroughs. They took over some of the Poor Law institutions and ran them as hospitals. Those that were left were managed by the public assistance committees of the local councils. Conditions in both types of institution, however, remained poor.

The development of local services after 1945 is described in Chapter 8, but 1946, 1948, 1962 and 1968 were important dates when the powers of local authorities were extended. Services for elderly people have expanded greatly, particularly since 1945. Some, such as holidays, telephones and free transport, were scarcely thought of as public services even 35 years ago. But the cost of these services, combined with the belief by some that the state should play a smaller role, has restricted any large-scale future expansion. Some contraction has taken place in the late 1980s and 1990s and the role has changed in many services from that of provider to enabler.

Central control of local authorities is an important issue. Three possible models have been identified (Clarke and Stewart 1990). The first is the relative autonomy model, where the emphasis is on giving freedom of action to local authorities within a widely defined framework of powers and duties. The second is the agency model, where local authorities are principally agencies for the carrying out of central government's policies mainly through detailed controls. Thirdly there is the interaction model where there is a complex pattern of relationships in which the emphasis is on mutual influence. In many ways the 1980s were a time when more local freedom was given, for example, to choose how central government grants were spent. But in other ways such as rate and poll tax/community charge capping central government has laid down firm boundaries, especially over spending.

In any discussion about local services the effect of local government reorganisation must be taken into account. Many attempts were made from 1945 onwards to change the structure for various reasons. Some local authorities were thought to be too small, some boundaries seemed meaningless and the division of responsibility between different types of authority hindered the provision of effective services. Under the Local Government Act 1972 the old all-purpose (unitary) county boroughs disappeared and a tiered system of local government was set up. In 1986 metropolitan county councils and the Greater London Council were abolished. Under the Local Government Act 1992 the Local Government Commission was set up to make recommendations for changes to the structure, boundaries and electoral arrangements of LAs. One of the reasons for the review was the belief by the Government (and others) that unitary authorities would improve the cost-effectiveness, quality and co-ordination of local services. The Government agreed to the Commission's recommendations for the setting up of 50 new unitary authorities with starting dates from April 1996 onwards.

In 1996 the position in England was as follows:

- *Providers of all local government services*
  Unitary authorities i.e. metropolitan district councils (36) and others (50) London boroughs (32) and City of London (1)
- *Local government services split between different LAs* i.e. county councils (39) (responsibilities include social services) and district councils (296) (responsibilities include housing).

Outside London, the metropolitan areas and the new unitary authorities, different LAs are responsible for two key services for older people – housing and social services. Although it is argued that division does not matter as long as there is co-ordination of services, both Conservative and Labour politicians were discussing the possible abolition of county councils in the late 1980s and early 1990s.

Responsibility for services for elderly people is also split between the NHS and local authorities. For local authorities the major change was in 1970 when the Local Authority Social Services Act created social services departments, bringing together many functions which had previously been scattered between health, welfare and other departments.

By the independent sector: The independent sector comprises voluntary bodies and the private sector. Voluntary bodies have pioneered provision for older people. Almshouses, charities and trusts to help older people date back at least as far as the Middle Ages. Old people's homes, financial help and the provision of meals are all examples of this.

Local authorities have sometimes used voluntary bodies instead of making provision themselves. Under the National Assistance Act 1948, for instance, a local authority may use accommodation such as a hostel provided by a voluntary body and make payment for it. They may also contribute to the funds of a voluntary body that provides recreation or meals for older people. What developed rapidly in the late 1980s was the contracting out of services by local authorities to the voluntary sector. For example local Age Concern organisations have become involved in providing services to older people such as day and residential care. In a similar way housing associations have found themselves taking over some public housing. The sudden acquisition of services has not been without its problems. These particularly concern the contraction of choice for the consumer, controlling standards and the difficulties small organisations may have in taking over new, and possibly larger, tasks than they have undertaken before (Morton 1990a).

A rapidly developing area of the welfare state is the private sector. In health, pensions, housing and residential care the role of the private sector has increased rapidly. The advantages include more choice, if only for those with the money, but disadvantages include problems of standards and difficulties in co-ordinating services.

Some changes in the nature of services

Greater entitlement as of right

One of the most striking subsequent developments after 1945 was the widespread adoption of comprehensive services. The major services, in particular health, were no longer provided for different categories of people depending on how much they could pay and from what source. Where a universal service was provided everyone was entitled to use it. For a generation of people used to highly selective services this was a major change.

Some of the services for elderly people, such as pensions and health, are provided as of right. There is no question of pensions or access to a GP being restricted to a limited number of people. Every old person (with a few exceptions in the case of pensions) has a right to these national services. The same is true in some areas of certain local services such as bus passes for free travel.

Eyden, in *The Welfare Society*, distinguished between three main types of service (Eyden 1971). First, services which are financed wholly or mainly out of general taxation and are used at will without any test of contribution (e.g. health). Second, services framed on a contractual basis with entitlement to benefit being dependent on being within the scope of a particular scheme and satisfying its relevant contribution test (e.g. pensions). Third, services where there is a needs test (e.g. local authority housing). As Glennerster has shown (see previous section) there are now other models.

The move to selectivity

Some services are provided on a selective basis – that is, certain criteria are laid down and people may apply. Services provided in this way include meals on wheels, chiropody, aids such as zimmer frames, and adaptations to houses. The arguments in favour of this sort of approach are that it ensures that those with specific needs have them met, that scarce resources can be rationed and that services are not 'wasted'. Against this it is held that there may be a low take-up if it is left to individuals to apply, there may be a stigma attached if only a few people receive the service, and such schemes are expensive to administer. An increase in selective services, referred to more often from the late 1980s as 'targeted', was evident during this period, for example, the new home improvement system which started in 1990. Whichever system is adopted, comprehensive or targeted services, there still remain the practical problems of access to services. These are explored by Foster in her study of welfare rationing (Foster 1983).

Moves to prevention

Those responsible for many services, for elderly people as well as for other groups, are attempting to move away from the sort of provision which aims to solve particular problems, that is, is crisis-centred, and goes no further.

This is specially noticeable in medicine, where people are being persuaded not to drink or smoke and to take greater care on the roads. This approach is in contrast to the provision of a health service which picks up the casualties after the damage has been done. Thus, it can be argued that chiropody and greater attention to the care of the feet may prevent elderly people becoming housebound. In *Prevention and Health: Everybody's Business* it is stated that: 'Prevention is the key to healthier living and a higher quality of life for all of us', and ways of prevention are outlined related to elderly people (DHSS 1976c: 96). The question that has to be asked is what is the object of prevention? Not the avoidance of death, because this is inevitable. One answer is that it may be possible if certain measures are taken early enough to prevent older people going into expensive forms of care. It is also held that preventing an accident or entry to institutional care saves money and human suffering and improves the quality of life. A strategy for prevention is laid out in *The Health of the Nation* (Sec. of St. for Health 1991).

Community care

One of the main developments has been the shift of emphasis in policy away from institutional care to what is loosely called community care or care in the community. This shift, and the reasons for it, are not just confined to older people but apply also to other groups such as children, offenders and mentally disordered people.

There seems to be a lack of satisfactory definition of community care and some confusion as to its meaning. This may be partly because a number of different theories and facts came together at roughly the same time. First, there were views about the positive value in terms of quality of life of being at home. There was also a general reaction against institutional care which led to the belief that alternatives ought to be made available for both existing and potential inhabitants of institutions. Second, there were practical problems increasingly associated with institutions such as the difficulty of getting residential staff. Third, there was less need to keep some people (including those who are older) in an institution away from society because much behaviour that was disturbed or bizarre could be controlled by drugs and other methods. Fourth, there was the cost of institutional care. Finally, there was a growing recognition that people had a right, where possible, to live among ordinary people in society and not to be in a separate institution. The institution was seen as a barrier to normal living.

In short, for both positive and negative reasons the fashionable swing towards attempting to look after people within society (or the community as it was usually put) snowballed. There can scarcely be a group of people now who do not have some form of 'community' service whether it is community (children's) homes, community health councils or (offenders') community service.

In the past it seems that community care has meant very much what people have wanted it to mean. There are two extremes of meaning. There is the narrow definition of community care as the provision of domiciliary rather than institutional services and there is the ill-defined cosy picture of a group of local people 'caring' for their neighbours.

The official view for a long time was nearer to the first description and has equated the concept with the provision of services by local authorities. The Ministry of Health's 1962 *Hospital Plan*, for example, was intended to be complementary to the local services 'for care in the community' (MoH 1962). Similarly, when local author-ities were asked to produce plans along these lines the title of the official publication was *Health and Welfare: The Development of Community Care* (MoH 1963) and so was the revision (MoH 1966). The introduction to the 1963 edition states: 'At the reorganisation of 1948, local government, while losing responsibility for any part of the hospital service, retained the environmental services, and took on much wider responsibilities for the prevention of ill-health and for care in the community (p. 1)'. But it went on to include a short section headed 'Voluntary Effort' which was an indication that something other than statutory help could be included in the definition.

A wider definition of community emerges from the Seebohm Report, although even here the official definition was: 'Community care has come to mean treatment and care outside hospitals or residential homes' (Home Office *et al.* 1968: 107). It is this concept of community which is so difficult to define and perhaps contributes to the extreme view of a caring group of people given above. As Clegg points out: 'There is no agreed definition of "community" among academic sociologists, social workers or the makers of social policy' (Clegg 1971: 16). She indicates that the sociological concept relates to: 'a small population in a defined geographical area whose social relationships are distinguished by the fact that they share a common culture which has emerged over a long period of time' (Clegg 1971: 16).

The chapter on The Community in the Seebohm Report starts with the definition of community both in the physical sense of location but also 'the common identity of a group of people' (Home Office *et al.* 1968: 147). However, it then goes on to introduce yet another factor: 'The notion of a community implies the existence of a network of reciprocal social relationships which among other things ensure mutual aid and give those who experience it a sense of well-being' (Home Office *et al*. 1968: 147). Although official thinking has moved beyond the narrow concept of domiciliary provision there is still need for a working definition of community care which needs to be spelled out with precision.

Major reports and legislation concerning community care are to be found in the chapter on health (Chapter 6) and that on personal and other social services (Chapter 8). The focus of them has been on enabling older people, and other vulnerable groups, to remain in their own homes for as long as possible and also to allow people in institutions to return to the community.

It will be suggested in Chapter 13 that any redefinition of community care needs to take into account, in a realistic way, the role both of the family and of older people themselves.

CHAPTER 5

The financial and employment position

The financial position

Introduction

Financial security in old age is a fundamental need because few older people are able to continue to earn their living. An adequate income may be secured from a number of sources including personal savings and state, occupational and private pensions. In the past older people who could no longer work and had no savings were thrown on the resources of the Poor Law or of their families.

Landmarks in legislation

The development of statutory provision of pensions from 1908 has been outlined in Chapter 4. Some points are elaborated below.

A major initiative was the Committee of Inquiry set up by the government in 1941 and chaired by Sir William Beveridge, to look at the whole system of social security. Its terms of reference were: 'to undertake, with special reference to the inter-relation of the schemes, a survey of the existing national schemes of social insurance and allied services including workmen's compensation, and to make recommendations' (Beveridge 1942: 5). The Committee's proposals for pensions must be seen against the background of an overall strategy for a system of insurance covering everyone, whatever their income, and for benefits including pensions to be paid to everyone who contributed based on a national minimum [Document 8]. Contributions were to be compulsory and benefits universal and not means tested. The responsibility of the state was seen to be the provision of a minimum income, while people were encouraged to supplement this on a voluntary basis. The monetary benefit was to be seen as just one part of 'a comprehensive policy of social progress' which included provision of better services in health, education and housing.

The Beveridge Report was accepted with one important exception. This was the rejection of the 'national minimum' standard of benefits, which would have meant frequent changes to keep up with the cost of living. Benefits were to be fixed and reviewed at intervals. National insurance became compulsory for everyone of working age except married women. Pensions were to be paid on retirement (65 for men and 60 for women). To encourage people to work beyond this age an addition to the basic rate was given for each year of deferment.

In 1948 the National Assistance Act set up the National Assistance Board (NAB) with a duty to assist persons in need, that is, those 'who are without resources to meet their requirements or whose resources (including benefits receivable under the National Insurance Act 1946) must be supplemented in order to meet their requirements'. For those who were not insured, or who needed additional help, this Act laid down the machinery and introduced the means-tested benefit known as National Assistance. It was the last break with the Poor Law [Document 9].

One of the provisions of the National Insurance Act 1957 was to enable retirement and widowed pensioners under the age of 70 (65 for women) to revoke their declaration of retirement if they wished and to earn additions to their retirement pensions to be paid when they ceased working.

In order that people might be able to receive a pension more closely related to the level of what they had been earning, as distinct from a basic minimum, a Graduated Pensions Scheme was introduced in 1961. Higher pensions were to be payable in return for higher contributions related to higher earnings. Employees might, however, be contracted out if their employers provided a comparable or better occupational scheme. Another change was the granting of a standard addition for supplementary pensioners and some other long-term cases. This was intended to reduce the number of discretionary additions to the weekly rate of benefit and to limit the need to ask detailed questions about special expenses. This Act replaced National Assistance with Supplementary Benefit (this was a Supplementary Allowance for those under pension age and a Supplementary Pension for pensioners).

In 1966 the NAB was merged with the Ministry of Pensions and National Insurance to become the Ministry of Social Security, and a semi-autonomous board, the Supplementary Benefits Commission (SBC) (which replaced the NAB) was set up under this Ministry. The SBC was an independent agency whose main function was to ensure that people got the supplementary benefit to which they were entitled.

The National Insurance Act 1970 provided three new social security cash benefits, one of which was for people aged 80 or over who were too old to come into the National Insurance Scheme when it began in 1948. The National Insurance Act 1971 authorised a further payment above the normal retirement pension for the over-80s. The following year a tax-free Christmas bonus for pensioners, and some others, was provided under the Pensioners and Family Income Supplement Payments Act 1972. This bonus has been paid in most subsequent years.

Following the Social Security Act 1975 the State Earnings Related Pension Scheme (SERPS) began in 1978 to provide pensions based on earnings, regardless of whether there were company schemes. There was provision for members of occupational pension schemes to be 'contracted out' of the additional pension of the state scheme by their employers. Contributions to the former Graduated Pension Scheme ceased in 1975. One of the main features was that pension rights should be protected during absence from work to look after children, old people or the sick. This was thought to be particularly beneficial to women.

The 1980 Social Security Act amended the Social Security Act 1975 so that in future all benefit increases were to be related to the movement of prices, and not to whichever was the higher of earnings or prices, as had been the practice previously. The system had fewer elements of discretion and the SBC, which had undertaken a great deal of guidance was thought to be no longer needed and was abolished. The Social Security Advisory Committee, which replaced the SBC, had a purely advisory role. In their first report they said that they regretted the decision to break the link between the growth of earnings and pensions (Social Security Advisory Committee, 1982: 2). Pensioners would no longer have a guarantee that their living standards would rise in step with those of wage and salary earners. While the Advisory Committee did not single out benefits for retired people as a priority topic, they emphasised their concern that the benefits for this group should be protected and improved as resources permitted. The Social Security and Housing Benefits Act 1982 provided for a change in the way in which pension increases were calculated.

In 1984 the DHSS announced that there was to be what the Minister called 'the most substantial examination of the social security system since the Beveridge report'. In 1985 the results were presented in a government Green Paper *Reform of Social Security* (Sec. of St. for Social Services 1985a). A particularly controversial proposal was to withdraw SERPS only six years after its introduction. However, the subsequent White Paper *Reform of Social Security: Programme for Action*, which virtually mirrored the Green Paper, proposed to modify rather than withdraw SERPS (Sec. of St. for Social Services 1985b). The aims of the White Paper were to achieve a simpler system of social security, to give more effective help to those who needed it, to reduce the poverty trap, to give individuals more choice and to take account, especially over pensions, of 'the very substantial financial debt that we are handing down to future generations' (Sec. of St. for Social Services 1985b: 1). The way this was to be done was to modify the SERPS scheme and to encourage the spread of occupational and personal (private) pensions. These modifications represented substantial reductions in the benefits paid out. Since 1988 people have been able to contract out of SERPS and take out a personal pension instead. The changes to SERPS were phased in over 10 years and affect people retiring on or after April 1999.

The Social Security Act 1986 also brought changes in the supplementary benefits system. This Act, which took effect in April 1988, replaced supplementary benefit with income support, changing the kind of help that had been available to people on long-term benefit. One of the main aims was to harmonise rules for calculating entitlement to supplementary benefit/income support and housing benefit. The main points were:

- replacement of long-term rates, special needs additions and householder/non-householder distinction with a series of client group premiums paid on top of basic allowances;
- introduction of capital limits;
- entitlements to be based on after-tax/national insurance income to alleviate poverty/unemployment traps.

In addition an innovation was the introduction of the social fund, which was to help people on low incomes meet exceptional circumstances (see p. 56). The reason was that ministers had concluded that the costs of previous systems of exceptional needs payments between 1966 and 1980 and single payments after 1980 were out of control (National Audit Office 1991).

Critics of the 1986 Act claim that the emphasis on targeting means-tested benefits marked a shift away from the aims of the Beveridge Report which guaranteed security against want without a means test (Social Security Consortium 1986). Fifty years after the Beveridge report an international conference *Social Security 50 Years After Beveridge* was held. Questions were posed about a system of insurance which had been based on a male, full-time employee. The many changes in society, such as the rise in female labour participation and different patterns of family formation and dissolution had been matched by changes in work which includes more which is part-time, temporary and contract, as well as self-employment (Baldwin and Falkingham 1994). There was general agreement that the system needed changing but not a consensus about how this should be done.

Much of the debate, but not exclusively, in the 1990s focused on equalisation of pension ages between men and women (Department of Social Security 1991, 1994, West 1994). The subsequent Pensions Act 1995 increased the state pension age of women to 65 to be phased in between 2010 and 2020. There has also been discussion about a minimum pension guarantee (by the Commission on Social Justice, 1994, which was similar to that put forward by the Retirement Income Inquiry of 1996). Changes on pensions have included compensation arrangements for people wrongly advised to transfer out of occupational pensions to personal ones and pension law/

regulation following the experience of the Maxwell pensioners (Goode 1993).

Other changes relate to the replacement of attendance allowance, mobility allowance and sickness and invalidity benefits (see p. 58) and income support and residential care (p. 59).

Some poverty and other studies

A noticeable feature of much research into poverty has been the prominence of older people. Some of these studies will now be referred to in chronological order.

The studies: As early as 1895 a Royal Commission had investigated 'the Aged Poor' and recommended some alterations to the Poor Law system. Then a notable researcher, Seebohm Rowntree, carried out a survey of poverty in York in 1899 and again in 1936 and 1948. He concluded that the main causes of poverty had been low wages in 1899, unemployment in 1936 and old age in 1948. In 1947 Rowntree chaired a Committee on the problems of ageing and the care of old people (Rowntree 1947) [Document 6]. One of their main conclusions was that acute poverty had been substantially abolished among 'the aged' and that state pensions were 'now probably adequate' (Rowntree 1947: 99). They felt that there was still a considerable measure of austerity, but the flexible administration of the National Assistance Board had been successful in adjusting benefits to need in a humane but not unreasonably extravagant manner. In 1953 an official committee chaired by Sir Thomas Phillips was set up: 'to review the economic and financial problems involved in providing for old age, having regard to the prospective increase in the numbers of the aged, and to make recommendations' (Chancellor of the Exchequer 1954). They considered the economic problems to be those resulting from the need to accumulate or free resources out of which adequate provision could be made for old people, and the financial problems to be those arising from the need to transfer to old people the purchasing power that would give them the appropriate command over those resources (Chancellor of the Exchequer 1954).

In 1962 Cole and Utting in *The Economic Circumstances of Old People* noted that all the problems they looked at – loneliness, ill health and poverty – appeared to be suffered in *extreme* form by only a relatively small minority (Cole and Utting 1962). Two periods were examined by Abel-Smith and Townsend and reported on in *The Poor and the Poorest* (Abel-Smith and Townsend 1965). Comparing 1953–4 and 1960 they found that 7.8 per cent of people in the United Kingdom (4 million people) were living below 'national assistance' level in 1953–4. About half of them were living in households whose heads were retired. In 1960 they found that

14.2 per cent of people in the United Kingdom (7.5 million people) were living below 'national assistance' level. About 35 per cent were living in households primarily dependent on pensions. One of the reasons for the apparent increase from 7.8 to 14.2 per cent living at this low level appeared to be the relative increase in the number of old people in the population. Another reason was the slight relative increase in the number of chronically sick middle-aged men and the relative increase in the number of large families. Abel-Smith and Townsend concluded: 'On the whole the data we have presented contradicts the commonly held view that a trend towards greater equality has accompanied the trend towards greater affluence' (1965: 66).

Townsend and Wedderburn in their 1962 survey of over 4,000 people, *The Aged in the Welfare State*, found that in general old people had income levels of half or more below the levels of younger persons in the population (1965). Few old people had substantial assets and over one third were solely dependent on state benefits. About two fifths of the men and of the couples and one tenth of the women received a pension from their employers, but these were relatively small. The very old were worse off as a result of inflation and because they were less likely to work.

There was mounting evidence that some old people were living on a smaller income than the scale provided by the NAB. The MPNI, in co-operation with the NAB, carried out an enquiry in 1965 to find out their numbers and the reasons why they did not apply for assistance. The enquiry consisted of a survey of nearly 11,000 pensioners and the findings, *Financial and Other Circumstances of Retirement Pensioners* (MPNI 1966), were similar to those of other researchers. Incomes of pensioners were low. Nearly half of the men had occupational pensions. The corresponding proportions were one quarter for single women other than widows, and one ninth for widows.

Turning to the main purpose of the enquiry, it was estimated that rather more than 700,000 pensioner households (about 850,000 pensioners) could have received assistance if they had applied for it (MPNI 1966: 83–4). The main reasons why pensioners did not apply for assistance were: lack of knowledge, the dislike of 'charity', a feeling that they were managing all right on what they had and (a small proportion) a dislike of going to the NAB (MPNI 1966: 84–5).

The Townsend and Wedderburn survey and that of the MPNI both found that the older the person the smaller the income, that few old people had substantial assets or savings and that single and widowed women were the worst off. In Townsend's 1968–9 national sample, older people comprised one third of those in poverty. One of his findings, reported in *Poverty in the United Kingdom*, was that: 'People tend to separate into two groups, one anticipating a comfortable and even early retirement, the other dreading the prospect and depending almost entirely for their livelihood on the resources made available by the State through its social security system' (Townsend 1979: 820).

Many of the findings of the 1976 OPCS survey for DHSS, such as the dependence of elderly people on state benefits and the decline of income with age, were similar to previous surveys (Hunt 1978). It is interesting, however, that financial difficulties did not figure prominently in the list of things they disliked, although suggestions about ways in which they could be helped *did* include a number having financial implications.

A survey of 1,174 people in Great Britain in 1983 provided information on the comparative living standards of the poor and attitudes to them (Mack and Lansley 1985). In the Townsend study elderly people represented about one third of all those in poverty. In the 1983 study the proportion was about one fifth. Moreover, it was not only the case that elderly people formed a smaller proportion of those in poverty generally, they also formed a smaller proportion of those in intense poverty. The researchers put the decreased proportion down to higher pensions, including a higher proportion having an occupational pension, but also attributed it to the dramatic rise in the numbers of unemployed people.

A similar finding about the drop in the proportions of pensioners in poverty was established in a special analysis of the *Family Expenditure Survey* which the government conducted for the 1984–5 *Social Security Review* (see Social Security Advisory Committee 1988). This revealed that there had been a shift in the composition of the lowest fifth of the income distribution, with a reduction in the number of pensioners and an increase in the number of families falling in the bottom group (see Dawson and Evans 1987 and Social Security Advisory Committee 1988: 50).

The OPCS *Surveys of Disability* in GB in 1985–8 also shed light on poverty. *The Financial Circumstances of Disabled Adults Living in Private Households* showed that a high proportion (69 per cent) of disabled adults were over the age of 60 compared with 29 per cent in the general population (Martin and White 1988). However, disabled pensioners had similar incomes on average to those of pensioners in general since all pensioners were largely dependent on state benefits and had on average lower incomes than non-pensioners. But the research makes it clear that disabled people have extra expenditure, although for disabled pensioners this was less marked than for non-pensioners.

Useful information was gained from the OPCS Survey of *Retirement and Retirement Plans* undertaken for DSS (Bone *et al.* 1992). The main purposes were to:

- identify factors which influence the ages at which people retire;
- aid prediction of the distribution of income after retirement for future pensioners;

- provide up-to-date information about the financial preparations people make for retirement.

The survey covered 3,543 people aged 55–69 and took place in 1988–9. The research showed that the groups receiving the highest income before retirement also received the highest post-retirement incomes. 'Thus among both the retired and non-retired: men, non-manual workers, people without disabilities and those in work currently or at the time they retire have higher incomes respectively than: women, manual workers, people with disabilities and people not working as they near retirement' (Bone *et al.* 1992: *x*).

Most studies of the financial position of older people in the 1990s have been secondary analyses of large annual government surveys – mainly the *General Household Surveys* and the *Family Expenditure Surveys*. Three inquiries that have made extensive use of secondary data are relevant. The Carnegie Inquiry into *Life, Work and Livelihood in the Third Age* (Carnegie Inquiry into the Third Age 1993) sponsored a number of pieces of research and the relevant one here is *Income: Pensions, Earnings and Savings in the Third Age* (Johnson *et al.* 1992). The Carnegie Inquiry took 50–74 as a working definition of the third age. The research showed great disparities in income in third agers. As might be expected it was found that income falls with age among the 50–74 year age group with the steepest falls during the early 60s as more retire. A worrying trend for the future, however, was the finding that some of the very poorest third-agers were under 60. Many of these were involuntarily unemployed with 'little time to re-establish themselves in work and earn a decent income' (Johnson *et al.* 1992: 34).

The second inquiry was set up by the Joseph Rowntree Foundation and was on *Income and Wealth* (Joseph Rowntree Foundation 1995). The purpose was to consider living standards, income and personal wealth of people of all ages. Key findings were:

- the gaps between rich and poor have widened;
- the growing gap has multiple causes;
- differences in income from work have grown rapidly;
- social security slowed the growth of inequality in the early 1980s, but has not since;
- the tax system did not slow inequality growth;
- particular groups and areas have done disproportionately badly;
- wealth inequalities have stopped declining and have now levelled out.

Pensioners were one of the groups singled out for comment. It was found that their incomes had risen but had become more unequal.

The third inquiry was on retirement income. Its terms of reference were to:

- review the present arrangements in the UK for the provision of retirement income;

- consider in particular the roles of the state, employers and individuals and the suitability of different financing mechanisms;
- consider, taking account of the economic and social implications, whether changes should be made to ensure the adequacy of retirement income in the longer term;
- make recommendations.

Their report was *Pensions: 2000 and Beyond* (Retirement Income Inquiry 1996). The familiar picture of growing disparity between better and worse off pensioners since 1980 was painted. The very old, single women, including a growing number who are divorced, were found to be especially likely to be poor.

Attempts are now being made to make comparisons with other countries. Laczko (1990) concludes that it is difficult to draw firm conclusions about poverty among older people in the European Community because of lack of comparative data. An international comparison of incomes and living standards of older people also found that determinants of living standards are complex and may differ significantly in different countries (Whiteford and Kennedy 1995). However, a study for the EC found both persistent problems of poverty and widening inequalities between younger and older pensioners in the EC (Walker 1992:178).

Laczko states that on the information available old age is still more associated with dependence on social assistance in Britain than in other northern countries of the EC. This, he says, is partly because the state pension in Britain is much less generous than in other EC countries. Whiteford and Kennedy found that: 'The average incomes of older people in the UK are lower as a proportion of the average income of the total population than in most other countries in this study' (Whiteford and Kennedy 1995: *xi*). However, there was a lower level of inequality in the incomes of the older population than in many other countries. 'This appeared to be because the UK has a more effective benefit safety net than several other countries' (Whiteford and Kennedy 1995: *xi*). Other research shows that slightly higher proportions of older people in the UK (45 per cent) said that their financial position was very comfortable or comfortable than the average for the 12 EC countries (36 per cent) (Walker 1993: 17).

Some definitions: The term 'absolute poverty' is not usually used to mean subsistence level but simply to mean a poverty level expressed in absolute terms (e.g. £50) rather than relative terms (e.g. half mean income). Some researchers have used as a guide supplementary benefit, now income support level, which is higher than would be needed for sheer physical survival. Others have claimed that a better yardstick would be a certain percentage above that level. Thus Abel-Smith and Townsend added 40 per cent, taking into account discretionary payments and statutory disregards (Abel-Smith and Townsend 1965).

These differing definitions make strict comparison between the poverty studies difficult. Taking gross or net incomes alone reveals only a crude indication of poverty. Even more sophisticated analyses which incorporate indirect taxes and make allowance for use of services funded through public expenditure, such as health, have their drawbacks. Any study relating to the incomes of older people has to start from the premise of caution. Evidence is conflicting and sometimes this is because some researchers use incomes of individuals and some of households. The DHSS abandoned the notion of a poverty line based on income support and replaced it with proportions of mean/median household income and analyses of the bottom fifth of the household income distribution, known as households below average income.

It is generally accepted that any definition must take account of more than just financial matters. Abel-Smith and Townsend considered that income and expenditure should be regarded as only one of a number of indicators of poverty and that differences in home environment, material possessions and educational and occupational resources must also be included. Townsend suggested a definition based on 'relative deprivation' – that is: 'the absence or inadequacy of those diets, amenities, standards, services and activities which are common or customary in society' (Townsend 1979: 915). A great deal of the debate on poverty since this study has been about the kinds of services and items which are essential to avoid poverty/deprivation. This wider definition, taking account of not just material deprivation but also of people's place in society and how far they are excluded from taking part in the normal pursuits of their peers, is an advance on previous measures.

Some studies are now asking questions about both income and expenditure and also about people's feelings about being poor. For example, the OPCS *Surveys of Disability* used two subjective measures of financial position and standard of living (Martin and White 1988). These were how people managed and how satisfied they were with their standard of living. They also asked about lack of particular items, as had Townsend and Mack and Lansley. But they went further and asked if this was because they did not want them or could not afford them.

A useful discussion of absolute and relative poverty, relative deprivation and inequality can be found in Alcock (1987) and details of the poverty debate in Oppenheim (1993). Another useful definition is 'modest but adequate' which was the title of a report (Parker 1995).

The present position

***The overall incomes of pensioners*:** The main need for older people is for an adequate income when they are no longer able to earn their own living. The current pension system is one where there is a universal (although strictly speaking it is only paid to people with a contribution record) flat-rate pension and a second-tier system where a person may belong to an approved occupational scheme, the state SERPS scheme or a personal pension. Before 1989 pensioners did not receive a full pension if they earned over a certain amount but this so-called 'earnings rule' has now been abolished. (Details of all benefits are given annually by ACE in their *Your Rights* booklet.) Anyone over 80 who is not getting a contributory retirement pension and who satisfies certain residence conditions, is entitled to a non-contributory pension. In 1993–4 8.1 million pensioners in Great Britain were receiving a retirement pension only and 1.4 million a retirement pension and income support (CSO 1996: 154).

There are powerful voices maintaining that poverty and deprivation in old age have persisted despite social recognition for over a century and more than 30 years of welfare provision (e.g. Walker 1990). Particularly criticised is the breaking of the link in 1979 between the level of the state pension and that of prices or earnings, whichever is the greater (e.g. Atkinson 1991). Detailed research based on the *General Household Surveys* and the *Family Expenditure Surveys* has emphasised the great diversity in the incomes of different groups of pensioners. During the 1980s the average real incomes of pensioners rose 15–30 per cent but the gaps between rich and poor, older and younger pensioners and those with and without occupational pensions all grew (Hancock and Weir 1994). As noted (on p. 50) *The Retirement and Retirement Plans* survey showed that the groups receiving the highest income before retirement also received the highest post-retirement incomes (Bone *et al.* 1992: *x*).

The components of income and the role of pensions: There seems little disagreement about the importance of state income to old people. For example, in a comparative study of the last 50 years it was found that at no time in recent years has the state played a subsidiary role (Falkingham and Gordon 1988). These researchers found that the role of the family has always been minimal. A telling statistic is the percentage of income from social security benefits. In 1993 72 per cent of all pensioner units (i.e. single people over state pension age or a couple where the husband is over state pension age) received at least half their income from state benefits (DSS 1995a: 15).

Many older people and academics have argued for an increase in the basic level of the state pension. A comparison of attitudes of pensioners between 1983 and 1991, based on the *British Social Attitudes Surveys*, showed that 40 per cent of them felt that the level of the state pension was 'very low' in 1991 compared with 25 per cent in 1983 (Askham, Hancock and Hills 1995). In 1996 67 per cent of pensioners and 61 per cent of the total population said that the current state pension was too low and should be raised even if it meant increasing taxes (ACE 1996: 5). Midwinter in *The Wage of*

Retirement: The Case for a New Pensions Policy suggested a single retirement wage in place of the contributory pension and means-tested benefits (Midwinter 1985). He also suggested that older people should be treated as citizen-pensioners rather than welfare bene-ficiaries and their income should be looked on as a wage of retirement.

In 1991 three fifths of retired people and half of non-retired people thought that the government should have the *main* responsibility for ensuring that people have an adequate pension (Askham, Hancock and Hills 1995). (But 30 per cent felt that the responsibility should be shared equally between employers and government.) There has, however, been a shift in the sources of pensioners' income. As Table 5.1 shows, while average gross income (adjusted to 1993 prices) rose from an average of £120.60 per week in 1981 to £170.20 in 1993 the percentage from benefits dropped from 61 per cent to 53 per cent and that from occupational pensions rose from 16 per cent to 25 per cent. But in 1993 38 per cent of pensioners had no occupational pension at all (DSS 1995a: 11 and see also Hancock and Weir 1994).

For some the combination of a private pension and home ownership will mean greater affluence in old age. But as the Joseph Rowntree Foundation (JRF) Inquiry into Income and Wealth found, 'a substantial minority of even new pensioners do *not* have occupa-tional pensions or private savings and remain heavily reliant on state pensions' (Joseph Rowntree Foundation 1991: 28). Both this inquiry and the Carnegie Inquiry into the Third Age called for wide public debate about pensions and other issues to do with income in old age so that action could be based on a political consensus. Clear recommendations did come from the Retirement Income Inquiry although they too called for public debate. The Retirement Income

Table 5.1 **Pensioners'[1] gross income: by source United Kingdom**

| | Percentages | | | |
	1981	*1990–1*	*1992*	*1993*
Benefits	61	50	50	53
Occupational pensions	16	22	24	25
Investments	13	20	19	16
Earnings	9	7	6	6
Other	–	1	1	–
All gross income (= 100%) (£ per week at July 1993 prices[2])	120.60	163.30	170.40	170.20

[1] Pensioner units.
[2] Adjusted to July 1993 prices using the retail prices index less local taxes.

Source: CSO *Social Trends*, No. 26, HMSO, 1996, p. 102.

Inquiry said that, although there are strong arguments for enhancing the value of the basic income, this is not possible within realistic resource constraints (Retirement Income Inquiry 1996: Ch. 6). Their solution was an assured pension. This is an arrangement under which the state tops up income in retirement to some minimum level. The components would be the basic pension and an additional income-related amount where necessary to increase total income to an adequate minimum level. The level would increase with age and assets would not be taken into account but savings and earnings would.

There have been other powerful advocates of change. Atkinson argues the re-establishment of earnings indexation for the basic pension and also compulsory membership of a defined benefit pension plan, restoration of the original SERPS formula and the introduction of a new minimum pension guarantee (Atkinson 1994, and see also the Commission on Social Justice 1994).

There does appear to be a measure of agreement among commentators and inquiries into the need for encouragement to be given to all income groups to accumulate private and occupational pensions over and above state entitlement.

Income support: Income support, formerly supplementary benefit, is a means-tested benefit. It is available to home owners, tenants and to people living with families. It may also be a passport to other benefits such as free dental treatment and grants from the social fund. The original Beveridge plan was for the national insurance retirement pension to be sufficiently high for pensioners not, in general, to have to rely on means-tested assistance. This has not happened and so large numbers of older people have had to apply for the latter. The safety net of income support has become an important element of pensioners' resources. Numbers of pensioner households claiming income support have remained relatively stable between 1989 and 1994, although they have declined as a proportion of claimants from 39 per cent to 31 per cent (derived from DSS 1995a: 18 Table 2.05).

Occupational pensions: Many public services and commercial organisations now run occupational pension schemes with pension based on final salary. In the 1994 *GHS*, of those working full-time 60 per cent of men and 54 per cent of women had an occupational pension. The figure for women working part-time was 19 per cent and for men 16 per cent (CSO 1996: 111). However, the amount received may be small. Membership of occupational pensions has now levelled off (Retirement Income Inquiry 1996). A number of problems over occupational pensions, including transferability, were highlighted by the Goode report (1993).

Personal (private) pensions: These pensions, which bring tax advantages, could become more important and have been encouraged by the government. They may be bought by anyone who has taxable earnings from employment or self-employment but who is not in an employer's contracted-out pension scheme. There has been a major expansion of personal pension plans following the Social Security Act 1986. In 1993–4 5.6 million individuals had opted to take up personal pensions (House of Commons Written Answer 4.12.1995, *Hansard* Column 90). Questions placed in the OPCS *Omnibus Survey* in 1995 aimed to gauge how much individuals themselves would or could pay to get higher pensions or retire early (Hancock *et al.* 1995). This showed that those who most needed to increase their pension contributions were least able or willing to do so. One third of those who considered their likely future pension to be definitely inadequate would or could not pay extra to increase it, while well over half those who regarded their likely future pension as definitely adequate would or could pay extra t' increase it. The *British Social Attitudes Survey* in 1991 showed that three quarters of people thought that the government should encourage people to provide *something* for their retirement themselves (Askham, Hancock and Hills 1995).

Personal saving: This is another way in which people can provide for their old age. The 1965 MPNI survey showed that few old people had much in the way of savings (MPNI 1966) and the position in 1976 was very similar (Hunt 1978). In part this may be due to low levels of wages and unemployment in the past, but in part it may also be due to the effect of inflation which erodes the value of savings. In 1982 two thirds of pensioners received income from their own savings and investments, though often this was a small proportion of their total income (Fiegehen 1986). The proportion of pensioner units with investment income rose from 62 per cent in 1979 to 73 per cent in 1993 (when the median was only £8.70 per week and the mean £37.40, DSS 1995a: 10). Table 5.1 shows that the percentage of pensioners' incomes from investments rose in the years to 1990–1 but has now fallen. This is likely to be due to changing interest rates. There are a growing number of ways in which savings can be made, such as personal equity plans.

The most important asset for older people is housing, which represents almost half of all wealth (McKay 1992). Few attractive means of accessing housing equity without the person moving have either been developed or taken up (McKay 1992).

Other forms of financial help

There are other ways in which financial help may be given and some of these are listed below.

The social fund: The social fund has both non-discretionary and discretionary elements. The former provides entitlements for exceptional expenses, such as funeral expenses, for certain people entitled to means-tested benefits, and help with the cost of heating during periods of cold weather for people receiving income support. The discretionary element, from a fixed budget, provides budgeting and crisis loans (about 70 per cent of the budget) and non-repayable community care grants (about 30 per cent of the budget). Budgeting loans are for people who have been on income support for at least 26 weeks and need items they cannot afford. Crisis loans are available for anyone (not just those on income support) who needs help in an emergency or disaster. The purpose of community care grants was: 'to help people re-establish themselves in the community, to avoid institutional care, or to ease particular exceptional pressure on families' (Sec. of St. for Social Services, 1985b: 42). They are available for help with moving out of institutional or residential care, help to remain at home (such as minor house repairs), help with certain travel expenses and help with exceptional pressures on families caused by disability, chronic sickness or a breakdown in a relationship.

In contrast to single payments, which were a legal entitlement governed by regulations, there are no legal entitlements to the discretionary parts of the social fund. The only part of the fund which is not cash-limited, and which is based not on discretion but on regulations, is for grants for funerals, maternity and cold weather. Although an applicant can ask for a review by a social fund officer, and then an inspector, if refused a grant or loan there is no right of appeal. There are great variations in the success of applications for grants and general ignorance about these grants. In 1989–90 more than half of applicants (53 per cent) were turned down for community care grants (National Audit Office 1991: 27). Subsequent research has criticised the tight cash limits, discretionary decision making and the emphasis on loans (Craig 1992).

Help with health costs: People aged 60 and over are entitled to free prescriptions. Pensioners and others on income support are entitled to help with certain other NHS charges. They may be eligible for help with the costs of eye tests, glasses, dental treatment, wigs and fabric supports and travel costs to hospital.

Help with heating costs: Housing surveys show that older people tend to live in older, poorer accommodation than many other households. This means that they will need to spend a higher proportion of their income on fuel than most households and therefore need heat for longer periods. These facts, as well as the great increase in the cost of fuel, have given rise to widespread concern about the many older people who are living in homes which are cold (see Chapter 6). Supplementary pensioners used to be eligible for help with extra heating costs but this amount has now been subsumed into the general amount given in income support.

However, for those on income support cold weather payments are automatically paid from the social fund for each period of seven days when the temperature has been, or is forecast to be, 0 degrees Celsius or below.

Help with housing costs: Financial help is available from local authorities (but according to national rules and national funding) in the form of housing benefit which is available for help with rent and certain service charges (see Brown, 1990 for a detailed account of the history of this).

A major problem faced by older owner-occupiers is the cost of repairs to the home. Income support can cover certain housing costs for home owners, including mortgage interest payments and interest on loans for some repairs and improvements. Some building societies and a small number of local authorities make available interest-only loans to older people who need to carry out bigger repairs and improvements. The capital is recovered from the sale proceeds of the property. Full interest has to be paid monthly, but in some circumstances income support assistance from DSS may be available to cover some or all of the interest. In certain circumstances a grant may be given by the local authority to repair or improve the home (see Chapter 7).

Council tax: The council tax replaced the community charge, or poll tax as it was more often called, which in turn had replaced local rates. Council tax benefit is available for people on low incomes and with savings below a certain level. There is also a second adult rebate for some people who have someone with a low income living with them.

Income tax: People aged 65 or over receive a higher tax allowance than younger people and allowances are still higher at age 75. However, these increased allowances are subject to an income limit. Older people may also qualify for other allowances such as the blind person's allowance or widow's bereavement allowance.

Attendance allowance: A tax-free attendance allowance is payable to people who need frequent attention or continual supervision both by day and at night. A lower amount is payable if the help is needed only for the day or the night. It is only available for people over the age of 65 or for people who become disabled earlier but do not claim until after reaching 66. People outside these ages may be eligible for the disability living allowance.

Disability living allowance: This has replaced attendance and mobility allowance for people under the age of 65 who need help with personal care, getting around or both because they are ill or disabled. There is both a care and a mobility component although the allowance can be spent as wished. The care component is payable at three different levels and the mobility component at two levels.

Paying for residential and nursing home care: Income support is available for elderly people with low incomes for both these forms of care (see Chapter 8).

Other financial concessions: Travel at a reduced rate, or free between certain hours, is subsidised by some local authorities. Some also give concessions for other services such as for pensioners attending further education courses or public entertainments. There is much variation between local authorities. British Rail allows pensioners to travel at reduced rates with a special railcard. Television licences at a reduced rate are available for pensioners in old people's homes and sheltered housing.

Expenditure

Pensioners have a slightly different pattern of expenditure to other households. The 1991 *Family Expenditure Survey* showed that compared with non-pensioners they spent more on fuel but less on housing, motoring, clothing, household goods and leisure services (Smeaton and Hancock 1995: 30). The largest component of pensioner's expenditure is food, followed by housing and fuel (Smeaton and Hancock 1995: 46).

Looking at overall spending between 1979 and 1991 pensioner's total spending levels increased, but by slightly less than non-pensioners (Smeaton and Hancock 1995: 46). In 1991 pensioners' weekly spending tended to be around two thirds of that of non-pensioners. Those over 75 and those living alone spent, on average, less than the under-75s and those living with others (Smeaton and Hancock 1995: 46).

The 1994 *GHS* showed that households containing at least one person over the age of 65 were less likely to own a telephone, deep freezer, washing machine, tumble drier, microwave oven or car than households containing no older persons (OPCS 1996: 158).

Some other issues

Public expenditure on pensions: In Great Britain expenditure on retirement pensions rose from £5,662 millions in 1976–7 (CSO 1991: 87) to an estimated outturn in 1995–6 of £30,146 millions (Sec. of St. for Social Security 1996). At least part of this was accounted for by the rise in the number of pensioners, and pressure will grow in the first quarter of the twenty-first century for the same reason. Of all social security benefits, retirement pensions are by far the largest, accounting for about half of total expenditure (Johnson *et al.* 1992: 45). The *British Social Attitudes Survey* in 1991 showed retirement pensions and disability benefits stand out as priorities for any extra spending amongst both the retired and non-retired, although more of the non-retired favour benefits for families and the unemployed (Askham, Hancock and Hills 1995: 26). In the 1994 *British Social Attitudes Survey* 78 per cent of the population surveyed wanted more government spending on pensions and 21 per cent said it should be the same as now (Taylor-Gooby 1995: 4).

Age for retirement: People can, of course, retire at any age but cannot draw a state pension until the minimum state pension age, namely 60 for a woman and 65 for a man. A few continue for longer (e.g. clergy, judges, those in domestic service, the self-employed) but they are the exception. Nearly half of those within five years of pension age are not in paid work (CSO 1995: 66, Table 4.4). Some people, especially those in heavy manual jobs, may wish for early retirement, while others would prefer to stay on for longer. The Sex Discrimination Act 1986 makes it illegal for men and women to be forced to retire from work at different ages. A flexible age for retirement may be more in keeping with the varying physical and mental capacities of old people and the case for this has been carefully set out in *Flexibility and Fairness* (Tompkins 1989). The disparity between the ages at which men and women are eligible for a state pension is another factor. Other countries also have unequal pension ages, although within the EC in 1996 nine out of the fifteen have equalised (France at 60; Germany, Ireland, Luxembourg, Netherlands, Finland, Sweden and Spain at 65; Denmark at 67, and Belgium gives flexibility to both men and women at 60–65). In Italy the age is 62 for men and 57 for women. In the UK, Austria, Greece and Portugal the age at which the state pension is paid is to be equalised at 65 for both men and women over specified periods.

Take-up of benefits: One of the regular findings of surveys has been that elderly people do not all claim the benefits to which they are entitled. Income support is currently not taken up by between a third and a quarter of pensioners who are entitled to it (Retirement Income Inquiry 1996: 25). Although the amounts are often small the value of this small weekly entitlement, stretching over years, may not be inconsiderable. The Retirement Income Inquiry said that because income support was part of the social security system designed to cover a much wider set of social needs than ensuring adequate income in retirement, 'it involves intrusive bureaucracy, is complex and expensive to administer, penalises unacceptably those who work and those who save, is often regarded as demeaning' (Retirement Income Inquiry 1996: 25). DSS estimates for 1993/94 show that pensioners had the lowest take-up for income support, housing benefit and council tax benefit (DSS press release 15.12.1995).

Abuse: There is great public concern about wrongful claims to social security and in 1971 the Fisher Committee was set up to report on this form of abuse. In *Report of the Committee on Abuse of Social Security Benefits* (DHSS 1973) they found that over non-disclosure of earnings there was abuse 'to a substantial extent' though no evidence was given about the extent among pensioners. The Committee considered how the DHSS attempted to make sure that pensioners were aware of the earnings rule and correctly reported any earnings which might affect the amount of benefit payable. They felt that there was little public sympathy for those who both worked and drew benefit, but added: 'More sympathy is felt for pensioners, for disabled men and for women without male support who do part-time or casual work and earn a little over the "disregard" limits. Though this is "abuse" it could take a lower place in the attentions of the Departments' (DHSS 1973: 277). Since this date there has been little in the way of systematic monitoring of abuse but the abolition of the earnings rule may have made this less relevant. During the 1970s there was a 'vigorous, and at times strident, public campaign against social security abuse' but in the early 1980s, possibly due to the use of special claims control and regular fraud teams, there was a sharp decline in the number of cases of prosecutions for suspected social security fraud (Barker *et al.* 1990). In 1995 it was estimated by the DSS that there was an annual fraud level of £1.4 billion for income support and unemployment benefits (DSS press release 31.1.1996). In 1995 cases of confirmed fraud among pensioners were 2.8 per cent, which was lower than for any other group (Sainsbury 1996: 19).

Employment

Introduction

Retirement from work can be viewed from a number of different standpoints – economic, medical, administrative and social. Economically, it implies the loss of trained and experienced workers and also considerable expenditure by the state on pensions. Medically, there may be the effect of ageing on productivity, although there is little evidence about this, and of retirement on the individual's health. Administratively, there is the problem of deciding what type of retirement policy should be adopted. Socially, it can be examined for its impact on the happiness of individuals and their families.

Decline in proportions of economically active older people

An important change took place in the economic activity rate (i.e. the percentage of the age group gainfully employed or seeking employment) of most older people between 1951 and 1995 in Great Britain.

Although the trends are slightly different between and within cohorts (Johnson *et al.* 1996) the overall trend is of a decline. This is true for people over the age of 50 as well as for those of pensionable age (Tillsley 1995). For those of pensionable age, 31 per cent of men were economically active in 1951 but in 1995 this had dropped to 8 per cent (Taylor and Walker 1995: 142). For women of pensionable age there was a rise for those aged 60–64 from 14 per cent in 1951 to 26 per cent in 1995 and a drop for the over-65s from 4 per cent to 3 per cent (Taylor and Walker 1995: 142). A similar picture of declining economic activity rates can be seen in the EU and in many other countries although there are wide variations (Moore *et al.* 1994 and CSO 1996).

The rise and fall in the number of older people in paid employment is to some extent related to the state of the economy. Comments on changes in government policy have been made thus: 'twenty-five years ago the labour shortage led to official encouragement of older people remaining at work, *inter alia* by promoting research to show that their capabilities were on a par with others; now the situation is different. The point has been made that official interest in the elderly employed has tended to be influenced by the state of the economy so that voluntary early departure from the labour force is now regarded as worth encouraging' (Jolly *et al.* 1980). In the 1980s and early 1990s the recession was one of the main influences for shedding older workers.

The House of Commons Employment Committee in *The Employment Patterns of the Over-50s* put it thus: 'When we began to plan the inquiry [1987], interest still centred on the development of schemes to ease older workers into early retirement. By the time we had finished taking our evidence there had been a dramatic shift of emphasis and there was a growing discussion of ways in which older people could be persuaded to stay at work in order to offset the impending shortage of young workers. The pendulum has rarely swung so swiftly' (House of Commons Employment Committee 1989: *ix*). They later argued that the nature of work would change as well as the nature of the workforce. 'As part-time work, self-employment and career mobility increase, the post-industrial revolution pattern of a lifetime of paid, full-time work in a single trade or occupation, frequently for one employer, becomes less dominant' (House of Commons Employment Committee 1989: *ix*). Currently the expected drop in the younger working population (see Ermisch 1990) is now encouraging some employers to woo older people back to work. This is particularly noticeable in the retail trade.

Why older people stop working: As might be expected, the percentage of people working decreases sharply at older ages. Most older people have to leave their jobs on reaching the official retiring age, unless they are self-employed. The trend to earlier retirement is shown in the OPCS Survey *Retirement and Retirement Plans* (Bone *et al.* 1992). There is now also some evidence that more people would like to retire earlier (Hancock *et al.* 1995).

Why do people leave their jobs before they reach retirement age? Ill health has always been a major reason. Surveys, such as *Reasons Given for Retiring or Continuing at Work* (MPNI 1954) and subsequent research, have confirmed that many who retire early do so for health reasons. In the OPCS *Retirement and Retirement Plans* survey, ill health was the main reason given (by 43 per cent of the retired men and 31 per cent of the retired women) for taking early retirement (Bone *et al.* 1992: 56). Ill health also featured highly in the Carnegie study of employment in the Third Age (Trinder *et al.* 1992).

A second reason is financial inducements but this is more likely to happen with men and with Social Classes 1 and 11 (Bone *et al.* 1992). The inducement of an occupational pension has been shown (e.g. Trinder *et al.* 1992). An international survey showed that 'An abundance of early retirement pension schemes have tended to lead to lower average retirement ages. Early exit from work has been welcomed generally by employee representatives' (Whitting *et al.* 1995: 147). A third reason is redundancy. However, redundancy has increased less among older workers than among other age groups (Dibden and Hibbett 1993). Other factors include, especially for women, wanting to spend more time with partner/family (Bone *et al.* 1992: 56). The decline in manufacturing and construction industries where many older men were employed, and a reduction in demand for unskilled workers, is yet another factor (Dibden and Hibbett 1993).

Another reason why older people stop working may be because of the views of society. The House of Commons Social Services Committee said: 'The strongest pressure (for early retirement) comes from the high rates of youth unemployment leading to individual and collective beliefs that older workers should retire to make way for younger people' (House of Commons Social Services Committee, quoted in Victor 1987: 174). Across Europe nearly one third of the general public agreed strongly or slightly that people in their fifties should give up work to make way for younger people (Walker 1993: 25). It is also worth noting that ending paid employment for a minority of people does not always mean that status is lost. Doctors and clergy, for example, can continue to use their titles.

Older people who want to continue to work: Work provides income, status, interest and companionship and the need for these does not necessarily become less on retirement. People may wish to continue in work for all these reasons. It can be argued that while many older people prefer to retire rather than continue in work, others would suffer a substantial fall in living standards and prefer to work. For people who are self-employed this is easier than for employees. The proportion of older people who are self-employed is higher than for other age groups. In 1994 of all people over the age of 16 who were employed 13 per cent were self-employed. The figures for those in employment aged 50 to state pension age was 17 per cent and for those of state pension age and over 25 per cent (Tillsley 1995). What is not known, however, is what proportion of older people become self-employed after retirement.

Older people are more likely to work part-time than other age groups. In 1994 between one fifth and one quarter of those aged under the age of 60 worked part-time compared with over one third of those aged 60–64 and two thirds of those aged 75 and over (Tillsley 1995). In all age groups, including old ones, women were much more likely than men to work part-time.

Those who have been compulsorily retired from their jobs may seek another one, and for those who have to retire in their 50s (e.g. from the police or armed services) a long spell in another occupation may be possible. The most likely outcome is part-time work. Some have suggested that jobs suitable for older people should be kept open for them and that special training should be provided. This, however, assumes that older people are alike and can be provided for as a group, whereas all the evidence shows that each is an individual with particular skills and differing levels of performance.

Why employ older workers? Some have argued that work after retirement should be encouraged. The Rowntree Committee, for example, pointed out that from the economic standpoint it was important for people of pensionable age to remain at work so long as they could make a worthwhile contribution to the creation of wealth (Rowntree 1947). However, these views have to be considered against the background of high levels of unemployment. As well as the argument about the creation of wealth, a growing number of other reasons are being put (e.g. by the Carnegie Inquiry into the Third Age 1993, Retirement Income Inquiry 1996, and by a variety of researchers such as Trinder *et al.* 1992, Itzin and Phillipson 1993, Institute of Personnel Management 1993, Taylor and Walker 1995, Local Government Management Board 1995). These include:

- a response to skill shortages;
- a response to the growing number of older consumers;
- the waste of investment in older worker's training;
- the value of older workers who may have different contributions and experiences to make;
- a decrease in the dependency ratio and the burden on those in work;
- the fact that staff turnover is lower for older workers than younger ones;
- the fact that older workers are more likely to accept the kind of work increasingly on offer i.e. part-time and lower paid.

Some problems

Attitudes: In Chapter 2 reference was made to society's perceptions of ageing and it was remarked that older people are often regarded as second-class citizens unable to make much contribution to the world around them. A blanket approach like this is unhelpful and inaccurate. Research in two particular spheres, the physiological and psychological aspects of ageing, demonstrates this in relation to employment.

Research into the physiological aspects of ageing is clearly important for the light that can be shed on physical and mental performance. The general conclusion seems to be that while performance in certain ways, such as physical strength, does decline with age, chronological age is by no means an accurate indicator of capacity to perform a task (Straka 1990, Trinder *et al.* 1992). A summary of much recent research concluded that age is not a sound basis on which to judge the ability to work or learn (Dibden and Hibbett 1993).

Psychological evidence is just as important, because the way in which both prospective employee and employer view the older worker will affect their attitudes. There is evidence that stereotypes about ageing are common and that these influence the behaviour of people in the employment market. These beliefs can affect recruitment, transfer, training and redundancy policies.

Age bars and age discrimination: Age restrictions applied to 28 per cent of all job vacancies in 1994 compared with 39 per cent in 1990 (*Hansard* 12.6.1995 col. 390–1). Evidence drawn from advertised job vacancies and in the recruitment process has shown that the incidence of age-qualified vacancies is fairly widespread (e.g. Equal Opportunities Commission 1989, quoted in McEwen 1990: 88, Trinder *et al.* 1992, Itzin and Phillipson 1993, Dibden and Hibbett 1993, Institute of Personnel Management 1993, Taylor and Walker 1995). Trinder's study was mainly of secondary sources of data and was for the Carnegie Inquiry into the Third Age. That by Itzin and Phillipson was of the situation of older workers in local government. The one undertaken by the Institute of Personnel Management included case studies of 17 organisations in both the public and private sectors in the UK, a survey of personnel practitioners and some information about European policies. All these give evidence about age bars and discrimination.

A number of reasons for age bars have been suggested: the presence of career structures and internal labour markets (people may be recruited and trained to fit in with the structure of a particular organisation); the likely age at which the peak of professional output is reached; the standard of health and fitness required; restrictive practices; length of training required; wage-for-age scales; a filter mechanism (to reduce the number of applicants); and problems over pension funds.

In a number of countries, including the USA but not the UK, discrimination on grounds of age has been outlawed in legislation. In 1996 a National Gallup Survey found that 58 per cent of both the total population and people aged 60 and over wanted the government to introduce legislation to outlaw discrimination against older people (ACE 1996: 11). Whether a change in the law would help is debatable. Laczko and Phillipson (1990) have shown that the impact of the American legislation must not be exaggerated. It has also been shown that older worker's participation rates in the countries where there is legislation are not markedly higher than in those where there is none (Whitting *et al.* 1995). Laczko and Phillipson nevertheless suggest that, while a variety of strategies may be needed, legislation would 'be important in terms of setting an agenda for change, challenging stereotypes, and for highlighting particular areas of injustice faced by older workers' (1990: 93). In 1993 two thirds of the general public in the EC thought that their government should introduce laws to try to stop age discrimination (Walker 1993: 26).

The House of Commons Employment Committee in their report *The Employment Patterns of the Over 50s* recommended a number of other things such as:

* the Employment Service should always ask employers seeking to impose age restrictions on recruitment if these are strictly necessary
* the Government should mount a campaign with the Confederation of British Industry to encourage awareness among employers of the potential worth to them of older workers and to challenge on practical grounds the discrimination being practised and should try to persuade employers of the benefits of considering older workers.
        (House of Commons Employment Committee 1989: *xvii–xviii*)

In 1992 the Department of Employment set up an Advisory Group on Older Workers. Its terms of reference were to advise the Secretary of State for Employment on questions of employment policy relating to older workers. The Department has subsequently tried to encourage employers to recognise the value of recruiting, retaining and training older people. The approach has been one of encouraging good practice and this is one of the roles being undertaken by the Employers Forum, which ACE helped set up in 1996.

Preparation for retirement: Studies of older people show clearly that many are ill-prepared to cope with what may be one third of their lives. In one of the classic studies, *Work, Age and Leisure*, Le Gros Clark argued that for most men the end of their working life no longer coincides with physiological old age (Le Gros Clark 1966 [in Document 5]). More recent research shows a general dearth of preparation for retirement (e.g. the Carnegie Inquiry into the Third Age 1993).

One answer might be to have a gentle transition to retirement. Some older workers already do this by changing to part-time work or self-employment. Research for the Retirement Income Inquiry also examined the possibility of 'bridge' jobs that permit part pensions to be drawn and where the employee continues to work part-time (Johnson *et al.* 1996).

Some organisations are beginning to pay more attention to the need for preparation for retirement. Some firms organise courses for their employees and some adult education institutes do the same for a wider constituency. The Pre-Retirement Association offer seminars, courses and individual counselling. Le Gros Clark took a wider view. He believed that advances in technology would mean fewer jobs and that other methods for prolonging working life outside industry, such as sheltered workshops, were little more than pilot schemes. He ended with a plea for active pursuits in retirement to be considered in the wider context of increasing leisure for people of all ages. But not everybody finds leisure pursuits alone to be fulfilling and prefer to work voluntarily to benefit the community (Chapter 12).

Until recently, what has been missing from much of the debate is any mention of gender differences. Women in later life may wish either to start a career, retrain or come to terms with a continuation of a domestic life. The experiences of retirement and the need for preparation may be very different for a man who has spent his whole life in full-time employment and a woman whose work-pattern may be very uneven or non-existent. Some men are now calling for 'portfolio careers' in which different jobs and unpaid work can be done at different times in their lives. Handy has long argued that the portfolio approach with a combination of part-time jobs, and perhaps voluntary work, means that no-one need finally 'retire' (Handy 1983). This pattern is, of course, well-known to many women already.

Current focus on the Third Age may mean that we should think of retirement *to* something rather than retirement *from*.

Conclusions

It is clear that older workers are not a group who can be neatly categorised according to skill, ability or physical strength. It would be helpful if employers could choose people for a particular job regardless of their age and train them accordingly. But for those older people who are disabled, special policies may be appropriate.

There may, however, be practical difficulties for employers. For example, an employer undertaking to train someone for a job expects that person to work in it for sufficient time to pay off the cost of the training. On the other hand, as we have seen, the employer may find that older workers provide stability and do not move on so quickly from one job to another as younger people sometimes do.

What has also to be remembered is that employment policies cannot be considered in isolation. Pension transfer schemes and the effect of the state pension age all have a bearing, both on what the individual older person chooses to do and on the retirement policy of employers. The issue is also part of the wider debate on the value that society currently puts on paid employment rather than the contribution which people make to society in an unpaid capacity. Martin argues that older people may be able to retire with the opportunity to pursue the mainstream activities of family, home and self-satisfaction now that the 'work ethic' is disappearing (Martin 1990). It is also part of the debate about opportunities for older people which is explored in Chapter 12.

CHAPTER 6

Health

Introduction

Health is a matter of prime importance for older people because it is
staying reasonably well, among other things, that helps them to
remain independent. As has been seen in Chapter 2, a common view
of ageing is of a steady decline in physical and mental powers.
Professional workers can be particularly prone to this negative view,
since it is those who are ill and frail whom they normally meet. This
chapter concentrates on physical health (see Chapter 9 for mental
health). Throughout this chapter it must be remembered that there are
often variations which include gender and social class.

The health of older people

General

Perceptions of health: The World Health Organisation (WHO)
defines health as a 'state of complete physical, mental and social
well-being, not merely the absence of disease and infirmity' and
although this is a useful starting point its limitations have been
pointed out (Bowling 1991). Increasing attention is being paid to how
people perceive both health and ill-health (see also Victor 1991: Ch.
6 and Allsop 1995: Ch. 6).

Sources of data and measures: Care must be taken in interpreting
data about health because it is often taken from surveys, such as the
General Household Survey, which ask people about their experiences, that is, they use subjective self-assessment. The results may be
different from those obtained from professionals through clinical
assessment. For example surveys are carried out in a sample of
general practices in England and Wales. The one carried out in
1991–2 was based on half a million patients and covered reasons for
consultation with their general practitioner (McCormick *et al.* 1995).
Both these types of surveys cover morbidity, that is, the amount of
sickness and disease. As the Medical Research Council (MRC) has
pointed out 'Current data sources do not provide adequate information on the real health status of the elderly population nor of the

changing health status over time' (MRC 1994a: 23).

Mortality, that is, deaths, is another measure of health in a population. The main causes of death for older people are circulation (heart disease and stroke), neoplasms (tumours) and respiratory diseases.

Increasing attention is being paid to measuring health status and the various measures of function and disability. Broader measures of health status and psychological well-being are included in an assessment of their use and validity (Bowling 1991, 1995).

In GB the first relevant OPCS study measured impairment and handicap (Harris 1971). Impairment was defined as: 'lacking part or all of a limb, or having a defective limb, organ or mechanism of the body' (p. 2). Handicap was the 'disadvantage or restriction of activity caused by the loss of functional ability' (p. 2). A later survey, which was of adults and children and took place between 1985–8, decided to use disability as its concept. It was defined as: 'a restriction or lack of ability to perform normal activities, which has resulted from the impairment of a structure or function of body or mind' (Martin *et al.* 1988: *xi*).

One measure of health is active life expectancy. As the Carnegie Inquiry reported: 'There is considerable controversy as to how far the gains, especially at older ages in recent years, have been gains in active life expectancy' (Carnegie Inquiry into the Third Age 1993: 6). Sometimes known as disability-free life expectancy (DFLE) it has been used as an indicator of health. DFLE is defined as 'the average number of years that a person of a given age may expect to live free of disability' (Colvez 1996: 41). Another measure is Healthy Active Life Expectancy (HALE). This expresses the average number of years that a fit person of a specified age can be expected to enjoy before suffering disability (MRC 1994a: 29, see also Evans 1993b). Another measure, used mainly for allocating services, is Quality Adjusted Life Year (QALY). See pp. 85–6.

The views of older people

Most older people consider their health good. In GB in 1994 39 per cent of the over-65s claimed that their health was 'good' and 38 per cent 'fairly good' (Table 6.1). There may be differences of opinion between their assessment of their health and that of doctors. Commenting on this, Johnson argues that self-referred illness is only the tip of the iceberg and is likely to have reached a fairly advanced state before consultation with a doctor is considered necessary (Johnson 1972).

What is 'normal' is a moot point. Does society distinguish between some sort of 'norm' and older people's perceptions of what is normally acceptable? Evans argues that there is at present no way of identifying those processes which constitute intrinsic ageing whose effects it might even be reasonable to designate as 'normal' (Evans 1988: 45).

Table 6.1 *A comparison of health in the year before interview between the under- and over-75s: Self-reported health in the year before the interview* Great Britain 1994

	Percentage		
	65–74	*75 and over*	*All 65 and over*
Self-reported health:			
good	44	31	39
fairly good	36	42	38
not good	21	26	23

Source: OPCS, *GHS*, 1994 HMSO, 1996, Table 6.12, p. 159.

Because there is a stereotype of old age which promotes expectations of ill-health and decrepitude it is little wonder that older people refuse as long as possible to be labelled as sick. In the OPCS *Disability Surveys*, commenting on the lower prevalence estimates of limiting long-standing disability of the *GHS* compared with their survey, the authors say that: 'many elderly people do not think of themselves as having health problems or being disabled; they consider limitations of activities a normal consequence of old age' (Martin *et al.* 1988: 21). In a study of over-90-year-olds only 8 per cent rated themselves as either unfit or very unfit although only 7 per cent had no chronic conditions (Bury and Holme 1991).

Patterns of morbidity

Older people differ in three major ways from the young: in the type and number of diseases and accidents, in their reactions to disease and in special features to do with their background (Hodkinson 1975). They often have a multiplicity of diseases, partly accounted for by the accumulation of non-lethal diseases such as osteoarthritis and deafness. They are more likely to fall than any other age groups except the under-fives (Department of Trade and Industry 1995) often with serious consequences (Askham *et al.* 1990, Lilley *et al.* 1995). On the other hand, as a recent study has shown, 'prevalence rates of most of the major health related behaviours (smoking, alcohol consumption, sexual behaviour and diet) were generally lower among older people' (DoH Central Health Monitoring Unit 1996:15).

There is clear evidence of a greater incidence of both acute and chronic sickness among older people than in other age groups, as the 1994 *GHS* shows (OPCS 1996: Ch. 3). For acute sickness the average number of days per year of restricted activity for people aged 65–74 in 1994 was 44 for men and 55 for women. For men aged 75 and over the figures were 51 and for women 72 (OPCS 1996: 55). The average for all ages was 24 for men and 31 for women. For chronic sickness 56 per cent of men and 57 per cent of women aged 65–74 reported a long-standing illness (OPCS 1996: 53). For men aged 75 and over the figures were 62 per cent and for women 64 per cent. The average for all ages was 32 per cent for both men and women. Figure 6.1 [and Document 10] show the estimated rises with age of limiting long-standing disability. There are also differences in the way older people react to disease (e.g. pain mechanisms and temperature response). General background, too, has an effect, for poverty, lack of status and disability can all lead to depression. Coronary heart diseases and many cancers, while strongly age-related, also have important environmental causes. Many researchers have also pointed to the dangers to older people of the potential toxic effects of the many drugs they have to take.

The health study for the Carnegie Inquiry found that on balance the evidence suggests that most of the years of life gained are without major disability, but that there is also a small increase in the period

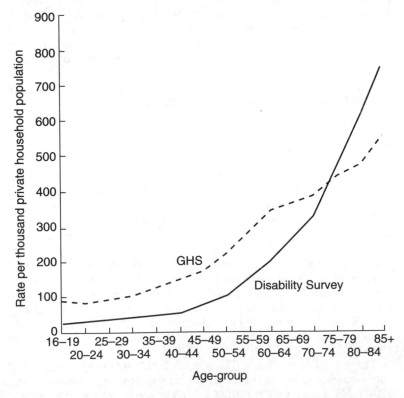

Figure 6.1 GHS estimates of prevalence of limiting long-standing disability by age (Great Britain 1985) compared with disability survey estimates: adults in private households
Source: Martin, J., Meltzer, H. and Elliot, D., OPCS Surveys of Disability in Great Britain, No. 1, HMSO, 1988, Figure 3.4, p. 20.

of disability, especially for women (Evans *et al.* 1992). This finding
has been endorsed by the MRC (1994a).

The very old and least mobile

In general there is an increase in ill health for the over-75s. In the
1994 *General Household Survey* 62 per cent of those aged 75 and
over reported that they suffered from a long-standing illness
compared with 56 per cent of those aged 65–74 (Table 6.2). Table 6.2
also shows that limiting long-standing illness and average number of
restricted activity days also rises with age. There is also a substantial
difference over falls. Among women aged 75 and over falls were the
cause of 82 per cent of all home accidents treated in hospital
compared with 61 per cent for those 65–74 in GB in 1992 (Wright
1994: 66). For men the comparable figures were 78 per cent for those
aged 75 and over and 63 per cent for those 65–74.

Sight declines with age and there is an increase in the prevalence
of eye diseases. In 1994 30 per cent of those aged 75 and over wore
glasses or contact lenses but still had difficulty with their eyesight
compared with 17 per cent of those aged 65–74 (Table 6.3). Hearing
also declines with age. In 1994 19 per cent of those aged 75 and over
had a hearing aid while 25 per cent did not wear an aid but still had
difficulty hearing compared with 8 and 22 per cent respectively for
those aged 65–74. For cognitive function (reasoning ability, memory
etc.) the *Health and Lifestyle Survey* in 1984–5 showed that, in
general, older groups performed more poorly than younger groups,
but age differences were reduced when differences in education were
taken into account (Cox *et al.* 1987). The cohort effect must also be
taken into account.

*Table 6.2 A comparison of self-reported chronic and acute sickness between the
under- and over-75s and all aged 65 and over Great Britain 1994*

		65–74	75 and over	All 65 and over
Chronic sickness	percentage with long-standing illness	56	62	59
	percentage with limiting long-standing illness	38	46	41
	percentage with non-limiting long-standing illness	18	16	17
	percentage with no long-standing illness	44	38	41
Acute sickness	average number of restricted activity days per person p.a.	49	61	54

Source: OPCS, *GHS*, 1994, HMSO, 1996, Tables 6.15 and 6.16, p. 162.

Table 6.3 A comparison of eyesight and hearing between the under- and over-75s
Great Britain 1994

	Percentage		
	65–74[1]	75 and over[1]	All 65 and over
Wears glasses or contact lenses, still has difficulty with eyesight[2]	17	30	22
Wears a hearing aid[3]	8	19	12[3]
Does not wear a hearing aid but has difficulty[3]	22	25	23[3]

[1] *Source:* Calculated from Tables noted below.
[2] *Source:* OPCS, *GHS*, 1994, HMSO, 1996, Table 6.17, p. 163.
[3] *Source:* OPCS, *GHS*, 1994, HMSO, 1996, Table 6.20, p. 164.

Surveys show that the main causes of loss of mobility are arthritic and rheumatic conditions, followed by cardiac and pulmonary conditions (e.g. Hunt 1978, OPCS *General Household Surveys*). Evidence about the least mobile is given in the study of disabled adults by OPCS. Figure 6.1 shows that the overall rate of disability rises with age, slowly at first then accelerating after 50 and rising very steeply after about 70. In the survey almost 70 per cent of disabled adults were aged 60 or over and nearly half were aged 70 or over. Among the most severely disabled adults very elderly people predominated.

Surveys also show that women are more likely than men to suffer impairment or disability in later life. For both chronic and acute sickness the 1994 *GHS* showed that there were higher rates for women than for men (OPCS 1996). The OPCS *Disability Surveys*, which, unlike the *GHS*, included people in institutions, found that for the over-75s the prevalence of disability, particularly severe disability, was higher among women than men. However, the study also showed that for the under-75s the prevalence of mild, and therefore overall, disability was slightly higher for men. Grundy suggests that possibly men of this age are more conscious of health limitations than women because of the effect on their ability to work (Grundy 1991a).

Use of services

Table 6.4 shows the use of some health and other services by people aged 65 and over. The trend since the early 1970s has been for a higher percentage of people of all ages to consult their GP (although the average number of consultations per person has changed little) and for people to attend hospital as an outpatient or casualty

Table 6.4 Use of health services by the under- and over-75s and people of all ages
Great Britain 1994

	65–74	75 and over	All ages
Consultation with an NHS GP in the 14 days before interview: percentage consulting GP	16·	18	12
Average number of NHS GP consultations per person p.a.	5	5	4
Percentage of persons who reported attending an outpatients or casualty department in a 3-month reference period	22	22	14
Percentage with inpatient stay in the 12 months before the interview	12	18	9
Average number of outpatient attendances per 100 persons p.a.	222	218	126
Average number of nights spent in hospital as an inpatient during the last 12 months	12	13	8

Source: OPCS, *GHS*, 1994, HMSO, 1996, Tables 3.19–3.33, pp. 66–74.

department more frequently. The 1994 *GHS* shows that for most services there is a steady increase in use of services by the over-75s. For all the health services women are greater users than men. Table 6.5 shows the increased use by people over the age of 75 of the services of a doctor (except at the surgery), district nurse/health visitor, chiropodist and optician. The exception was the dentist.

Table 6.5 Use of some health services in the three months[1] before interview
Great Britain 1994

	Percentage		
	65–74	75 and over	All 65 and over
Hospital doctor	19	22	20
Doctor at surgery	48	46	47
Doctor at home	7	19	11
Nurse at surgery or health centre	16	18	17
District nurse/health visitor[1]	3	11	6
Dentist	18	11	15
Chiropodist	16	35	24
Optician	11	14	12

[1] District nurse/health visitor in the month before.

Source: OPCS, *GHS*, 1994, HMSO, 1996, Table 6.44, p. 184 and Table 6.47, p. 187.

People living alone also make greater use of services. It should also be noted that although there are references to families and other carers in this chapter many older people live on their own and may have different kinds of problems in dealing with disabilities such as incontinence.

Some related health issues

Some health problems faced by older people have attracted a good deal of multidisciplinary research and have a particular relevance to social policy. Five of these are accidents, nutrition, incontinence, hypothermia and osteoporosis.

Accidents

The number of accidents that older people have is difficult to estimate because most figures are based on people who go to t᷉ ⁓ Accident and Emergency department of a hospital. In this case the main national figures are based on the Home Accident Surveillance System (HASS). For accidents where people do not go to a hospital information has to be collected from the GP (but not everyone goes to a GP after an accident) or from a sample in the population.

Looking first at deaths, falls are the leading cause of accidental deaths of the over-75s. The main type of non-fatal accident for older people is also a fall. Very elderly people and women are most likely to fall and there are many causes (Askham *et al.* 1990, Lilley *et al.* 1995). In many cases it is difficult to disentangle the main cause. They include:

- medical (this may include non-specific ill-health);
- medication (this may have a direct or indirect effect on the brain); a wide range of drugs are implicated including tranquillisers, diuretics and sleeping tablets;
- alcohol;
- housing and the environment (such as homes in poor condition, stairs, uneven surfaces);
- social and psychological factors (rarely considered in studies but some evidence).

The consequences of accidents may be physical but may also be psychological. Physical consequences include a loss of mobility but may also lead to a loss of confidence. They may also be a reason for entry to institutional care. Accidents, such as falls, are an important factor in the use of health services by older people as the *Health of the Nation Key Area Handbook: Accidents* points out (DoH 1993b). Accidents may also affect relatives and professionals, who may become overprotective.

Accidents have been identified as a major problem in all the *Health of the Nation* documents and were chosen as one of the five main areas for concern in the 1992 strategy (DoH 1992a). A target was set for a reduction of 33 per cent in accidents to the over-65s by 2005.

Nutrition

The health of individuals is clearly affected by what they eat. As Khaw has pointed out, there are three main factors influencing nutrition and health (Khaw 1996: 181). They are:

- food intake factors (such as socio-economic e.g. income; and physiological e.g. dentition);
- nutritional status factors (such as environment e.g. sunlight; behavioural e.g. physical behaviour; and metabolic e.g. digestion);
- health outcome factors (such as host factors e.g. genetic susceptibility; and environment e.g. smoking).

The early poverty studies (e.g. those by Rowntree) showed that many old people did not enjoy a diet which enabled them to remain healthy. More recent evidence suggests that this is now no longer the case.

Surveys in 1952 and 1962 indicated that the popular idea that many old people who live alone exist almost entirely on bread, butter, jam, biscuits and cups of sweetened tea was not substantiated. In 1972 *A Nutrition Survey of the Elderly* found that older people followed a dietary pattern that was similar to that of the general population except that they ate smaller quantities (DHSS 1972). Nevertheless, some old people were malnourished. Similar findings were reported in 1979 (DHSS 1979). A study of the nutrition and well-being of older people rejected the simple approach to meeting nutrition needs pointing out, for instance, that the provision of meals on wheels will not automatically increase the food intake in those who are ill or neglecting their diet (Davies 1981).

Khaw concludes that those who are at 'high risk of poor nutrition and health include those who may already have poor health, with poor dentition or inability to swallow, those with physical disability, mental illness, malabsorption, those who are taking medications that interfere with nutrition, and those who are poor or isolated or in ignorance of basic nutritional facts' (Khaw 1996: 182).

Changes in diet towards a 'healthy eating' pattern are beginning to be noticeable. The 1993 *Health Survey for England* showed that older people were more likely to eat vegetables or salad, fruit, wholemeal bread and high fibre cereal than those between the ages of 16 and 44 (CSO 1996: 138). On the other hand they were more likely to use solid cooking fat, add salt when cooking and usually drink whole milk.

Maclennan argues for a variety of ways of identifying those at risk of subnutrition and points to the lack of evidence about the pros and cons of nutrient supplements and diet supplementation (Maclennan 1986). Another growing concern in all age groups is obesity. *The Health Survey for England* in 1993 (CSO 1996: 132) showed that:

- of those aged 65–74 54 per cent of men and 41 per cent of women were overweight and 15 per cent of men and 21 per cent of women were obese;
- of those aged 75 and over 46 per cent of men and 42 per cent of women were overweight and 11 per cent of men and 16 per cent of women were obese.

Nutrition for older people is an underresearched area. There is, for example, little knowledge about the nutritional needs of older people compared with younger and the nutritional needs of different kinds of older people such as those who are active, bedbound or terminally ill.

Incontinence

There are few reliable estimates of urinary incontinence in old age and much depends on the definition (McGrother and Clarke 1996). Summarising the research, Tobin estimates that most studies have found between 3 and 7 per cent of elderly people suffer from 'frequent' urinary incontinence (Tobin 1992: Ch. 3). He also found that the prevalence of incontinence rises with age, with women on average being twice as likely to be affected. High proportions are reported in nursing homes and hospitals (Tobin 1992). The studies also show that between 50–70 per cent of elderly people who were incontinent were unknown to nursing or social services.

Even less is known about faecal incontinence. In one study faecal incontinence was found to affect 10 per cent of residents in local authority residential homes (Tobin 1987).

Often sufferers do not get assistance because society treats incontinence as a taboo subject; sufferers themselves are reluctant to discuss this problem. But incontinence can prevent an old person from living an independent life. For instance it is sometimes laid down that no-one who is incontinent can be accepted in sheltered housing. Unresolved problems related to caring for an incontinent person can also lead to stress on relatives and may be the determining factor in whether or not a family feels able to continue to care.

It is therefore important to identify the cause of the incontinence and to treat it or take other steps. There is need for careful diagnosis and then for both medical and social factors to be taken into account. A report by the Royal College of Physicians on incontinence examined the causes, management and provision of services (Royal College of Physicians 1995). It recommended that whenever possible a medical diagnosis should be made. A recent review suggested that there is uncertainty about the relative merits of treatments and the organisation of services, particularly the role of specialist nursing (McGrother and Clarke 1996). Practical considerations like stairs to negotiate or the absence of a conveniently placed lavatory may suggest the need for adaptations to the home. Good practice by health authorities should include the availability of a continence advisor, provision for regular and adequate supplies of continence aids and reasonable access to a urodynamic unit. Although there is much more awareness by local authorities now (e.g. Norton 1989) there is wide variation in the provision of incontinence services by health authorities. Useful guidance on the provision of services has been published by the Association for Continence Advice (1993).

Hypothermia

Unlike incontinence, hypothermia (low body temperature) is a subject which is discussed in public. Hypothermia means low body temperature. It is usually defined as the condition present when the body temperature falls below 35°C, or 95°F, but there is no sharp cut-off point at this temperature. There are two main causes: diseases and conditions in the body (such as a failure in the temperature-regulating system) and environmental factors such as cold winters and lack of heating.

The importance of hypothermia as a medical condition seems to have been noted only comparatively recently. In the 1950s articles appeared in medical journals reporting hypothermia in babies and these were followed by accounts relating to old people. The British Medical Association (BMA) reviewed existing knowledge and the Royal College of Physicians undertook a screening survey. Research followed with the aim of measuring the body temperatures and the social and environmental conditions of a sample of 1,020 old people (Wicks 1978). This study was replicated in the winter of 1991 when 916 people over the age of 65 were interviewed. The results are presented in *Cold Comfort* (Salvage 1993). It was found that, despite the increase in central heating, 81 per cent of respondents still had living room temperatures in the morning below those recommended by the WHO. Although there had been some improvements since 1972:

- approximately three quarters of a million older people in Britain may be at risk of developing hypothermia in the winter;
- one third of the sample did not use any heating in their bedrooms;
- the main reason for not feeling warm enough was inability to afford more heating and inadequate heating systems;
- substantial proportions had housing problems such as condensation and draughts.

In a summary of the research evidence Salvage points out that death where hypothermia is a primary cause is rare (Salvage 1993). However, there is considerable evidence that large numbers of people suffer from cold conditions and some die from them. Cold-related illnesses are a major problem. For example the increase in deaths from coronary thrombosis occurs mainly 24–48 hours after a cold day. In GB, mortality statistics for older people show that a larger proportion die in winter compared with summer and this proportion increases with age (McManus 1985). In countries with similar or colder winters, such as Sweden and Canada, numbers are spread more evenly throughout the year. This suggests that there are special factors at work in this country. Collins concludes that winter mortality may be due both to outdoor exposure and cold indoor temperatures – outdoor exposure being associated with deaths related to heart conditions and cold indoor climates being responsible for deaths related to respiratory conditions (Collins 1989).

Many people lack adequate heating facilities in the home. Although more widespread use of central heating would help it is clear that other things are important. Wicks concluded that, while specific policies such as using electric blankets and insulating housing would help, a more general approach was needed. He emphasised the need for more small units of accommodation and housing specially built for older people and for a significant increase in pensions to enable them to meet heating bills. Salvage also endorses the need for more income in old age, the importance of housing, the value of insulation and energy-efficiency measures (Salvage 1993).

Gray (1987) also stresses the importance of training for all who have contact with older people especially home helps. Kafetz (1987) advises GPs that there should be prompt treatment of acute illness (visiting today and not tomorrow) and monitoring function. The new GP contract should help identify illnesses.

Osteoporosis

Osteoporosis, the loss of bone tissue resulting in the thinning and weakening of bones, is one of the most important age-related diseases and causes of disability (Riggs and Melton 1988, MRC 1994a, 1994b). It is estimated that the lifetime risk of a fracture caused by osteoporosis is 40 per cent for women and 13 per cent for men (Maggi 1996). Not only may osteoporosis contribute to fractures, including fractures of the hip, but it can also cause painful and disabling fracture of the wrist and spine. In addition, the risk of dependency or death and the large costs incurred by health services in treating fractures have been identified (Maggi 1996). Osteoporosis has been described as the 'silent epidemic' (Riggs and Melton 1988: 129); preventative action, especially attention to diet and exercise in early life and the avoidance of smoking, is recommended and the advantages of hormone replacement are stressed.

Trends and priorities in health care

Health care and specialism

The growing interest by doctors from many different disciplines in the treatment of older people was noted in Chapter 3. The development of geriatric medicine, defined by the British Geriatrics Society as 'that branch of general medicine concerned with the clinical, rehabilitation, social and preventive aspects of illness and health in the elderly', has been rapid. The MRC provide a neat summary of the current situation:

Geriatric medicine has developed in the UK in such a way that three models of service now exist, namely, 'traditional', 'age-defined' and 'integrated'. The essential feature of the traditional model is that patients entering the geriatric service are selected by non-geriatricians, usually by the GP. The age-defined model, which is now the type of service most widely espoused in the UK, admits all medical patients above a certain age, the commonest being around 75 years of age. The integrated model includes 'physicians with special responsibility for the elderly' as members of multi-consultant medical teams who are also responsible for providing a comprehensive range of specialist geriatric services including rehabilitation, long-stay, day-hospital, outpatients and hospital/community liaison work. There is controversy as to the relative cost-effectiveness of these models of care. There have been no formal randomised trials in this country to demonstrate which patients have the best outcome and at what cost. Studies in the USA and Canada have suggested that some patients do benefit if offered evaluation by geriatric teams or geriatric evaluation units, but it cannot be inferred from these studies that the same will be true in the UK where practice differs significantly. Research to confirm or refute these findings in the UK NHS would therefore be timely.

(MRC 1994a: 55–6)

Health promotion, the prevention of ill health and rehabilitation

'Current policy reflecting both modern medical practice and the wish of most elderly people to remain in their own home is to promote an active approach to treatment and rehabilitation' (DHSS 1978a: 37). This statement, taken from *A Happier Old Age*, is an indication of a positive approach towards the health of older people that has been a theme of government policies during the 1980s and 1990s. *The Health of the Nation* was a consultative document published in 1991 by DoH to develop a health strategy for England (Sec. of St. for Health 1991). A main objective was 'to focus as much on the promotion of good health and the prevention of disease as on the treatment, care and rehabilitation of those who fall ill or who need continual support' (Sec. of St. for Health 1991: *vii*). It has, however, been criticised as putting too much emphasis on individual responsibility and less on wider issues such as poverty and housing.

To enable older people to remain healthy, attention has to be given to prevention, detection and rehabilitation. Health promotion may contain all these elements and will be referred to last. Prevention has already been mentioned (Chapter 4) as an objective of many services. The aim is the prevention of disability. This is important for cancer and non-cancerous health conditions (Kennie 1993). Enhancing functional status is also important. The pioneering work by Gray on the importance of paying attention to the older person's ability to function has been refreshingly practical (for example, Gray 1987, 1996). Measures to prevent unfitness (e.g. encourage exercise: the motto is 'use it or lose it') and social problems are proposed. Outlining a strategy for preventive medicine, the Royal College of Physicians concludes that maintaining mental and physical activities and social contacts is important as well as more obviously medical measures (Royal College of Physicians 1991). To get over preventive messages Gray favours a normal primary care consultation (because most elderly patients will contact the practice at some time during the year) rather than full-scale screening. The general value of screening is controversial but there seem to be a number of areas where it is worthwhile for older people (Carpenter 1996). These include hypertension, cervical cancer and breast cancer.

An opportunity for a consultation, which may enable some screening to be done, is now given in the GP contract. From 1990 patients over the age of 75 must be offered a consultation and a domiciliary visit to see whether medical or other services are needed. The Royal College of General Practitioners has issued a practical guide to help members of the primary health care team to carry out effective health checks (Williams and Wallace 1993). In a survey of GPs and nurses about the usefulness of these routine assessments, giving advice (67 per cent), giving reassurance (64 per cent), and social needs (54 per cent) were seen to be the most important (Chew *et al*. 1994a). In the survey of the people aged 75 and over it was found that:

- three quarters of those offered an assessment accepted it;
- 88 per cent felt that the assessments were fairly or very useful;
- one quarter were referred to other services;
- less than half who had an assessment could remember the nurse or doctor discussing the result with them (Chew *et al*. 1994b).

Prevention must also take into account iatrogenesis, which is when disease is caused by diagnosis or treatment. The therapeutic use of drugs is one of the most common instances of this. Swift describes iatrogenesis as 'a major issue of health care in late life' (Swift 1996). Because older people are the highest consumers of prescribed medication and because of the problems of iatrogenesis, Swift argues for a range of measures including drug regulation, prescribing audits and professional and public education. On the latter point he argues: 'Prescribers, particularly those in general practice (primary care) are in the forefront of demand from both patients and their carers. Some of the demand is built into cultural perceptions, is often fuelled by media material of dubious value, is difficult to withstand and is an undoubted contributor to overmedication' (Swift 1996: 406).

Detection to pick up early signs of illness is important because not all old people report their medical conditions. This can lead not only to serious illnesses being unnoticed in their early stages but also to failure to treat minor conditions which later can have a cumulative effect. Reliance on patient-initiated contact with GPs has resulted in health problems remaining unrecognised until a crisis occurs; a screening programme can anticipate problems.

Recent research underlines the importance of rehabilitation, which is generally defined as the achievement of the optimum level of independence for the individual. There is also agreement that rehabilitation must be started as early as possible. Despite the need for more research on many aspects of rehabilitation, especially on outcomes and innovations (e.g. MRC 1994a), most experts agree that a successful outcome owes more to mental factors than to the degree or nature of the physical disability (Hodkinson 1975). Good motivation may lead to recovery in the face of quite severe physical difficulties. Most experts also underline the value of a multidisciplinary approach from professionals (e.g. Squires 1991).

In 1995 the WHO launched a programme on ageing and health which aimed to carry forward its earlier programmes. Part of this involved a programme of health promotion which focused on ageing well/healthy ageing. Kalache (1996) points out that health promotion not only covers health education and disease prevention but health maintenance (such as treatment to prevent a decline in health status) and public policies (such as fiscal and transport policies). He gives examples of the many varied programmes that are being undertaken across the world. These include physical exercise, healthy nutrition, empowerment and prevention of accidents. Most are targeted at older people living in their own homes.

Expenditure

Costs of health services are greater for older people than other age groups. While people over the age of 65 represented 16 per cent of the population in England in 1994, expenditure on hospital and community health services for this group was 42 per cent and 28 per cent for family health services (NHS Executive personal communication 1996). Comparative annual costs of hospital and community health services and family health services per person are given in Table 6.6. From this it will be seen that, apart from births and

Table 6.6 Estimated costs[1] of health services for different age groups England

	1994/5 Hospital and community health services £	1993/4 Family health services authorities £	Total[2] £
Births	1855	130	1985
Aged 0–4	435	130	565
Aged 5–15	195	120	315
Aged 16–44	250	135	385
Aged 45–64	375	135	510
Aged 65–74	815	235	1050
Aged 75–84	1500	325	1825
Aged 85+	2205	325	2530
All ages[3]	455	155	610

[1] Figures are in cash terms, rounded to the nearest £5.
[2] Note that they are different years but this gives a rough estimate of total costs.
[3] The all ages figures excludes births.

Source: DoH, personal communication, 1996.

children aged 0–4, costs increase with age. Those aged over 85 cost twice as much as those aged 65–74. One contributory factor to cost is that older people are more likely to spend longer in hospital. The average number of nights spent in hospital as an inpatient in GB in 1994 was 12 days for people aged 65–74 and 14 for those over 75, compared with an average for all ages of 8 (Table 6.4). Hospital outpatient attendance, consultation with GPs and other health and social services also increase with age, as has already been seen. Elderly people also account for 25–30 per cent of the NHS drug bill (MRC 1994a: 22).

When considering future expenditure it is clear that the projected increase in numbers of very old people means that extra resources will be needed just to maintain, let alone improve, standards. DoH economists estimate that expenditure on older people will need to increase by around 0.7 per cent over the next 10–15 years just to keep up with demographic change (Robins and Wittenberg 1992).

In early cost benefit analyses of health there was a tendency to measure the output of intervention as the ability of patients to return to work and contribute to the economy. Cost-effectiveness procedures now use the health state of patients as the value, so that older people are not disadvantaged (Robins and Wittenberg 1992).

Inequalities

Equality, as the DoH have stated, is about comparisons between the level of health, or ability to obtain access to health care, of individuals and communities (DoH, Chief MOH 1995: 8).The MRC have stated that there is growing concern regarding possible inequalities in health care for older people (MRC 1994a: Ch. 10). They relate equality to access, use, expenditure, processes or outcomes of care between and within different groups such as the young and old. The kinds of inequalities they identified were:

- clinical trials, i.e. older people are less likely to be included than other age groups;
- explicit inequality, e.g. exclusion of women over the age of 65 from regular invitation to breast screening and the exclusion of older people from admission to specialist coronary care units or referral to specialist care for diabetes (other examples of inequality and discrimination are access to good modern treatment for cancer and for end-stage kidney failure, Evans 1994: 19–20, see also the report of the Royal College of Physicians, 1994);
- implicit inequality, i.e. an implicit assumption that older people will receive less appropriate care (the MRC claim that more evidence is needed).

They point to the lack of evidence over the extent of inequalities and the need to research variations in health status and health care. On the other hand it must also be recognised that older people, even at very advanced ages, have gained from many interventions such as hip replacements and cataract operations.

The reasons for inequalities are many. In health care they were illustrated in the DHSS Black Report *Inequalities of Health* subsequently reproduced with comments (Townsend and Davidson 1982). The Report points to inequalities in health as being a direct reflection of inequalities in occupational class during working life. A report by the King's Fund shows how some inequalities, such as between different towns and districts, is growing. They also show how disadvantaged circumstances clearly lead to poor health among older people (Benzeval *et al.* 1995). Preferring the word 'variations' to 'inequalities' DoH also published a report on health in 1995 (DoH 1995b). Both reports concluded that broad policies were needed.

Some of the implications of inequalities in services are taken up in the last chapter.

Outcomes of care: QALYS, performance indicators and medical audit

Outcome of health services: This is defined by DoH as '*any* end result (health or otherwise) which is attributable to a health services intervention' (DoH 1992b: 81). It is important to have some way of measuring the effectiveness of different forms of health care. One measure which can help health authorities direct resources to areas which will derive most benefit is the *QALY* measure. QALY (quality-adjusted life years) is an estimation of expected life years gained from consumption of a healthcare procedure, in addition to a judgement on the quality of expected life years gained. It has been argued that QALYS are not an appropriate way of measuring quality of life of older people requiring long-term care, mainly because it is based on a scale (Rosser) which uses disability and distress as its main indicator and it has never been studied in people over the age of 60 (Donaldson *et al.* 1988). Others have shown the dangers of relying on a single measure of the quality of life and question economic approaches (Baldwin *et al.* 1990). Other critics point to the assumption that the only outcome of health services is health, the necessity for value judgements and the assumption that there is the same value to each year gained (MRC 1994a: 30–1).

Performance indicators: These are another useful tool. They arose from concern by the Public Accounts Committee in 1981, and subsequently by DHSS, about the monitoring of activities by health authorities (House of Commons Social Services Committee 1981). The purpose of the indicator is to provide health service managers with systematic information so that they can compare their perform-ance with other areas. Criticisms of them have been on the grounds that they do not measure performance, that they do not compare like with like, that the data used is inaccurate and that, even if the indicators were accurate, there would be variations between districts because of random factors (Allen 1987). Research has shown that, despite these criticisms, they did result in districts changing their performance; however they are blunt instruments and need to be supplemented by other means (Allen 1987).

Medical audit: This is the systematic critical analysis of the quality of medical care, including the procedures used for diagnosis and treatment, the use of resources and the resulting outcome for patients. Since 1994 the emphasis by DoH has been on multiprofessional clinical audit.

The development and types of services

General

The origins of the NHS were described in Chapter 4. Specific general points relating to the development of services are now discussed. The development of primary health care is discussed later in this chapter and services for people with mental disorder in Chapter 9.

An early matter of concern was the cost of the service which in 1946 had been estimated at £110 million, but by 1951–2 had grown to £384 million. The Guillebaud Committee in their *Report of the Committee of Enquiry into the Cost of the NHS* had concluded that in practice there was no objective and attainable standard of adequacy in the health field, that there was no evidence of extravagant spending, and that in some cases (e.g. hospitals, capital expenditure) more money needed to be spent (MoH 1956). For older people they drew heavily on a paper on costs prepared for them by Abel-Smith and Titmuss which concluded that: 'by-and-large, the older age groups were currently receiving a lower standard of service than the main body of consumers and that there were substantial areas of unmet need among the elderly' (MoH 1956: 40). The Committee examined the pattern of care between the different parts of the NHS and laid down guidelines.

The Guillebaud Committee referred to a survey on chronic sick patients which was then being carried out: *Survey of Services Available to the Chronic Sick and Elderly 1954–55* (MoH 1957). The wide-ranging conclusions of this survey covered both medical and other provision. In regard to the former, the Report indicated that the number of hospital beds for the chronic sick was sufficient in total but needed to be properly used and better distributed. Their recommendations about other provisions arose out of their conviction that: 'the key to the problems stemming from an ageing population lies with preventive and domiciliary services' (MoH 1957: 37).

The Hospital Plan 1962 (MoH 1962) laid down standards for geriatric patients of 1.4 beds per 1,000 total population and it was visualised that the main hospital services would be brought together in district general hospitals (of 600–800 beds) designed to serve a population of 100,000–150,000. Although the plan was subsequently modified in 1966 many new hospitals were built and conditions for patients and staff greatly improved. More of these general hospitals had geriatric units providing treatment and rehabilitation so that older people would not need long-term hospital care. More day hospitals were established.

In 1962 local authorities were asked to take part in a long-term planning exercise similar to that for the hospitals (MoH 1963, 1966). Wide variations were disclosed in what they planned to provide for health and welfare services.

The administration of the NHS had ... since its inception ... been the subject of much comment and criticism and it was reorganised in 1974. Then followed what Abel-Smith (1978) has called 'the lean years following reorganisation: 1974–8', with a shortage of resources and criticisms of the new tiered system of administration. Geographical equality was one matter of concern: the Resource Allocation Working Party (RAWP) made suggestions for financial allocations to be based on criteria which included age and mortality (DHSS 1976b). The question of priorities formed the subject of two consultative documents – *Priorities for Health and Personal Social Services in England* in 1976 (DHSS 1976e) and *The Way Forward* in 1977 (DHSS 1977). Both consultative documents visualised an expansion in community services, and advice by the DHSS to local authorities and health authorities in 1979 acknowledged the growing pressure on services.

The Royal Commission on the NHS, which reported in 1979, had a great deal to say about the demands of older people on health and local authorities for the rest of this century (Royal Commission on the NHS 1979). They agreed with current national priorities, including the emphasis on older people and community care for them [Document 11], but found that there were considerable practical difficulties to be overcome in shifting the resources from one patient or client group to another.

In 1982 the NHS was reorganised following the Health Service Act 1980. The main effect was to reduce the tiers of management from five to three.

A positive flood of documents came from the DHSS in the early 1980s, most with 'community' or 'care' in the title and all concerned with two issues. One was the need to give priority to increasing and improving provision for older people and the other to promoting care at home rather than in institutions. These documents continued the theme of the mid-1970s following the concentration in the 1960s and early 1970s on hospital provision.

In February 1981 *Care in Action* was published (DHSS 1981a). This was a handbook providing national guidance for health and personal social services. It stated that priority was to be given to four groups, one of which was 'elderly people', especially the most vulnerable and frail (DHSS 1981a: 20). Four objectives were given (DHSS 1981a: 32). First, to 'strengthen the primary and community care services, together with neighbourhood and voluntary support, to enable elderly people to live at home'. Second, to 'encourage an active approach to treatment and rehabilitation to enable elderly people to return to the community from hospital wherever possible'. Third, to 'maintain capacity in the general acute sector to deal with the increasing number of elderly patients'. Fourth, to 'maintain an adequate provision for the minority of elderly people requiring long-term care in hospital or residential homes'. In December 1982 the Government stated that these priorities had not changed (DHSS 1982b). *Care in Action* drew on material included in a *Report of a Study on Community Care*, written by DHSS officials based on research and published in September 1981 (DHSS 1981b). It concentrated on assessing whether there had been any shift away from long-term hospital or residential provision for those people whose needs put them on the boundary between institutional and non-institutional care and also the contribution of the voluntary sector to all forms of community care. Some interesting findings and expressions of doubt emerged. The authors found little shift from hospital and residential care for elderly people on the margins of institutional and community-based care and they noted that there may have been a tendency to underestimate the number of elderly people who will always require long-term residential care. There was an acknowledgement that: 'community-based packages of care may not always be a less expensive or more effective alternative to hospital or residential provision, particularly for those living alone' (DHSS 1981b: 3). They also made some salutary points about the voluntary sector, which they wanted strengthening, and included the warning that 'it is important not to assume that the amount of informal care can be limitlessly increased' (DHSS 1981b: 5). Some of the general pointers to emerge from this study were that it may be necessary to shift NHS expenditure from hospital inpatient to community health services, that labour constraints (e.g. a shortage of district nurses) may become as important as financial constraints, that social and demographic changes may reduce the number of people who have traditionally provided the mainstay of informal care, and finally that demand for all community-based services were likely to continue to increase over the next decade.

Published simultaneously were two complementary studies on hospitals. *The Respective Roles of the General Acute and Geriatric Sectors in the Care of the Elderly Hospital Patient* indicated that an important area of concern was the impact on the acute sector of the shortfall in provision for elderly patients in departments of geriatric medicine (DHSS 1981f). The *Report of a Study on the Acute Hospital Sector* also showed that between 1968 and 1978 most of the increase in activity rates throughout the acute sector were accounted for by services to elderly people (DHSS 1981e). In between *Care in Action* and the three reports came (March 1981d) the White Paper *Growing Older* (see p. 32) with its firm commitment to community care, but again with the warning that community services and families: 'cannot be expected to provide a solution to every problem and should not normally be used to support people who can only properly be cared for elsewhere' (DHSS 1981d: 32).

Then in July 1981 *Care in the Community* was published (DHSS 1981c). This was subtitled 'A consultative document on moving resources for care in England' and it was concerned with how patients 'together with resources for their care', may be transferred from the NHS to the personal social services in addition to existing joint finance arrangements. As a subsequent DHSS explanatory note explained (DHSS 1983b), the policy thrust was different from before: 'The joint finance arrangements have assisted the development of community care and in doing so have contributed to the important objective of enabling people to *remain* in the community instead of having to be taken into hospital. But the *Care in the Community* initiative has a different and quite specific aim: to help long-stay hospital patients unnecessarily kept in hospital to *return* to the community where this will be best for them and is what they and their families prefer' (DHSS 1983b: 1). While no estimate could be given of numbers of older people who might be more suitably cared for by the personal social services it was stated that each patient cost the NHS on average about £8,000 in 1979–80.

A number of suggestions were put forward, including the transfer of hospital buildings, lump sum or annual payment, central transfer of funds and extending joint finance arrangements. In a subsequent DHSS circular (note that details of all circulars are given in the text but not in the bibliography) in March 1983 *Health Service Development: care in the community and joint finance* (DHSS 1983 HC (83)6 and LAC (83)5), District Health Authorities were empowered to offer lump-sum payments or continuing grants to local authorities or voluntary organisations for people moving from hospital into community care. In addition joint financing was extended from 7 to 13 years. A further decision was the extension of joint financing to housing departments and housing associations. This needed legislation and was part of the Health and Social Security Adjudications Act 1981. A programme of pilot projects was started.

It is clear that joint financing has provided a welcome additional source of funds for older people. There is a lack of information about joint finance. It appears from published information that there was a 3.9 per cent real increase in expenditure from 1983–4 to 1993–4 (House of Commons Health Committee 1995a). Health authority expenditure on joint finance was £132 million in 1994–5 compared with £123 million in 1991–2 (NHS Executive personal communication 1996). The total percentage spent on elderly people was 16 per cent in 1994–5.

But a simple shift of resources away from hospital care may not always be in the best interests of older people. More advanced and safer anaesthetic procedures, together with more refined surgical techniques, have enabled surgical treatment to be given to patients who would previously have been considered too frail for major surgery.

A Management Inquiry Team chaired by Sir Roy Griffiths (Griffiths 1983) said that a small, strong management body was required at the centre and that responsibility should be passed down the line as far as possible. They recommended a Health Services Supervisory Board at the centre to decide overall objectives and budgets, an NHS Management Board to run the Health Service and, at regional and district health level, managers to take charge of services. At district level each unit was to have its own manager too. In 1984 the new system was set up. Aimed mainly at hospitals, the new system seemed torn between the political imperatives of the NHS, the principles of business management and the caring values necessary for the health needs of the population (Leathard 1990).

In 1986 and 1987 a consultation paper and then proposals for changes in primary health care were published by the government and these are discussed in the next section (on primary health care).

In 1989 the government's proposals for a review of the NHS were published in a White Paper *Working for Patients* (Sec. of St. for Health *et al.* 1989a). The stated objective was to give patients better health care and greater choice of services and to give greater satisfaction and rewards for those working in the NHS. Others argue that the main aim was to contain costs and to achieve greater value for money by allowing competition to supply services (Allsop 1995: 193). The White Paper stated that the founding principles of an NHS open to all, regardless of income, financed mainly out of taxation and generally without charges at the point of service, would remain.

On organisation the Supervisory Board and the NHS Management Board were replaced by a new Policy Board and new Management Executive. There was to be delegation of power and responsibility as far as possible. The District Health Authority (DHA) was to have an enhanced purchasing role and would enter into contracts or agreements with those hospital and community health units which could best provide high quality, value for money services. A key principle was the separation of the responsibility for managing services and for purchasing those services. The DHAs were to assess the health needs of the population, decide the pattern of service provision, appraise service options, choose between providers and place contracts, monitor the contracted services and control expenditure within the district. A central feature was that hospitals and units would be funded for work they actually did, that is, the money would follow the patient.

Service providers would include the district's directly managed hospitals and units, those from other districts or the private sector, and the proposed NHS Trusts. The latter were to have greater freedom than directly managed hospitals, for instance to determine the pay and conditions of their staff, borrow money and acquire, own and dispose of assets. They were to earn revenue for the services they provided through contracts with health authorities, GP practices with their own budgets, private patients and insurance companies. Another change proposed was to make Family Practitioner Committees accountable to Regional Health Authorities and to rename them Family Health Services Authorities (FHSA). Other changes were planned for GPs who could apply to manage their own general practice funds.

The proposals were made law in the National Health Service and Community Care Act 1990 and implemented in April 1991. Critics pointed to the upheaval of yet another reorganisation, the danger of treating health as a business and not a service, the emphasis on management and the encouragement of private provision, all of which might lead to a two-tier service.

Since 1991 the development has continued on the lines outlined above. The structure has been even more streamlined (Figure 6.2) with the abolition of Regional Health Authorities from April 1996 and the setting up of regional offices, which now come directly under the NHS Management Executive. District Health Authorities and Family Health Authorities were amalgamated and became Health Authorities. The dominant relationship became that between those who purchased (now sometimes referred to as commissioning)

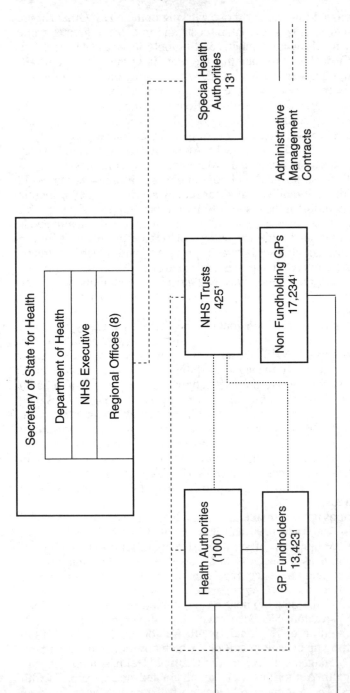

Figure 6.2 **Structure of the NHS 1996**
Source: NHS Executive (previously unpublished – personal communication August 1996).

[1] Numbers used are indicative of health bodies, GPs etc. and are subject to in-year fluctuation.

services and those who provided them. The need for involving local organisations was acknowledged with the encouragement of local health alliances. (See Allsop 1995 for a more detailed account of the changes.)

The commitment to a better service for patients was one of the reasons for producing *The Patients Charter* (DoH 1991b). This set out the existing rights of patients and added three more. These were the right to have detailed information on local health services, to be guaranteed admission for virtually all treatments by a specific date no later than two years from being placed on the waiting list and a simplified complaints system.

On policy, the Government's strategy was set out first in a 1992 White Paper *The Health of the Nation* (DoH 1992a). This emphasised the benefits and importance of preventing ill-health as well as treating it. A major theme was that people must, as far as possible, take responsibility for their own health. The relative neglect of elderly people has been noted. One of the major objectives of the Health of the Nation initiative has been to set targets for improvements in health. The five main areas of concern were cancer, HIV/AIDS and sexual health, mental illness, accidents and coronary heart disease. As subsequent Health of the Nation reports have shown, some of these targets have been achieved (DoH 1993a, DoH 1995a). Cynics maintain that this would have happened anyway without any action by the Government.

Overall, the central themes of the NHS, namely that it is funded by taxation and that it is universal and comprehensive, have not changed. Very little evaluation of the NHS since 1991 has taken place although there have been some useful studies such as that by the Audit Commission on the new role of the District Health Authority (Audit Commission 1993a). The role of the Health Advisory Service (HAS) is also useful. Originally it was set up as the Hospital Advisory Service which then became the NHS Health Advisory Service. The emphasis and extent of its role became wider in 1992 and its main thrust now is to monitor and advise upon the quality of services delivered by purchasers and providers responsible for mentally ill and older people.

What is clear since reorganisation is that numbers of administrative, clerical and managerial staff have increased. Allsop comments on the divergent trends now evident: 'The rhetoric is about devolution, local autonomy and diversity but central government nevertheless continues to dictate the agenda' (Allsop 1995: 188).

Primary health care

Primary health care includes all those services provided outside the hospital by the family practitioner services (family doctors, dentists, retail pharmacists and opticians) and by the community health services (community nurses, midwives, health visitors and other professions allied to medicine). The WHO has emphasised the importance of primary health care which they described in the Alma-Ata declaration of 1978 as 'the first level of contact of individuals, the family and community with the national health system, bringing health care as close as possible to where people live and work, and constitutes the first element of a continuing health care process' (WHO 1978, quoted in Andrews 1990: 346). Looking at the international picture Andrews summarised some of the important principles in any system (Andrews 1990). These included:

* a teamwork approach;
* the need to consider older people in relation to their family, local and community relationships;
* continuity of care;
* a medical and social perspective;
* a preventive component;
* appropriate referral mechanisms to ensure full access to more technical care.

General practitioners (GPs) play a crucial role in maintaining the health of older people but they may not always take a positive approach. Elderly people are more likely than any other age group except for the under-fives to consult their GP and are likely to need more home visits than average. They are also more likely to receive a home consultation than other age groups. In 1994 31 per cent of consultations for the over-75s took place at home (the figure was 13 per cent for those aged 65–74) compared with figures ranging from 4 per cent for those aged 16–44 to 15 per cent for the under-fives (OPCS 1996: 71). The higher numbers may be partly due to difficulty in getting to a surgery because of lack of transport. A number of different developments have taken place since the early days of the NHS which have affected elderly people.

The number of patients per doctor has dropped from 2,300 in 1961 to 1,900 in 1993 (CSO 1996: 138) but there is an increase in demand for out-of-hours visits. There has been a shift away from single-doctor practices (half in 1950 and 11 per cent in 1994) to group practices and health centres (Dorrell 1996). These make it possible to experiment with different methods of providing primary health care, and they can also house a wide range of services, such as consultant outpatient clinics and diagnostic and paramedical services. For elderly people their advantage is that they are more likely to be purpose-built premises which are more comfortable and have better facilities, and it is more likely that a range of both medical and non-medical staff are employed. The elderly person may therefore be able to see a nurse for dressings and not join the queue to see the doctor. However, there are disadvantages. The grouping of doctors in one building inevitably means that it is less likely that patients will have their own GP just 'round the corner'. A group or health centre practice is also likely to run an appointments system, although there may be an open surgery as well. A rigid appointments system may cause problems for elderly people who are less likely to be on the telephone than the rest of the population and who may just 'turn up' at the surgery. Elderly people may also feel that they get a more personal service from a doctor practising alone whom they will see on every occasion except when he or she is ill or on holiday. Some single-handed doctors, however, are still in poor, lock-up premises in inner-city areas and may not be as accessible as a group practice. The move to group practices has also been accompanied by greater audit and computerisation.

Another development has been the growth in the number of staff other than doctors in primary health care and the establishment of teamwork working (Pringle 1993, British Medical Journal 1992). [See Document 12 for the history of the practice team.] The number of practice nurses in England grew from 1,920 in 1984 to 9,100 in 1994 (Dorrell 1996: 40). Practice nurses are playing a growing role and undertake a wide range of tasks including health promotion, chronic disease management and health checks. This may include visiting elderly people at home and making follow-up visits on a regular basis. It is not known how many social workers are members of primary health care teams, but progress has been slower, possibly due to a different approach to patients between the professions and some mutual distrust. The importance of receptionists and secretaries is also being increasingly recognised for they can act as 'gatekeepers' – that is, be a help or a barrier to contact between the older patient and the doctor.

Greater emphasis on primary health in the UK is also due to a number of factors. These include the decreased length of stay by many patients in hospitals (either after operations or after childbirth), the closure of many psychiatric hospitals, developments in services and technology which allow even seriously ill people to be nursed at home, the desire by patients to be at home and not in hospital, and the lower costs of home care.

In 1986 the Government published *Primary Health Care: An Agenda for Discussion* (Sec. of St. for Social Services *et al.* 1986). After discussions, *Promoting Better Health: The Government's Programme for Improving Primary Health Care* came out in 1987 (Sec. of St. for Social Services *et al.* 1987). The aim was to shift the emphasis from treatment of illness to promotion of health and prevention of disease (see also *The Health of the Nation*, Sec. of St. for Health 1991: Ch. 4). One of the ways this was to be achieved was by giving incentives to GPs, proposing help with premises and ensuring that patients got a wider choice of doctors and more information about them. Large GP practices (those with over 11,000 patients) could apply for their own budgets to cover certain diagnostic, outpatient, inpatient and day care costs together with practice team staff costs, improvement to practice premises and prescribing costs. These were called fundholding practices (see below). Other GPs would have a drugs budget set by the FHSA. In response to criticisms that GPs would not want to take on elderly people or would be reluctant to prescribe expensive drugs the Minister said that there was no question of GPs having to stop treating their patients but if they exceeded their budget they would have to justify this (Kenneth Clarke in a DoH press release 9.3.1989). As noted before, patients aged 75 years and over must be offered a consultation and domiciliary visit by the GP to assess whether personal medical services are needed.

The new GP contract, which came into force in April 1991 following the NHS and Community Care Act 1990, implemented these proposals. A report which resulted from a consultation exercise, *Primary Care: The Future*, stressed the importance of primary care and underlined the principles of quality, fairness, accessibility, responsiveness and efficiency (Dorrell 1996).

One of the most interesting innovations has been fundholding. This scheme started in 1991. The aim was to improve the quality of care by enabling GPs to choose the most appropriate response to the needs of their patients and to stimulate hospital and community services to be more responsive. From 1996 practices with 5,000 patients have also been eligible to become fund holders. In 1991, 7 per cent of the population in England were served by fundholding practices but by 1995–6 this had gone up to 41 per cent with half GPs being fundholders (DoH press release 23.9.1995).

The new system has given fundholders more autonomy with freedom to choose and pay for a range of services. Their budgets allowed them to buy:

- specific hospital services (such as certain surgical procedures e.g. cataract and hip replacement operations), outpatient services, diagnostic services (such as X-rays), physiotherapy, occupational therapy, speech therapy and counselling services;
- drugs and appliances;
- non-medical staff employed within the practice;
- (from 1993) community health services including community nursing, health visiting, dietetics and chiropody.

Fundholding has advantages for GPs and for their patients and has attracted generally favourable comments in two research reports (National Audit Office 1994, Glennerster *et al.* 1994). But it has also brought an increase in bureaucracy and some other problems. The Audit Commission concluded: 'The best managed and outward-looking practices achieve most benefits for their patients. A few fundholders have made achievements across the board and are at the leading edge of purchasing; but the majority have achieved only a small proportion of the benefits potentially available for their patients' (Audit Commission 1996b: 86).

Satisfaction with the GP services is higher than for hospital services although approximately one in five (of all ages) felt that there was room for improvement in the quality of medical treatment, being able to choose which GP to see and the amount of time each GP gives to each patient (CSO 1996: 150). At the same time, but not necessarily linked of course, is the rise of interest in complementary medicine such as acupuncture, herbal medicine and osteopathy.

Community services

Community services include community nursing, occupational and speech therapy, physiotherapy and pharmaceutical, ophthalmic, chiropody and dental services and services for people with hearing loss. The Association of Community Health Councils for England and Wales says that these services are highly valued by patients but are:

- often overlooked in long-term planning;
- poorly resourced and not considered a high priority by NHS managers;
- likely to be fragmented by the internal market;
- unlikely to be able to cope with any additional workload unless they receive additional funding (Association of Community Health Councils 1994).

Another general change is the widening role seen for community services. For example, pharmacists are being encouraged to give more advice and in 1994 nurses in some pilot areas were given the authority to prescribe simple remedies and medicines. A government report stated: 'There is potential for non-medical professionals to develop their roles to provide more of the care currently provided by doctors and to extend services generally. This requires a change of public and professional attitudes as well as changes to professional education and training' (Dorrell 1996: 52).

The Audit Commission in *Homeward Bound: A New Course for Community Health* commented on the uneven pattern of services and the need to get better value for money (Audit Commission 1992a). They argued for a more coordinated approach by professionals. One of their minor recommendations was replacing some home visits by sessions at local clinics and health centres except where there is no affordable public transport. Critics of this approach point to the value of visits to old and vulnerable patients in their own homes.

The effect of purchasing on community services is not known but it may make evaluation of these services more likely. An example of advice to NHS purchasers and providers/professionals on ways in which planning and delivery of services might be improved is that put out by DoH on foot care – *Feet First* (DoH NHS Executive 1994). The involvement of community health professionals, such as nurses, in purchasing health care services is the other side of the coin.

Community nursing: This includes district nurses, health visitors, community psychiatric nurses, school nurses and their support staff of registered and enrolled nurses and nursing auxiliaries. Over half of community health expenditure is spent on nursing but there are great variations; for example people over the age of 75 have two or three times as many staff available to them in some areas as others (Audit Commission 1992a: 4).

District nursing: Many district nurses work in group practices or health centres and are registered nurses with additional training who provide care for people in their own homes. In some areas this extends to a night nursing service. In 1994 2 per cent of older people aged 65–69, 12 per cent of those aged 80–84 and 19 per cent of those aged 85 and over had used the services of a district nurse or health visitor in the previous month (OPCS 1996: 186). New roles include nurse-led minor injuries clinics and nurse prescribing (Dorrell 1996: 41).

Health visiting: Health visitors are nurses with additional training, who are concerned with the promotion of health and the prevention of ill health. They usually work in an advisory supportive role rather than in a nursing capacity.

The Cumberlege report in 1986 was about community nursing (Cumberlege 1986). It studied health services provided outside hospitals and reported on how resources could be used more effectively. The major recommendation was that nurses outside hospitals should come under a neighbourhood nursing service, which would plan, organise and provide community nursing services, and that subsidies to GPs enabling them to employ staff to perform nursing duties should be phased out. Nurses working in the community may either be employed in the primary health care team or in 'neighbourhood' teams. A number of districts did set up the latter after the Cumberlege report but this model still allows for the attachment of nurses to GPs within a primary health care team.

An expansion of the role of district nurses and health visitors had been recommended by the Royal Commission on the NHS and this was also a theme of the Cumberlege report, which included the adoption of nurse practitioners in primary health care. Nurse prescribing has been referred to in the section on primary health care.

The Cumberlege report included a useful checklist of ways of monitoring and improving community nursing services (Cumberlege 1986: 44). Stilwell discusses the demarcation between nurses and doctors and highlights the role of nurses as health educators (Stilwell 1986). Role boundaries between nurses and other health and care workers is becoming increasingly blurred, which leads some authors to argue for qualified 'transdisciplinary' workers (Hollingbery 1993, Nolan 1994).

Occupational therapy (OT): This is another invaluable service. It is usually arranged through a hospital, but many local authorities have occupational therapy services associated with the provision of aids and appliances. Occupational therapists now play an important role in assessment of levels of independence, maintenance of these levels and of rehabilitation, as well as providing advice on, and arranging for, aids and adaptations. Although numbers of OTs have grown rapidly in recent years there has also been a serious drain of qualified staff. Shortages are widespread as demand for their services grows.

Speech therapy: This is another profession which is increasingly being regarded as having an important contribution to make to the well-being of older people. Speech therapists are concerned with communication and speech problems.

Physiotherapy: Physiotherapists usually work in a hospital rehabilitation unit, but are sometimes available to treat a patient at home. Their main concern is with mobility. They play a crucial role in the assessment, rehabilitation and treatment of illness and conditions that affect older people (Wagstaff and Coakley 1988). Physiotherapists themselves are now suggesting that there is need for evaluation of their work which may lead to a greater appreciation by purchasers of their value (Squires and Livesley 1993).

Pharmaceutical services: Two matters are of particular concern here – access to the service and the role of the pharmacist. Both of these were considered by the Royal Commission on the NHS (1979). They found that while few people experienced difficulty in getting a prescription dispensed there were some problems in rural areas. Problems have subsequently been reported in other areas. The role of the pharmacist has traditionally been to dispense medicine on the prescription of doctors. The Royal Commission on the NHS found that this role had expanded and that the pharmacist was now regarded as a main source of advice in relation to minor ailments. An extended use of the pharmacist's skills was also recommended by the Nuffield report (Nuffield Foundation 1986) and the White Paper *Promoting Better Health* (Secs. of St. for Social Services *et al.* 1987). A Working Party of the DoH and the pharmaceutical profession also argued for a wider role where advice would be offered on the best treatment and monitoring its effectiveness (Royal Pharmaceutical Society 1992). Research shows that most doctors would favour an extension of the role of community pharmacists but worry about their role in screening and counselling patients and prescribing (Spencer and Edwards 1992). A government document considered that community pharmacists could make a greater contribution to primary care but 'there were also limitations because there is no continuity' (Dorrell, 1996: 36).

Ophthalmic services: Many older people have eye problems and these increase with age (Weale 1989). The main problems are cataracts, glaucoma and age-related macular degeneration. Patients may be dealt with under the NHS by hospitals or by the general ophthalmic service, which provides sight testing and the supply, replacement and repair of spectacles. The 1994 *GHS* showed that 12 per cent of people over the age of 65 used the services of an optician in the three months before the interview (Table 6.5). A particular need, however, of many old people is for a domiciliary consultation.

Chiropody: National surveys have confirmed that one of the greatest unmet needs of older people is chiropody. Problems are those to do with systemic disease such as diabetes, disabling foot conditions and inability to cut nails. Foot conditions affect mobility inside and outside the home. A detailed survey which investigated foot problems and treatment among older people found that one quarter reported severe or moderate pain or discomfort with their feet and almost half should have been referred to a chiropodist (Cartwright and Henderson 1986). The study recommended a doubling of current facilities, a screening service for the over-65s and a foot care clinic at health centres employing better trained foot care assistants. The importance of this service has also been emphasised by other researchers.

Dental services: These are also important to older people. In 1993, 43 per cent of people aged 65–74 and 62 per cent of those aged 75 and over in GB had no natural teeth (OPCS 1995: 105). There is evidence, too, of poor dental health. In general there is a lack of awareness of regular dental care for older people both with and without their own teeth, and of the relationships between dental health and comfort and nutritional well-being. Fifteen per cent of people over the age of 65 used the services of a dentist in the previous three months in 1994 (Table 6.5). Fewer people are now being treated by NHS dentists as the latter increasingly opt for private practice and charges to NHS patients increase.

Services for people with hearing disorders: These are also important. In the UK one third of those aged 61–70 and 60 per cent of those aged 71–80 had a hearing impairment at a level for which a hearing aid would confer benefit (MRC 1994a). Many old people do have hearing loss but it is difficult to isolate the effects of ageing on hearing from other factors such as noise, medication and so on. It is sometimes assumed that an older person has decreased cognitive function when they cannot hear or communicate properly. It is suggested that half of the people who are sufficiently hearing impaired to be considered as disabled are over the age of 65 (Noffsinger *et al.* 1990). A variety of services, including the widening range of assistive devices, are necessary.

Hospital services

Numbers in hospital: Very few old people (less than 1 per cent in the 1991 census) are in hospital at any one time. However, people over the age of 65 account for 60 per cent of all days spent in hospital in the four largest specialties – general medicine, general surgery, trauma and orthopaedics and urology (Audit Commission 1995: 58). Admissions of elderly people to hospital are increasing at about 4 per cent per annum and almost two thirds of patients admitted to combined specialties of general and geriatric medicine are over the age of 65 (Royal College of Physicians 1994). In 1995 of all patients over the age of 75, 20 per cent were waiting to be discharged and of these one third were waiting for a placement in a residential or nursing home (House of Commons Health Committee 1995b: *xxiii*). The effect on hospitals of the increasing number of very old people in the next 20–25 years will be marked (see section on continuing care for figures for long-term beds).

Types of hospital and standards: The importance of acute care for older people who need medical care has been underlined in many reports (e.g. The Royal College of Physicians 1994, MRC 1994a). The Royal College of Physicians argue that there must be no distinction or negative discrimination on grounds of age and there must be immediate access to investigation and treatment by appropriately trained medical and nursing staff (Royal College of Physicians 1994). As has been mentioned earlier, there are three main patterns of service provision – traditional, age-defined and integrated (see p. 81 for the advantages and disadvantages). Elderly people now go either to geriatric hospitals (some of which were formerly workhouses, though some are modern), to psychiatric hospitals or to general medical or geriatric or specialty wards (such as orthopaedics) in acute types of hospitals. One of the objectives of policy has been to bring the three types of hospital together. This has been for a number of reasons; not least to even up standards and to bring the first two types of hospital into the mainstream of modern medicine. The development of geriatrics, which is the study and treatment of diseases common to old age, as a medical speciality, also has a bearing on the service provided. The Royal Commission on the NHS felt that the development of geriatrics had in many places enhanced the quality of care of elderly people but that it had also influenced some physicians to take less interest in elderly people and to look to geriatricians excessively for their care (Royal Commission 1979:

216). In the early 1990s '80 per cent of persons who are admitted with a medical condition are cared for by physicians in the specialty of general medicine rather than in geriatric medicine. For persons aged 74 to 84 years the proportion is 50 per cent and in the very elderly (aged 85 years or over) it is 30 per cent' (Royal College of Physicians 1994: 2).

There is general agreement that conditions for elderly people in hospitals have improved greatly. New buildings, more patients being nursed in wards of acute hospitals and growing medical interest in old age have all contributed to this improvement. Nevertheless, there are still some problems and these are mainly to do with buildings, staff and lack of suitable accommodation for patients who should be discharged. The problem of old buildings and the lack of small community hospitals for people who do not need the facilities of the district general hospital is still acute. Staff problems are related to shortages, lack of trained personnel and negative attitudes towards the benefits of working with older people. Redfern, for example, explains reasons why nurses choose not to work with elderly patients (Redfern 1989).

A further dilemma is 'bed-blocking' which comes about when a patient cannot be discharged from hospital because no suitable accommodation is available (see Victor 1990). The development of other forms of housing, such as very sheltered housing (see Chapter 7), and NHS nursing homes is helpful but there is only limited provision of either (McCafferty 1994; Bond *et al.* 1989). An evaluation of the first three experimental NHS nursing homes found that residents were: 'not disadvantaged in terms of outcomes; this form of care was preferred by both residents and their relatives; and it was no more expensive than continuing care provided in NHS hospitals' (Bond *et al.* 1989: 3).

Day surgery and day hospitals: The development of day surgery is a trend which will require changes in policy, especially more community services. Another development has been connected with maintaining elderly people in their own home while at the same time providing them with hospital treatment. This can often relieve the pressures on a family who are looking after a frail older person. It can be achieved through short-term care in hospitals, for example admitting an old person for a specified period on a regular basis, or through day hospitals where treatment is given on certain days to patients who continue to live at home.

Hospital discharge: The other key issue is discharge from hospital. When patients leave hospital there is need to ensure that the conditions they will move to are suitable. Whether this is their own home or somewhere else the physical condition of the home (perhaps the need for a ramp or modifications to a bathroom) are as important as the need for help with personal and care tasks (see also Chapter 8 for community care services). What is not sensible is to discharge patients too soon only to have them readmitted; concern has been expressed about this and about the lack of research in this area (e.g. Colledge and Ford 1994, Tierney and Worth 1995).

The greatest need is for discharge planning. A study of acute hospitals by the Audit Commission outlined five areas of concern and one of these was discharge (Audit Commission 1992b). On discharge they said: 'Close attention should be paid to planning and co-ordinating discharge for patients needing domiciliary support or places in residential or nursing homes. This involves establishing close links with local community services and GPs' (Audit Commission 1992b: 2). There may be a need for rehabilitation but the Royal College of Physicians warn against using this as a disguised request for a 'waiting period' while social support arrangements are made (Royal College of Physicians 1994: 11).

Useful guidance was given in a 1989 DoH Health Circular HC (89)5 *Discharge of Patients from Hospital* but this has now been superseded by community care arrangements and advice on continuing care (see next section). The *Hospital Discharge Workbook* also provides examples of good practice (DoH 1994). However, as the House of Commons Health Committee commented, it seems that some elements in the circular have been downgraded from guidance to advice on good practice (House of Commons Health Committee 1995b: *xxii*).

In some cases hospital discharge may be the equivalent of hospital care provided at home and may embrace intensive nursing care as well as a high technology service right through to palliative terminal care (see Marks 1991).

Continuing care

With the closure of many long-stay hospitals and beds, attention has increasingly turned to what is sometimes called continuing care and sometimes long-term care. Both expressions are used for hospitals and beds. However, they are now also interpreted as anywhere where long-term care is given and this includes at home (see evidence by the author, Tinker 1995, and by Emily Grundy 1995b, to the House of Commons Health Committee 1995b).

The reasons for the decline in hospital provision is because of the cost, evidence that some elderly people do not need constant medical care and because it is considered preferable for them to be in a less restrictive/institutionalised environment. Two current issues arise: what care is available outside the hospital for inpatients who need to be moved out; and how people are to be looked after who need continuing care but not constant medical attention. Of major importance is the question of cost. Whereas care in hospitals under the NHS is free at the point of delivery (i.e. no charges are made), care in any other situation, provided by local authorities or privately, is subject to charges. A particular anomaly is that people who live in nursing homes have to pay for nursing care, which is not the case in hospitals, residential care or for people living in their own homes. (See Chapter 8 for the financing of long-term care in residential care and at home.) It is this issue of cost which has exercised many bodies in the early 1990s including the House of Commons Health Committee (see below), the Joseph Rowntree Foundation and the Royal College of Physicians (1994).

Long-term care may be funded in a variety of ways including the state, paid for through taxes or national insurance, private long-term care insurance (compulsory or voluntary) or some kind of partnership between the two (Nuttall *et al*. 1993 and House of Commons Health Committee 1996).

In the UK 57 per cent of the general public thought that the best way of providing for long-term care was by public provision financed through taxes, whereas this was the choice of only 34 per cent across the EC where 37 per cent favoured compulsory public insurance (Walker 1993: 31).

The Department of Health issued *NHS Responsibilities for Meeting Continuing Health Care Needs* in early 1995 (DoH Circular 1995 HSG(95)8 LAC(95)5). This provided a national framework for local health authorities to base their own policies on. It laid down what responsibility the NHS had for 'people who require continuing physical or mental health care' and required health authorities to develop local policies and eligibility criteria which set out clearly:

* the criteria which will be used as the basis, in individual cases, for decisions about the need for NHS funded care;
* the range, type, location and level of services to be arranged and funded by the NHS to meet continuing health care needs in their area.

Later in the year the DoH produced guidance *Discharge from NHS Inpatient Care of People with Continuing Health or Social Care Needs: Arrangements for Reviewing Decisions on Eligibility for NHS Continuing Inpatient Care* (DoH Circular 1995 HSG (95)39 LAC (95)17). In 1996 the government issued a consultation paper, *A New Partnership for Care in Old Age* (Chancellor of the Exchequer *et al*. 1996). The main proposal was that if older people take out certain kinds of insurance to pay for some long-term care they will be able to keep more of their assets if they then have to rely on state funding. The aim is to encourage people to provide for their own long-term care.

The House of Commons Health Committee set up an inquiry in 1992 to review 'the current and future arrangements for providing and funding long-term care in England' and produced their first report in 1995 (House of Commons Health Committee 1995b). They pointed to the decline in the number of NHS beds for older people from 55,600 in 1976 to 37,500 in 1994 but the almost doubling in places overall for long-term care from 225,597 in 1976 to 482,820 in

Table 6.7 *Long-term care places for elderly people England*

Year	NHS beds general patients, elderly	Private/voluntary nursing homes, hospital and clinics	NHS beds, mental health, elderly	Local Authority Part III residential homes	Voluntary sector residential homes	Private sector residential homes	Total all sectors
1976	55,600	n/a	n/a	110,796	32,789	26,412	225,597
1986	55,300	33,900	n/a	115,609	36,000	92,605	333,414
1994	37,500	148,500	18,200	68,899	45,513	164,208	482,820

Source: House of Commons Health Committee *Long Term Care: NHS Responsibilities for Meeting Community Health Care Needs*, Vol. 1, HMSO, 1995 p. viii.

1994 (Table 6.7, House of Commons Health Committee 1995b: *viii–ix*). The main reason for the latter was the significant increase in the number of private sector residential and nursing home places (Table 6.7). (See also Chapter 8 for a discussion of residential care.) Their figures also showed a rise in the overall number of long-term care places per thousand population for the over-75s from 92.8 in 1976 to 144.2 in 1994, and for the over-85s from 491.5 in 1976 to 558.8 in 1994. The Health Committee expressed concern about:

- the content and implementation of continuing care policies;
- the setting of local eligibility criteria;
- hospital discharge arrangements;
- independent advisory panels;
- the role of the Centre i.e., the DoH.

They wanted national criteria, clearer definitions of specialist care, a charter specifying minimum standards of care, and no patients to be discharged from hospital without an adequate aftercare package. They also wanted the NHS to take responsibility for funding all types of continence supplies and for the care of people in nursing homes who need palliative care. In 1996 they produced their recommendations (House of Commons Health Committee 1996). They considered that 'the problems the country faces in relation to paying for long-term care, although real, are more manageable than many recent commentators have suggested' (1996: *vii*). They endorsed policies of allowing people to remain in their own homes and stressed the importance of housing, domiciliary and preventative services as well as more effective liaison between housing, health services and social services. They also concluded:

We make clear that the status quo of funding long-term care mainly from general taxation is a defensible option, which is both possible and affordable, but go on to discuss the pros and cons of possible alternative approaches. We call for the long-term care insurance market to be properly regulated. We state that until such a time as the Government divulges its own estimates of the likely cost of each option – including the likely costs of its preferred option of partnership schemes – it will not be possible to reach a final decision on the best way forward. Decisions on whether long-term care should be funded through general taxation or through insurance, and if the latter whether the system should be voluntary or compulsory, touch upon fundamental questions concerning the future of the Welfare State, and cannot be tackled in relation to long-term care in isolation.

(House of Commons Health Committee 1996: *lxiv*)

The Joseph Rowntree Foundation Inquiry reported later in 1996 (JRF 1996) and called for free care in old age backed by compulsory care insurance. They recommended that:

- older people living in institutions should not be charged for the health and personal care they receive, and there should be no local authority charges for domiciliary care;

- means-tested charging should be restricted to the costs of accommodation (including meals etc.) in residential and nursing homes;
- a National Care insurance scheme, based on compulsory contributions, should be introduced in partnership with the private sector;
- a National Care Council should regulate the new system with responsibilities for deciding the level of contributions and set national standards for care services. ·

Useful guidelines for long-term care in all settings have been produced by the Royal College of Physicians (Royal College of Physicians 1992).

Private health care

Private medical insurance was taken out by just over 2 million people in the UK in 1971 and this rose to 7.6 million in 1990, but since then it has fallen back to 6.8 million in 1994 (CSO 1996: 152, and personal communication Office for National Statistics). The number of NHS beds authorised for private inpatients' care dropped from 4,400 in 1971 to 3,000 in 1990–1 (CSO 1993: 108) but this is a very small proportion of all NHS beds (200,000).

It seems unlikely that elderly people will contribute much more to the costs of their health care over the next 10 to 15 years (Robins and Wittenberg 1992). Tax relief on private health insurance for elderly people, introduced from April 1990, may encourage some increase in the number of policy-holders; but premiums are high, such that only a minority are likely to be able to afford them, and conditions requiring long-term care, often the most costly conditions, are in any event generally excluded from coverage (Robins and Wittenberg 1992: 16).

Collaboration between services

Teamwork and co-ordination within the NHS

It is vital that there is co-operation between the various parts of the NHS, especially between primary and secondary care. A few examples demonstrate this. When an elderly person is referred to hospital, the hospital must be made aware of all the relevant medical and social circumstances which only the GP will know. When the patient is discharged the primary health care team needs to be alerted in good time and advised what, if any, treatment is needed. Those working in community nursing and other services also need to be kept in the picture and the development of primary health care teams should aid this.

Links between health and other services

Links between health and other services are crucial in a number of situations. For example, when elderly people are discharged from hospital they probably need the support of some of the domiciliary services. Equally there can be occasions when an elderly person is incapable of remaining either at home or in residential care and the hospital is unwilling or unable to admit them. The closure of long-stay hospitals without adequate community provision is a matter of deep concern.

One of the key links is with social services. After the reorganisation of the NHS in 1974 the health of older people became the responsibility of the NHS, and welfare that of local authority social services departments. The latter took the responsibility for the medical social workers employed in hospitals and certain other services. There are areas now where there should be close links, especially over community care. For example, there is a clear role for GPs over assessment when they should have an input into what should be a multidisciplinary exercise. This is both at the individual level of the patient and at the macro level of providing data from the practice for overall planning purposes. The changing role of some staff also has implications for relations between services. For example, the increased duties that some home helps have may encroach on the work of nurses and there is need for a clarification of roles. The divide between health and social care is not always clear but some guidelines need to be worked out by health and social services authorities. What is unhelpful is when local authority boundaries are not coterminous with those of health authorities.

The new local and health authorities were required to set up joint consultative committees, made up of members from both authorities, to advise on arrangements for collaboration and the planning and operation of services of common concern. Authorities were recommended to set up joint care planning teams, one of whose tasks was to plan and co-ordinate for groups such as elderly people. Joint finance which was introduced in 1977 (DHSS, *Joint Care Planning: health and local authorities* Circular 4C(77) 17/LAC(77) 10 1977) has helped this co-operation (see earlier section). A working party representing local authority associations and the National Association of Health Authorities with full participation from DHSS produced a report *Progress in Partnership* (DHSS 1985). But, as Westland commented, joint planning requires at least two willing parties and this cannot be achieved by legislation (Westland 1986). Later developments are discussed in Chapter 8.

Equally important are links with the independent sector. Both private and voluntary organisations are included in advice by the government to health authorities to make healthy alliances. Sometimes these will be formal links when, for example, the health authority purchases services from the independent sector.

The link between housing and physical and mental health, accidents, homelessness and hospital discharge are clear (see Lowry 1991). The importance of housing for the health of older people, so long neglected, is increasingly being acknowledged (House of Commons Health Committee 1996, Tinker in press). It is housing that is the concern of the next chapter.

CHAPTER 7

Housing

Introduction

Any discussion about housing for older people should recognise that most live in their own homes and not in any form of institutional care. There has been little change since 1948. Approximately 90 per cent live in ordinary accommodation either owned by themselves or rented, 5 per cent live in their own home in sheltered housing with a resident warden and 5 per cent live in some form of institutional care – mainly old people's homes or hospitals.

Adequate housing is important to older people in many ways. Such features as the absence of stairs may enable even a very frail person to continue living independently. There is growing recognition of the link between poor health and housing (summarised in Tinker, in press). Warmth, too, is particularly necessary for less active people. Familiar surroundings and nearness to shops, post office, pub and church also contribute to their ability to live alone. What is shown more clearly than anything else by surveys in the UK and elsewhere is the desire of older people to be able to live in the way they want in their own home (Tinker 1994). The psychological aspects of home are also increasingly being recognised (Sixsmith 1990, Gurney and Means 1993) as is the need to take a life course approach recognising that an older person's housing must be related to their previous housing history (Clapham *et al.* 1993). At the same time community physicians have been pointing to the benefits for older people of the physical and mental activity involved in housework, shopping and generally caring for themselves.

Many old people, however, live in less than desirable housing and some groups have particular problems. There is evidence, too, that some people remain in residential care only because alternative accommodation is lacking (Wagner 1988b, Allen *et al.* 1992).

The development of policies

Policies for older people

There has been remarkable consistency in policies for housing older people, irrespective of which political party has been in power. Advice from central government, given mainly in circulars, has emphasised the need to provide small units of accommodation, to allow older people to maintain independent lives in their own homes and make movement from larger to smaller dwellings easier. Other points made have been the importance of siting dwellings near amenities and, between 1944 and the early 1980s, the value of grouping accommodation, usually referred to as sheltered housing, with communal facilities and a warden [Document 13]. Another piece of advice regularly given is the need for effective co-operation between all the authorities and departments concerned [Document 14].

In 1956 the Ministry of Housing decided to find out whether old people were receiving a reasonable share of the accommodation provided and whether this was of the kind best suited to their physical needs and financial circumstances (Circular 32/56, *The Housing of Old People*). The following year advice was given (Circular 18/57, *Housing of Old People*) which stressed the need for adequate provision of small dwellings and a sympathetic and efficient system for moving tenants from larger to smaller homes. Observations were made about the success of local authority (LA) and housing association (HA) schemes for accommodating 'less active elderly people' in bedsitters or flatlets in converted large houses where some shared facilities could be provided. Handbooks were then issued (*Flatlets for Old People* and *More Flatlets for Old People*, Ministry of Housing 1958, 1960) illustrating sheltered housing schemes, and the hope was expressed that councils would consider carrying out such schemes. In 1961 general advice was given in a joint Ministry of Housing and Local Government (MHLG)/Ministry of Health (MoH) circular, *Services for Old People* (Circular 10/61) [Document 14].

The Ministry then became involved in an interesting experiment in which they built (for Stevenage Development Corporation) a prototype sheltered housing scheme and monitored reactions to it. The results were published in three MHLG Design Bulletins (1962a, 1962b, 1966).

The following year Circular 36/67, MHLG, *Housing Standards, Costs and Subsidies*, established what have become known as the Parker Morris Standards (minimum standards of design and construction). Then in 1969 the principal circular (MHLG/Welsh Office (WO), *Housing Standards and Costs: Accommodation Specially Designed for Old People*, Circular MHLG 82/69, WO 84/69) came out [Document 15]. Two types of accommodation were declared eligible for subsidy. Category 1 was self-contained dwellings for old people who were more active. The standard was Parker Morris with some additional features. Limited communal facilities could be provided and so could a warden. Category 2 accommodation, for less active older people, was smaller than Parker Morris standards and comprised grouped flatlets with full communal facilities and a warden. The circular was withdrawn in the 1980s and is no longer a standard to be adhered to.

As a preliminary to a new circular, *Housing for Old People: A Consultation Paper* in 1976 stressed the importance of widening the choice of accommodation available for old people (DoE 1976). DoE research on innovatory ways of enabling older people to stay in their own homes and very sheltered housing (see pp. 121 and 126–7) added to the debate. The circular *Housing and Community Care* (DoE 10.92, DoH LAC (92) 12) finally appeared in 1992. (See last section of this chapter [and Document 14].) The National Federation of Housing Associations (NFHA) also issued policy advice *Rented Housing for Older People: Implementing a New Framework*, which emphasised accessible housing, flexible support and, for those who can no longer live on their own, supported housing (NFHA 1993). The Housing Corporation has produced policy guidance, *Housing for Older People*, for housing associations which ranged over all types of housing both specialised and non-specialised (Housing Corporation 1996).

Underpinning much policy now is the DoE research *Living Independently: A Study of the Housing Needs of Elderly and Disabled People* (McCafferty 1994). The objectives included providing estimates of housing need for subsidised accommodation by these groups. The research included national surveys of housing provision and large surveys of older and disabled people and their carers. It stressed the variety of housing needed and that provision must not just keep to existing classifications of sheltered housing.

It is interesting, and encouraging, that older people are now not necessarily seen to be a group in need of subsidised (social) housing and are included in discussions about all tenures.

General housing policies

General housing policies have also had an effect on provision, for example the 1963 White Paper, *Housing*, laid great stress on new building and in particular of small units for older people (MHLG 1963). A White Paper, *The Housing Programme 1965 to 1970*, in 1965 set out the first stage in formulating a national housing plan but stated that more needed to be known about the needs of older people (MHLG/Welsh Office 1965). Meanwhile a committee was set up by the MHLG to review the practice of authorities in allocating tenancies. Their report, *Council Housing Purposes, Procedures and Priorities* (the Cullingworth Committee), appeared in 1969 (MHLG 1969). Concern about the need for more and better homes led to another White Paper (in 1973), *Widening the Choice: The Next Steps in Housing*, which expressed disquiet about the many people who had no choice at all (DoE/WO 1973a). When considering the way in which provision could be made the government proposed a range of measures to expand both owner-occupation and the role of housing associations. However, the view was expressed that local authorities had a special responsibility for groups who had 'general needs or suffer from special disadvantages'. Included among these were elderly people. A further White Paper, *Better Homes: The Next Priorities*, in 1973 proposed a range of measures to tackle the worst housing conditions and in particular outlined changes in the improvement grants system (DoE/WO 1973b). The setting up of housing action areas and general improvement areas, recommended in the White Paper, took place after the Housing Act 1974 which also expanded the role of the Housing Corporation. The importance of these changes was the attempt to help urban areas with poor property (where incidentally many older people lived) and to expand the role of housing associations (which were fast becoming major providers of accommodation for elderly people). The Rent Act 1974 gave security of tenure to tenants in furnished accommodation, many of whom were elderly.

The growth in small households, including older people, was one of the reasons for *Housing Needs and Action* (DoE Circular 24/75) in 1975 which stressed the need for more small accommodation and showed how better use could be made of existing dwellings. The latter theme was expanded in 1977 in *Better Use of Vacant and Under-Occupied Housing* (DoE Circular 76/77) which sought to bring into full use empty and underoccupied dwellings, whether or not they belonged to the local authority, and to ensure that the accommodation people occupied accurately reflected their housing requirements. In the same year the new system for deciding on capital allocations to local authorities by central government was put forward by the DoE in *Housing Strategies and Investment Programmes* (DoE Circular 63/77). In the annual strategy statement which local authorities were requested to complete, they were asked to include any measures 'to meet the housing requirements of groups with special needs, for example, the aged and disabled'.

In 1977 a Consultative Document, *Housing Policy*, endorsed previous policies for elderly people, and the proposed abolition of local authority residential qualifications was stressed as was the need for co-operation between authorities (DoE 1977b).

Of major importance was the Housing Act 1980 which affected people in all tenures. The right to buy provisions enabled council (and some housing association) tenants to buy their homes at a discount from the local authority or housing association. In England between 1979 and 1994 1.5 million LA and HA tenants bought their homes, 1.25 million under the right to buy legislation (Secs of St. for Environment and Wales 1995a: 14). Purpose-built or adapted accommodation was specifically excluded, but this covered only a small proportion of the stock. Opponents of the Act argued that council housing would become a residual service and that some families would lend or give their parents the money so that they could eventually sell the home at a profit or use it as a second home.

Older people gained from some of the other provisions of the Act such as security of tenure, greater freedom over conditions (e.g. the right to take in lodgers) and the statutory duty of authorities to give information about allocations and to consult tenants. The Act also widened the grant system so that more owner-occupiers became eligible for improvement and repair grants and grants were made more flexible.

The mid- and late-1980s saw the publication of a number of important reports, surveys and also legislation relevant to the housing needs of older people. The Housing Act 1984 extended the right to buy. The 1985 Green Paper on home improvement policies stressed the importance of targeting grants to those in need, partly to help older owner-occupiers (DoE 1985). The basic thrust of policy in the early 1980s concentrated on controlling public sector spending and providing incentives for privatisation (Whitehead 1989). Neither of these measures were particularly helpful, probably the reverse, for older people.

In 1985 the influential report of *An Inquiry into British Housing*, chaired by the Duke of Edinburgh, declared that there were deep-seated problems in housing which were the product of policies going back over several decades (NFHA 1985). The authors stated that old and poor owner-occupiers emerged as a clear target for assistance and encouragement. Unusually for an inquiry there was a second report which recommended that overdependence on owner-occupation be reduced, that Mortgage Interest Tax Relief be phased out, a targeted allowance be introduced for home owners as well as tenants and measures be taken to boost the quantity and quality of rented housing (Joseph Rowntree Foundation 1991).

The 1987 White Paper, *Housing: The Government's Proposals*, set out the Government's proposals (DoE 1987). These were to:

- reverse the decline of rented housing and improve its quality;
- give council tenants the right to transfer to other landlords if they choose to do so;
- target money more accurately on the most acute problems;
- continue to encourage the growth of home ownership.

These led to the 1988 Housing Act.

The main thrust of policy since 1988 has been designed to encourage owner-occupation, limit the role of local authorities and to stimulate an independent rented sector. Under the Housing Act 1988 provision was made to deregulate new lettings in the private rented sector, finance for housing associations was restructured, public sector tenants were offered the opportunity to change landlords and Housing Action Trusts could be established. The Local Government and Housing Act 1989 made certain changes to the right to buy as it related to housing for older people. Sheltered housing, and other housing deemed to be particularly suitable for older people, was still excluded from the right to buy unless it was first let after 1 January 1990. The Act also stipulated that LAs seeking to exempt a property from the right to buy must first seek the approval of the Secretary of State.

The Local Government and Housing Act 1989 also introduced a new mandatory grant system to bring properties up to a new fitness standard with discretionary grants for work above this. However, the level of income threshold and the treatment of savings has meant that some older people were excluded from a grant or eligible only for a reduced one. A useful addition though was the introduction of minor works grants for minor but essential repairs, improvements and adaptations (Bookbinder 1991: 77–8). Since 1988 older home-owners in receipt of income support have also been eligible for grants from the DSS's social fund for essential repairs, although these are discretionary and only available in certain circumstances.

In 1992 Compulsory Competitive Tendering was introduced for LA housing management (Franklin and Clapham 1995). In 1993 the Leasehold Reform, Housing and Urban Development Act brought about leasehold reform and extended further the right to buy as well as certain other measures. In 1994 three new rights for LA tenants were introduced. They were the Right to Manage, the Right to Repair and the Right to Compensation for Improvements. These are now included in the Council Tenants Charter. Other landmarks included the issue by the government of a White Paper, *Our Future Homes*, followed by a Consultation Paper, *More Choice in the Social Rented Sector* (Secs of St. for Environment and Wales 1995a). There continued to be stress on the expansion of owner-occupation and ways of sustaining renting. There was also continued commitment to the involvement of the private sector and to the transfer of LA housing to new landlords. By March 1995 40 LAs had transferred their stock (Wilcox 1995: 62). On council housing the recent developments have been described as residualisation or, summarised by others, as:

- a virtual stop to new build;
- privatise wherever possible, by disposing to individuals through right to buy and to organisations through bulk disposals (with tenants' consent);
- privatise the management of the remainder by compulsory competitive tendering;
- change the role of LAs from providers to enablers and purchasers.

(Page 1995: 10)

Condition, new build, tenure and type of accommodation

Amenities and the condition of housing

Overall the condition of the housing stock has improved. In England only 1 per cent of dwellings lacked basic amenities in 1991 but 7.6

per cent were still found to be unfit (this includes the interior and exterior of the building and defects relating to fitness for human habitation as well as lacking basic amenities) (DoE 1993). The position of households composed of older people improved relatively to some others. For example, whereas 30 per cent of households occupying the worst housing were either a lone person of pensionable age or two persons at least one of whom was of pensionable age in 1986 this proportion had dropped to 20 per cent in 1991 (Table 7.1). However, it is estimated that almost 700,000 older households lived in the worst housing in England in 1991 (Rolfe *et al.* 1993: 29). A great deal depends on tenure. Lone older households are the most likely to live in private housing in the worst condition and both they and two-person older households are disproportionately represented in pre-1919 stock in the worst condition (DoE 1993: 8). On the other hand older households are more likely to occupy some of the best housing in the social rented (LA and HA) sector.

New build

Another factor which has affected older people has been the decline in house building. There were 426,000 dwellings built in the UK in 1968 but this had dropped to 189,000 in 1994 (CSO 1996: 178). However, the proportions of small accommodation have increased. In England and Wales in 1971 23 per cent of housebuilding completions were two bedrooms compared with 34 per cent in 1993 (CSO 1995: 175). The proportion of one-bedroom dwellings was

Table 7.1 The proportion of households in the worst dwellings in 1986 and 1991 identified by household type England

	1986 For each household group – % of households in the worst dwelling	1991 For each household group – % of households in the worst dwelling
Household type		
Lone adult	16.0	17.5
Two adults	8.5	9.1
Lone parent	8.8	11.2
Small family	6.3	9.1
Large family	6.3	8.3
Large adult	8.6	7.6
Two older[1]	11.4	7.6
Lone older[2]	18.2	12.4

[1] Two persons (related or unrelated) at least one of whom is of pensionable age.
[2] Lone person of pensionable age.

Source: DoE *English House Condition Survey* 1991. HMSO 1993, p. 270, Table A11.24.

Table 7.2 Number of specialised dwellings completed for elderly people in 1981 and 1992 England

	Sheltered			Other			All			
	Priv	HAs	LAs	Priv	HAs	LAs	Priv	HAs	LAs	Total
1981	130	1,929	5,558	62	261	4,636	192	2,190	10,194	12,576
1992	1,339	1,442	751	404	564	94	1,743	2,006	85	4,594
1995	419	779	62	37	477	41	456	1,256	103	1,815

Priv – Private sector.
HAs – Housing associations.
LAs – Local authorities and new towns.

Source: CSO (1994) p. 111, Table 8.7; 1995 Provisional Housing Data Statistics (personal communication DoE 1996).

15 per cent in 1971, increased to 22 per cent in 1981 but has now dropped back again to 15 per cent (CSO 1995: 175). Specialised dwellings completed for elderly people in England show an overall drop between 1981 and 1995 from 12,576 to 1,815 as Table 7.2 indicates. Over the period completions by councils (LAs) have dramatically declined and those by HAs halved.

Tenure

For all households the major change has been the rise in owner-occupation and the decline of the private rented sector. Whereas 40 per cent of all households owned their own homes in 1961 that figure had risen to 67 per cent in 1994 (CSO 1983: 114, OPCS 1996: 229). A lower proportion of elderly than all households were owner-occupiers but more older households were outright owners and fewer had mortgages. Whereas 67 per cent of all households were owner-occupiers in 1994, 67 per cent of people aged 65–69, 63 per cent aged 70–79 and 56 per cent of the over-80s owned their own homes (Table 7.3). Figures from the *English House Condition Survey* in 1991 indicate that there was a higher level of satisfaction with owner-occupation than with other tenures (DoE 1993; 9) and the 1993–4 *Survey of English Housing* showed similar findings (Green and Hansbro 1995: 31). Older people also express greater satisfaction with their dwelling than other age groups (Hedges and Clemens 1994: 158) although this is often bound up with a number of other factors (Wilson *et al.* 1995).

Older people are not only less likely to own their own homes but are less likely to have considered buying. In 1993–4, 23 per cent of all tenants in England were expecting to buy their own or other accommodation whereas only 2 per cent of the over-65s were (Green and Hansbro 1995: 150).

New forms of owner-occupation have been developing whereby older people can buy part of their home and rent the rest. A study of some of these schemes (flexible tenure, shared ownership and leasehold) concluded that they were particularly valuable for a significant group of older people who were 'not rich, not poor' (Oldman 1990). They allowed older people to use their own resources supplemented by public subsidies for the rented part.

A higher proportion of people aged over 70 were local authority tenants than other age groups in the population as a whole in GB in 1994 (Table 7.3). In the council sector the poor and the disadvantaged are disproportionately represented and this includes older people (Page 1995: 11).

Although a great deal more is now known about the private rented sector as a result of the *Survey of English Housing* (Carey 1995) there is still very little research specifically on older people in this context. Carey's research showed that 'private renters are predominantly a

Table 7.3 Tenure by age of head of household – percentages 1994 – Great Britain

Age of head of household	Owner-occupied			Rented				
	owned outright		with mortgage	from local authority	from housing association	privately furnished	privately unfurnished	with job or business
Under 25	1	(25)	24	24	9	26	15	2
25–29	1	(56)	55	21	5	8	6	3
30–44	4	(69)	65	18	4	3	4	2
45–59	21	(77)	56	15	2	1	2	2
60–64	49	(76)	27	20	2	0	2	1
65–69	57	(67)	10	25	4	1	3	1
70–79	57	(63)	6	27	4	0	6	1
80 and over	54	(56)	2	27	7	1	8	0
All	25	(67)	42	20	4	3	4	1

Source: OPCS, General Household Survey 1994, HMSO 1996, p. 233, Table 11.9.

young, mobile population and are becoming more so' with the proportion of the under-30s increasing from 29 per cent in 1988 to 39 per cent in 1993 (Carey 1995: 28). At the same time the proportion of renters aged over 60 declined from 33 per cent to 21 per cent (Carey 1995: 101). In one of the few studies specifically about elderly private renters Smith (1986) found that many were living in very poor conditions but 81 per cent preferred to stay in their own homes and were reluctant to move from familiar surroundings.

A new feature has been the growth of housing association tenancies. Housing associations are non-profit-making organisations providing low cost housing for people in housing need. Some go back to the beginning of the twentieth century. Their expansion dates from 1964 when the Housing Corporation was set up to make loans to cost-rent and co-ownership housing associations. Under the Housing Act 1974 the Housing Corporation was given wider powers which included the supervision and registration of housing associations. Wilcox describes HAs as moving 'centre stage' since 1989 (Wilcox 1995: 45) and the White Paper, *Our Future Homes*, made this explicit when it was stated that they would have 'a continuing role as the main providers of social housing' (Secs of St. for Environment England and Wales 1995: 11). By mid-1995 HAs passed the million mark in the provision of homes in the UK (Wilcox 1995: 45); they have now become the main new providers of new homes and own almost one fifth of social housing in England (Secs of St. for Environment and Wales 1995a: 28). Local authorities often nominate the tenants in housing association schemes. In 1989/90 one third of all new lettings were to people aged 60 and over but in 1994/95 it was only one fifth (NFHA Statistics 1995). The shift has been towards homeless and/or unemployed households.

The overall picture for social housing (LA and HA) is of a decline in the numbers of homes: in 1981 there were 7 million social housing dwellings in the UK (6.9 million in GB), while in 1993 there were 5.8 million social housing dwellings in the UK (5.6 million in GB). This represented a percentage fall of 18.7 per cent for the UK (18.9 per cent for GB) (Wilcox 1995: 104). In 1981 HA dwellings represented 6 per cent of the stock of social housing but this had risen to 15 per cent in 1993 and it was here that there had been major growth compared with a dramatic drop in LA dwellings. In England in 1994 17 per cent of LAs stock was for older people (8 per cent sheltered and 9 per cent other) and 24 per cent of the stock of HAs (*Hansard*, Parliamentary Answer 29.1.1996, Column 571).

Types of accommodation

The majority of people (80 per cent of all households in 1994) in Great Britain live in houses and so do elderly people (OPCS 1996: 230, Table 11.4). In 1994 88 per cent of all households containing two adults, of whom one or both were aged 60 or above lived in houses, 10 per cent in a purpose-built flat or maisonette and 2 per cent in a converted flat, maisonette or rooms (OPCS 1996:230). Fewer single people of that age occupied houses (67 per cent) and more occupied purpose-built flats or maisonettes (29 per cent) or a converted flat, maisonette or rooms (4 per cent). Five per cent of elderly households lived in flats on the second floor or above and of those 60 per cent were without a lift (OPCS 1996: 156).

What many old people, but not all, seem to want, is somewhere small and easy to manage. In the DoE survey elderly people living in bungalows were more positive (72 per cent said that they were very satisfied) than those living in other types of housing, particularly flats and maisonettes (56 per cent) (McCafferty 1994). As has been seen, a higher proportion of new build is now smaller accommodation following a swing away from the building of three-bedroom houses that took place between the wars.

Non-specialist and specialist housing

Non-specialist (mainstream) housing

Research consistently shows that most older people want to remain in homes of their own and this 'ageing in place' as it is often called is an international issue (see, for example, Tinker 1994 and Heumann and Boldy 1993). In the large DoE survey of elderly people in mainstream housing, 69 per cent expressed a preference for their own home exactly as it was, 15 per cent required repairs and adaptations to be carried out, 8 per cent wanted a smaller property, 4 per cent wanted alternative accommodation of the same size, 2 per cent wanted somewhere larger and 1 per cent wanted to move in with relatives or friends (McCafferty 1994: 96).

Research for DoE and DHSS, *Staying at Home: Helping Elderly People*, was an evaluation of some innovations (now mainstream services) by housing and social service departments to enable elderly people to remain in their own homes (Tinker 1984). The national sample of 1,310 older people were found to be, on average, more dependent than elderly people in sheltered housing. Nearly all the elderly people wanted to stay in their own homes and the innovatory schemes were successfully providing help to enable them to do this. However, the schemes needed to be provided as part of a package of statutory and informal support. The findings of the research supported a growing body of other evidence that, for some frail elderly people who do not need full-time surveillance, these schemes were a successful option [see also Document 16].

Other research which also pointed to ways in which elderly people could remain at home were the Kent Community Care Scheme (see Chapter 8) and agency schemes for owner-occupiers (see pp. 133–4).

Also to be taken into account in policy development was research which raised question marks about sheltered housing. In the 1980s Butler and colleagues identified some of the reasons which include danger to health and psychological well-being because of relocation, creation of geriatric ghettos, cost, over-provision of support, schemes beginning to resemble the institutions they were intended to replace and independence undermined rather than fostered among tenants (Butler *et al.* 1983).

Specialist housing

Sheltered housing: Sheltered housing, in various forms (usually including a warden, communal facilities and an alarm system) accounts for just over three quarters of all specialised units of accommodation (McCafferty 1994: 36). In Great Britain in 1995 there were over half a million (512,007) sheltered housing units. They were provided as follows:

local authorities	293,888;
housing associations	172,097;
other public sector	1,867 (provisional);
private	44,115 (provisional)

(DoE Housing Investment Programme 1995 Returns, Personal communication DoE).

Five per cent of people aged 65 and over in private households lived in sheltered housing in 1994 but this figure rises to 10 per cent if those with a peripatetic (non-resident) warden are added (OPCS 1996: 157). People who live in sheltered housing have many advantages. They have their own flat (although not all – particularly in early schemes – are self-contained) or a bungalow with communal facilities and a warden on hand for emergencies. Levels of satisfaction are high and many enjoy living in groups with people of their own age, and this type of living arrangement. Table 7.4 shows that, compared with elderly people in mainstream housing, they are more likely to be older, female, not married and of a higher level of dependency. The tenants also appear to be more likely to be in receipt of some health and social services at all levels of dependency than elderly people in mainstream housing (McCafferty 1994: 117).

Most of the early literature concerned design features, but in the 1970s and early 1980s a more critical approach to other aspects became apparent and these issues are still topical in the 1990s, not just in the UK but also throughout the world (see Dooghe and Vanden Boer 1993 and Kaye and Monk 1991). Research in the 1970s and 1980s (Page and Muir 1971, Boldy *et al.* 1973, Griffin and Dean 1975, Attenburrow 1976, Bytheway and James 1978, Wirz 1982 and Butler *et al.* 1983) showed that sheltered housing, although ideal for some people and giving high levels of satisfaction, was not quite the

Table 7.4 Age, gender, marital status and dependency of elderly people in non-specialised and specialised housing England 1991–2

	Non specialised housing %	Specialised housing %
Age of respondents		
Up to 65	not interviewed	4
65–74	56	28
75–84	36	48
85+	8	20
Gender		
Male	40	23
Female	60	77
Marital status		
Married	44	16
Widowed	44	67
Divorced/separated	4	6
Single	7	9
Dependency profile (Clackmannan scale of dependency)		
A/B (none)	58	36
C	9	17
D	–	33
D/E	26	
E/F	–	1
F/G	8	–
G (high)	–	10
Number	8,901	3,569

Source: DoE Surveys
Non-specialised housing McCafferty (1994) p. 80 calculated from Table 4.1, p. 84
Table 4.8 and DoE (1995) Report No. 7 p. 2.
Specialised housing McCafferty (1994) p. 104, Table 5.1, p. 105 and DoE (1995)
Report No. 8 p. 30.

panacea that some had envisaged. In the late 1980s there was a national study of sheltered housing in Scotland (Clapham *et al.* 1988) and a study of Anchor housing association schemes in England (Fennell 1986) and in two housing associations in Scotland (Fennell 1987) where there were similar findings. A follow-up study of Anchor schemes in England found that there were still high levels of satisfaction but a higher proportion of tenants were older and frailer, they had higher expectations (such as for a separate bedroom) and there were features that could be improved including more involvement with tenants (Riseborough and Niner 1994).

Three crucial questions relate to the purpose of sheltered housing, the design and layout and the problem of frail tenants. It is clear from Circular 82/69 that sheltered housing was conceived as a form of accommodation where older people could maintain independent lives. The less active were supposed to form the main body of tenants although there was believed to be value in mixing ages and states of dependence. Sheltered housing has been seen as having a preventive role (tó prevent people going into Part III accommodation; [see Document 9]), a social role (primarily for those who are isolated and have no or few relatives) and a housing role in offering an attractive alternative to older people who were underoccupying or who needed to be rehoused for some other reason. In reality research has shown that clear criteria for selection do not appear to be applied. The national study by Butler *et al.* queried the lack of clarity about the purpose of sheltered housing and disproved some of the benefits claimed (e.g. that it increased longevity and broke down isolation) (Butler *et al.* 1983). The national study in Scotland suggested clear grounds for reviewing the concept of a balance of tenants and recommended allocation on grounds of need (Clapham and Munro 1990). The NFHA in their Policy Report *The Future of Sheltered Housing – Who Cares?* (Fletcher 1991) and their *Practice Guide* (Fletcher and Gillie 1991) advocate priority in tenant selection to more dependent people. They also recommended that, where appropriate, LA social services departments should play a role in assessment and that an appropriate care plan should be put in place before the tenancy is taken up. What is increasingly being questioned is the high proportion of new entrants who appear to have no mental or physical frailty (McCafferty 1994, Tinker *et al.* 1995).

A relatively new phenomenon is difficult-to-let sheltered housing. A national survey in 1994 in England and Wales found that 92 per cent of local authorities and 79 per cent of large housing associations had some difficult-to-let sheltered housing. In the main this was Category 2 (i.e. sheltered) but there was some very sheltered as well (Tinker *et al.* 1995). The problem was usually caused by a combination of factors which included bedsits rather than separate bedrooms, shared bathrooms, letting difficulties where schemes were located in 'problem' areas or where local shops or public transport were lacking. Overprovision and the growing number of ways in which older people can remain in their own homes were also reasons. Nearly all the housing organisations had attempted, with mixed success, to do something about the problem including refurbishment, marketing, lowering the age limit, providing a higher level of care and admitting another group such as younger old people discharged from long-stay hospitals (see also Roose 1994).

On design and layout, questions have been asked about the need for communal facilities and research indeed seems to indicate that their use depends to some extent on the warden. The Scottish study found underuse of communal facilities, especially the common room, and recommended using them as a local resource (Clapham *et al.* 1988). The study by Butler *et al.* (1983) concluded that while most tenants were satisfied with their housing, this satisfaction was generally linked to the wish for small, warm, easy-to-run accommodation rather than the provision of an alarm and warden.

In both the Anchor studies and the DoE one (McCafferty 1994) property-related reasons were given as a major reason for leaving their previous accommodation. There is more discussion now about the use of communal facilities by people outside the scheme. The study of very sheltered housing advocated caution (Tinker 1989b) but the NFHA recommended its use (Fletcher 1991) and a study for Anchor found that the experience had so far been largely positive (Riseborough 1995).

The question of what should happen to tenants as they become older and more frail is a difficult one. The Butler study showed that on average tenants were not more dependent than other old people in the community, but what seems to have happened since then is a greater polarisation with both a growing core of highly dependent tenants and an increasing proportion with no physical or mental dependency (McCafferty 1994: Table 7.5, 175). Those who are frail cannot be forced to move (because they are either tenants with rights or owners) even though they might need to be in residential care or hospital. The answer seems to be to provide extra care in the existing scheme (see next section) or to provide 'floating support' as HAs do for tenants as and when they need it (Morris 1995).

Private sheltered housing has developed rapidly during the last 10 years. Reasons for the growth include the growing number of older owner-occupiers who want to remain home owners in smaller homes, and the growing realisation among developers of the possible size of this new market (G. Williams 1990). The latter was fuelled by a number of reports which estimated a huge market (Baker and Parry 1983, 1984, 1986). Very few schemes have been built during the 1990s because of the collapse of the market.

Research reveals general satisfaction with schemes but, as with public sheltered housing, it was generally the wish for more suitable housing rather than the sheltered features which were important

Table 7.5 Dependency (Clackmannan scale[1]) profile of elderly people in different kinds of specialised housing[2] England 1991–2

Category of accommodation	Percentage				
	A/B	C	D	E/F	G
1/Other (specially designed with optional communal facilities)	48	16	25	1	8
1.5/2 (Sheltered)	37	17	32	1	10
2.5 (Very sheltered)	19	16	47	1	14

[1] The Clackmannan scale of dependency ranges from A independent to G very dependent.
[2] The % figures in Columns A/B to G do not add up to 100% because 3% of the elderly people had missing information.

Source: McCafferty, P. (1994), p. 108, Table 5.5.

(Fleiss 1985). There were problems, especially over management charges and the small size of units. A survey of residents in Guardian Housing schemes found high levels of satisfaction but 'consumers are increasingly aware of the costs of private sheltered housing, including the acquisition costs, service charges, and the costs associated with disposal' (Rolfe *et al.* 1995: 67). In Fleiss' study almost one fifth of owners said that they would consider moving again (10 per cent in the Guardian study), while one in six said that they would not have moved if they had known as much about their sheltered scheme as they did when interviewed (Fleiss 1985). The building industry has responded to criticism in a positive way and has drawn up a *Sheltered Housing Code of Practice* (National House Building Council 1990) which is complemented by a *Guidance Note on Management and Services* (House Builders Federation 1990). Guidance on the location and design of private sheltered housing has also been produced (House Builders Federation/National Housing and Town Planning Council 1988). The Association of Retirement Housing Managers (ARHM) has issued a *Code of Practice* with helpful annotations on the legal requirements, and this is statutorily approved by the Secretary of State (AHRM 1996). ACE, with the NHTPC, has published *A Buyer's Guide to Retirement Housing* (ACE and NHTPC 1995). ACE also set up an advisory service for residents in private sheltered housing schemes, formerly called the Sheltered Housing Advisory and Conciliation Service (SHACS) and now called AIMS (Advice Information and Mediation Service for Retirement Housing).

The role of the warden has been the subject of some research and comment. The original idea was that the warden would be a good neighbour and, despite evidence that some wardens perform more duties than others, the general conclusion in the 1980s was that the warden should be the enabler and should not perform duties, such as home nursing, that are the responsibility of others. However, the move to keep sheltered housing more for frail older people points to a greater involvement of wardens especially in liaising with other services. The NFHA go further than this and suggest that the role should 'encompass initial assessment, referral to statutory services for detailed assessment, key worker, monitoring, co-ordination of care delivery for individuals, acting as advocate, and providing emergency or defined short-term care for individuals' (Fletcher 1991: 28).

Very sheltered housing: Very sheltered housing is sheltered housing with extra facilities, usually extra communal rooms, some meals and 24-hour cover by staff. The DoE survey showed that although only 2 per cent of subsidised special accommodation was very sheltered it was the fastest growing form of provision and that there was a shortfall in provision (McCafferty 1994: 36, 180). Research, *An Evaluation of Very Sheltered Housing*, which included a national survey of LAs and HAs and interviews with 1,089 elderly people, showed that they were popular with management, older people and staff. Because of its expense (confirmed in the McCafferty study [Document 17]) it was considered that it should only be provided for people who both wanted and needed it (Tinker 1989b) [Document 16]. Such needs might be high dependency, strain on relatives or lack of ability to live in ordinary non-specialised accommodation. Bringing extra care to existing sheltered housing was one way of making provision. There were a number of problems which needed to be taken into account and these included dissatisfaction of some staff with pay and conditions of work and unrealistic expectations by some elderly tenants, relatives and other professionals.

Granny annexes: Another form of special housing is granny annexes. These are self-contained homes next to a family home. The idea is that the older person will be able to live independently yet be able to give and to receive help from their family next door. In an evaluation of local authority schemes some problems of flexibility were found when either the family had to move or the grandparent died (Tinker 1976). Private schemes seem to be becoming increasingly popular as families see the advantages of having a grandparent next door. Some owner occupiers use the granny flat for a nanny, au pair or teenager when they do not need it for a grandparent, or else they just let it. There is a good deal of international interest in granny annexes (Lazarowich 1991) but there are problems over the design of the property, the need to get planning permission, legal issues of ownership and insurance.

Hostels and group living: In hostels, shared rather than self-contained accommodation is provided. One variety is that run by Abbeyfield societies where 8–10 older people live in bedsitters in one house. A housekeeper provides the main meals and some of these schemes now provide extra care facilities.

Comparisons between different types of accommodation

Comparisons between different kinds of housing for older people are in their infancy. Pioneering work was done by Wager (1972) and Plank (1977). The DoE study (McCafferty 1994) showed that staying at home options were cheaper than specialised housing at all levels of dependency. The average gross costs (including housing, care and state benefits) per person per year are shown in Table 7.6. However, if help from relatives and friends (informal care) was costed and added then staying at home options became more expensive than sheltered housing but cheaper than very sheltered [Document 17]. Costings were also produced by the Audit Commission which showed that staying at home options were cheaper than alternatives

Table 7.6 *Average gross costs per person per year for different types of housing*

	Average for all levels of dependency £	The most dependent £
Staying at home	7,353	7,890
Living in Category 1 housing	8,436	9,537
Living in Category 2 housing	9,618	11,034
Living in Category 2.5 housing	14,825	16,378

Source: McCafferty (1994) calculated from p. 197, Table 3.14.

(Audit Commission 1986). Caution is, however, needed in any costings exercise because if the salaries of the mainly low paid women working in various housing and care situations was increased, the position would change dramatically. It is also possible that the cost of providing 24-hour surveillance and services for people in their own home could exceed that of alternatives.

Some costings have included residential and hospital care (Tinker 1984, updated in 1989b). These showed that staying at home with a package of innovatory and other statutory services was cheaper on average than sheltered and very sheltered housing or residential care and hospitals [Document 16].

Some issues

Assessing and meeting needs

One dilemma facing central government when allocating public money is how to assess what sort of housing is needed and by whom, and then how these needs may be met. It is also an issue faced at a local level by local authorities and housing associations and a problem which private developers are increasingly facing. For the public sector it is the extent of subsidised (social) housing that is the issue.

The National Housing Forum, in *Housing Needs in the 1990s*, discussed the complex matters that have to be taken into account when assessing needs (Niner 1989). These include the number of existing, potential and concealed (e.g. couples and lone parent families living as part of someone else's household) households, the condition and suitability of the housing and homelessness. This work has been taken further by Alan Holmans in *Housing Demand and Need in England 1991–2011* (Holmans 1995a, see also Holmans 1995b). He demonstrated the effects of population change, including the effects of an ageing population, mortality and migration, and other factors. He predicted a slower rate of growth of owner occupation because of uncertain incomes, more mortgage defaults and fewer LA and HA tenants being able to afford to buy even under right to buy terms. He estimated an overall need in England of a little under a quarter of a million additional new homes a year between 1991–2011 and argued that the need for additional social housing will average 90,000 homes a year in 1991–2001 and 100,000 a year in 2001–11. This is higher than DoE estimates.

At local authority level the Cullingworth Committee in 1969 put forward certain criteria to be used as a basis for assessing housing need (MHLG 1969). This included some of the ideas now used by social services departments, such as looking at the needs of the whole community and not just those with whom they were in contact (i.e the housing waiting list) and regardless of whether the solution to any problems lay in their own hands or elsewhere. As early as 1978 the DoE, in *Organising a Comprehensive Housing Service*, pointed out that needs are not necessarily best met by the local authority itself (DoE 1978).

Local authorities use a number of different methods for allocating accommodation. Some work on a points basis, some work strictly on a date order of first come first served, while others have separate categories for different people and different kinds of accommodation. Two studies of waiting lists for LA accommodation have shown that they are poor indicators of need with only four in ten applicants still living at the registered address and wanting housing when records were checked (Prescott-Clarke *et al*. 1988, 1994). In 1978 the DoE Housing Services Advisory Group in *Allocation of Council Housing* suggested various criteria such as the need to treat all applicants equitably and for the rules to be easily understood by both applicants and staff (DoE Housing Services Advisory Group 1978). Under the Housing Act 1985 councils must publish a summary of their rules relating to allocations, transfers and exchanges. The Housing White Paper *Our Future Homes* in 1995 stated that: 'Each authority will also be required to operate an allocations scheme, to ensure that these long term tenancies go to the households on the register with the best claim to them' (Secs of St. Environment and Wales 1995a: 36).

It may be necessary to treat particular groups in a special way for housing, but that does not necessarily mean that they will need special types of housing. Some may need a special design, or special location, or to be grouped in some way, but not all. A study of underoccupation concluded that special accommodation for elderly people was 'likely to attract only a very small minority' (Barelli 1992: 73). Nor should the assumption be made that those who are already housed are necessarily in the most appropriate form of accommodation. Most surveys of elderly people in whatever situation find a proportion who appear to be in the wrong place. For example, both the Butler *et al*. (1983) sheltered housing research and the very sheltered housing research (Tinker 1989b) showed that one quarter would have preferred to have stayed where they were. Studies of residential care invariably show a proportion of people who do not need to be there (see Chapter 8). In addition, research on people who shared accommodation showed that a majority of the over-60s, in common with other age groups, would have preferred separate accommodation (Rauta 1986).

For elderly and disabled people there is now guidance from the DoE based on the study both of provision and of levels of dependency and views of these groups. This concluded that:

• two out of three elderly households have no assessed need for any form of subsidised specialised housing, or other housing with care support;
• of those households that do have a need for provision, seven out of ten wish to remain at home and can be enabled to do so with repairs and adaptations to their homes and/or domiciliary support;
• there is evidence of overprovision of traditional or ordinary sheltered housing and an underprovision of very sheltered housing (McCafferty 1994).

While criteria for various forms of provision were suggested no numbers (e.g. so many units per thousand elderly people) were suggested. In Scotland the Scottish Development Department undertook a piece of research based on interviews with 1,750 people over the age of 65 to estimate their requirements for housing and support (Hart and Chalmers 1990). There was a high degree of satisfaction with existing housing and only one quarter of the sample expressed a wish to move. As a result of the research the Department issued guidelines (which had not been updated by 1996) of:

• sheltered housing – 46 dwellings per 1,000 aged 65 and over population;
• other medium dependency housing – 80 dwellings per 1,000 aged 65 and over population;
• very sheltered housing – 20 dwellings per 1,000 aged 65 and over population.

It may be possible to solve some housing problems simply through a more flexible and sensitive use of existing stock. Even a small amount of building of one- and two-bedroom homes may lead to a general shifting round of people to a more appropriate size of accommodation. But this raises the question of underoccupation, where accommodation is located and whether older people should be encouraged to move.

Underoccupation

Many older people occupy only a part of their home after their family move away or a spouse dies. This can be a problem when it comes to repairing, decorating, cleaning and heating the home. 'Under-occupation', although it has no statutory meaning, is usually defined as having two or more bedrooms above the bedroom standard and half a million LA and HA tenants were in that situation in 1995 (Secs of St. Envir. and Wales 1995a: 42). 'The household type that is *most* likely to be underoccupying contains two adults rather than one and is not necessarily elderly – households in which at least one person is still below retirement age are more likely to have "spare" rooms than other households' (Barelli 1992: 7). In 1994–5 half of two-person households where one or both were aged 60 or over underoccupied as did one in three single adults of that age (CSO 1996: 180). Elderly couples from all tenures are particularly likely to underoccupy (McCafferty 1994: 90–3).

There may be a shortage of accommodation for families in those same areas where older people are underoccupying. Yet many local authorities may do nothing to encourage older people to move. The reasons are not hard to find. There is a general reluctance to persuade people to move from a home in which they have lived for many years and, as a study of underoccupation has concluded, it would be 'very hard to devise a policy (e.g. in respect of rents or benefits) that did not result in considerable hardship and injustice' (Barelli 1992: *vii*). Various strategies that could be adopted, including incentive schemes to provide grants to tenants who move and setting differential rents, are recommended by DoE (Secs of St. for Envir. and Wales 1995a: 42–3).

Moving

General: The 1991 Census showed that about 3 per cent of people aged 70–74 moved during the previous year but that this rose to 8 per cent among the over-85s (Warnes and Ford 1995). Most moves are of short distances. Recent research indicates that those who move at or around the age of retirement tend to do so for housing reasons whereas those who move at older ages do so with care and surveillance in mind (Warnes and Ford 1995).

In 1993/94 in England 10 per cent of council and housing association tenants (9 per cent of HA and 11 per cent of LA tenants aged 65 or over) intended to move, compared with 80 per cent of those aged 16–29, 62 per cent of those aged 30–44 and 32 per cent of those aged 45–64 (Green and Hansbro 1995: 157). The DoE research showed that 8 per cent of elderly people living in mainstream housing said that they were very or fairly likely to move in the next year as did 7 per cent of those in sheltered housing (McCafferty 1994: 101, 115).

While many older people move willingly, this is not always the case, as has been seen in the previous section.

To another tenure: There are several reasons why people may wish to switch tenure as they become older. They may, for example, have to give up tied accommodation when their employment ends. They may be worried about the upkeep of their home and garden and willingly accept a council or housing association tenancy. They may need some special form of accommodation only provided in the public sector. However, most changes in tenure are associated with changes in domestic circumstances, such as moving to live with relatives. Some of the new forms of tenure such as equity share and housing co-operatives may prove attractive to older people.

To a retirement area: While the majority of older people remain in the same neighbourhood area, others may choose to move to the seaside, country or other retirement area. Recent years have seen a clear dispersal of the most favoured destinations for retirement-age migrants. East and West Sussex and Dorset have declined in their relative popularity as Norfolk and Cornwall have climbed. During the 1980s, Lincolnshire, Powys in central Wales and North Yorkshire emerged as attracting high rates of people of retirement age.

Retirement migration may have some effect on the recipient area and therefore on older people who move there. Karn found that while the majority of her sample were happy in their new environment, and would have made the same decision again, there were problems for health and social services (Karn 1977). Karn (1977) and Law and Warnes (1982) in their retirement studies have established that elderly migrants were less likely to have younger relatives to help them. These older movers were predominantly owner-occupiers, childless or had few children, and they had retired at or before pensionable age. Other research indicates that institutionalisation rates were slightly above average in 1981 in counties with large proportions of retirement migrants and high rates were found in areas with high densities of elderly people (Harrop and Grundy 1991).

Very little is known about retirement migration to other countries. If the existing rights of free movement for workers and their families in EC countries extends to retired people, more older people may want to settle abroad.

Retirement communities are beginning to be developed by the private sectors. In the United States, and to a lesser extent in Australia and Germany, retirement communities have developed with a number of different kinds of accommodation and care on one site. The idea is that people do not have to move from the site. There has been little evaluation of such schemes.

To be near relatives: One of the groups identified by the Cullingworth Committee as wanting to move was elderly people wishing to join their relatives (MHLG 1969). In most cases this was to enable them to give mutual support. Research on migration, particularly on very old people, shows that a major concern is to be near relatives.

In research on every housing authority in England and Wales and a number of housing associations, *Housing the Elderly near Relatives*, it was found that although many elderly people already lived near their families, there was a demand from those who did not to move closer (Tinker 1980b). Two groups who faced particular problems over moving were owner-occupiers who wanted to move into council accommodation in their own area and people from any tenure who wanted to rent in another local authority area. A number of schemes sponsored by central government exist to help local authority and housing association tenants move, and wishing to receive support from, or give support to, relatives is one criterion.

Some problems of particular groups

Six groups who may be particularly vulnerable in the housing market are those who are disabled, those from black and ethnic minorities, owner-occupiers, private renters, homeless people and tenants in tied accommodation. The first two groups are discussed in Chapter 9 and private renters on pp. 118–20 and the other groups here.

Owner-occupiers: Older owner-occupiers may face particular problems. Among problems identified as early as 1969 by the Cullingworth Committee were physical inability to cope with maintenance, cleaning, stairs or garden; too large accommodation; financial problems of upkeep; the need to move to a more convenient area; inability to cope with improvements (MHLG 1969). Many of the studies of sheltered housing give these problems as reasons for moving. Some specific problems faced by this group, in addition to those mentioned above, are lack of knowledge about the grant system, lack of money, difficulty in finding builders to carry out the work and dislike of the upheaval of having workmen in the house. Help may be needed to improve, repair and adapt the home. In addition to the main housing renovation grants, other grants including minor works assistance (of which 88 per cent were estimated to go to people over the age of 60 in 1994 – *Hansard*, 12.2.1996 column 399) to help older people remain in their own homes or move in with relatives have become available from local authorities. Most are discretionary. The total number of renovation grants to private owners in England and Wales rose from 9,139 in 1990 to 105,710 in 1994 (Wilcox 1995: 47, 110). Legislation going through Parliament in 1996 make Disabled Facilities Grants the only ones which will be mandatory.

A great many schemes have been developed to help with the problems of owner-occupiers in the last 10 years. The biggest development has been in the setting up of home improvement agencies, usually called agency services. These provide advice and practical assistance to householders seeking to repair and maintain the fabric of their homes. Their help is usually technical and financial and can include assistance with raising money (through grants, loans, etc.) for the work, help with choice, organisation and supervision of builders and checking the work has been satisfactorily completed.

Agency services can be provided by local authorities, housing associations, voluntary bodies and the private sector. Thomas (1981) pointed to the role of local authority schemes and the first scheme provided in the voluntary sector was in Wales (Morton 1982). This was quickly followed by others. Some of the first schemes provided by Anchor Housing Trust were evaluated by Wheeler in her study *Don't Move: We've Got You Covered* (Wheeler 1985). Her research stressed the poor housing conditions of applicants to the schemes, but they were not, on the whole, unaware of or satisfied with this. Most had low incomes and were unable to pay for repairs. The research confirmed the value of these schemes and recommended that more should be provided. In 1986 the DOE announced a £6 million initiative with the government offering half the costs of setting up around 50 new services. More help was given subsequently. A large number of publicly funded agency services were monitored and further expansion was encouraged (Leather and Mackintosh 1990). Subsequent evaluation showed that they provided a responsive and valuable service (Mackintosh and Leather 1993, Mackintosh *et al*. 1993, Fielder *et al*. 1994). Long-term funding through local authorities was agreed in 1990 and Care and Repair Ltd were given a national co-ordinating role. In 1992 elderly and disabled people had access to home improvement agencies in one in three local authorities in England (McCafferty 1994: 23). The development of handyperson schemes have also been useful (Appleton 1996).

Another helpful development has been the development of schemes allowing older people to use the equity in their homes (Leather and Wheeler 1988). The plight of low income home-owners has become known as 'house rich, income poor'. Of course older home-owners can realise their equity by selling and trading down to a cheaper home but, if they want to stay where they are, some form of re-mortgage is now possible. Home equity release schemes, often called 'reverse mortgages' in the USA, allow some or all of the value of the home to be realised to generate a lump sum or regular income, at the same time enabling owners to stay in their own homes (Hinton 1995). The most widely available type available involves an insurance company providing a mortgage loan on part of the value of an older owner's home. The loan is used to purchase an annuity, part of which goes to paying off the loan interest, the remainder providing the older owner (annuitant) with an income for life. Research has shown that these schemes had on the whole successfully provided an additional source of income for older owners (Fleiss 1985). Subsequent research looked at home income, maturity loans and home reversion schemes (Leather and Wheeler 1988). The conclusion of a subsequent study found that equity withdrawn was minimal and that schemes were inflexible

(Mullings and Hamnett 1992). However, a study in 1995 found that home income schemes had the potential to enhance the incomes and lifestyles of older people (Davey 1995). ACE produces an annually updated guide on the schemes available and they stress the need to take professional advice.

Homeless older people: Surprise is often expressed that some older people are homeless. But in one of the most detailed studies carried out in the 1960s, older people figured prominently (National Assistance Board 1966). The survey for the NAB, *Homeless Single Persons*, found that of those sleeping rough (nearly 1,000) 18 per cent of the men were aged 60 and over. Research has continued to highlight the problems of older people who are homeless. *Single and Homeless* found that 8 per cent of the sample were over retirement age (Drake *et al.* 1981). In a survey of rehoused hostel residents, *A Home of their Own*, 39 per cent of the sample were 60 or over (Duncan *et al.* 1983). Although there are a few homeless applicants for housing who are older (2 per cent of applicants in a 1992–4 study, O'Callaghan *et al.* 1996) what is of concern is the number of those who do not apply, especially those who sleep rough. There are now a number of pieces of research specifically on older homeless people, which show the very poor physical and mental health of this group (Crane 1990, Crane 1993, Kelling 1991).

Under the Housing (Homeless Persons) Act 1977, later consolidated in the Housing Act 1985, with minor amendments in the Housing and Planning Act 1986, local authorities in Great Britain were given a statutory duty to secure accommodation for applicants who are homeless and who are in priority need. In 1994 in GB 5 per cent of homeless households who were found accommodation by local authorities were in the category of vulnerable because of old age (CSO 1996: 186). In research on policies and practices of local authorities variations were found in the age at which older applicants were accepted as being in priority need (Evans and Duncan 1988). For the majority this was retirement age but some used 60 for both men and women. The Audit Commission pointed to the need for more affordable permanent housing, a lack of co-ordination between agencies and the need for changes in practice (Audit Commission 1989). The government's *Review of the Homelessness Legislation* (DOE 1989) led to a revised *Code of Guidance* which has been assessed as, on the whole, achieving better practice (Niner *et al.* 1996) but legislation going through Parliament in 1996 would mean that LAs no longer had a duty to secure permanent accommodation for priority need homeless people.

Tenants in tied accommodation: Those who live in accommodation provided by their employers generally lose their right to their home when they stop working. Their employer may try to find them alternative accommodation, but will need their home for the next employee.

Some older people will have managed to save for a retirement home, but others will have to apply to a local authority or housing association for a tenancy. In GB in 1994 1 per cent of the population (such as farm workers, clergy and the police) lived in tied accommodation compared with 5 per cent in 1971 (OPCS 1996: 229).

Affordability

Affordability of rents is important to older people because about one third of those aged 65 and over rent accommodation. The Housing Act 1988 and the Local Government and Housing Act 1989 have resulted in higher rents in both the public and private rented sectors. There is now a convergence between the costs of renting and buying. The progressive withdrawal of housing subsidy has caused a substantial rise in LA and HA rents. Despite this only 3 per cent of retired LA and HA tenants were in arrears with their rent in 1993/4 in England compared with 17 per cent of all tenants (Green and Hansbro 1995: 169). Since 1988 housing benefit has been available to people with less than £16,000 capital. Housing Benefit is intended to help people on low incomes to pay their rent and 71 per cent of LA and HA retired tenants received this in 1993/4 (Green and Hansbro 1995: 163). While most attention tends to be focused on rich and poor older people, the housing options for those on middle incomes should not be forgotten and is examined in *Not Rich Not Poor* (Bull and Poole 1989).

Paying for Britain's Housing, a nationwide survey of 100,000 households in 1988, concluded that savings of elderly LA and HA tenants were very small (Maclennan *et al.* 1990). They point to the devastating correlation of old age, social rental status, low incomes and negligible assets – assets that are barely enough, they say, to cover the cost of a pauper's funeral. A study of housing association older tenants expressed concern about their levels of resources in relation to the affordability of their housing (Marsh and Riseborough 1995).

The need for advice

For many of the issues just discussed, such as whether to move or not and how to get repairs done, advice is important. It is important to ensure that staff in housing departments, housing advice centres and housing associations, as well as those in health and social services authorities, are fully briefed on the needs of older people and the means available to help them. Publications such as ACE's *Housing Options for Older People* fulfil an important role in giving informa-tion to old people (Bookbinder 1991).

Links with other services

To offer choice and to avoid duplication and omissions, housing and social service departments and health authorities need to collaborate to plan whatever services are appropriate for their areas. The recognition that housing is 'the foundation of community care' (to quote from the title of a book – NFHA/MIND 1989) has been slow in coming. The Griffiths report (see Chapter 8) played down the role of housing. However, in the NHS and Community Care Act 1990 there is a requirement for local authorities to consult every housing authority and 'such voluntary housing agencies and other bodies as appear to the local authority to provide housing and community care plans'. A joint DoE/DoH circular (DoE 10/92 and DoH LAC (92) 12), *Housing and Community Care*, in 1992, stated clearly: 'The Government wants housing authorities to play a full part, working together with social services departments and health authorities so that each can effectively discharge their responsibilities' (para 1). A 'seamless service' must be the aim (para 19). Some of the points in this circular were elaborated in a subsequent draft circular *Joint Guidance: Community Care, Housing and Homelessness*.

In the overall planning of particular forms of housing, and especially over the criteria for acceptance to sheltered housing and Part III accommodation, co-operation is essential. Staff in each agency must be clear about this policy. Problems over co-ordination are not unique to the UK. A study of housing policies for frail elderly people in the 26 OECD countries found a lack of co-ordination between agencies concerned with housing, health and social services at both national and local levels (Tinker 1994).

Research on the relationship between housing and social services points to an improving situation but some problems still exist, including housing managers feeling that they are left to pick up the pieces from social services, hostilities at the level of front line staff and question marks over the role of support staff in housing where it was thought that the costs might not be recovered from rents under housing benefit regulations (Clapham and Franklin 1995). Although there are some encouraging signs of co-operation (e.g. the Housing Corporation's Strategy) there is still a long way to go (Arblaster *et al.* 1996) with health and social services. It is to the latter that the next chapter turns.

CHAPTER 8

Personal and other social services

The development of local social services

In comparison with services concerned with income maintenance, health and housing, local authority personal social services are of more recent origin. Much of the provision before 1946 was by voluntary bodies. One of the first post-war acts to give local authorities powers to intervene in this field was the National Health Service Act 1946 which, amongst other things, allowed local authorities to employ home helps [Document 18]. It also gave very general powers for the care and aftercare of persons suffering from illness and preventive measures relating to health. So services such as chiropody and laundry became possible.

Under the National Assistance Act 1948 local authorities were enabled to make arrangements for 'promoting the welfare' of people who were deaf, dumb, blind or substantially handicapped [Document 19]. The provision of workshops, hostels and recreational facilities were specifically mentioned. Older people who came into any of these categories benefited from this legislation. Power was also given to local authorities to make contributions to the funds of voluntary bodies providing meals or recreation for old people [Document 19].

Under the 1948 Act a duty was laid on local authorities to make accommodation available for all persons who by reason of age, infirmity (amended to 'illness, disability' in the NHS and Community Care Act 1990, para 2), or any other circumstances are in need of care and attention not otherwise available to them [Document 20]. Because residential accommodation is provided under Part III of this Act it is often just referred to as Part III. Before this date some local authorities had been providing residential care on an experimental basis, but they now inherited large workhouses from public assistance committees. Local authorities were also given power to arrange residential care in homes run by voluntary bodies.

Under the National Assistance Act 1948 (Amendment) Act 1962 local authorities were themselves enabled to provide meals and recreation for old people in their homes or elsewhere, as well as day centres, clubs and recreational workshops. They might, however, continue to employ voluntary bodies as agents, if they so wished.

It has been noted (Chapter 4) that the development of local services was seen as being complementary to the hospital service. In

1962 local authorities were asked by the Ministry of Health to draw up plans for local health and welfare services for the next 10 years. The advice given (in Circular 2/62, *Development of Local Authority Health and Welfare Services*) was that:

Services for the elderly should be designed to help them to remain in their own homes as long as possible. For this purpose adequate supporting services must be available, including home nurses, domestic help, chiropody and temporary residential care. These supporting services will also often be needed for those who live in special housing where there is a resident warden. Residential homes are required for those who, for some reason, short of a need for hospital care, cannot manage on their own, even in special housing with a resident warden.

Specific standards were not laid down.

The general power for local authorities to provide welfare services for elderly people was not given until the Health Services and Public Health Act 1968 [Document 21] which came into force in 1971. They include powers to provide home helps, visiting, social work and warden services, arrangements to inform elderly people about services and to carry out adaptations. Local authorities may use voluntary bodies (widened in 1990 to include private organisations) as agents and may make charges. Another section of the 1968 Act which came into effect in 1971 made mandatory the provision of domestic help on an adequate scale. Power was also given to provide laundry services.

There was concern about the lack of a co-ordinated approach to families because of the different responsibilities of departments involved – welfare for elderly and mentally disordered people, children's for children and health for home helps and other domiciliary provision. This was one of the reasons for the appointment of a committee in 1965: 'to review the organisation and responsibilities of the local authority personal social services in England and Wales, and to consider what changes are desirable to secure an effective family service'. Its report, *Local Authority and Allied Personal Social Services* (the Seebohm Report) was published in 1968 (Home Office *et al.* 1968). Its main recommendation concerning administration was the establishment of a single social services department in each authority. This took place in 1971 following the Local Authority Social Services Act 1970.

The overall philosophy of the Report was that the new departments should be less concerned simply to meet individual needs in crises and more concerned about ensuring a co-ordinated and comprehensive approach to people's problems [Document 22], detecting need and encouraging people to seek help. In this way they would be better able to attract and use scarce resources and to plan systematically to best advantage for the future (Home Office *et al.* 1968). The need to support families caring for old people was also a consideration [Document 22].

Following the Act the main services for elderly people for which social services departments became responsible were: provision of domestic help, residential accommodation, general welfare, meals and recreation, registration of old people's homes and social work support. Another change which came about as a result of the Seebohm Report was an increase in the number of generic social workers instead of specialists (see section on social work support).

Developments since 1972 have included further attempts at long-term planning. In 1972 (Circular 35/72) ten-year plans were requested by the DHSS for health and social care but in 1977, three-year plans were introduced. Financial constraints have subsequently made planning more difficult.

In Chapter 4 the reasons for the development of community care policies were given. There were several subsequent initiatives by the DHSS to promote these policies. These included legislation in 1974 imposing a duty on health and local authorities to co-operate in planning services (joint planning), the introduction of joint finance in 1976 to enable NHS funds to be used on collaborative projects with local authorities, and the introduction of financial arrangements in 1983 to enable the transfer of funds from the NHS to local authorities to pay for services for people moving from hospitals to the community. These and other measures were discussed in Chapter 6.

The 1980s brought a number of very influential reports which, together with a new thrust to government policies, brought about legislation to change the role and funding of local social services departments. A report of the House of Commons Social Services Committee, chaired by Renee Short MP, *Community Care*, presented a critical picture of services for people, many of whom were elderly, mentally ill or mentally handicapped (House of Commons Social Services Committee 1985). The Committee argued wholeheartedly for community care policies but were concerned at the lack of local services. It expressed particular worries about people discharged from institutions and quoted one of their witnesses who said: 'patients should not be removed until the alternative facilities actually exist in the community. It seems to me it is like asking a passenger to jump off an elderly ship into the stormy sea with the assurance that the lifeboat will be along in a few months time' (House of Commons Social Services Committee 1985: *lviii*). It maintained that no-one should be discharged without an individual care plan. It also concluded that some people would need institutional care.

The Audit Commission's *Making a Reality of Community Care* was highly critical of community care in practice (Audit Commission 1986). Its grounds for concern were the slow progress that had been made and the uneven response of authorities, despite some very encouraging local schemes. Pointing to some fundamental underlying problems [Document 23] the Commission suggested a number of courses of action. At the core of its recommendations was the principle that the 'perverse incentives' (there being DHSS funding for care in residential and nursing homes, but no similar level of funding for people in their own homes) must be removed. Drawing on this study the National Audit Office (NAO) examined progress in implementing community care policies, including that of shifting support from long-term hospital care to community-based care (NAO 1987). It found that there had been a shift from long-stay provision and an increase in community facilities but it was less clear whether this had gone far enough, particularly with regard to the unknown numbers of people in the community who formerly would have been admitted to long-term care.

The Secretary of State for Social Services then asked Sir Roy Griffiths to: 'review the way in which public funds are used to support community care policy and to advise me on the options for action that would improve the use of these funds as a contribution to more effective community care' (Griffiths 1988: *iii*). Building on both the Short and Audit Commission reports the conclusion of Griffiths was that 'community care is a poor relation; everybody's distant relative but nobody's baby' (Griffiths 1988: *iv*). The key-stones of his proposals were:

- the appointment of a minister responsible for community care;
- a clear framework for co-ordination between health and social services with ring-fencing of funds for community care and the transfer of any necessary resources between central and local government;
- local social services departments to be in the lead over planning and providing community care (but funding dependent on satisfactory plans);
- local social services departments should be responsible for ensuring that 'packages' (the combination of support and services) of care are devised for individuals and, where appropriate, a care manager assigned; they should also be responsible for assessing the need for moves to residential care where public funding may be required.

Other proposals included one for public housing authorities to be responsible only for 'bricks and mortar' and not for care through wardens or other means.

After some delay the White Paper, *Caring for People*, subtitled 'community care in the next decade and beyond', was published at the end of 1989 (Secs of St. for Health *et al.* 1989b). This report acknowledged that progress in community care had been: 'slower and less even than the Government would like, and the arrangements for public funding have contained a built-in bias toward residential and nursing home care, rather than services for people at home' (Secs of St. for Health *et al.* 1989b: 4). The major objectives of policy were affirmed as enabling people: 'to live as normal a life as possible in their own homes or in a homely environment in the local community; provide the right amount of care and support to help people achieve maximum possible independence and, by acquiring or reacquiring basic living skills, help them to achieve their full potential; give people a greater individual say in how they live their lives and the services they need to help them to do so' (Secs of St. for Health *et al*. 1989b: 4). The key objectives of the proposals were:

• to promote the development of domiciliary, day and respite services to enable people to live in their own homes wherever feasible and sensible;

• to ensure that service providers make practical support for carers a high priority;

• to make proper assessment of need and good case management the cornerstone of high quality care;

• to promote the development of a flourishing independent sector alongside good quality public services;

• to clarify the responsibilities of agencies and to make it easier to hold them to account for their performance;

• to secure better value for taxpayers' money by introducing a new funding structure for social care.

(Secs of St. for Health *et al*. 1989b: 5)

Reference was made to housing in the White Paper which went beyond the 'bricks and mortar' approach of Griffiths, but it was not clear what action was to be taken.

The key proposals were made law in the National Health Service and Community Care Act 1990. It was subsequently decided that the provisions in the Act would be introduced in three phases and they were fully implemented from April 1993. The main changes were that local authorities:

• must produce and publish community care plans (but must consult health and housing authorities, the independent sector and care service users and their carers);

• must make the maximum use of care providers in the independent sector (see DoH/SSI 1993c);

• are responsible for assessing needs (in collaboration with users, carers and medical, nursing and other caring agencies);

• must design packages of care in the most cost-effective way;

• are responsible for checking the standards of all residential care homes;

• must develop social care services for people who are seriously mentally ill (local authorities were given a specific grant to do this).

Implicit in the new system was the expectation that not all services would be provided by the local authority (the mixed economy of welfare) and that there would be a separation of responsibility for commissioning and providing services (the purchaser–provider split). Services that are commissioned are usually either by an individual or spot contract where a service is provided for a specified time at an agreed price, or a block contract where the purchaser buys access to a service or facility for a specified price. In addition a grant was given which was called the special transitional grant (STG). This was mainly made up of funds transferred from social security which would previously have gone to individuals going into independent residential or nursing homes. Of this grant 85 per cent had to be spent in the independent sector. A new funding structure was introduced for residential and nursing homes (see p. 156–8).

Policy guidance was issued by the DoH, *Community Care in the Next Decade and Beyond: Policy Guidance* (DoH 1990a) and much more detailed guidance in a series of implementation documents.

What has been remarkable since the Act has been the outpouring of advice from the DoH. Some of this has been in the form of letters and circulars; the most influential of which were probably the two joint NHS Management Executive and Social Services Inspectorate (SSI) (Foster/Laming) ones. The first in March 1992 (EL (92) 13 and CI (92) 10) gave detailed key tasks for 1992/3 and the second, in September 1992, updated the first and gave further advice (EL (92) 65 and CI (92) 30). (These can both be found in McCreadie 1994.) In addition the SSI, sometimes in conjunction with the NHS Executive, have produced advice in the form of reports or research from inspectors and research by people outside the DoH. The early advice was in advance of the implementation of the Act but subsequently the focus has been on progress and developments. The series in 1993 was entitled *Monitoring and Development*, and that in 1994 *Implementing Caring for People*. The reports from 1993 onwards were based on inspections. Also of interest are the Annual Reports of the Chief Inspector of the Social Services Inspectorate. Their titles give the flavour of their concerns. The first was *Concern for Quality*, the second *Raising the Standard*, the third *Putting People First*, the fourth *Partners in Caring* and the fifth *Progress Through Change* (DoH/SSI, Chief Inspector's reports 1992, 1993, 1994, 1995, 1996). Although there is increasing attention paid to older people in these reports, issues of child care dominate. The House of Commons Health Committee in their report *Community Care: The Way Forward* recommended 'a more explicit recognition of the centre's role' and 'clear guidance from the centre' (House of Commons Health Committee 1993a: *xlviii*).

The findings of the DoH reports on the success of community care are brought together with those of others later in this chapter under the heading 'Some issues'.

Domiciliary and home support services

General

The need: Surveys consistently show the inability of a minority of elderly people to perform domestic and self-care tasks (Table 8.1).

The purpose of domiciliary services, now sometimes referred to as 'home support services', is to provide personal and practical help to people in their own homes. Townsend and Wedderburn commented: 'The domiciliary services therefore perform two main positive functions. They furnish expert professional help which the family cannot supply, and they furnish unskilled or semi-skilled help for persons who do not have families and whose families living in the household or nearby are not always able or available to help' (Townsend and Wedderburn 1965: 135). This role of providing services for older people who have no relatives and of supplementing what the family does comes out in many studies.

No norms are laid down by the Department of Health for these services but they suggested in 1977 that the need for meals, home helps and chiropody services would be greater than previously envisaged because of the difficulties in increasing the supply of residential care (DHSS 1977). The SSI have, however, produced a framework for developing standards for home support services so as to provide quality services (DoH/SSI 1993d). The values, beliefs, attributes (i.e. reliable, flexible, affordable, sufficient and co-ordinated) and principles (such as user control) that underpin a quality service were spelt out. (See also Chapter 9 on elderly people

Table 8.1 Percentage of elderly people unable to manage on their own: locomotion, self-care, and domestic tasks Great Britain 1994

	All aged 65 and over	85 and over
Locomotion		
Going out of doors and walking down the road	13	37
Getting up and down stairs and steps	9	23
Getting around the house (on the level)	1	3
Getting to the toilet	1	3
Getting in and out of bed	2	4
Self-care		
Bathing, showering, washing all over	8	21
Dressing and undressing	3	6
Washing face and hands	0	1
Feeding	0	1
Cutting toenails	31	60
Domestic tasks		
Household shopping	16	47
Washing and drying dishes	2	6
Cleaning windows inside	20	53
Using a vacuum cleaner to clean floors	10	30
Washing clothing by hand	7	14
Dealing with personal affairs	7	21

Source: OPCS, *GHS*, 1994, HMSO, 1996, p. 166 Table 6.22, p. 171 Table 6.28, p. 173 Table 6.30.

who are disabled and the impact of the Chronically Sick and Disabled Persons Act 1970.)

Use: The 1994 *GHS* showed that most domiciliary services are used by the over-75s, by women and by people living alone. This is true of home helps, meals on wheels, and visits to day centres (OPCS 1996: 186–7). The greater use by women is partly explained by the greater number who live alone. However, there is evidence that some people in need are receiving little or no help from community services (Allen *et al.* 1992). Charges are referred to at the end of the chapter.

Costs: Looking at public expenditure on elderly people by health and social services in real terms the percentage on non-residential services by local authorities has altered little. It was 11 per cent in 1986/7 and 13 per cent in 1993/4 (figures calculated from CSO 1996: 152, Table 8.19). Over three quarters was spent on hospital care and community health services in both years. There was a 130 per cent increase in current personal social services expenditure in England in real terms between 1978/9 and 1995/6:

- 1978/9 outturn £1062 million (real terms at 1995/6 prices £3183);
- 1995/6 budget £7323 million (DoH/SSI Chief Inspector's Fifth Annual Report 1996: 81).

Almost half (46 per cent) of local authority gross expenditure on personal social services in 1993/4 was spent on elderly people compared with 28 per cent on children (DoH personal communication 1996). Public expenditure in England on personal social services rises with age as the estimated annual figures per person for 1996/7 shown in Table 8.2 indicate.

Table 8.2 **Public expenditure on personal social services: estimated annual figures per person 1996/7 England**

Years	£*
All ages	150
0–17	155
18–64	50
65–69	90
70–74	210
75–79	445
80–84	890
85+	1,930

*All figures rounded to the nearest £5.

Source: Personal communication from DoH, Economic Advisers Office, March 1995.

Research on some of the services which follow is summarised in Robbins 1993.

Home helps and home care

The mandatory duty to provide a home help service was imposed on local authorities by the Health Service and Public Health Act 1968, as part of their general responsibility to promote the welfare of elderly people. There is evidence from numerous studies that home help and home care services are among the most popular and effective elements of community care (summarised in Sinclair and Williams 1990).

Home helps undertake a range of tasks including cleaning, laundering, shopping and cooking, and sometimes give help with dressing and washing. They also often informally provide companionship and advice. Almost 90 per cent of the users of home helps are elderly. Home carers are relatively new (see below) and their role is to provide a more intensive service which may include care which is of a personal rather than a domestic nature.

By 1949 all the English and Welsh local authorities provided home helps. There has been little variation in the percentage of people over 65 who receive the services of a home help. It was 9 per cent in 1976, 1980, 1985 and 8 per cent (excluding private home helps) in 1994 (Table 8.3). Over one third of people over the age of 85 in England received home help or home care in 1994 (CSO 1996: 153). Just over half a million households in England received home help or home care in 1995 and 72 per cent were aged 75 or over (Govt. Statistical Service 1996a: 4). One third of households in England had only one visit per week of less than two hours duration in 1995 but 21 per cent had six or more visits with a total contact of five or more hours in a week (Govt. Statistical Service 1996a: 4). In 1995 the figures showed a slight shift since 1992 towards a more intensive service with fewer households receiving more hours of service (Govt. Statistical Service 1996a: 1). The Audit Commission found that most local authorities had increased both the total amount of home care and, by increasing targeting, provided more hours per household but there was wide variation between authorities (Audit Commission 1996a). The Audit Commission had also commented on this uneven provision in the 1980s (Audit Commission 1986: 24).

Research in the 1960s, 1970s and more recently suggests that there is a substantial amount of unmet need. In 1987 the SSI stated: 'If increasing numbers of very elderly people are to be enabled to continue living in their own homes, or in sheltered housing, rather than having to move into residential care, either a higher volume of domiciliary services will be necessary, or the currently available resources will have to be more specifically targeted on those in most need, and those for whom most can be achieved' (DHSS/SSI 1987:

Table 8.3 Use of some services by elderly people aged 65 and over

	1976[1] England		1980[2] GB	1985[3] GB	1994[4] GB
Home help	9[5]		9[5]	9[5]	8[6]
Attendance at day centre			5	5	3
Lunch at lunch club or day centre	17	social centre for the elderly	3	4	3[7] 3[8]
Meals on wheels	3		2	2	3

[1] Visits received during the past six months. Hunt, A., *The Elderly at Home*, HMSO, 1978, p. 87 and p. 103.
[2] In the month before interview, OPCS, *GHS*, 1980, HMSO, 1982, p. 211 and p. 213.
[3] In the month before interview, OPCS, *GHS*, 1986, HMSO, 1989, p. 210 and p. 212.
[4] In the month before interview, OPCS, *GHS*, 1994, HMSO, 1996, p. 185 Table 6.45 and p. 188 Table 6.48.
[5] The question was different prior to 1991.
[6] Excluding private home help.
[7] Lunch club only.
[8] Day centre only.

26). Unmet needs were found in the research noted above by Allen *et al.* (1992).

Problems identified in the 1970s and early 1980s included the number of visits elderly people received per week (i.e. the service was spread too thinly) and restrictions on what home helps could do. Research raised questions over whether home helps should be domestic cleaners or personal carers (Hedley and Norman 1982). It was partly to meet these criticisms and partly because of the growing frailty of clients that home care or intensive domiciliary care schemes developed. Aimed at elderly people who needed more than a cleaning service, innovatory schemes grew up around the country. Some of the early ones were evaluated and found to be a popular and cost-effective element in a package of care (Tinker 1984). In some areas it is now difficult for elderly people to find help with the 'traditional' home help tasks, such as cleaning or shopping, if they do not have more intensive care needs. A study of elderly people discharged from hospital showed the value of home helps and stressed the value of the housework part of the work (Neill and Williams 1992).

Most recent work has focused on management issues (DHSS/SSI 1987, 1988a) and these are important. The SSI identified three strategies for home care services: incremental change; radical change towards a more professional, flexible and targeted service; and parallel change with a new type of service developed alongside the traditional home help service (DHSS/SSI 1987; see also Morton 1989b). Particularly acute are political issues. A service which changes from one provided for a large number of people and targets it on a few may not endear itself to councillors and the public.

Despite the trend towards privatisation of social services, 82 per cent of home help and home care services were provided directly by social services in 1995 while 15 per cent was provided by the private sector and 3 per cent by the voluntary sector (Govt. Statistical Service 1996a: 8).

Meals

Meals, usually lunch, are provided for some older people either at day centres or clubs or are delivered to their homes. Sometimes a meal is cooked by a neighbour who may receive payment from the local authority. The meals service is a good example of co-operation between local authorities and voluntary bodies. As has been seen earlier, voluntary provision came first and local authorities were given powers to contribute to their costs under the National Assistance Act 1948. In 1962 this Act was amended to allow local authorities to provide meals themselves, as well as widening their powers to help voluntary bodies with the cost of vehicles, equipment, premises and staff. The independent sector makes a significant contribution, providing 42 per cent of meals to people's homes and 62 per cent of the meals to luncheon clubs in 1995 (Govt. Statistical Service 1996a: 5).

The percentage of people over the age of 65 receiving meals on wheels has changed very little. In 1976 it was 3 per cent, in 1980 and 1985 it was 2 per cent and in 1994 it was 3 per cent (Table 8.3). More very old people receive the service: i.e. 12 per cent of the over-85s compared with 1 per cent of those aged 70–74 in 1994 (OPCS 1996: 186). Thirty-four per cent of all those receiving meals at home in England in 1995 were aged 85 and over (Govt. Statistical Service 1996a: 11).

Among the reasons stated for the provision of meals are the nutritional one and that of enabling someone to keep an eye on recipients to make sure all is well. In a review of provision of all kinds of meals Dunn's starting point was to consider why an older person might be in temporary or permanent need of a meal provided by someone else (Dunn 1987). She looked at possible problems of finance, isolation, environment, cooking and cultural barriers. Only when these are analysed can an appropriate response be made; this may be help with shopping, advice on cooking or equipment or the provision of a microwave oven rather than meals on wheels. A helpful development is that many home care staff prepare meals in the home and help people with eating.

Day care

Day care is care provided on a daily basis not in the older person's home. Attendance may be daily or less frequently. Sometimes this is provided in a day hospital where it is usually short-term and with a specific clinical or rehabilitation aim (see Chapter 6), sometimes in a residential home and sometimes in a day centre or club. Voluntary organisations are the biggest providers of clubs for older people and a wide range of recreational facilities are offered. Both in 1980 and 1985 5 per cent of people aged 65 and over attended a day centre but in 1994 this had gone down to 3 per cent (Table 8.3). In 1993/4 18 per 1,000 people aged 65 and over were attending a day centre and being paid for by local authorities (CSO 1996: 154). In 1994 229 places per 10,000 population aged over 65 were provided in England (Govt. Statistical Service 1995a: 111).

The purpose of day centres and clubs is to provide a means of social contact and recreation, and in some of the former, other services such as meals, laundry facilities and chiropody are available. Services provided may be for different sorts of need, including physical (meals, chiropody, etc.), emotional (companionship, advice, etc.), recreational (drama, choir, etc.), advice and further education. Day care may also be helpful in relieving relatives of their care of an older person for a few hours each day. A more recent innovation is care in the evenings, at night and at weekends. The growth of special day centres, for example, for people with Alzheimers disease is important because people like this may be excluded from general day centres.

The value of day care is underlined in research, but so are a number of problems. In 1974 Morley in *Day Care and Leisure Provision for the Elderly* pointed to problems of transport, location and type of buildings (Morley 1974). A national study was carried out by Carter, *Day Services for Adults: Somewhere To Go* (Carter 1981), and this was complemented by a number of local studies. Goldberg and Connelly have summarised research up to 1981 and they concluded that the most important issue was how to integrate day care into a continuum of community services (Goldberg and Connelly 1982). The second main issue concerned the effective organisation of day care and the third related to staffing. A later review of the literature (Brearley and Mandelstam 1992) concluded that day care:

- had developed in a piecemeal fashion;
- was not adequately integrated into coherent local planning between agencies;
- did not reach those most in need;
- had not been exploited to the extent of its potential.

There has been a renewed questioning of the role of day care. Pahl's study, for example, found little difference between users of hospital and other kinds of day care (Pahl 1988). This is clearly an anomaly as hospital care is more expensive to provide and yet free to the user. Tester's national survey in 1989 showed the variety of provision, the problems and some of the anomalies (Tester 1989). Other current issues such as timing, transport and who should provide are raised in Morton (Morton 1989c). Both Pahl and Tester argue for clarity of purposes of day care, but while Pahl veers towards a general kind of provision with a range of activities, Tester would like to see services become more specialist. The SSI have issued advice which stresses the need for a collaborative approach between agencies and that day centres must embrace the full range of community services (DoH/SSI 1992b).

Good neighbour and similar schemes

Although the official Good Neighbour Campaign sprang into life in 1976, good neighbour, street warden and similar schemes had been in existence for many years. Some are run entirely by voluntary bodies, often churches, but some social services departments contribute money or staff to help.

The reasons for visiting older people may vary. They range from just talking to shopping and cooking. In some cases payment may be made to a good neighbour. Some of these schemes have been evaluated and been found to be popular and good value for money (Tinker 1984). A more recent study acknowledged the role of paid care schemes in the provision of local and highly personal care, but showed that it was difficult to detail the contribution to total provision in terms of numbers or characteristics of clients served (Leat and Gay 1987). The morality of paying some people to care, while others are expected to care for nothing and more often at a considerable loss, is also discussed by the authors.

Telephone and alarm systems

Old people, particularly those living alone and those who find difficulty getting out of their homes, may need to summon help in an emergency. They may also want to communicate with professionals such as their doctor or with relatives, friends and shopkeepers.

The most versatile means of two-way communication is the telephone. In 1994 93 per cent of households over the age of 65 in GB had a telephone compared with 61 per cent in 1980 (OPCS 1996: 157). Some local authorities supply these to older people under the Chronically Sick and Disabled Persons Act 1970. The value of telephones for emergencies (Tinker 1984), but also as a means of enabling older people to keep in touch with people outside the home (Tinker 1989a), is well established.

There is growing provision of alarm systems. A survey in 1994 found that 75 per cent of local authorities in the UK and 21 per cent of the larger housing associations provided community alarms and that over a million people – living in sheltered housing and in individual homes in the community – had the use of one (Calling for Help Group 1994). Overall coverage is not known but it is known that 3 per cent of all disabled people have a personal alarm (Martin *et al.* 1989: 56). A national survey showed their value, especially that of ones that can be worn on the person (Tinker 1984). But the same research also showed that alarms need to be provided as part of a package of care. Subsequent research by the Research Institute for Consumer Affairs (RICA) offered advice on dispersed (i.e. not in sheltered housing) alarms to organisations (RICA 1986) and to individuals (Consumers Association 1986). Useful advice on developing alarms in the context of community care was given in another research study (Thornton and Mountain 1992).

Holidays

Some older people, who might not otherwise have had a holiday, have been able to enjoy one through schemes organised by local authorities. Before 1962 there was no power to do this and schemes were mostly organised by voluntary bodies. Some authorities meet the cost of a holiday taken independently, but most offer holidays for groups of older people. Some run their own homes but more use ordinary holiday accommodation, usually out-of-season, in the spring or autumn. In some schemes the organisation and accommodation are provided by voluntary bodies while the social services department selects the individuals and pays all or part of the cost. Net expenditure on holidays and recreation by LAs in England declined from £6 million in 1991/2 to £3 million in 1993/4 (House of Commons Health Committee 1995a: 79).

Social work

Before the creation of social services departments, most statutory work with older people was done by welfare officers, few of whom were qualified, from the welfare department of the local authority. In contrast many social workers working with children were trained and were in the children's department. The Seebohm Committee recommended a radical alternative to the previous pattern of specialisation whereby social workers dealt with one client group only (Home Office *et al.* 1968). They suggested that generic training should be the norm and this became the subsequent pattern. The Younghusband Committee in the *Report of the Working Party on Social Workers* had previously also come down in favour of a generic approach (MOH/

DoH Scotland 1959). However, they considered that some specialisation would be necessary above the basic field level.

A study for the DHSS, *Social Service Teams: The Practitioner's View*, found that four types of specialisation had developed (Stevenson and Parsloe 1978). They were informal specialisation within social work teams, formal specialisation at practitioner level, organisational specialism at team level (e.g. sub-teams concerned with particular groups of clients) and formal 'advisory' specialisms outside the teams (Stevenson and Parsloe 1978). Despite the aims of the Seebohm reforms, a national survey in 1986 found a return to client group specialisation which: 'reflects a desire to prevent the deskilling of social workers and improve professional standards in a hostile climate' (Challis and Ferlie 1988: 20–1).

Stevenson and Parsloe found social workers to be preoccupied with the needs of families and children to the exclusion of other groups such as older people. The Barclay Committee set up to review the role and tasks of social workers commented: 'If an elderly person has problems of these kinds, we consider they are as much in need of social work help as a child might be. We cannot accept what in effect is rationing by age' (National Institute for Social Work 1982: 47). Rowlings in *Social Work with Elderly People*, discusses some of the reasons for the reluctance of social workers to work with this group (Rowlings 1981). An increase in legislation and more attention to child abuse have also led to a high priority being given to social work with children.

The nature and aims of social work are a matter of controversy. The Younghusband Committee saw the function of social workers as including the assessment of problems and the offer of appropriate help of a practical or supportive nature (e.g. practical assistance, giving information or bringing about environmental changes). Stevenson and Parsloe described case-work as: 'broadly concerned with helping the individual or family with a range of problems rather than narrowly directed to discussing the client's emotional functioning and interpersonal relationships' (Stevenson and Parsloe 1978: 133).

The debate about the purpose of social work continued with the Barclay Committee favouring a community, locally based approach (NISW 1982). However, Pinker, in a powerfully argued note of dissent to the report, pointed out the dangers of this with the possibility of conflict between social workers as 'advocates' of 'community needs' and their employers. He also argued for the continuation of the trend towards specialised social workers rather than community workers.

The range and complexity of skills required by social workers have been spelt out in a number of helpful books about social work and older people (e.g. Bowl 1986, Scrutton 1989, Froggatt 1990, Marshall 1990).

A more detailed statement by the British Association of Social Workers (BASW) laying down guidelines for work with older people also gave a summary of the role of the qualified social worker [Document 24]. This role was based on social work values of acceptance, self-determination and confidentiality.

More recent policy developments have identified other roles including that of care manager responsible for organising packages of care. The White Paper *Caring for People* argued for a 'case' manager to ensure that the needs of individuals were regularly reviewed, resources managed effectively and that each service user had a single point of contact (Secs of St. for Health *et al.* 1989b: 21). It was envisaged that the case manager would often be employed by social services but not always. It was stated that: 'The Government does not wish to be prescriptive about the background from which the case manager should be drawn. A range of backgrounds could be possible, although social workers, home care organisers or community nurses, as the professionals in most regular contact with the client, may be particularly suitable' (Secs of St. for Health *et al.* 1989b: 21–2). The policy guidance following the NHS and Community Care Act 1990 substituted 'care' for 'case' management (DoH 1990a; Appendix B/2). The care manager was defined as: 'Any practitioner who undertakes all, or most, of the "core tasks" of care management, who may carry a budgetary responsibility but is not involved in any direct service provision' (DoH 1990a; Appendix B/2). The care manager was distinguished from the key worker who is to carry the main service-providing role (DoH 1990a: 25). It was considered that the skills of the care manager could be found in a number of professions in both statutory and non-statutory agencies.

Whether the social worker is the care manager or key worker or performs any other task he or she must know about local resources and welfare rights and be able to negotiate with other agencies on behalf of older people. An enhanced role in supporting carers has also become apparent with the growing recognition of the importance of the latter culminating in the Carers (Recognition and Services) Act 1995. An expanding role is also likely in work with older people with dementia, those who are abused and those from ethnic minority groups. Social workers are also likely to have to pay more attention to user participation in services. All these elements in the social worker's job will call for new skills and must be reflected in training. It is encouraging that the Central Council for Education and Training in Social Work have taken a lead in giving advice on training and that this has stressed the need to work with older people themselves (e.g. Winner 1992, Ahmad-Aziz *et al.* 1992).

A discussion of the role of social workers cannot take place outside the context of the organisation of personal social services and in particular, that of social services departments (Webb and Wistow 1987) (see p. 171).

The assessment of social work practice has been attempted by only a few researchers. One study which took place between 1965 and 1970 found that trained social workers did not bring about any further change in physical circumstances but did create a general improvement in morale (Goldberg 1970). A small study of older people living alone, which compared those allocated to social workers with those in touch with home helps, showed the complex nature of the tasks which the former undertook (Sinclair *et al.* 1989). Social workers had not made much impact and users often did not understand what they were trying to do. However, in the Kent Community Care Project, elderly people with a social worker as care manager fared better on the criteria laid down compared with a control sample who did not have a care manager (Challis and Davies 1986). One summary of research on the effectiveness of social work concluded that:

- social work backed by practical resources can sustain or improve the morale of old people, reduce their practical problems and possibly lessen the likelihood that they will die or be admitted to residential care in a given period;
- social work is likely to be most effective with those who have particular difficulties but are either fit enough to manage on their own or, if severely dependent, have the support of a caring relative;
- the likelihood of effective social work may well be reduced by the pressures on social workers in area offices (Sinclair and Williams 1990: 151).

Very few older people are seen by a social worker or care manager. In 1994 only 2 per cent of people in GB aged 65 and over had seen one in the last three months and the figure for the over-85s was only 5 per cent (OPCS 1996: 183). Extensive research on care management has been undertaken by the Personal Social Services Unit, University of Kent (e.g. Challis and Davies 1986).

Residential care

The nature of residential care

As noted on p. 138 residential care is for old people who, even with domiciliary support, cannot manage to live in their own homes, but who still do not need intensive nursing care. The respective roles of residential home and hospital were laid down by MoH (1965) in Memorandum for Local Authorities and Hospital Authorities, *Care of the Elderly in Hospitals and Residential Homes*. In 1980 the Residential Homes Act consolidated certain legislation relating to the registration, conduct and inspection of private and voluntary homes but made no changes in powers. Under the Health and Social Services and Social Security Adjudications Act 1983 a new classification of residential care homes, as distinct from nursing homes, was set up for establishments which provided residential accommodation with both board and personal care by reason of old age, disablement and certain other categories. Each home looking after four or more residents had to be registered with the local authority, which might impose conditions and might refuse or cancel registration. Since April 1993 residential homes with less than four places come under the Registered Homes Act but registration depends only on whether the person in charge is a fit person rather than direct inspection.

The Registered Homes Act 1984 defined a residential care home as: 'any establishment which provides or is intended to provide, whether for reward or not, residential accommodation with both board and personal care for four or more persons in need of personal care by reason of old age, disablement, past or present dependence on alcohol or drugs or past or present mental disorder'. The Act required homes to be registered with the local authorities and subject to inspection by them. The local authority may impose conditions and may refuse or cancel registration. Homes can have dual registration as a nursing home (this is where nursing care is provided as compared with residential care where it is personal care that is provided). The Secretary of State for Health has made the *Residential Care Homes Regulations*. In addition *Home Life: A Code of Practice for Residential Care* was published in 1984 as a result of a Working Party sponsored by DHSS and convened by CPA (CPA 1984). This was updated by CPA in 1996 in *A Better Home Life: A Code of Practice for Residential and Nursing Home Care* (CPA 1996). The issue of what is residential and what is nursing care often has to be decided at local level. Local authorities may place people in nursing homes as well as residential care. The boundary between very sheltered housing and residential care has also become blurred now that the former has to be registered under the Registered Homes Act 1984 if care is provided (see Chapter 7 and NFHA/Special Needs Housing Advisory Service 1987).

Changing pattern of provision

Residential homes for elderly people are provided by local authorities, voluntary bodies and the private sector. While the overall proportion of elderly people in residential care has remained constant at about 2 per cent for some years there has been a dramatic shift towards private provision (Fig. 8.1). A comparison of places for nursing, residential and long-stay hospital care of older, chronically ill and physically disabled people between 1970 and 1995 shows:

- *overall* a doubling in places from 270,300 in 1970 to 563,000 in 1995;
- *for residential care* a steady drop in local authority provision from 137,200 places in 1984 (there was a rise from 1970 to 1984) to 80,800 in 1995), a dramatic rise in private provision (from

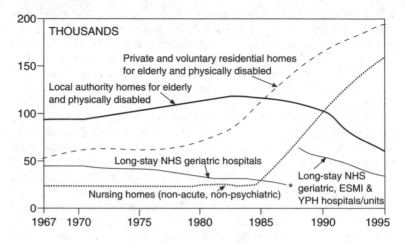

* Discontinuity at time of change to Korner aggregates. After 1988, separate figures for acute/rehabilitation geriatric beds and long-stay geriatric beds are no longer available. Long-stay beds have, therefore, been estimated since 1988 on the assumption that acute/rehabilitation geriatric beds in England have remained constant and all the decline in beds in England in the speciality of geriatrics overall is attributable to loss of long-stay beds.

Figure 8.1 Nursing and residential care places for elderly, chronically ill and physically disabled people by sector, England, April 1967–95
Source: Laing and Buisson *Care of Elderly People: Market Survey 1996*, Laing & Buisson 1996, p. 25 Table 8.1.

23,700 places in 1970 to 167,800 in 1995), a slow growth in voluntary provision (from 40,100 in 1970 to 52,800 in 1995);
* *for nursing homes provided by the private and voluntary sectors* a rise from 20,300 places in 1970 to 208,000 in 1995 (92 per cent of this was in the private sector);
* *for NHS long-stay geriatric places* a drop from 52,000 to 33,200;
* *for NHS long-stay psycho-geriatric places* a drop from 23,000 to 18,500 (Laing and Buisson 1996: 18, Document 25).

Between 1984 and 1994 there was an increase in numbers of residents aged 65 and over in England from 180,576 to 233,688 but whereas the percentage increase for residents in private homes was 157 per cent it was only 29 per cent for voluntary homes and there was a decrease in local authority homes of 43 per cent (Govt. Statistical Service 1995b: 14–15). In 1995, 75 per cent of residential places in homes primarily for elderly people in England were in independent homes (Govt. Statistical Service 1996b, Older People section: 2). This has been mainly a result of government policy (see below). Another development has been the transfer of Part III homes by local authorities to the private and voluntary sector where little is known about the effects on residents.

The main reason for the increase in private provision was originally the availability of a board and lodging allowance by DHSS which was paid to all those under certain capital limits without sufficient income to cover the fees but with no test of disability. Until 1980 most residents in voluntary sector homes received public funding from 'sponsorship' by local authorities in addition to the money that residents paid themselves. After this, supplementary benefit board and lodging payments (later to be known as income support) became available and: 'there was an accelerating switch to this funding system accompanied by a massive increase in the number of private sector homes' (Peaker 1988: 3, see also NAO 1987: 24–30, Bradshaw 1988). Social security expenditure on income support for recipients in private residential care and nursing homes in GB was £10 million in 1979, rising to £2,575 million in 1993 and dropping to £1,754 million in 1995 (Laing and Buisson 1996: 110). Numbers of people receiving this benefit increased from 11,000 in 1979 to a peak of 281,200 in 1993 and then a fall to 181,000 in 1995 (Laing and Buisson 1996: 110).

A Working Party report in 1985 recommended that local authorities' multidisciplinary assessment arrangements for admission to their own homes should be extended to those claiming supplementary board and lodging allowance for residential care in private and voluntary homes (DHSS, Joint Central and Local Government Working Party 1985). The Audit Commission concluded that, at best, there had been a shift from one pattern of residential care based on hospitals to an alternative supported in many cases by supplementary benefit payments, missing out more flexible and cost-effective forms of community care altogether (Audit Commission 1986: 2). A subsequent committee (the Firth report) of a joint central and local government working party, *Public Support for Residential Care*, concluded that a system in which local government provided public support, rather than the social security system, for people in residential care homes offered the best way forward (DHSS Joint Central and Local Government Working Party 1987). They recommended that local authorities should take over assessment of need, setting of standards and responsibility for finance.

The Griffiths report also recommended that local authority social services departments should be responsible for assessing the need for residential care (Griffiths 1988). It also recommended that local social services departments should, if they judged it appropriate, meet the costs of caring for people who cannot pay themselves in residential (including nursing) homes above a basic level of support. This basic support should continue to be available as a social security entitlement, at a level broadly in line with that available to people in the community (Griffiths 1988: 1–2).

The DoH White Paper *Caring for People* followed the recommendations outlined above and proposed that local authorities should take over responsibility for financial support of people in private and voluntary homes but that the new arrangements should not apply to existing residents (Secs of St. for Health *et al.* 1989b). (Existing residents subsequently became known as those with 'preserved rights'.) Social services departments would become responsible for the assessment of people who sought care and wanted financial help and should secure the delivery of services, not simply by acting as direct providers, but by developing their purchasing and contracting role to become enabling authorities (Secs of St. for Health *et al.* 1989b: 17).

The subsequent National Health Service and Community Care Act 1990 made these proposals law and also required the setting up of inspection units within local authorities to cover local authority residential homes, previously excluded from inspection, as well as those currently being inspected in the private and voluntary sector. These provisions took effect in April 1993 and funds were transferred from social security to local authorities.

Another factor in the decline of local authority provision was that residents who qualified on financial grounds in independent homes became eligible for the Residential Allowance (an allowance in addition to income support) but those in LA homes were not. If someone is placed in a Part III home the LA has to make up the shortfall in fees itself.

The influence of the Wagner report

In 1985 an independent review of residential care was set up by the Secretary of State for Health and Social Services. Its terms of reference were to review all forms of residential care and to make recommendations. The Committee, chaired by Lady Wagner, reported in 1988 (Wagner 1988a). Some of their recommendations are referred to later in this section [and see Document 26]. In a critical account covering every aspect of residential care for all groups they concluded that entry must be *A Positive Choice*, the sub-title of their report. To make this choice, they said, there is need for:

- adequate information about options;
- realistic alternatives to choose from;
- help, if necessary, in making choices;
- the initial choice to be tested by a trial period with an option to return to the previous situation if possible, or to another setting;
- a review of the chosen service at appropriate intervals;
- ways to appeal against inadequate, inappropriate or enforced services (Wagner 1988a: 26).

An accompanying volume to the Wagner report, *Residential Care: The Research Reviewed* (Wagner 1988b), contains a summary of research on residential care for elderly people (Sinclair 1988). The

Wagner Development Group was formed in 1988 to carry forward the recommendations, and continued until 1992. As well as issuing useful guidance on standards in homes (DoH/SSI 1989, 1990) DoH set up the Caring in Homes Initiative in 1989 to carry forward the recommendations of Wagner. The Initiative included four research programmes; they were on quality assurance, training for care staff, the provision of information and 'Window in Homes' (about links with the community). This programme was evaluated and the report *Raising Voices* showed the value of the guidelines and practice manuals, the support for planning and implementation of change from the grassroots and the help that was given to residents in setting and monitoring the quality of care (Youll and McCourt-Perring 1993).

The residents

Who they are: Most elderly people in residential care are women, frail (often with multiple disabilities), aged over 75, have their entry arranged by someone else and nearly all (89 per cent) are single, widowed or divorced (Laing and Buisson 1996: 79). Table 8.4 shows the growing proportion of very old people (over the age of 85) in residential care – 35 per cent in 1980 and 51.6 per cent in 1994. In 1995 90 per cent of older people in residential care in England were aged 75 or over (Govt. Statistical Service 1996b, Older People section: 5). The trend is for people to be older on admission. In 1994 85 per cent of admissions of elderly people in England were over the age of 75 (Govt. Statistical Service 1995c, Older People section: 12–13). However, one large research study found that the level of resident dependency had no effect on the homes' overall quality of care (Bland *et al.* 1992).

Why they are there: Evidence has already been presented that some elderly people were in residential care in the 1960s only because of a lack of alternative housing (e.g. Townsend 1964) [Document 27].

*Table 8.4 **The growing percentage of very elderly people in residential homes 1980–1994 England***

	Percentage of residents aged 85 and over in local authority, private and voluntary homes
1980	35.0
1985	40.4
1989	45.6
1994	51.6

Source: Government Statistical Service DoH Personal Social Services *Local Authority Statistics, Residential Accommodation for Elderly and for Younger Physically Handicapped People. All Residents in Local Authority, Voluntary and Private Homes, Year ending 31.3.89.* RA/89/2, DoH, 1989, Table B and year ending 31.3.94 RA/94/2, DoH, 1995b Table B and DoH personal communication.

Research in the 1980s showed that some older people were inappropriately placed in most forms of care (e.g. Wade *et al*. 1983). This was particularly so in the case of residential care (Audit Commission 1985, DHSS, Joint Central and Local Government Working Party 1987). Much of the evidence is summarised in Neill *et al*. (1988). Research, mainly from the local authority sector, shows that the idea of residential care often begins with someone other than the applicant. Applicants have often not been given sufficient information to make an informed choice and only rarely do they make a positive choice (Sinclair 1988: 264). A summary of more recent evidence on why some older people enter residential care and others stay at home shows that, although for some people residential care is a positive and appropriate solution, for others 'admission may be accepted only with regret and community-based options may not have been fully explored, utilised or developed' (Warburton 1994: 1). A field study by the NHS Executive and SSI found that one of the main reasons why older people chose residential care was *The F Factor* (this is the title of their report). The F stood for fear – fear of falling, fear of attack, fear of being unable to cope and general anxiety (DoH/SSI/NHS Executive 1994c).

The pressure for a move away from residential care is based on the views of older people themselves, the development of alternatives and the cost. However, some argue that an expansion of residential care is needed bearing in mind the expected growth in numbers of very old people. Grundy and Arie have suggested that residential care is needed for those who need round-the-clock support and live alone (Grundy and Arie 1982) and others that there will always be a minority who, for whatever reasons, can be most appropriately cared for in an institution (Higgs and Victor 1993). Research by Allen and colleagues showed that an important group of elderly people had made a choice to enter residential care and that it should not be regarded as a 'last resort' by professionals (Allen *et al*. 1992).

Most elderly people move to institutional care voluntarily or with persuasion. But in certain circumstances – such as where old people are physically incapacitated or are living in insanitary conditions and are unable to devote to themselves, and is not receiving from other people, due care and attention – the local authority may apply for a court order for their compulsory removal to a hospital or other suitable place (under Section 47 of the National Assistance Act 1948). This power is rarely used.

Some important factors

Important aspects with residential care to be considered include setting up standards and monitoring the quality of care, staff training, numbers and deployment, design and adequacy of buildings, use by residents who are not long-term and costs.

Standards: Concern about standards in residential homes is considerable. These relate particularly to privacy, the rights of the residents and their opportunities for self-determination, availability of choice over many everyday matters, and arrangements for health care. These were highlighted in the Wagner report. A mixed picture was presented of LA provision in 1993 with the quality of care in most homes being good to excellent; in many homes there was an emphasis on choice but care planning was relatively underdeveloped, and in some there was a tendency to respond to the needs of the group rather than the individual (DoH/SSI, Annual Report of the Chief Inspector 1995: 41).

Many ways have been suggested to make life more satisfying and individual for both residents and staff. For example DHSS in *A Lifestyle for the Elderly* looked at ways in which staff and buildings could meet the real needs of residents (DHSS 1976d). The point of the title of the report was that elderly people are not just consumers of a service. How quality of care can be measured is discussed by Kellaher, who then suggests that the available evidence indicates that residents are more satisfied with, and express definite preferences for, those care arrangements which allow a fundamental rather than a token measure of control over their range of life domains (Kellaher 1986). A study by Counsel and Care (1991), the aptly named *Not Such Private Places*, examined private and voluntary residential and nursing homes in Greater London. It pointed out the lack of privacy which some residents experienced and offered guidance on standards. In a second study in Greater London the wish for a single room, en-suite toilets, personal furniture, locks on bedroom doors and more choice on timing of getting up and over meals were among the requests (Counsel and Care 1992). A large research study in Scotland endorsed the value placed on privacy, especially single rooms and improved toilet arrangements (Bland *et al.* 1992). This study also raised the interesting question about the ethos and objectives of residential care and 'the extent to which they should adopt a "hotelier" approach, in which the principal objective is to respond to the service needs of the consumer, or one which deliberately takes responsibility for residents' welfare' (Bland *et al.* 1992: 15).

The importance of residents being involved in decisions was confirmed in the follow up to the Caring in Homes Initiative where it was found that:

- established care practices and routines were often out of line with what was needed by residents;
- fulfilment of social and emotional needs were found to be at least as important as physical or medical needs;
- residents and relatives could be too accepting of what was on offer (Youll and McCourt-Perring 1993).

A study of LA homes showed that, while privacy was generally respected, there was less awareness of other rights of residents, such as managing their own financial affairs (DoH/SSI 1995b). The whole issue of the importance of choice was underlined in an inspection of LA homes ((DoH/SSI 1995b).

Concern about arrangements for health care, and especially the lack of community nursing staff, have been expressed by the Royal College of Nursing especially that 'nursing needs of people in residential (and sometimes nursing homes) are not being met' (Royal College of Nursing 1992: 21).

Staff: Availability of adequate number of staff may be related to the low status of residential social work and a lack of appropriate training (Willcocks *et al.* 1986, Sinclair 1988). The 1994 *Social Services Workforce Analysis* showed that 76 per cent of all care staff in community homes (this excludes homes mainly for children) had no relevant social work qualification although the figures for officers in charge is more encouraging – 78 per cent *did* have a relevant qualification (Local Government Management Board and Association of Directors of Social Services 1995: 66). Among the recommendations of the Wagner Committee were that care staff should no longer be graded as manual staff but that their posts should be redefined as officers or the professional equivalent and that every establishment should have staff training plans. Perhaps more important was their recommendation that 'residential staff are the major resource and should be valued as such. The importance of their contribution needs to be recognised and enhanced' (Wagner 1988a: 114).

An independent inquiry into staff in all kinds of residential care reported in 1992 (Howe report 1992). Entitled *The Quality of Care*, it made detailed recommendations about training, status, pay and conditions and the management of residential care staff. Some of these were directed towards the enhancement of links between residential and field staff. The need for more training to enable staff to be more responsive and confident in their relationships with residents and to be more involved in decision making were points made in the evaluation of the Caring in Homes Initiative (Youll and McCourt-Perring 1993).

The buildings: One major study has widespread implications for buildings. *A Balanced Life* is a consumer study of residential life in 100 local authority homes (Peace *et al.* 1982, Willcocks *et al.* 1986). The researchers concluded that a major problem was lack of privacy and recommended that future homes should allow for more private and less communal space. They argued for residential flatlets which are more akin to very sheltered housing. Conditions have improved and in 1995 three quarters (74 per cent) of residential places in homes for elderly people in England were single rooms. A survey of the private sector showed that 34 per cent of nursing homes and 29 per cent of residential homes had rooms with en-suite toilet in 1995 (Laing and Buisson 1996: 85).

Use by older people who are not long-term residents: Few residential homes are now used exclusively for long-term residential care. In some homes residents only stay for a short time, perhaps while relatives have a break, or for rehabilitation between hospital and their own home. Three per cent of places in residential homes for elderly people in England were occupied by short-stay residents in 1994/5 (Govt. Statistical Service 1996b, Older people services section: 10). In 1994 70 per cent of admissions to residential homes for elderly people were short stay and over three quarters (78 per cent) of these were in LA homes in England in 1993/4 (Govt Statistical Service 1995c: 12–13). In 1995 74 per cent of private residential homes and 78 per cent of private nursing homes offered respite care compared with 35 per cent and 52 per cent respectively in 1989 (Laing and Buisson 1996: 85). Allen, in *Short-Stay Residential Care for the Elderly*, found that the needs of short-stay residents were often different from long-stay and that a separate home or wing was likely to meet the different needs of the two groups (Allen 1983). The main beneficiaries seemed to be the carers. The use of residential provision as a community resource was supported by the Wagner Committee but with some reservations (Wagner 1988a: Ch. 5). A literature study following this report showed a complicated picture (Elkan and Kelly 1991). For example on the use of volunteers it was pointed out that residents do not always want volunteer help, the contribution of volunteers is not always of benefit to residents and they should not be used as a substitute for staff. On the wider issue of links between homes and the community there was a patchy and ad hoc picture. A national study of LA multipurpose homes, where residential care homes were used to provide services for non-resident older people and their carers, found that, although there were obvious advantages in allowing these facilities to be used by a wider group, there were problems and the policy was less popular with the elderly residents themselves who felt that their home was being invaded. Staff found problems too in dealing with people who had different needs (Wright 1996).

Costs: On costs there is no doubt that institutional care is not cheap. In 1993/4 the weekly expenditure on residential care for older people per supported resident was £265 (Govt Statistical Service 1996b, Unit costs section: 2). Comparative costings of the overall public expenditure costs have already been given [Document 16]. It will be seen that Part III accommodation was less expensive than hospital care but more expensive than very sheltered housing and staying at home with a package of care (Tinker 1989b: 114).

A problem for residents with 'preserved rights' in the private sector is the gap between income support levels and the fees charged so that they have to 'top up' their fees from relatives or charities (Wright 1992). One study found no direct relationship between the cost of providing care and the quality of that care (Bland *et al.* 1992). There are also local differences, for example, in some areas spouses are financially liable but not in others.

Supported lodgings schemes

It has already been seen that both hospital (Chapter 6) and residential homes (p. 163) provide short-stay and respite care for older people. Another kind of provision is supported lodgings which is: 'a general term covering a range of schemes such as: adult placement schemes, adult fostering, boarding out, home finding and so on. The common feature of all such schemes is that a care agency places people who need care (referred to as clients) in a living situation where they receive care or support as well as board and accommodation' (Young 1988: 1). Where there have been schemes in the past they were often labelled by the press as 'rent a granny' or 'foster a granny'.

In a handful of towns voluntary organisations ran schemes like this in the late 1940s, but there was little public provision. A survey in 1977 of all social services departments in England and Wales revealed that less than 10 per cent had schemes operating (Rattee 1977). A survey in 1980 found only 23 schemes in England and Wales. Some were long-term and some short-term with a wide range of objectives, from providing a cheap form of care to enhancing the quality of life of older people (Thornton and Moore 1980). The researchers reported satisfaction by both older people and their carers. They emphasised the importance of selecting and matching the older person and the person caring for them.

By 1982 just over one third of English local authorities were running supported lodgings schemes (Tait 1983) and by 1987–8 it had risen to 81 per cent in England, Wales and Scotland (Young 1988). In the latter study 41 per cent of providers had only one scheme and most were quite small. Only 20 per cent had 20 or more carers and 40 per cent had under five. One third of schemes placed older people. Carers provided a high level of physical and personal care and many clients received a level of care one would expect in a registered residential care home.

A slightly different kind of scheme is one using volunteers as opposed to employed individuals and research has found that the most likely model was an unpaid volunteer providing a regular day-time sitting service which was not necessarily what was wanted (Thornton 1989).

In a summary of the research on all kinds of short-term care it is noted that spouses, who seem very reluctant to give up their caring role, rarely used it (Sinclair and Williams 1990). The evidence also suggests a need to increase the quantity of short-stay care; increase the variety of ways it is provided; pay attention to the wish of carers for a shared approach, for example by passing on information about treatment; and ensuring that rotating care is part of a combination of services (Sinclair and Williams 1990).

Mobility and transport

The mobility of older people, which affects their access to facilities, may decrease with increasing age. Not only do many of them become physically less able to move about but fewer own cars than other age groups. This may be less to do with age than with that generation of old people. Travel declines with age and this is sharper for women than for men (Pharoah and Warnes 1992). In 1994 only 46 per cent of households containing at least one older person had a car, compared with 78 per cent containing no older people (OPCS 1996, 157–8). Elderly women, many of whom probably never learnt to drive, were less likely to have a car than men, and people living alone were also likely not to have a car (OPCS 1996: 158). The Carnegie Inquiry into the Third Age, however, was concerned about the likely rise in car ownership by the next cohort of people, which could cause a further decline in public transport and local amenities (Carnegie Inquiry into the Third Age 1993).

Many older people make their journeys by walking. However, pedestrian casualty rates are much higher among people over 60 compared with younger adults, and fatalities of people aged 75 and over account for a quarter of all pedestrian fatalities (ACE 1990a). In 1991 about two thirds of people aged 65 and over made use of public transport (Jarvis *et al.* 1996: 74). The main reasons for not using it were related to having a car and ill health and disability. The study of disabled adults, of whom the majority were elderly, found that for those in private households the largest number (76 per cent) had used a private car the previous year, 57 per cent a bus, 27 per cent a taxi and smaller proportions other forms of transport (Martin *et al.* 1989: 24).

A Department of Transport (DTI) report included recommendations about vehicle design, traffic calming and road signs (DTI 1991). Suggestions made by ACE to improve access of older people include improving public transport, developing new forms of transport such as dial-a-ride buses and taxi-card schemes and ensuring that older people can afford transport (ACE 1994). Concessionary fares (Chapter 5) are helpful, but less so for older people who live in areas with an infrequent bus service. Recommendations based on a survey of nearly 1,000 elderly people came to similar conclusions and also stressed their dependence on families for transport (Jegede 1993). An original set of recommendations is based on cross-sector benefits of accessible transport (Fowkes *et al.* undated). This is when making an improvement for the person involved may also result in a benefit (often a saving) for another sector. For example if more older people could get out to a day centre then some domiciliary services such as chiropody and the provision of meals would not be needed.

Some issues

Some points of concern about local social services are discussed elsewhere. These include variation between authorities (Chapter 13) and the role of voluntary organisations (Chapter 11). Others which are more specific are discussed below.

Community care and how it is working

There was a general welcome for the emphasis on community care and the eventual removal of the perverse funding incentives following the 1990 Act. There has been considerable research on the new system and this has come in the main from DoH itself, the Audit Commission, the House of Commons Health Committee, academics and the voluntary sector. However, much of this is descriptive and there is need for more evaluative work especially on cost-effectiveness (MRC 1994a). Some of the monitoring and evaluation is documented in Henwood and Wistow (1994). Attention has focused on the following topics.

General: There are a number of problems in assessing the success of community care and they include the lack of baseline information on the services before the reforms, the lack of national standards and other changes (e.g. in health and local government) which have had an effect on it (Meredith 1995). A general point that was made after the implementation of the 1990 Act was the need to have some measurable standards and one recommendation was for a Community Care Charter (House of Commons Health Committee 1993a: *xlvi*).

The immensity of the task facing social services departments was made clear in the Audit Commission's report *Community Care: Managing the Cascade of Change* (Audit Commission 1992c). This report reiterated the main problems facing social services departments as did *The Community Revolution: Personal Social Services and Community Care* (Audit Commission 1992d). Looking at solutions to these problems, the latter report exhorted social services departments to gain the commitment of members and staff, develop systems to support strategic and operational aspects of implementation and to achieve good collaboration with other agencies. In the

Audit Commission's 1993 report *Taking Care: Progress with Care in the Community*, 'cautious but steady progress' was reported (Audit Commission 1993b: 1) but some authorities were 'rather slower than others, and a few are in danger of lagging well behind' (Audit Commission 1993b: 14). The 1994 Audit Commission report *Taking Stock: Progress with Community Care* stressed the need for more sensitivity, flexibility and responsiveness (Audit Commission 1994b). Findings from surveys in social services and the NHS were that progress in general had been made in most areas but disquiet was expressed about the uneven provision by the independent market and about the link between hospitals and community services (especially over hospital discharge arrangements) (DoH/SSI/NHSE 1995). In 1996 the Audit Commission (1996a) in *Balancing the Care Equation: Progress with Community Care* concluded that progress continued but financial issues dominated. Some fundamental criticisms of community care has come from some researchers (e.g. Walker 1994). In 1996 it was announced that the Audit Commission and the Social Services Inspectorate would undertake joint reviews to 'provide an independent assessment for local people of how well served they are by their social services authority' (Audit Commission/DoH/SSI 1996: 3). The reviews were also intended to assist LAs to improve the quality of their services.

Community care plans: The first plans were very largely descriptive but there is now more consultation, collaboration and greater clarity (Kennedy and Stewart 1994). After analysing the first two years of plans it was held that 'the overall aim should be to produce a statement of purchasing intentions within a framework of need and supply mapping and priority setting' (Wistow and Hardy 1994: 48). Age Concern have found planning patchy (Meredith 1994).

Maximising the use of the independent (private and voluntary) sectors: The White Paper *Caring for People* stated: 'The Government will expect local authorities to make use whenever possible of services from voluntary, "not for profit" and private providers insofar as this represents a cost effective care choice' (Secs of St. for Health *et al*. 1989b: 22). Ways of developing a mixed economy of welfare would include taking steps to stimulate the setting up of not-for-profit agencies, identifying areas of their own work which were sufficiently self-contained to be suitable for 'floating off' as self-managed units, and stimulating the development of new voluntary sector activity (Secs of St. for Health *et al*. 1989b: 23). A programme *Caring for People Who Live at Home* was set up in 1992 by the government to encourage developments in day and domiciliary care, particularly in the independent sector. It is being evaluated.

Residential care is one service where there had long been provision by the independent sector but it remains less common for other services such as domiciliary care and this is considered ripe for expansion (Laing and Buisson 1996: 90). In 1994 research showed that social services departments were beginning to recognise the benefits of the independent sector but that genuine partnerships with the private sector were uneven, with more stress on the voluntary sector (Wistow *et al.* 1994). Another study showed that social services were adopting a more pragmatic approach to the independent sector because of the need to expand community services (Henwood 1995). While many would agree with a variety of local providers, critics point to the dangers of overdependence on the private sector (e.g. Glennerster *et al.* 1990) and the problems for voluntary bodies (see Chapter 10).

There is a great lack of hard information about the private sector but it is already known that it differs from public care in a number of ways including organisation, finance, use, regulation and the kinds of people it caters for (Parker 1990).

It is claimed, but with little evidence, that private care enables older people to be more in control and more able to choose the kind of service (including tasks done and timing) than in publicly provided services. The dangers are that there may be abuse unless standards are monitored and some kind of inspection takes place. A DoH study found that it was of concern that some authorities did not have service specifications to use with private providers and that there needed to be a more systematic approach to purchasing and setting contracts for all providers (including in-house) (DoH/SSI/ NHSE 1994b). There may also be problems when there are few competitors, and large organisations move into areas where profits are to be made, undercut their rivals and then raise prices (Glennerster *et al.* 1990). For residents in private and voluntary residential care there is the possibility of closure due to financial failure, and so on. Three per cent of homes for elderly and physically handicapped people closed in 1995 (Laing and Buisson 1996: 31). Problems over the lack of monitoring of private domiciliary agencies have been expressed (DoH/SSI/NHSE 1994b). Some have argued that regulation and inspection can be done by the providers as is done with private sheltered housing. The Joint Initiative for Community Care produced detailed guidance and advice (Bell and How 1996).

Assessing need: Assessing the population needs of an area is not easy and has to take account of national demographic and other data alongside local information. What also needs to be done is to cost possible options and ways have been devised of doing this (Hancock 1994). At an individual level people's needs for services have to be assessed but, as with planning for the area, there are variations in procedures, eligibility criteria and the experiences of older people (Meredith 1994).

Providing packages of care: A central thrust of the new system was that individuals should receive a package (combination) of care (services) if they were assessed as being in need. A study of elderly people living on the margin of community and residential care found that most older people had only one or two services and some had none at all (Allen *et al.* 1992). In this study few had much choice in what services they received, any say in the time of delivery, the person who delivered it, or how much they received. The package of care should be needs-led, that is, not just based on existing services. A study in 1994 found a variable picture with care management 'enabling more people with complex needs to remain in the community, but it was too early yet for the needs-led dimension of the process to be a major driving force in the development of new and different community-based services' (DoH/SSI/NHSE 1994a: 6). The SSI reported a variable picture a year later where 'in some instances users were being helped to organise their own care packages. Other staff were still overwhelmed by all the changes and sceptical of the future' (DoH/SSI 1994c: 1). A specific study, *Community Care Packages for Older People*, found that there was a clear commitment by both social services and health authorities on care packages but that users and carers were not satisfied with the system for providing the service where issues of flexibility, consistency, the need for information and charges needs to be addressed (DoH/SSI/NHSE 1994b). Similar findings are reported in Henwood (1995), whose study found that pressure on resources was leading to reduced levels of service and a tightening of eligibility criteria.

***The involvement of users and carers*:** A study for DoH in 1993 found that much was being done to inform users and carers but that there needed to be 'better opportunities for user and carers to participate and be involved in information creation, publication and dissemination' (DoH/KPMG Peat Marwick undated: 4). A 1994 study found that involving older people was less developed than involving carers (DoH/SSI/NHSE 1994b). However, a study for the Carers National Association found that the majority had not noticed any change in their circumstances since the 1990 NHS and Community Care Act and over half were dissatisfied with the assessment of their needs (Warner 1994). The implementation of the Carers' Recognition and Services Act in April 1996 gave carers a statutory right to have their needs assessed.

In addition to more emphasis on users and carers, the 1990 Act included a requirement that local authorities must establish and publicise a complaints procedure for social services departments. Policy and practice guidance were issued (see DoH/SSI 1994b). (See also Chapter 9 for legislation to give disabled people cash payments and Chapter 12 for a discussion of empowerment and the contribution of older people to policy making.)

***Finance*:** Sceptics have suggested that financially stretched local authorities will find it difficult to provide a reasonable standard of community care without the injection of large amounts of extra money. However, considerable extra resources became available with the special transitional grant money (Audit Commission 1994b. See also p. 145 for details of the increase in expenditure between 1978/9 and 1995/6). Taking into account *all* spending on community care in England (including domiciliary care, community health, social security benefits etc) expenditure rose from £7,352 million in 1988/9 to £11,311 million in 1992/3 (all at 1992/3 prices) (House of Commons Health Committee 1995b: 61–2). Nevertheless one study indicated that support for community care was being undermined by resource shortfalls (Henwood 1995). The Audit Commission in March 1996 found that local authorities were giving priority to community care and that spending was 7 per cent more than that proposed or funded by the Government (Audit Commission 1996a).

The involvement of other agencies: What is vitally important is that all the services should be planned together. Policy guidance from the DoH in 1990 noted that the NHS and Community Care Act 1990 requires social services to bring apparent housing and health care needs to the attention of the appropriate authorities and invite them to assist in the assessment (DoH 1990a: 29). An evaluation after two years of the new system found that improved working relations were widely reported (Henwood 1995), but problems around the health and social care divide, including hospital discharge, have also been found (Henwood and Wistow 1994). The importance of involving housing is emphasised in much of the early research (e.g. Audit Commission 1992d) and the variable pattern of relations is stressed (e.g. DoH/SSI/NHSE 1994b). Guidance on staff training by the SSI even went as far as noting that 'organisations and individuals hitherto marginalised will need to be brought into centre stage' (DoH/SSI 1993d: 6). This included housing agencies, the others being users and carers, providers and purchasers of acute and primary care, the independent sector and other 'key local authority players' (p. 6). (See also Chapter 6 for more on links between social services and health, Chapter 7 for housing and also Chapter 9 for services for mentally disordered people.)

Levels of provision

It is likely that more of all the supportive services are needed: more home helps, better laundry services, more adequate meals services and so on. While the provision of community services have increased quite substantially they have barely kept pace with the demographic changes (Tinker *et al.* 1994: Ch. 3). This is especially the case for very elderly people (House of Commons Health Committee 1995a: 137–8). Age Concern maintain that in some areas there are 'simply not enough services or a high enough level of resourcing' (Meredith 1994: 73). There is also concern about the move to more short-term hospital care which indicates that older people are spending more time in the community with the consequent need for additional community services (NAO 1987: 31).

Comparative data about levels of provision of local social services are difficult to find. The National Audit Office commented that there was a general lack of information (NAO 1987). There is also need for caution with statistics. For example, there has been an overall increase in public expenditure (in real terms) on elderly people in England and Scotland which increased from £2,225 million in 1989/90 to £2,248 million in 1992/3 (CSO 1995: 148). What these increases might mean is that the number of staff had risen or there had been a rise in salaries. The number of staff employed in personal social services in Great Britain has indeed risen – in 1981 there were 240,000 and in 1994 293,000 (CSO 1996: 147). One indication of unmet needs is in the OPCS disability surveys where disabled people were asked whether they needed some kind of domiciliary service they were not getting (Martin *et al.* 1988). The most common service needed was a chiropodist (34 per cent) followed by a home help (21 per cent) (Martin *et al.* 1988: 39, 41).

Standards

One development in the 1980s was the move away from norms (i.e. quantity) of provision laid down by DHSS. Although these have not all been explicitly dropped much more recognition is being given to local conditions. In 1982 the position was made even clearer when DHSS were asked by the House of Commons Social Services Committee whether some indication could be given of the informal minimum personal social services standards which they used (House of Commons Social Services Committee 1982). They replied that they did not have any formalised or precisely quantified minimum standards. However, as has been seen, the SSI have taken a much more forceful role in giving informal advice in the 1990s. The need for standards is increasingly made (e.g. by Age Concern, see Meredith 1994).

The organisation of social services departments

A formidable problem of size was posed when local authority departments were not only amalgamated but took on fresh responsibilities at the time when the new social services departments were created. Many departments attempted to get over the problem of size by creating area teams and patch organisations but some have now reverted to a more centralised system.

Another major change to their working has been the split between purchasing and providing. While some services are still provided by social services departments the 1990 NHS and Community Care Act encouraged provision by the independent sector.

Staff

Numbers of staff in local authority social services departments rose overall 8 per cent between 1985 and 1995 as Table 8.5 shows. Social work staff increased by 55 per cent and domiciliary and day care numbers also went up but those in residential work dropped (Table 8.5). Another change between 1984 and 1994 was the increased percentage of senior directing and professional staff, support and other staff where it rose from 11 per cent to 16 per cent and this was matched by a decline of staff in residential care (for adults from 30 per cent to 24 per cent) (DoH/SSI 1996, Chief Inspector's Report: 96).

Lack of trained staff is a major problem in social services departments. The importance of training for the changes brought about by community care have been shown in some of the SSI reports which show some progress but also the problems, including the low status of training and the lack of commitment from senior managers (DoH/SSI 1993a). Issues which need to be addressed include

Table 8.5 **Comparison of staffing[1] numbers 1985–95 in local authority social services departments England**

	1984	1995	% change
Total staff	217,013	233,862	+8
Social work staff[2]	20,557	31,926	+55
Domiciliary services[3]	54,705	56,961	+4
Day care:			
Children	9,392	8,622	–8
Adults and elderly	15,680	20,407	+30
Mixed client groups[4]	–	2,081	–
Total	25,072	31,109	+24
Residential provision:			
Children	19,852	13,407	–32
Adults and elderly	65,603	54,753	–17
Mixed client groups[4]	–	490	–
Total	85,455	68,651	–20
Occupational therapists	979	1,560	+59

[1] Whole-time equivalent.
[2] Includes team leaders and assistant team leaders, but excludes care managers.
[3] Includes home help/home care organisers and assistant organisers.
[4] Not separately identified in 1984.

Source: Government Statistical Service, DoH Personal Social Services Local Authority Statistics S/F 95/1 *Local Authority Social Services Statistics: Staff of Local Authority Social Services Departments at 30.9.95, England*, DoH, 1996c, Table 7.

assessment and abuse, the needs of older people with dementia, and race and culture (DoH/SSI/NHSE 1994b). In 1988/9 DoH introduced the Training Support Programme specific grant of £7 million for the training of staff working with elderly people and this has now been expanded to cover staff working with all client groups. This sum has risen to £33.35 million in 1994/5 (DoH/SSI, 1995c).

Residential staff, of whom few are trained (see p. 172), face particular problems. The Williams report, *Caring for People: Staffing Residential Homes* commented on the lack of a career structure, the variation in accommodation provided and the need for skills (NCSS 1967). These views were endorsed by the Wagner Committee which particularly stressed the need for training (Wagner 1988a). Demands on residential staff are likely to increase as a higher proportion of residents accepted are very frail and also possibly confused. Three quarters of residential care staff were employed in homes for elderly people in 1994 (Local Government Management Board and Association of Directors of Social Services 1995: 15).

Charges for services

Charges may be made by local authorities for community social services. The current power to make discretionary charges for adult social services was given under the Health and Social Services and Social Security Adjudications Act 1983 (Section 17). Any charges must be 'reasonable' (not defined) and individuals may ask for a reduction or waiver of the charge if they have insufficient means. Once someone has been assessed as needing a service, that service should not be withdrawn even if that person refuses to pay the charge. Details are given in *Charging for Non-Residential Services* (ACE 1995). After the NHS and Community Care Act 1990 it was stated that detailed guidance would follow but an SSI note in 1994 gives only vague comments on the need to set a 'reasonable' charge, the need to provide information and how charges might be monitored (see National Consumer Council (1995) for details).

A national survey in 1994/5 showed a picture of 'sometimes ambiguous guidance at national level and widely variable, often confused and confusing practices at local level' (NCC 1995: 2). Local authorities used different criteria and users lacked information. Similar findings were reported by Baldwin and Lunt (1996). The Audit Commission in 1996 found that most authorities were increasing charges but there were wide variations between them (Audit Commission 1996a). The types of services now being charged for include home help, home care, day centre care, sitting services, transport to and from day centres, meals, adaptations to the home, aids to daily living and orange badges for parking for people with disabilities.

Innovations

As Isaacs has pointed out, an innovation has three components: a good idea, making it work and demonstrating that it works (Isaacs and Evers 1984). In *A Happier Old Age* stress was laid on exploring innovatory methods, especially in providing practical help to meet personal needs (DHSS 1978a). In the 1980s many such schemes did develop and have since been incorporated in mainstream services. They included intensive home care and alarm schemes, the Kent Community Care project and others designed to help carers. A major finding of a national survey on what were then innovatory schemes was that they needed to be provided as part of a package of care which included formal and informal services (Tinker 1984). The lessons of the Kent scheme have been influential in policies to give managers budgets to buy in care. In this scheme community care was targeted on people on the margins of residential care (Challis and Davies 1986). Social workers with small caseloads were given a budget of two thirds the cost of residential care and were able to buy in services. The clients were matched with a control group who received the usual range of services. On various criteria, including cost and quality of life, the elderly people in the scheme were significantly better off.

Innovations may be a completely new service, or one provided at new times, in a new location, by new organisations, catering for new client groups, using different staff or novel in some other way. Innovations need to be evaluated before it is decided whether they should be expanded, abandoned or incorporated into mainstream services. Interest is growing in the process of innovation and in the culture of the organisation to see why some become 'thrusters' and others 'sleepers' (Ferlie *et al*. 1989). The importance of innovations, such as those in home care and in the use of residential homes by people from outside has been stressed (Audit Commission 1994b).

Conclusion

At the end of the 1980s questions were being raised about the future of personal social services if they became enablers and managers (e.g. Allen 1989). Many of these questions remain unanswered on current evidence. Will LA services become residual with all the likely stigma? Has contracting out meant more or less choice? How realistic is the marrying of formal and informal care? It is with this last question that Chapters 10 and 11 are concerned, but before that some groups who may have special needs are discussed in Chapter 9.

Some groups with special needs

There are some groups of older people about whom there is particular concern. These include those people who are disabled, mentally disordered, dying, bereaved, abused and from black and minority ethnic groups.

Older people who are disabled

Definitions

Evidence has already been presented that the incidence of disability increases with age (Chapter 6). Because older people are the largest proportion of physically disabled people, 69 per cent in 1984–6 (Martin *et al.* 1988), it is appropriate to consider any special provision that has been made for this group. Generalisations about disabled people are as dangerous as those about other older people but there is an important distinction between those who become disabled as a result of ageing (disabled older people), and those who were either born with a disability or who acquire it in earlier life (older disabled people) (Zarb and Oliver 1993). A study of the latter group found serious problems related to health, income and lack of services, with feelings of isolation and low levels of satisfaction with the quality of their lives (Zarb and Oliver 1993).

Of course there are other differences too. Older people with impaired hearing or vision may need different services from those in wheelchairs. There are also the distinctions discussed in Chapter 6 between impairment, handicap and disability. Most services are based on the degree of disablement, for example, Disability Living Allowance.

Policies

Disabled people of all ages are increasingly demanding the right to run their own lives with a minimum of interference from others. Many of these arguments are put in *Disabling Barriers – Enabling Environments* (Swain *et al.* 1993). In this book the contributors, many of whom are disabled, argue that disabled people are faced with numerous social, structural and economic barriers which deny them the opportunity of full citizenship and equal opportunities.

The main way in which provision can be made by social services departments is under the Chronically Sick and Disabled Persons Act 1970. This Act extended the powers of local authorities and placed a duty on them to find out the numbers of disabled people in their area, to publicise the services available and, where there was need, provide the services described in the Act. These included practical assistance in the home (including aids such as walking frames), television and radio, help with travel, holidays, meals, telephones and adaptations to the home. The latter is now the main responsibility of housing departments (see Chapter 7). A DHSS circular (12/70) stated that local authorities were to assess need in the light of their resources. Charges could be made for services. 1981 was the International Year of Disabled People. Some have argued that, although attitudes may have been changed, little was achieved in practical terms. Despite attempts in the 1980s to enforce the 1970 Act, provision is patchy. The 1986 Disabled Persons (Services, Consultation and Representation) Act was an attempt to give more power to disabled people. The parts that have been implemented include the duty placed on social services departments to decide about the needs of disabled people for welfare services, the duty when assessing these needs to take into account the carer's ability to continue to care and the duty to give disabled people information about relevant services. The government announced in 1991 that it was not planning to implement the sections giving rights to disabled people to have an advocate, who would have right of access to meetings, or the right of disabled people to make their views known to social services and have account taken of these views. Ministers argued that the NHS and Community Care Act 1990 would enhance the rights of service users in general through community care plans and complaints procedures. Disability groups did not agree but there are now rights to assessment and other changes (see Chapter 8).

In 1994 the government issued a Consultation Paper on *Government Measures to Tackle Discrimination Against Disabled People* (Disability Unit 1994) and the Disability Discrimination Act was passed in 1995. This covered people whose disability had a long-term effect, was substantial and could be physical, mental or sensory. It contained new rights of access to goods, facilities and services, and provisions were to be phased in.

Services

Income: One of the main problems is lack of income which is often due to the inability to work throughout life. Added to this is the likely additional expenditure arising from the disability. One useful source of income for disabled people themselves was the government-funded Independent Living Fund which made cash payments. This operated from 1988–93 and was intended to pay for practical help with everyday personal and domestic tasks. When this ended money was made available to local authorities through their transitional community care grants. Other details of financial provisions were given in Chapter 5. The Community Care (Direct Payments) Act 1996 gives LAs the powers to give disabled people under the age of 65 cash payments to enable them to make their own arrangements for their community care services.

Social services

(See previous section for the 1970 and 1986 Acts.)

Housing: The housing problems of disabled people may differ widely. Early evidence was given in the OPCS study, *Work and Housing of Impaired Persons in Great Britain* (Buckle 1971). The DoE Housing Services Advisory Group's *The Assessment of Housing Requirements* advised that for many disabled people the adaptation of the home in which they live usually provides the quickest, cheapest and best solution (DoE Housing Services Advisory Group 1977, see also Goldsmith 1974, 1975 and Statham *et al.* 1988). That has become more possible with greater powers given to housing departments, especially since the Housing Act 1975, now consolidated into the Housing Act 1985. In a circular published in 1978, *Adaptations of Housing for People who are Physically Handicapped*, housing authorities were asked to take responsibility for structural modifications and social services, under the Chronically Sick and Disabled Persons Act 1970, for non-structural features and aids (DoE Circular 59/78 DHSS LAC(78)14 WO 104/78). New disabled facilities grants were introduced following the joint DoE/DoH circular *House Adaptations for People with Disabilities* (DoE 10/90 and DoH LAC(90)7) and 71 per cent of these are estimated to go to people over the age of 60 (*Hansard* 12.2.1996: column 399). The OPCS disability surveys showed that of all disabled adults 31 per cent of those with a locomotor disability (i.e. problems moving around such as getting up and down stairs) and 38 per cent of those with a personal care disability (such as washing or feeding themselves) had some adaptation to their home (Martin *et al.* 1989: 59). The DoE research showed that almost two fifths (38 per cent) of elderly households have had adaptations made to their homes (McCafferty 1994). All the research on adaptations shows the crucial role, and shortage, of occupational therapists. Research on users shows the very variable provision by LAs and that adaptations do not diminish the need for appropriate home care (Heywood 1994). What would be helpful would be if all homes were built to a standard accessible to people of all ages and disabilities (Bonnett 1996).

Mentally disordered older people

Definitions

One of the most difficult situations facing families and professionals alike is in caring well for a mentally disordered older person. The term 'mentally disordered' is usually taken to cover both people who are mentally ill and those who are mentally handicapped (now usually referred to as having learning difficulties or disabilities).

The World Health Organisation has suggested a broad definition of mental illness which covers all forms of illness in which psychological, emotional or behavioural disturbances are the predominating features. The DHSS distinguished three main groups among elderly people with mental illness symptoms to whom the term 'psychogeriatric' is often loosely applied (DHSS Circular HM (72)71 *Services for Mental Illness Related to Old Age*, Oct. 1974). These are patients who entered hospitals for the mentally ill before modern methods of treatment were available and have grown old in them, older patients with functional mental illness and older people with dementia. It is dementia, however, which dominates old age psychiatry. Dementia involves the irreversible degeneration of brain tissue and resultant loss of intellectual function. There are two main types – cerebrovascular (or multi-infarct dementia) which is progressive brain damage often resulting from something like a mini-stroke, and neurodegenerative dementia. The best known example of the latter is Alzheimer's disease. Some of the symptoms of dementia are associated with other problems. For example confusion may be the result of dehydration, adverse drug reactions or a chest infection.

Depression: This is another state which needs careful investigation to find out the causes which may or may not be due to physical causes. Murphy concludes that adverse life events, lifelong personality traits, and lack of self-esteem may also play a role but the relationship between social factors and genetic and biological ones needs further exploration (Murphy 1986).

Mental handicap: For people with mental handicap, now usually referred to as people with learning difficulties or disabilities, a definition is: 'those whose intelligence in relation to their age is so far below average that they are incapable of assuming the kind of responsibilities accepted as normal' (Clegg 1971).

Numbers

It is difficult to estimate the number of older people who are mentally ill, but 34 per cent of admissions to mental hospitals and units in England in 1986 were of people aged 65 and over (Taylor and Taylor

1989: 15). The OPCS disability surveys showed that the prevalence of problems with intellectual functioning in Great Britain in 1985–8 was 40 per thousand for people aged 60–74 and 152 for those aged 75 and over, compared with 20 for those aged 16–59 (Martin *et al.* 1988: 26). The prevalence of dementia increases with age. A rate of four to five per cent of people aged 65 and over is estimated (Taylor and Taylor 1989: 13) and 20 per cent for people over the age of 85 (Lindesay 1996). About half a million people suffer from dementia in the United Kingdom but the growth in the population aged 80 and over could increase this by 20 per cent in the early years of the next century (Taylor and Taylor 1989: 11).

There is little evidence that older people are *per se* more vulnerable to depression than younger adults. Extreme depression may lead to suicide. Death rates from suicide increase with age but not so steeply as rates for other causes of death (Bulusu and Alderson 1984). For females, the rates fall after the age of 70 but rates rise slightly for males. Since 1960 the suicide rate among the older population, particularly men, has dropped dramatically while the rate for men below the age of 45 has risen (MRC 1995: 9). Numbers of suicides of people with learning difficulties are difficult to estimate.

Policies

The DoH have long expected that the number of older people suffering from mental disorder will grow (DHSS 1978a). In the past the care of mentally disordered people has been mainly by the family and in institutions, often isolated from society. In the 1950s, however, a number of factors combined to emphasise the trend away from hospitals and towards community care. There was dissatisfaction in many quarters about the effects of institutional care. There were also major developments in drug treatment, allowing symptoms of mentally ill patients to be controlled so that their behaviour became less disturbing. The aim of the Mental Health Act 1959 was to establish a comprehensive community care service for mentally ill people who did not need hospital treatment.

In 1971 *Better Services for the Mentally Handicapped* (DHSS 1971) explained why services needed to be extended and improved. It showed that there had been a large growth in numbers of older people in hospitals, but also that considerable numbers had been discharged: 'Many of these probably required residential rather than hospital care'.

In 1972 the DHSS, in a circular, *Services for Mental Illness Related to Old Age*, (DHSS HM (72) 71) stressed the importance of assessment, defined the groups involved and examined their needs in turn. It advised that those needing hospital treatment were best treated in the psychiatric departments of district general hospitals. For the rest the emphasis was on rehabilitation with the use of day hospitals and, where necessary, residential care. The importance of co-ordination and joint planning with local authorities was stressed. The eventual closure of hospitals for mentally ill people was envisaged.

In 1975 the White Paper *Better Services for the Mentally Ill* (DHSS 1975) recognised that adequate support facilities in the community had not generally become available owing to the limits on resources and increasing and competing demands for new developments. In 1978 *A Happier Old Age* acknowledged that places in some large mental hospitals were being reduced ahead of alternative provision in local hospitals (DHSS 1978a) and a DHSS National Development Group gave advice [Document 28]. In 1981 *Care in the Community* gave estimates of how many mentally ill and handicapped people could be returned to the community if services were available (DHSS 1981c). In 1982 the Mental Health (Amendment) Act expanded the range and degree of safeguards for patients and set up the Mental Health Commission as a watchdog on the new legislation.

The Rising Tide in 1982 was an aptly named report by the NHS Health Advisory Service (HAS) which claimed that rising numbers and increased expectations meant that 'the flood is likely to overwhelm the entire health system' (HAS 1982: 1). Particular emphasis was given to stressing that the problem was not just one for specialist psychiatric services. The difficulties of people attempting to care for older people at home, in private nursing homes or residential homes were acknowledged. The report called for extra resources and in 1983 an extra £6 million was given by the government to finance 30 demonstration projects in the community which were assessed as successful (Cambridge and Knapp 1988).

The emphasis on community care was endorsed in the Short report *Community Care*, which called for a wide variety of facilities in the community and stressed that none of this would be cheap (House of Commons Social Services Committee 1985). A further influential document was the Audit Commission's *Making a Reality of Community Care* (Audit Commission 1986). The House of Commons Social Services Committee advocated a range of policy changes in *Community Care: Services for People with a Mental Handicap and People with a Mental Illness* (House of Commons Social Services Committee 1990b). These included the need for some form of 'asylum' service provision, adequate financial provision for community care to be transferred to local authorities from the Social Security budget and the need to monitor the community care programme. The philosophy behind the NHS and Community Care Act 1990 was to enable vulnerable people to live in the community or homely surroundings. It introduced a specific grant to local authorities for the development of social care services for people with a mental illness.

The Care Programme Approach, introduced in 1991, involves a single plan being worked out for the individual which all the relevant services agree on (DoH Joint Health/Social Services Circular, *The Care Programme Approach*, HC(90)23/LASS (90)11, September 1990) and it is supported by the Mental Illness Specific Grant mentioned above.

In DoH's *Health of the Nation* (see Chapter 6) the section on mental health stated that there was 'a firm commitment that Ministers will not approve any hospital closures until they are satisfied that adequate alternatives have been developed' (DoH 1991a: 86). In the *Health of the Nation* initiative, mental illness was one of the five areas where attention was to be focused (DoH 1993e, Key Area Handbook). What was emphasised for older people was continuing and terminal care for those with dementia with respite care and practical support for carers. In 1993 DoH set up the Mental Health Task Force to help ensure 'the substantial completion of the transfer of services away from large hospitals to a balanced range of locally based services, including community-based beds' (DoH 1993a: 82). A useful critical report of services was produced by the House of Commons Health Committee in 1994. This was *Better Off in the Community? The Care of People who are Seriously Mentally Ill* (House of Commons Health Committee 1994). In 1994 the Audit Commission in *Finding a Place: A Review of Mental Health Services for Adults* critically reviewed mental health services for adults but excluded services for older people with dementia (Audit Commission 1994a). They argued that hospital care should be reserved for those with the most serious problems. They showed that the number of hospital beds has declined markedly since the 1950s and so had the length of stay in hospital, but also that most NHS expenditure on mental health services was still on inpatient care, that is, in 1992/3 66 per cent went on inpatient care, 24 per cent on day hospital and community services, and 10 per cent on social services (Audit Commission 1994a: 6–7).

In 1995 the Law Commission produced a report, *Mental Incapacity*, which suggested that a major overhaul is needed of the law (Law Commission 1995). Particular areas where they felt there was need for reform were over substitute (when the mentally incapacitated person cannot make a decision), decision making and the protection of vulnerable people from harm.

A more extensive account of the development of services can be found in Tinker (Norman and Redfern (eds) 1997).

Services

Health: The effect of changes in policy can be demonstrated by the fact that at the end of the 1950s about 40 per cent of NHS hospital beds were occupied by people suffering from mental illness. In 1986 the figure was 20 per cent (Taylor and Taylor 1989: 14–15). There has been a decline in the number of large psychiatric hospitals – from

130 in 1960 to 89 in 1993 – with more planned to close (House of Commons Health Committee 1994: *v*). The number of beds for mentally ill people in England has declined from 149,000 in 1955 to 50,278 in 1991–2 (House of Commons Health Committee, 1994: *v*). However, while long-term places for elderly people with mental health problems have declined in the NHS hospital sector, they have risen overall due to an increase in private and voluntary provision in nursing homes (as well as hospitals and clinics) (Table 9.1).

Mental illness outpatient attendances on the other hand have risen by 50 per cent in the last decade and there has been a significant rise in short-stay admissions and in numbers of consultants and nurses in the field of psychiatry (Taylor and Taylor 1989: 15). One of the most encouraging developments in the care of older people is the development of old age psychiatry. The case for a comprehensive psychogeriatric service geared to the needs of older people and their carers has been forcibly put (Royal College of Physicians and Royal College of Psychiatrists 1989). This has been matched by a growth of academic interest in the subject including the value of a multidisciplinary approach (e.g. Arie 1985, 1988, 1992, Jacoby and Oppenheimer 1991, Burns 1993). Key elements in the service are that it is multidisciplinary, and for those who need it there is inpatient assessment and treatment, day and respite care, rehabilitation and long-term care (Lindesay 1996). Equally encouraging is the growing interest expressed by nurses in this field (e.g. Norman and Redfern 1997).

Much that has been written about mental disorder in old age has focused on dementia. Bergmann and Jacoby say that until scientific research provides a means of altering the prognosis of dementia fundamentally, the main focus has to be on maintaining the autonomy and viability of the older person for as long as possible (Bergmann and Jacoby 1983). In the absence of the family, or when it collapses, homelike institutional settings in the community can substitute. Arie has argued that there are some patients, and he includes some with dementia, for whom institutional care is the only humane and proper answer (Arie 1986).

Social services: The last few years have seen a mushrooming of developments by social services departments and voluntary bodies. Particularly interesting have been innovatory projects (e.g. Hunter *et al*. 1987, Osborn 1988, Morton 1989a, Askham and Thompson 1990). They stress the importance of treating people as individuals with the same rights as other citizens. These include rights to dignity, choice, respect, being treated as an adult, participation and high professional quality services. A survey of elderly people with dementia found that there were three main areas of need:

• help with everyday tasks (or, in more severe cases, performance of those tasks for the sufferer);

Table 9.1 Long-term care places for elderly people with mental health problems England

Year	Private/voluntary nursing homes, hospital and clinics	NHS beds, mental health, elderly	Local authority Part III residential homes	Voluntary sector residential homes	Private sector residential homes	Total all sectors
1988	2,300	26,500	3,012	574	3,836	36,222
1991	7,600	22,500	3,238	445	4,417	38,200
1994	16,300	18,200	2,943	723	5,629	43,795

Source: House of Commons Health Committee Long Term Care: NHS Responsibilities for Meeting Community Health Care Needs, Vol. 1, HMSO, 1995 p. x.

- supervision, to ensure their own and other people's safety;
- social contact, support and reassurance.

The authors concluded that: 'From the sufferer's point of view, all three would, ideally, be fulfilled by the care of one person (preferably a familiar, loved person) for 24 hours a day' (National Consumer Council 1990). The most important issue which they and other researchers have identified is how to support the carer. Work done by Levin and others has shown that there is a heavy burden upon families supporting demented elderly people at home (Levin *et al.* 1989, Askham and Thompson 1990). Over one third of the supporters in the Levin study were so stressed as probably to be in need of psychiatric help themselves. The particular gaps in provision for carers appear to be early diagnosis; information and advice, especially at the early stages; counselling; a sitting service; information about possible residential care (for long-term planning); and a prompt reliable transport service for those needing day care (NCC 1990: 29). (See Chapter 8 for residential care.)

The reviews of the Mental Illness Specific Grant found that it supported 'many innovative projects which were contributing significantly to the provision of community care for people with severe mental illness' (DoH/SSI 1995a : 8)

Housing: Most older people with dementia live in their own homes but, for those who cannot, very sheltered housing may be a sensible solution (Tinker 1989b).

Dying older people

Numbers

Over half a million people die in Great Britain each year and a high proportion are in the upper age ranges. Nearly one quarter of those who die do so in their own homes, and many of those who die elsewhere may have spent many months seriously ill at home before going to hospital (Thorpe 1993). Dying at home has, however, become less common and the rise has been in people dying in residential and nursing homes although over half of deaths still occur in hospital.

Problems

The care of dying people is a major social challenge, not only for those faced with death but for those who attempt to provide support and help. Until recently there was little in medical or social work education about the care of the dying, nor was there much public concern. Now the subject is more openly discussed (e.g. Dickenson and Johnson 1993). A pioneering study enunciated the likely responses from someone who is dying as denial, anger, bargaining, depression and acceptance (Kubler-Ross 1970). Another study is Hinton's book *Dying* (Hinton 1972). Hodkinson points out that the attitudes towards death of staff, patients and the community at large have a considerable bearing on terminal care: 'Thus doctors and nurses are at risk of being so geared to the philosophy of cure that death is regarded as a humiliating failure' (Hodkinson 1975: 61).

Services

In *Life Before Death* the last 12 months in the lives of 785 adults is described (Cartwright *et al*. 1973). This study shows that relatives often struggle on with inadequate help from the professionals and community services. The message is for more and better co-ordinated services (see also Gilmore and Gilmore 1988). One of the authors of *Life Before Death* undertook another one, *The Year Before Death* (Seale and Cartwright 1994), which concluded that services were still far from good and that one fifth (the figure was higher for carers of old people) of the carers involved thought that it would have been better if the person who had died had done so earlier. To enable dying people to remain at home they need:

- adequate nursing care;
- a night sitting service;
- good symptom control;
- confident and committed GPs;
- access to specialist palliative care;
- effective co-ordination of care;
- financial support;
- terminal care education (Thorpe 1993).

One of the pioneers in this country in care of the dying is Dr Cicely Saunders. Her approach, outlined in *The Management of Terminal Disease*, is based on the control of pain, allaying the fear of a painful death, and a positive and caring approach to patients who are encouraged to feel that their lives are still worth living (Saunders 1978). The hospice movement has grown rapidly in the last decade and some of the issues were outlined in *The Hospice Movement in Britain* (Taylor 1983) with later research evidence presented by Seale (Seale 1989). Many people seem to equate 'terminally ill' and hospices with people in the final stages of cancer. Less attention seems to be paid to the needs of people dying from other causes. The NHS is paying more attention to terminal (palliative) care and in 1987 issued guidance (Circular (HC) 87/4 *Terminal Care*) and requested health authorities to undertake joint planning with the voluntary sector. The National Association of Health Authorities

(NAHA) also produced guidance in *Care of the Dying: A Guide for Health Authorities* (King Edward's Hospital Fund and NAHA 1987).

The National Council for Hospice and Specialist Palliative Care Services have produced useful reports on such topics as ethical issues and contracts with the NHS. There has been a phenomenal growth in the provision of palliative care ('the active total care of patients whose disease no longer responds to curative treatment' Gaffin 1996: 221) since 1980. The number of NHS patient units rose from 59 to 121, the total number of beds doubled and home care teams increased from 32 to 261 (DoH 1990b). There are now over 3,000 inpatient hospice/specialist palliative care beds in the UK and five out of six are in the voluntary sector (Gaffin 1996). There are also well over 200 day hospices and 400 home care nursing teams (Gaffin 1996).

Living wills, advance directives and euthanasia

Another aspect of dying concerns the use of life-sustaining treatment for patients who are no longer able to consent to, or refuse, medical therapy. *The Living Will* is the report of a Working Party on the current legal and medical practice (Kennedy *et al.* 1988). It examines the potential for competent individuals to make certain stipulations about their future health care. The report highlights the range of options available and calls for changes in current practice so that advance directives can be made for those who wish to use them (see also The Law Commission 1995 and *EAGLE* – the journal of the Exchange on Ageing, Law and Ethics, Feb/March 1995).

The growing technological ability to 'save' life or to intervene also raises questions about euthanasia and the quality of life. The UK contribution to the World Assembly on Ageing stated: 'There is a small body of opinion which believes that euthanasia should be legalised. Most people believe that legalised euthanasia could expose very vulnerable people to undesirable pressures, and would not wish to see it made possible. The Government considers euthanasia unacceptable, and is firmly opposed to changing the law to allow it' (DHSS 1982a: 11). Cartwright suggests that 'as the pressure for patient control increases and is accepted it seems likely that interventions related to the end of life will rise' (Cartwright 1996: 413).

Bereaved older people

To bereave is defined as 'to rob of'. Older people are more likely than other age groups to be robbed of the life of someone close to them. Those who lose a partner or who see their contemporaries dying may feel grief, shock, anger and bitterness. In 1994 49 per cent of women over the age of 65 were widows in Great Britain, whereas only 20 per cent of men over 65 were widowers (OPCS 1996: 152). The gender differences for the over-85s are even more pronounced. Whereas only 47 per cent of men of this age were widowers, 75 per cent of women were.

The importance of understanding mourning and the need for skilled professional help is underlined by Parkes in his book *Bereavement* (1975) and by Pincus in *Death and the Family* (1974). A comprehensive book on the subject is *The Anatomy of Bereavement* by Raphael (1984). Older people may need counselling to face their own and others' dying, as do their families. It is also helpful to understand the ways in which death and bereavement are treated in different cultures, as Neuberger has demonstrated in *Caring for Dying People of Different Faiths* (Neuberger 1987). A new issue is that of older people who are carers of people with HIV and AIDS (Stewart and Askham 1995). In *Bereavement and Grief: Supporting Older People Through Loss*, the author extends the definition of bereavement to include other losses in old age such as health, independence and social status (Scrutton 1995).

Elder abuse

A group who have received increasing attention are older people who are subject to abuse. Once called 'granny battering', the term 'elder abuse' is now usually used. It took its place in the matters of concern taken up by journals, and then by the wider media, in the 1980s. Non-accidental injury to children has long been a subject researched and written about, but the identification of older people as victims of abuse is relatively new. A survey of the literature until 1990 concluded that, despite concern expressed in this country over a period of almost 15 years, almost no systematic or reliable research has been carried out, in contrast to North America (McCreadie 1991). There is still little empirical research in the UK but more is taking place (see McCreadie 1996, for an updated extensive review of the literature; see also Pritchard 1992, Decalmer and Glendenning 1993). There is no standard definition but abuse is generally distinguished by type: physical, psychological, sexual, neglect and financial. The only study of prevalence is by Ogg and Bennett who used the OPCS Omnibus Survey in 1992. They found that of the 593 people aged 65 and over 5 per cent reported that they had been verbally abused by a relative, 2 per cent reported physical abuse and 2 per cent financial abuse (quoted in Bennett and Kingston 1993: 148).

Abuse is increasingly being seen in the context of the wider picture of family violence in this country (e.g. Kingston and Penhale 1995) and in Europe (Council of Europe Study Group on Violence against Elderly People 1993). Research is also moving from studies of the abused person to the abuser and from the simplistic view that abuse is largely a result of caregiver stress (see McCreadie 1996, Bennett and Kingston 1993).

Abuse in residential or other communal settings is seriously underresearched (Eastman 1994, McCreadie 1996). The front line provision for its prevention are the registration and inspection powers of LAs and Health Authorities. Their capacity to do their job effectively depends significantly on the resources available to them (McCreadie 1996).

More attention is being paid to advice to professionals. DoH have taken a lead (DoH/SSI 1992a, 1993b, 1994a) and increasingly LAs and Health Authorities are developing policies (Action on Elder Abuse 1995). There has also been a substantial growth in training packages.

There are concerns that, with the increasing numbers of older people, particularly women, who are mentally frail there is increasing vulnerability to financial abuse (Langan and Means 1995) and this relates also to issues of financial assessment and charging for both community and residential care.

The legal options available in relation to abuse are considerable although some, particularly in relation to incapacity and public law protection of vulnerable adults, are unsatisfactory (Law Commission 1995). The key statutes for the prevention of elder abuse in the domestic setting are Section 47 of the NHS and Community Care Act 1990 and the scope for carer assessments under the new Carers (Recognition and Services) Act 1995 (see Chapter 10).

Action on Elder Abuse was formed in 1993 to promote changes in policy and practice and it runs a national information and enquiry service.

Older people from black and minority ethnic groups

Numbers and needs

The projected increase in numbers of older people from black and minority ethnic groups has implications for services. Although it was seen in Chapter 2 that numbers of people in this group are small, they are expected to grow as the present generation of middle-aged people reach old age. As with any group, there are dangers in generalising. While most studies concentrate on black elders and those from the Indian sub-continent, there is also need to consider other groups such as the Chinese who, because of their ethnic origin, language, cultural or religious differences share a common experience (J. Williams 1990, National Association of Health Authorities 1988). Barker's account of the different groups of people who came to this country from the Caribbean and South Asia is revealing (Barker 1983) (Figure 9.1). Not only have people come for different reasons and from different parts of the world, but their experiences here vary too.

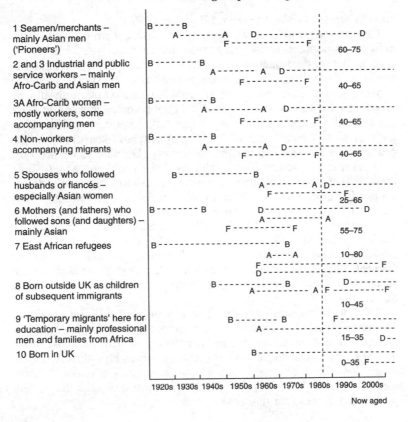

KEY
B = Birth date
A = Date of arrival in UK
F = Date of reaching age of 55
D = Death date

Figure 9.1 Ageing cohorts of black and Asian-origin people in Britain: a study of people aged 55 and over from the Caribbean and South Asia in 1982
Source: Barker, J., *Black and Asian Older People in Britain*, Age Concern England, 1984, Figure 1, p. 19.

Many of these differences for people of working age will have an effect on them when they are older. For example Pakistani and Bangladeshi women are less likely to be in paid (full and part-time) employment than white women (18 per cent of those of working age compared with 67 per cent of white women in 1994 – CSO 1996: 83). Black ethnic minority groups are less likely to be owner-occupiers (in 1992–4 40 per cent compared with 67 per cent of white households and 84 per cent of Indian households – CSO 1996: 184). The need to consider both diversity and differences between cohorts must be stressed (Blakemore and Boneham 1994).

Cultural or religious customs may be different from those of the indigenous population and may mean that there are particular needs such as dietary ones or support in certain circumstances. For example meals need to reflect these differences and so does design in sheltered housing where different forms of cooking and worship should be taken into account. Assumptions should not be made that services are not needed. For example the myth that 'ethnic minorities look after their own' can result in a lack of awareness and sensitivity in the provision of services to a multiracial society (DHSS/SSI 1988b: 1).

A number of studies have highlighted the problems which some members of ethnic minority groups face. Alison Norman's *Triple Jeopardy: Growing Old in a Second Homeland* (Norman 1985) paints a vivid picture of some of these problems, as have other researchers (e.g. CPA 1982, Bhalla and Blakemore 1981, Barker 1983, Blakemore 1985, Donaldson 1986, Fennell *et al.* 1988, Blakemore and Boneham 1994). These include language difficulties, negative attitudes, isolation, a marked underuse of some mainstream services, a lack of knowledge of services and insensitivity in how these services are provided.

The specific health problems of this group are difficult to assess. For the population as a whole DoH point out in their Strategy that for all their five Key Areas of concern: 'Rates of ill-health and death amongst the black and ethnic minority groups show differences to those for the white population and between individual ethnic minority groups' (DoH 1992a: 120). Ebrahim indicates that health problems fall into four main categories:

- influences of the old country (e.g. tuberculosis);
- influences of the new country (e.g. some such as asthma and stroke appear to be associated with changes in the way of life, especially the move from rural to urban);
- selection of who migrates (the theory that the process of migration requires fitness);
- the process of migration and adaptation (the theory that 'the multitude of non-specific symptoms that many migrants present to their doctors is almost certainly a reflection of the process of adaptation to the uncertainties and pressures of a new life that is complicated by prejudice and racism' – Ebrahim 1996: 206).

Services

Health and social services: Levels of access to services are lower in general for social services but higher for some health services such as consulting the GP. Research is beginning to uncover ways in which health and social services are planning to meet the health and social care needs of this group. One helpful study looks at specialists in health care professions, such as social workers, speech therapists and dieticians, and identifies specific issues and then considers how services can be planned. The recommendations include the need to plan services based on a population profile, involving older people themselves, realising that information and communication is essential, stressing the need for education for professionals and for research (Squires 1991). Research on primary health care for elderly people from black and minority ethnic groups was based on a survey of Family Health Service Authorities and GPs and interviews with members of primary health care teams (Pharoah 1995). Among the findings were:

- high GP consultation rates but not attributed to greater health problems;
- low uptake of community health services;
- the need for interpreting (usually performed by the patient's family);
- the need for staff to help with health promotion and education;
- the need for women doctors for older women patients;
- little liaison with other services;
- the need for training and education for health staff.

In the area of social services, the research reports a number of innovations in provision but these often face major problems including those of funding (Bowling 1990). Monitoring of services can help to show if there is discrimination, and the employment of staff from ethic minority groups is important.

Housing: Little attention has been paid to the housing conditions of black and minority ethnic elderly people but they now form a growing group. What evidence there is shows that not only are there differences between groups but also between men and women (Molnar and Davies 1993). Research also confirms that some live isolated and often unhappy lives in inappropriate accommodation and circumstances. A Working Party concluded that common assumptions regarding the ability of families to care for their elders, and the accepted policy of integration, combine with racial disadvantage and discrimination to deny an appropriate response from housing and care providers (ACE and Help the Aged Housing Trust 1984). A subsequent Working Party suggested that there should be more assessment of needs, including measuring whether there is underrepresentation in all forms of housing (Jeffery and Seager 1993). It was also recommended that there should be separate provision where there was local need, greater links with the community, more information to get better take-up of services, the monitoring of provision, employment of ethnic minority staff where possible and training for all staff. In one of the few pieces of research on housing for this group (albeit only on sheltered housing and only by housing associations), the complexity of need was outlined and the fact that, as with other groups, a range of housing is needed including sheltered housing that is specific for that group and that is mixed (Jones 1994). There has been a significant development of specialist sheltered housing by the black HA movement and one or two very sheltered schemes.

Separate provision?: One of the central issues is provision of, and need for, mainstream, specific or separate services and the advantages and difficulties surrounding each of these three different forms of care (J. Williams 1990). This was one of the issues addressed by a study of health and social services (Askham, Henshaw and Tarpey 1995) that covered District Health Authorities, social services departments and the views of a sample of middle-aged and older people from Asian and Caribbean groups. The different kinds of provision were defined as:

- mainstream – services are available equally to all ethnic groups, but without any recognition of special or specified needs on grounds of race or culture;
- specific – specific attention is paid to the needs of black and minority ethnic elders within a service available to all (e.g. special meals within a hospital's catering service);
- separate – black and minority ethnic elders receive a separate service (e.g. a day centre specially for that group) (Askham, Henshaw and Tarpey 1995: 4).

The main conclusion of this study was that there should be continued development of specific services and facilities within mainstream provision. Separation was not the preferred option of elderly people themselves. Detailed information is given on various services. More generally it was found that there was great variation between authorities, provision of services was patchy, the existence of completely separate services was low, special facilities within mainstream were more widespread and take-up of most social services was poor. However, as has been seen, some do prefer separate provision such as sheltered housing.

The discussion should not be all about problems, for there needs to be an appreciation of the contribution which black and minority ethnic groups bring to a multiracial society and their views on policies (Standing Conference of Ethnic Minority Citizens 1986).

CHAPTER 10

Community care – the family

Introduction

When planning the provision of any service three fundamental questions have to be asked. What is the need? How is it to be met? Who is to provide?

The first and second questions were discussed in Chapters 5–9, which dealt with particular needs and services, and a wider examination of need is to be found in Chapter 13. Chapters 5–9 paid special attention to developments in the statutory services. But there are other sources of help which are both more numerous and of longer standing. They are: first, the family; second, the community, expressed through voluntary organisations, volunteers and the wider network of neighbours and friends; and third, older people themselves. These three will be examined in this and the next two chapters.

It is proposed to look first at the rise of the Welfare State in relation to the family (in particular the extended family and the three-generation household). Then some factors which are changing the pattern of family care will be discussed. Recent policy developments will be described. Evidence will then be presented about the degree of contact older people have with relatives and the extent of care by families. Finally, questions will be asked about support for families in their caring role.

The rise of the Welfare State in relation to the family

Before examining the part that families play in providing help for older people, some consideration must be given to the debate about the rise of the Welfare State and the alleged consequent decline of the family as a caring group.

If it is argued that the Welfare State is a 'state which has a policy of collective responsibility for the individual's well-being' (Clegg 1971) with social services provided on behalf of society then, some have argued, the state must have taken over at least part of the role of the family. This issue was being debated in the 1960s and 1970s. For example Fletcher, while not holding this view himself, reported that some believe that: 'since much is now publicly provided for old people ... responsibility on the part of their families for the care of the aged has fallen away' (Fletcher 1966: 160). Wright and Randall summarised the position of the family in pre-industrial England and gave some reasons why the state had taken over some (but not all) of the functions of the family (Wright and Randall 1970). But after weighing the evidence they concluded that, in spite of all the forecasts about its imminent dissolution, family care continues.

The conclusion of an extensive examination of the family and the state by Moroney was that: 'on balance, the evidence does not support the view that the modern family is giving up its caring function, or transferring its traditional responsibilities to the state' (Moroney 1976). This view is supported by studies in the 1980 and 1990s. For example Qureshi and Walker, in their study in Sheffield, said that they had found that family care is 'alive and well' (Qureshi and Walker 1989: 244). This finding is echoed by other studies. In *Family Obligations and Social Change*, Finch said: 'If anything it has been the state's assuming some responsibility for individuals – such as the granting of old age pensions – which has freed people to develop closer and more supportive relationships with their kin' (Finch 1989: 243) [Document 29]. Later studies have also shown the extent of family care, as will be shown later in the chapter. The view that family support to older people has been jeopardised by demographic trends, geographic mobility and socio-cultural change is refuted by Bengtson *et al.* in an extensive review of the literature (1990).

The difficulty in trying to make comparisons with the past lies in the lack of available data. Great care must be exercised in drawing conclusions when the picture of past conditions is so fragmentary. Finch says: 'If we take a fairly long historical perspective, we can see that people in the present are not necessarily any more or less willing to support their relatives than in the past; but the circumstances under which they have to work out these commitments themselves have changed and created new problems to be solved' (Finch 1989: 242). Most of such evidence as there is about family care of older people is set in the context of two separate situations: the extended family and the three-generation household.

The extended family and the three-generation household

The extended family

The extended family is not easy to define. Stacey attempts this definition: 'The extended family has generally been used for a persistent group of relatives, wider than the elementary family. Empirical evidence suggests that the numbers and categories of kin included in such social groups are highly variable. It is not therefore susceptible of precise definition' (Stacey 1969: 36). Many studies have stressed the importance of the extended family in exercising a mutual caring role (see pp. 201–2). The importance of this network of kinship relations, which extends beyond the immediate household, is also a feature in the USA and elsewhere (Bengtson *et al.* 1990).

The three-generation household

Much discussion has centred on the living arrangements of families, and it is often assumed that the common pattern used to be one of three generations living together as one household. The further assumption is then made that if people live under the same roof they will care for one another. Whether many families did live like this is uncertain. There certainly have been many statements made that the three-generation household was fairly common. For example Cullingworth stated: 'The increasing break-up of three-generation households into two separate units . . . involves the provision of two or even three dwellings for every one that would have been required 50 years ago' (Cullingworth 1960). Beyer and Nierstrasz likewise talk about 'the days when the three-generation household was the norm' (Beyer and Nierstrasz 1967: 11).

But research in the late 1960s and early 1970s casts doubts on whether the three-generation household ever existed widely in England and Wales, although there is no doubt that the size of households has declined. Hole and Pountney in *Trends in Population, Housing and Occupancy Rates 1861–1961*, suggest that the larger households in Victorian times were due partly to a large number of children and partly to apprentices, domestic servants and lodgers. They say: 'Considerable doubt has been thrown on the popular conception of the Victorian household . . . it seems that a household consisting only of parents and children was as typical then as it is today' (Hole and Pountney 1971: 27). The size of households has declined. In GB in 1961 11 per cent of all households (4 per cent of whom were under pensionable age and 7 per cent over) were one person and in 1994/5 one-person households had risen to 27 per cent (12 per cent under and 15 per cent over pensionable age) (CSO 1996: 51).

Laslett also concludes that the nuclear family was the normal arrangement even before industrialisation (Laslett 1989). He points out how few people survived to old age anyway, making the three-generation household a physical impossibility in most cases. His explanation of the myth of this type of household is that it was probably due to a cherished mythology and a wish to believe in the large and extended household.

There has undoubtedly been some decline in co-residence between older people and their children in the UK and in most OECD countries (Sundström 1994). In 1994 5 per cent (8 per cent in 1980) of people over the age of 65 in GB lived with a son or daughter

(OPCS 1996: 153, OPCS 1994a: 12). But whereas only 2 per cent of men were in this position, 7 per cent of women were. The extent of this co-residence increases with age and 9 per cent of the over-85s lived with sons or daughters.

The desirability of close links and changing factors

Two important issues about family care are the desirability of close links and whether this situation is likely to continue.

The desirability of close links

Little is known about standards of care by families. A number of studies hint at the tensions when families and older people live under one roof (e.g. Willmott and Young 1960, Brandon 1972, Pruner 1974, Lewis and Meredith 1988, summaries of research in Twigg and Atkin 1994). There is also the point that: 'Close kinship relationships have their value but they can also be limiting, confining, frustrating, so that the loosening of these ties, for some people at any rate, may constitute a desirable improvement' (Fletcher 1966: 171). A study of 684 older people in Wales found that 133 (19 per cent) lived with their younger relatives (Wenger 1984). Among this group loneliness was more common than among other sub-groups (Wenger 1984: 190). It is interesting that in Europe the proportion of those who often felt lonely was highest in countries where there are higher rates of co-residence (e.g. Greece 36 per cent often felt lonely) compared with those with low rates (e.g. Denmark less than 5 per cent) (Walker 1993: 11). Older people living with their families may be subject to abuse (McCreadie 1996). Ungerson's qualitative study of 19 carers concluded that married women carers found care in the extended family was potentially destructive of the nuclear family of which they were a part (Ungerson 1987). Older people living with their relatives may also find themselves less likely to get help from statutory services (Charlesworth *et al.* 1984, Levin *et al.* 1989, Evandrou 1987, Jarvis *et al.* 1996). Nor should it be forgotten, as Askham points out, that not everyone may be able to provide care for many reasons including lack of strength or knowledge (Askham 1989: 112).

Of prime importance are the preferences of older people. In a national survey of 764 people over the age of 55 on Attitudes to Ageing respondents were asked 'if you need extra help, to whom, if anyone, do you turn' (Midwinter 1991: Statistical Appendix, Table 33). While 50 per cent said that they did not need to turn to anyone the next largest group (32 per cent) said that they would turn to family. However, any discussion about preferences should be set in the complex picture of family responsibilities which go way beyond a simple concept of obligation (Finch and Mason 1993). What seems to be happening is greater stress on the independence of older people, as happened earlier with disabled people. In *Paying for Care: Lessons from Europe*, evidence is given that 'disabled people with care needs are increasingly arguing for the right not to be dependent on the good graces of family members for their ability to carry out activities of daily living' (Glendinning and McLaughlin 1993: 9). As Twigg and Atkin put it, 'People with disabilities should be able to make and have personal and family relationships, but these should not become the basis for caring. The recent emphasis on the needs of carers, in this view, diverts attention and resources from what is the real issue, that of the support of disabled people' (Twigg and Atkin 1994: 6). There is some evidence that there is a growing preference in some countries for public services compared with those provided by the family (Daatland 1990). This is often preceded by provision of such services as home care (Sundström 1994).

Turning specifically to living with their families, the limited research in Northern Europe (summarised in Salvage 1995) indicates that older people do not, in general, want this. Arber and Ginn found that the least preferred option for older people was care given by a married child in the caregiver's home (Arber and Ginn 1991).

Changing factors

The second issue is whether family links are likely to continue. Pessimists point to the reduction in the size of families, which will mean that older people will have fewer children to turn to; the non-availability of the family when everyone is out of the house all day at school or work; the growing complexity of family life; the emergence of the four-generation family and their mobility. Yet a closer examination of all these factors shows that the position is not as bleak as might be supposed and that there are other factors emerging that potentially may lead to more help being available.

Taking first the reduction in family size in GB, the most striking point is that from the 1870s 'average family size had declined from five or six children to today's two child family within 60 years' (Coleman and Salt 1992: 61). Since then the numbers have altered little and are now well below two. This shows that smaller families are not a new phenomenon but have been in evidence since around the beginning of the century.

What is more significant is that today more children survive. A mother having seven children in 1860 would not expect that number to be still alive when she was old. There has been a remarkable decline in the infant mortality rate. This is most pronounced for infants under one year, but still appreciable for all ages of childhood. It is now the exception rather than the rule for a mother not to have her children survive to adult life. Expectation of life at birth has increased dramatically, as was seen in Chapter 2. This means that there will be more people in middle and early old age who may be able to assist their own parents as they move into extreme old age.

The alleged diminution in the pool of family care is also a more complex matter than would appear at first sight. On the one hand there are trends to suggest that sources of family help may be diminishing. There are fewer unmarried women to remain at home to care for aged relatives. There are also fewer women at home because many more now go out to work and it is expected that this will increase (see Chapter 5). So a lower proportion of potential family carers *may* be available than in the past. On the other hand, the decline in the number of single women means that more are marrying and therefore will probably have children to support them when they are older (although there has been a rise in childlessness among women (CSO 1996: 61). While there is a great increase in the number of married women working there is little evidence to support the hypothesis that they are less likely to provide care (Grundy 1995a: 10). Indeed their greater financial independence may well enable them to buy in help for their older parents or give assistance with labour-saving devices such as ways of contacting the family if they are alone. Another changing factor is the role of men as carers. A shorter working week, the increased possibility of flexible working hours and the greater sharing of tasks between men and women may all contribute to more men being able to help.

Another potentially complicating factor is the growing complexity of family life. Increased rates of divorce, remarriage and co-habitation mean new sets of in-laws, step-parents and varying relationships. To which older people will the younger feel bound?

The emergence of the four-generation family must also be taken into account. The reduction of the age gap between generations may mean that a grandparent is far from being a dependent; she may be an agile women who goes out to work full-time. A four-generation family can mean that a grandmother in her 60s is torn because her life is divided between the demands of her mother and her own children who may expect help with their children.

Family ties are also affected by mobility. Most studies have found, not surprisingly, that the closer children live the more complete the assistance they are able to give in time of need.

Other changing factors include the likelihood of families transferring more resources to their adult children because 'age at leaving the parental home has increased, the proportion of young adults in employment has plummeted, participation in further and higher education has increased, the real value of student grants has fallen' (Grundy 1995b: 90).

What is known about extended families and three-generation households does not provide enough evidence of greater family care in the past to justify the theory that the Welfare State has caused a decline in family care. Perhaps the factors mentioned in this section are the real reasons for any changes in family care, rather than any theory about the consequences of the rise of the Welfare State or the supposed breakdown of family care.

Policy developments

Public policy recognition of the family came into even greater prominence in policies in the 1980s and 1990s. The White Paper *Growing Older* not only recognised that families were still the principal source of support but held that there was 'no evidence to suggest that the modern family has given up its caring functions or transferred its responsibilities to the State' (DHSS 1981d: 37). The emphasis in policy was to be on providing support for families. The family became a major theme for political speeches.

Among the actions taken by DHSS was the issuing of models of practice for planners and practitioners (DHSS Social Work Service Development Group 1984), the setting up of demonstration projects to support informal carers (Hills 1991) and advice on setting up services for carers (Haffenden 1991). It was argued that all these initiatives were but a drop in the ocean and what was needed was far greater provision of services (e.g. Hicks 1988).

Both the Griffiths report and the White Paper *Caring for People* (see Chapter 8) underlined the importance of carers. The NHS and Community Care Act 1990 obliged LAs to consult organisations representing carers when drawing up local plans for community care. The Policy Guidance after the NHS and Community Care Act 1990 stressed the role of carers in assessing services for elderly people. It stated: 'The preferences of carers should be taken into account and their willingness to continue caring should not be assumed. Both service users and carers should therefore be consulted – separately, if either of them wishes – since their views may not coincide' (DoH 1990a: 28). The Policy Guidance also states that the local authorities' plans should set out targets, one of which should cover the desired outcomes for service users and carers. A subsequent evaluation gave detailed advice on consultation with carers, information, assessment, planning and providing services (DoH/SSI 1995e).

The all-party House of Commons Social Services Committee in *Community Care: Carers* (House of Commons Social Services Committee 1990a) reported that the Minister had told them: 'we say very clearly and explicitly that we think practical help for carers is called for ... Although not enshrined in legislation, the role of the carer most clearly will be given the priority that they deserve in all our guidance about assessment, about community care plans and about all the other aspects of these proposals' (House of Commons Social Services Committee 1990a, para 4). The Committee believed that the government should set three long-term objectives for carers. These were improved income maintenance, improved opportunities to combine work with caring and improved availability of domestic and nursing services (House of Commons Social Services Committee 1990a: para 104).

The Carers (Recognition and Services) Act 1995 marked an important milestone. From April 1996 carers who provide a substantial amount of care on a regular basis gained the right to ask their local authority for an assessment for themselves when the needs of the person for whom they are caring is being assessed. The Act also requires the LA to take into account the results of that assessment when making decisions about any service to be provided.

All the recent changes have to be put in the context of the many changes mentioned in other chapters. These include the trend away from statutory services to the independent sector (how will they take account of carers?), emphasis on community care (what will the effect of early discharge from hospitals and tighter boundaries around continuing care mean for families?) and growing discussion about the legal position of carers. On the latter, comparative studies of European Union countries points out that there are several European countries, such as Germany, where families are legally responsible for the care of older relatives (McGlone and Cronin 1994, Salvage 1995).

Contact with relatives

The importance of social networks and support is clear (Grundy 1996b). Most social surveys both in this country and elsewhere find that elderly people have frequent contact with a relative (e.g. see Sundström 1994, Salvage 1995). On average nearly four out of five older people in the original 12 EC countries saw a member of their family at least once a week in 1992 (Walker 1993: 11).

Unfortunately the *General Household Survey* asks about the frequency of seeing 'relatives or friends' and does not distinguish between them although there is information on help given. The 1994 figures show that 77 per cent of people over the age of 65 saw relatives or friends at least once a week and this is a slight decline from 1980 when the percentage was 85 per cent (OPCS 1996: 180, OPCS 1994a: 40).

With children

In most cases contact is with a child. This is as true now as it was in the earlier sociological studies such as those by Willmott and Young (1960). The *British Social Attitudes Survey* in 1986 showed that over a third of people over the age of 60 with daughters had some form of daily contact, while one in seven had similar contact with a son (Jarvis *et al.* 1996: 61). Nine in ten had some form of monthly contact with both sons and daughters. Frequent visits by children have been reported in all the studies of the community including sheltered and very sheltered housing. Growing concern about elderly people going into residential care is also expressed by relatives, usually children, who still wish to care in some way.

It must also be remembered that some old people will have no children or will have outlived them. Abrams found that 30 per cent of his sample of the over-75s had no children (Abrams 1978: 19). Wenger's study of the over-65s showed a similar picture with 15 per cent never having married and 15 per cent never having had, or having no surviving, children (Wenger 1984: 72). Even younger groups do not necessarily have children. *The Retirement Survey* in 1988, for example, found that 16 per cent of men and 15 per cent of women between the ages of 55–69 had no children (Jarvis *et al*. 1996: 64). Comparisons of developed countries show that the percentage of people over the age of 65 with children varies from 68 per cent in Ireland (70 per cent in the UK) to 92 per cent in Japan and Turkey (Sundström 1994: 31).

With other relatives

Nevertheless, old people do compensate for the lack, or the loss, of children. Many studies (e.g. Willmott and Young 1960, Shanas *et al*. 1968, Wenger 1984, Bengtson *et al*. 1990) have noted that older people provide replacements for intimate kin lost through death or in other ways. It seems that few people claim to have no living close relatives. Brothers, sisters, nieces and nephews can take the place of children and grandchildren.

Evidence about care by the family

Research confirms that social services do not undermine self-help or responsibility. The family still plays a major role in meeting the needs of older people. Evidence accumulated in the sociological studies of the 1950s and 1960s (e.g. Townsend 1957, Young and Willmott 1957, Willmott and Young 1960, Willmott 1963) which confirmed the strength of family ties, as did a comparative study between the United States, Denmark and Britain (Townsend and Wedderburn 1965). The latter study concluded that there was little evidence that health and welfare services were misused or undermined family responsibilities.

The 1980s brought new studies which have all shown the extent of family, mainly female, care. An Equal Opportunities Commission (EOC) report in 1980 found that two thirds of their sample of carers were giving help to elderly people, mainly relatives (EOC 1980). Only two fifths of carers lived in the same home and the others often had awkward expensive journeys to contend with before they could give help. Wenger's study of old people in Wales (Wenger 1984) and one in Sheffield (Qureshi and Walker 1989), together with the work of Finch and Groves (1980, 1983) and Lewis and Meredith (1988) have all demonstrated the role that women play in caring. More recent research such as the large DoE one of housing needs also demonstrated the extent of caring – mainly by women (McCafferty 1994).

General Household Surveys over the years confirm that families are the main source of help for most personal and domestic tasks [see Document 30 for 1994]. The greatest source of national information results from a series of questions about caring in the 1985 and 1990 *GHS* to identify people looking after a sick, handicapped or older person (Green 1988, OPCS 1992). A 'carer' was defined as a person looking after, or providing some regular service or help for one of the groups just mentioned living in their own home or in another household. (It should be noted that as service or help covers a range of activities from 'helping' to substantial involvement it is argued that the figures are inflated – see Parker 1992.) In the 1990 *GHS* it was estimated that 15 per cent of people aged 16 and over were providing informal care. This represented 6.8 million carers and was an increase of 15 per cent compared with 1985. More than half the carers provided care for someone aged 75 or over. Between 1985 and 1990 the proportion of carers whose main person cared for was aged 85 or over increased from 15 per cent to 20 per cent (OPCS 1992: 2). The main source for people aged 65 and over who needed help with domestic, self-care and locomotive tasks in 1991 was a son or daughter (two fifths) with one third receiving help from their spouse (Jarvis *et al.* 1996: 48).

The debate about family care has moved on from simple descriptions to a consideration of the link with paid work, the rights of those cared for and about the complexity of family links, responsibilities and obligations (see Twigg and Atkin 1994, Finch 1995).

Who carers are

Research on carers emphasises that they do not constitute a homogeneous group of people and failure to appreciate this can lead to inappropriate expectations of their role. This point was underlined in a book by two carers. They said:

A common fallacy is that the experiences of caring are similar to those of 'normal' child-rearing, and indeed there are shared problems – isolation, low income, lack of sleep ... The most important difference, however, is that of time-scale. The parent looks forward to the child leaving home, becoming independent, perhaps marrying. This is how parental success is measured and is the reward for years of caring and loving. The carer of a person with a disability can only see her task ceasing on the death of either his or her dependant, and this can bring with it the most crippling guilt.

(Briggs and Oliver 1985: 112–3)

The peak age for caring was 45–64 in 1990 (OPCS 1992: 2). Women were more likely to be carers. The 1990 *GHS* found that 17 per cent of women were carers compared with 13 per cent of men (OPCS 1992). However, since there are more women than men in the total adult population in Great Britain, the number of women caring was considerably greater than of men – 3.9 million compared with 2.9 million. A closer look at the figures shows that female carers were more likely than male carers to be sole carers, and sole carers were more likely to provide a greater number of hours of care over a longer period. Men under the age of 60 were far less likely to spend substantial weekly amounts of time caring and the proportion of women who spent at least 35 hours a week caring was twice that for men (Jarvis *et al.* 1996: 67). Carers who were married women under 65 obtained the least domestic and personal health care support (Arber *et al.* 1988). Research has also shown that discrimination by statutory services against women carers is primarily on the household composition of the older people rather than on gender *per se*. There is some evidence that service provision is biased against those who have resident carers (Parker and Lawton 1994).

Mutual care by older spouses is common and most co-resident carers are spouses. There are particular expectations and problems of spouses (Askham 1992, Atkin 1992, Sundström 1994). The extent of care by older spouses and the effect this subsequently had on their lives is documented in *Life After a Death* (Bowling and Cartwright 1982). Older people who had cared for a spouse not only lose the person they cared for but may have to come to terms with anxiety, loneliness and adjustment to their lives. It must also not be forgotten that older people do provide a substantial amount of other informal care in the community including to spouses, brothers and sisters, parents and often to younger older people (see Chapter 12).

There is little research on school-aged children as carers but they feature as well as the groups mentioned.

The nature of care and some effects

Attempts have been made to define exactly what care means. It may include physical, financial and emotional care. Parker makes the useful distinction between 'care' and 'tending' (Parker 1981). He says that the word 'care' is used to convey the idea of concern about people. But it also describes the actual work such as feeding, washing, lifting, cleaning up the incontinent, protecting and comforting. He prefers the word 'tending' for these activities. The nature of the caring role will have an effect too. A son or daughter may feel embarrassed at performing personal tasks for a parent which may be easier for a professional. The parent may also feel embarrassed.

While caring is often undertaken willingly and there are many rewards (summarised in Askham 1992, McGlone and Cronin 1994) an analysis of some of the long-term effects of caring show considerable effects on the lives of carers which last long after caring has ceased (Hancock and Jarvis 1994). For example, past carers are more likely to receive means-tested benefits, spend less time as members of occupational pension schemes and tend to live in families that are less well-off than families of non-carers. They may also suffer from depression (Butler and Madeley 1995).

Costing the time of the carer is complex and must take account of the costs both to the carer and to society (Tinker *et al.* 1992, Netten 1993). The costs of caring include expenditure on items needed because of the disability, the time spent on the care and the opportunity costs of lost earnings (McCafferty 1994). Using these three types of cost the DoE study showed how costs vary according to the level of dependency of the person being cared for, the type of carer and the kind of household the carer is in (McCafferty 1994). The annual gross cost ranged from an average of £2,800 for someone of medium dependency to £5,500 for someone of high dependency (McCafferty 1994: Ch. 3). If these informal costs are added to the other costs then the cost for an elderly person at home is more expensive than sheltered housing (but cheaper than very sheltered housing) (McCafferty 1994: 197). The costs for co-resident carers was more than double that of those who lived in another household. This was not because the elderly person was more dependent but because more help was given. Both the 1985 and 1990 *GHS* also showed that co-resident carers gave far more help than those outside the household (OPCS 1992: 7).

Supporting and involving carers

The last 15 years have brought a growth of interest in the position of those who do the caring. Indeed the word 'carer' was one increasingly used. It had not become familiar enough to be used in the 1981 White Paper *Growing Older* but it was used in *Care in Action* later that year. The formation of the Association of Carers in 1981 (later to become the Carers National Association) gave another boost towards recognition of this group of people, most of whom are family members. These developments were helped by an upsurge of research reports in the UK (although there is still a dearth in some areas – Parker 1994) and the United States, some of which have already been mentioned, compared with interest but less research in Europe.

Research on the needs of carers shows that these vary according to the type of carer but that common needs are recognition for what they are doing, time off and receipt of services (see, for example, Parker 1992, Twigg 1992, Twigg and Atkin 1994, Salvage 1995). A review of research on services for carers (Twigg *et al.* 1990: 13–15) suggests that these services fall into five broad categories. These are to:

- relieve the pressure of caregiving and help the carer to manage more adequately the emotional strains that arise from it;
- assist the carer with practical tasks;
- provide relief from caring;
- enable the carer to get more from the care system and from his or her own abilities;
- provide a high level and quality of services to the dependant.

Four useful typologies of carers in relation to service providers are:

- carers as resources (providing care);
- carers as co-workers (when formal services work alongside carers);
- carers as co-clients (carers are regarded as people in need of help in their own right);
- the superseded carer (when the emphasis is on the person cared for and how to make them more independent) (Twigg and Atkin 1994).

Practical suggestions about ways carers could be helped have been put forward and schemes started. The work of researchers on carers of dementia sufferers has shown not only that more services are needed but that greater flexibility would help, as would an explanation from a professional about what is happening to the person they are caring for (Levin *et al.* 1989, Askham and Thompson 1990). What is needed is a realistic assessment of how families willing to care for an elderly relative can be supported. Making it easier for families to move closer or enlarge their homes are two ways. Another is to give adequate professional support, such as extra nursing help, incontinence services and holiday relief. A night sitting service is often essential if carers are to get their sleep. Alternating care in a hospice can prove to be another great support. In employment a more flexible approach to the working week and domestic responsibilities and extended leave would be helpful (Carnegie Inquiry into the Third Age 1993). Self-help groups or opportunities to meet and discuss problems with fellow carers are what some carers want. Wenger's (1984) study, *The Supportive Network*, calls for an interweaving of family and informal support which needs tact and diplomacy. Qureshi and Walker (1989) argue for shared care, which implies the provision of resources to supplement and, where necessary, substitute for family care. As Allen and colleagues concluded: 'Essentially, carers of all types wanted good professional help and support, as well as help and support from relatives, if there were any' (Allen *et al.* 1992: 306). Ways in which these and other objectives can be met are usefully summarised in the findings *Caring Today: National Inspection of Local Authority Support to Carers* by the SSI (DoH/SSI 1995e) and in the results of another project (DoH/SSI 1995d).

More practically there are strong arguments for more financial help. Whether carers should receive direct payment is controversial.

An international report pointed to the absence of programmes that compensate carers and concluded that there can only be speculation about the social and service consequences of any large-scale compensation scheme (Sundström 1994). The Invalid Care Allowance (ICA) is the only benefit currently paid. There are strong arguments that any payment should go to the person being cared for. A comprehensive study *Paying for Care: Lessons from Europe* concluded that there were many good features about the British system but that improvements could be made including raising the ICA and introducing some element of direct payment to disabled people (Glendinning and McLaughlin 1993).

Giving up caring

There are some problems which may particularly lead to carers giving up their task. These include aggression, disturbance at night and behavioural problems. Evidence from residential care suggests that some families relinquish the care of an elderly person very reluctantly (see Warburton 1994). But it is only fair to recognise that other generations have their rights too. Who can argue that a disturbed grandparent in a family should be cared for at the cost of a mother's breakdown in health with the consequent effect on her children? Hopefully women's role will be shared more by men but even so it is likely that the future will continue to be one where middle-aged women look after other women a generation older. If present evidence is anything to go by they will receive less statutory help than their male counterparts. Finch and Groves raised serious question marks over community care based so much on families (e.g. women), claiming that equal opportunities were not being given (Finch and Groves 1980). They felt that the forces pulling women back into the domestic caring roles were an inevitable consequence of community care policies. Unless there were a greater degree of financial and practical support for the carers and changes in employment patterns (e.g. the development of job-sharing, 'caring' leave, etc.) women will continue to be disadvantaged. Finch returns to this issue with Mason in another study and suggests reasons why 'women are more firmly locked into sets of family responsibilities than are men, and usually more finely tuned to issues of negotiations, identity, reputation and the like' (Finch and Mason 1993: 175). They argue that these do not result from some inherent differences but '*emerge* as women and men negotiate their own relationships with their relatives' (Finch and Mason 1993: 176).

The dividing line between a family being able to cope or not is a fine one. There is little disagreement that policies in the future must concentrate on a partnership between families and the statutory services. DHSS concluded in *A Happier Old Age*: 'Although family links are irreplaceable we cannot assume that the family can carry the whole responsibility for caring for the growing numbers of very old people. We may therefore need to look increasingly to the wider community to give more support of the kind traditionally expected of the family' (DHSS 1978a: 6). And in the White Paper that preceded the NHS and Community Care Act 1990 DoH stated: 'The Government acknowledges that the great bulk of community care is provided by friends, family and neighbours' (Secs of State for Health *et al.* 1989b: 4).

It is with this wider community that the next chapter is concerned.

CHAPTER 11

Community care – support from the wider community

Introduction

In the last chapter it was suggested that, if family support is lacking, older people may turn to 'the wider community'. But what do we mean by 'the wider community'? And, if it is possible to define this group, what is its role and what are its limitations?

There are three seemingly distinct groups: voluntary organisations, volunteers and friends/neighbours. Each of these will be considered in turn.

Voluntary organisations

Type

A voluntary organisation is defined by Clegg as: 'Any organisation which relies for its funds at least in part on voluntary subscriptions ... It is to be distinguished from (a) statutory authorities and (b) businesses run for profit' (Clegg 1971). The complexity of defining this sector is thoroughly discussed in *The Voluntary Sector in the UK* (Kendall and Knapp 1996) and by other researchers (e.g. Hems 1996). DoH defines voluntary organisations where 'surpluses are re-invested into the work of the organisation and managed by unpaid management committees, trustees or directors' (DoH 1990a: Appendix B/7). They are therefore not statutory bodies like local authorities nor commercial organisations such as those which run private nursing homes. They can be divided into organisations which are *not* registered as charities (such as campaigning societies or small groups meeting together for mutual support e.g. a local stroke club), or registered charities which may or may not be registered charitable companies. Charities may be ecclesiastical, educational or relief of needs and the objectives are usually clearly set out, such as 'for the relief and welfare of older people'.

Many of the early voluntary organisations, such as almshouses, were concerned primarily with providing for older people and so are many, such as Age Concern, of those established more recently. The different purposes of these groups give an indication of their strengths and weaknesses today.

Some charities are solely *distributive*, that is, grant-giving when a benefactor has provided money for a very specific purpose. Some of the oldest charities were set up to provide money, fuel and food for such older people as satisfied certain conditions, usually relating to age, sex, place of birth or area of residence. These charities are often administered by churches which may interpret their brief widely. In place of the specified bag of fuel, money may be given to help pay the fuel bills. However, there are problems caused by restricted funds and the Charity Commissioners work to enable wider use of funds. The modern counterparts, though often of a more transitory nature, are organisations giving food parcels to older people at Christmas or harvest time.

A second type of charity is both *grant-giving* and *fund-raising*. It is set up to further some particular cause or help some particular group and raise the necessary funds for it (e.g. Age Concern and Help the Aged). They may also campaign, provide services and give advice.

A third type is a body which has one major objective but which also engages in voluntary social service. The churches, for example, may have worship as their primary purpose, but they also provide many services for older people in such ways as sponsoring housing associations, opening their crypts or providing food and shelter for those in need (many of whom are old). Businesses may help by giving help in cash or kind or by seconding staff.

A fourth type is a charity set up with broad aims and little or no restriction on who may benefit. This gives the trustees considerable freedom to seek out and support worthwhile and often pioneering causes. The Nuffield Foundation, which has in the past given core funding to the Centre for Policy on Ageing, and the Joseph Rowntree Foundation, are good examples of this type.

Some of these voluntary organisations are tiny charities while others, such as the City Parochial Foundation, handle millions of pounds a year. Sources of income include central and local government, individual giving (including legacies), the National Lottery, charity shops and companies (Charities Aid Foundation 1996). A large element of funding remains the charities' own fund-raising efforts. A voluntary organisation may make a profit on some activities such as a service contract but, unlike a private organisation, the profit is not distributed. It is used wholly for the purposes of the charity. A new development is the power which health authorities have had since the NHS and Community Care Act 1990 to have charitable funds transferred to them and for them to run charitable appeals (Holly 1996). But whatever the size of voluntary bodies there is need to see what they do for older people in the widest context. In order to do that one needs to look in more detail at their functions and their problems.

Development and functions

Throughout the centuries individuals and groups have responded in various ways to the social conditions of their time. Some have worked through the state and tried to get services provided publicly (either by a statutory body or through public finance for non-statutory organisations). Others have set out, either alone or with others, to provide the service themselves. For older people this voluntary provision has embraced housing, residential homes, hospitals, pensions and many other kinds of service.

There has never been a time when it was foreseen that the state would take over total provision. Indeed Beveridge in his report, which formed the basis of much of post-Second World War provision, went out of his way to stress the need for voluntary action alongside that of the state (Beveridge 1942: 6–7). Subsequent investigations such as that by the Wolfenden Committee (1978) and the Seebohm Committee have endorsed this view (Home Office *et al.* 1968: 152–4). The Home Office report *The Individual and the Community: The Role of the Voluntary Sector* talked about its vital role which 'occupies the ground between those areas which are properly the responsibility of individuals and those which are properly the responsibility of Government' (Home Office 1992: 5). More recently an independent commission set up by the National Council for Voluntary Organisations (NCVO) has reported (NCVO 1996). This said clearly that voluntary organisations in all their diversity are a major national resource and their independence must be safeguarded.

The greatest recent change has been the expansion of the role of voluntary bodies in social care which was planned as part of the emphasis laid on the independent sector after the NHS and Community Care Act 1990. Policy advice following this encouraged the development of formal contracts for services (DoH 1990a). This role was differentiated from other aspects of work, such as social advocacy (i.e. speaking on behalf of older people) supported through grants.

Another feature has been the growing partnership between statutory and voluntary agencies. An illustration of this was the extension of joint financing where health authorities could give money to voluntary bodies, for example, to enable older people to move into the community. The Health and Social Services and Social Security Adjudications Act 1983 provided for additional members of consultative committees to be appointed by voluntary organisations. Participation in health authority joint care planning teams can be effective for joint planning. Under the NHS and Community Care Act 1990 voluntary bodies must be consulted over planning services for an area (Chapter 8). The encouragement of the voluntary sector has not been specific to the Conservative Government. In 1994 Tony Blair called on the Labour Party to 'ditch its traditional preference for

State welfare services' (*The Times* 3.11.1994). The 1996 NCVO report said that voluntary bodies must work in partnership with other agencies but need to preserve their independence.

What then is the special contribution of voluntary organisations to the care of older people? There are a number of functions that can be identified.

Providing services: filling gaps or supplementing services? In the early years of the post-1945 Welfare State the emphasis was on the state as a provider with voluntary organisations seen as fillers of gaps. Since the late 1970s there has been more emphasis on the role of voluntary organisations as professional providers, and many mainstream services, such as day care, are now contracted out to them. But there are still services which voluntary bodies provide which supplement those of the statutory sector. For example the Red Cross lend medical equipment for people at home and provide many services, such as a mobile library or shop, for older people (and others) in hospital.

Giving a choice: When a voluntary body gives a service slightly different from that provided by the state this in theory offers choice. The various types of accommodation, for example, provided by voluntary bodies range from nursing homes, old people's homes and hostels to self-contained flats and bungalows. Voluntary bodies also offer choice to the staff, though this is less often noticed. Social workers who wish to specialise in older people may prefer to work in a specialist organisation rather than in a local authority team organised on a generic basis (although there is a good deal of specialisation now in local authorities).

Pioneering and experimenting: Many social services for older people have been started on an experimental basis by a voluntary body. This is still the case (Osborne 1994) and is officially commended (Home Office 1992). Chiropody, meals on wheels and good neighbour schemes are three examples. However, pioneering and experimenting are not necessarily the prerogative of voluntary organisations. Sometimes both statutory and voluntary organisations may be trying similar new schemes alongside each other. This was the case with very sheltered housing in the 1980s.

Harnessing individual and community enthusiasm: Many voluntary bodies seem able to attract voluntary help through the personal appeal of the organisation concerned. Age Concern, for example, estimate that there are about a quarter of a million volunteers involved in local Age Concern organisations.

Providing information and doing research: Another traditional role for voluntary bodies has been the collection of information and the presentation of research findings. At the end of the last century voluntary bodies led the way in recording and analysing social conditions. This role has been continued in this century. For example the Age Concern Research Unit, and its successor the Age Concern Institute of Gerontology, King's College London fulfil this role. The Centre for Policy on Ageing concentrates much of their work on the dissemination of research, which is a much neglected area of social policy. It has a library and information data base and produces regular reviews of the literature as well as a directory of social research.

Acting as pressure groups: Many voluntary bodies attempt to influence policy by acting as a lobby on special issues. When they are closely involved with the group they represent their views may carry considerable weight. A voluntary organisation may represent the needs and interests of a whole group (social advocacy) or a particular person (client advocacy).

Giving advice: Not every older person likes to go to an official agency for advice. They do not, for example, use housing advice centres to any great extent. Voluntary bodies (such as the Citizens Advice Bureau) are often more acceptable as they are thought to be one step away from the agencies providing the services. Research on the information needs of older people showed their important role (Tinker *et al.* 1993). The Goodman Committee considered that the giving of advice in appropriate cases was a charitable objective (Goodman 1976: 32). But the Wolfenden Committee felt that 'the relationship between casework for individuals and wider ranging pressure group activities is a delicate one for organisations in this field' (Wolfenden 1978: 49). The Charity Commission has produced some guidance in this area (Charity Commission 1994).

Others: It is also claimed that voluntary organisations save tax-payers' money, that they perform a valuable role in supporting the informal caring system and that they can be a catalyst for self-help groups. They may also offer practical experience for individuals (Home Office 1992). It is also said that their freedom makes them more flexible than statutory agencies, which may be useful when an older person does not fit exactly into the rules for a particular state service. For example, a local authority may exclude owner-occupiers from council accommodation while a voluntary body such as a housing association may feel able to accept them. It is also argued that flexibility may be more possible for bodies not subject to public election and the vagaries of party politics. However, voluntary organisations, which do not have external pressures to change, may themselves become traditional, set in their ways and inflexible.

Some problems

What is the role of voluntary organisations vis-à-vis statutory bodies? The most significant activities of voluntary bodies are social care (37 per cent) and accommodation and housing (19 per cent) (NCVO 1996). The question of which services can best be provided by voluntary bodies and which by statutory authorities is particularly difficult to determine. As one study put it, will they be 'partners, competitors or also-rans in the provision of social care?' (Lewis 1993: 191). The NCVO commission felt that voluntary work must not substitute for activity which is properly the responsibility of the state or the market (NCVO 1996). Questioning the expanding role of voluntary bodies, Leat maintains that it seems often to be based more on potential than actual strengths (Leat 1990a).

The growing dependence on voluntary bodies to provide contracted out local social services (Chapter 8) is not without its dangers, especially when public funding becomes a main source of income (although it could be argued that there may be greater financial security arising from contractual agreements). The NCVO commission argues that the monitoring of grants and contracts by LAs should not be heavy handed (NCVO 1996). Another danger is that voluntary bodies may be loath to bite the hand that feeds them through taking a critical stance. Grants from public bodies inevitably mean that voluntary bodies have to tread a delicate line. Not only may they have to provide exactly what the local authority lays down, rather than experimenting, but they may be pressed to take on a task such as running a day centre which would otherwise be the local authority's responsibility and to do it more cheaply and with lower standards. Financial insecurity and loss of autonomy may follow, although the increase in fund-raising and marketing activity amongst voluntary organisations is enabling them to develop core activities which can allow them to retain some independence. They may also be competing with the private sector which may initially put in lower bids to gain business. Some of the new challenges to voluntary bodies were spelt out before the reforms and have proved to be accurate (Harding 1990). These include the need to:

- take into account the time and skills required for the processes of planning, costing and tendering for services;
- consider their own management capacity and be prepared to learn new skills;
- obtain sources of advice and support;
- make clear distinctions between their different roles and to separate service provision from other development and advocacy functions (Harding 1990: 30).

Are there variable standards? When there are a number of different voluntary bodies working in the same field, standards may be uneven partly because so much depends on the energy and enthusiasm of individual people and committees. The NCVO commission underlined the importance of setting standards of good practice and effectiveness (NCVO 1996). However, standards also differ between local authorities.

To whom is a voluntary body responsible? Statutory bodies such as social services departments are responsible to elected councillors. They also have to work within legally authorised limits and are accountable for the expenditure of public money.

The Wolfenden Committee, taking into account also the evidence of the Goodman Committee, did not feel that the restricted acceptability normally led to serious problems, although they thought that some smaller organisations needed advice and help on how to keep and present accounts (Wolfenden 1978: 148). The Charities Acts 1992 and 1993, which cover activities such as fund raising as well as accounting, have given a tighter regulatory framework. As Deakin put it: 'Public accountability is no longer an option but a necessity' (Deakin 1996: 7).

Are there overlaps between organisations? Critics of voluntary bodies sometimes point to the number of voluntary organisations apparently working in the same field and suggest that there is duplication. However, there may well be valid reasons why one organisation is more appropriate than another.

In the case of older people three of the major national organisations are Age Concern, Help the Aged and the Centre for Policy on Ageing. A closer look at them shows that their aims and the way they carry these out are different. Also they have combined for various purposes when circumstances seemed appropriate.

Do they take the heat out of problems? It is argued that even the existence of a voluntary body, in however small a way, may give the impression that a need is being met. The voluntary body may be making only a minimal provision, but there is the feeling that something is being done and therefore others (perhaps the state) need not act. The Home Office have stated: 'the Government does not see the voluntary sector as a cheap alternative to statutory bodies. Nor is the Government seeking to abdicate responsibility for services which the community needs' (Home Office 1992: 15). Some charities are becoming worried that demands are being made on their funds when the state should act (Utting 1994).

Do they have a 'charity' image? Some voluntary organisations founded as charities in previous centuries are said to have a lingering image of providing for the 'undeserving poor'. But this image may not be attached only to voluntary bodies since one reason why older people do not claim the statutory benefits to which they are entitled seems to be the feeling that they are accepting 'charity'. The emphasis on user involvement may help overcome this problem.

What about lack of resources? The services that voluntary organisations can provide, and their independence, is partly affected by the amount of money they can raise. The main sources have already been mentioned and the subsequent possible dependence on statutory funding. A particular problem is core funding. The 'volatility' of local funding has also been found (Russell *et al.* 1996). Another fear is that the availability of lottery funding will have a negative effect on other funders such as government. New sources of finance are needed (NCVO 1996).

Does what is provided depend more on the personal appeal of the voluntary organisation rather than the value of its work? Voluntary organisations concerned with older people, children and blind people attract a good deal of public support because there is much public sympathy for these groups. Older people are fortunate to come into this category for there is evidence that some organisations operating in difficult or contentious fields find virtually no public response.

Can an adequate supply of clients be found? In a summary of research on voluntary organisations, Leat maintains that some of the difficulties experienced by voluntary projects appear to be related not so much to the problem of recruiting sufficient volunteers, but rather to finding an adequate supply of appropriate clients (Leat 1990a: 274). She feels this may be related to the wider issue of public knowledge of the voluntary sector and the acceptability or confidence in voluntary provision.

Conclusion

Despite the problems of voluntary organisations there are both positive and negative reasons for the continuation of their role in making provision for older people. What is essential is for them to be constantly questioning and redefining their roles. A crucial question is whether some of the potential advantages of the voluntary sector will continue to exist if its role is expanded to carry out more functions of the statutory sector.

Volunteers

Definition and developments

A volunteer is someone who makes a voluntary offer of his or her services. The *General Household Survey* in 1992 defined voluntary work as unpaid work, except for expenses, done through a group or organisation but not for a trades union or political party. An important source of information is The Volunteer Centre UK which was set up in 1973 with funds from trusts and central government to promote and encourage the use of voluntary workers. In their survey in 1991 they used a slightly broader definition than the *GHS* (Davis Smith 1991). The Home Office have distinguished between:

- the philanthropic model, i.e. the strong helping the weak;
- the community activist model (usually very localised) such as neighbourhood watch schemes;
- the self-help model where people with similar needs work together (Home Office 1995: 39).

Various initiatives in the 1980s impinged on the voluntary sector (Leat 1990a). These included the various Manpower Services employment programmes and the Opportunities for Volunteering programme. A major reason for these programmes was to increase opportunities for unemployed people to undertake paid or unpaid work. This was often through a voluntary organisation. The 1984 Helping the Community to Care programme was to help volunteers, families and others to care for people who needed support. In 1994 the Home Office set up a committee to encourage and enable people to become and remain volunteers, to maximise their involvement, to improve the organisation and infrastructure of volunteering and to communicate the importance, effectiveness and value of volunteering (Home Office 1995).

Across Europe 'the past decade has seen an upsurge in support for both individual and collective forms of civic action, as a response to declining confidence in public institutions and the formal mechanisms of democracy' (Davis Smith 1996: 181). In the United States there are extensive initiatives for older volunteers such as the foster grandparents programme.

Who volunteers and why?

In the 1992 *GHS* it was found that almost a quarter (24 per cent) of people over the age of 16 had acted as a volunteer in the previous 12 months (Goddard 1994: 4). This was slightly more than in 1987. Women were more likely to have done voluntary work – 27 per cent compared with 21 per cent of men. However men spent more time doing it. There are great class differences. In 1992 40 per cent of people in professional groups had participated compared with only 12 per cent of unskilled manual workers (Goddard 1994: 6). 'Those doing voluntary work were not drawn predominantly from those who it might be thought would have more time available, such as people without children, the unemployed, and perhaps the recently retired: on the contrary, these were the groups least likely to do voluntary work' (Goddard 1994: 1). (See Chapter 12 for a discussion of older people as volunteers.)

Volunteers who received full out-of-pocket expenses were more likely to volunteer on a regular basis and so were individuals who were motivated to meet people or make friends (Knapp and Davis Smith 1995).

As for the motives of volunteers, these seem very mixed and range from a genuine desire to help others, to the wish to further a particular cause and the satisfaction of their own personal needs. Both the Aves Committee (set up to examine the role of volunteers – NCSS and National Institute for Social Work Training 1969) and the Wolfenden Committees (1978) agreed that motives are always mixed. The Aves Committee felt that most volunteers worked to meet some need or combination of needs, and the Wolfenden Committee felt that most of them would not understand about introspection or self-examination about motives. Mixed motives have also been found in a study of volunteering in Europe (Davis Smith 1996). Obtaining special skills, for example, may be the aim of the volunteer. Before looking too deeply for motives it is worth noting that one research study showed that most people became volunteers by accident – they took it up on the spur of the moment because a friend or relative asked them to (Social and Community Planning Research 1990). The Home Office committee suggested a range of ways to make it easier for people to volunteer (Home Office 1995).

The contribution of the volunteer

The 1992 *GHS* (Goddard 1994: 9) shows that the most frequently mentioned activities for those who had done voluntary work in the last year were:

- fund raising (45 per cent);
- serving on a committee (31 per cent);
- collecting money (30 per cent);
- helping at a club (26 per cent).

Activities that are also likely to affect older people were visiting people in institutions (10 per cent), other practical help (10 per cent) and giving advice (8 per cent).

Much of the work of volunteers with older people in the past was concerned with visiting services and practical tasks. Much more important now is voluntary work in hospital discharge and aftercare services, advocacy and counselling. Volunteers can add greatly to the well-being of older people, but what do they actually do and what is their special contribution?

Supplementing the statutory services: In general the role of the volunteer is seen as providing something that paid workers for various reasons, such as lack of resources or time, cannot offer. It is important to consider exactly what this may mean. Both the Aves and NCVO committees were clear that volunteers should not be used as substitutes for paid professionals (NCSS/NISWT 1969: 195, NCVO 1996) and this has been endorsed in guidelines drawn up by The Volunteer Centre UK. In practice there is much blurring of the distinctions between professionals and volunteers.

Continuity: Since statutory workers move jobs, especially in order to gain promotion, the volunteer may be in contact with an old person over a longer period of time. This will not, of course, always be the case since younger volunteers may also move frequently.

Less identification with authority: Many people, older ones included, seem reluctant to go to official sources for advice. They seem more likely to go to an organisation, such as the CAB, which is staffed almost entirely by volunteers.

Helping older people keep in touch with the outside world: Older people in institutional care are surrounded by officials of various kinds and all of these occupy some part in the hierarchy. A volunteer coming in from outside represents a different perspective.

Some problems

The need to define the role of the volunteer: What seems to emerge from studies of volunteers are two clear recommendations. First that the respective roles of paid and voluntary workers should be more clearly defined. It is especially important that unions are involved in discussions. Volunteers must not be used as a cheap substitute for paid workers (e.g. Carnegie Inquiry 1993: 86). Second, these definitions must be kept under constant review because the roles may change.

Relations with statutory bodies: Although most voluntary workers work for voluntary organisations some work under the umbrella of statutory bodies. When this is the case the role of the voluntary worker needs to be clearly defined and help and support given where necessary by statutory workers.

Age barriers: The Carnegie Inquiry into the Third Age found age barriers in the recruitment and use of volunteers and felt that decisions should be taken not on age but on individual capacity (Davis Smith 1992: 56–7, Carnegie 1993: 85).

Training and organisation: It is not enough for volunteers to know what their tasks are. They must also know how to go about them, what the limits of their job are and in what circumstances they should call on professional help. This particularly entails a knowledge of the needs of older people and of the services that can be called in to help them. The main reason why people drop out of volunteering is because of dissatisfaction with the way that voluntary organisations manage them and the lack of training and support, in effect the exploitation and the amateurishness (SCPR 1990). One study pointed to problems of 'burn out' when volunteers had too many demands on them (Knapp and Davis Smith 1995). In a study in Europe it was found that only three in ten volunteers received training and that volunteering was not taken seriously by many organisations (Davis Smith 1996). The need for greater training is also endorsed in recent studies (Home Office 1992, NCVO 1996). However, in many voluntary organisations in the UK there is a strong acceptance of the need for training, professional standards of management and competent evaluation. Recruiting, training, monitoring and supporting volunteers requires professional and trained full- or part-time workers to have to keep up-to-date themselves.

Paying volunteers and the issue of insurance: Most (84 per cent) voluntary bodies reimburse expenses to their volunteers (Blacksell and Phillips 1994). Payment of volunteers has been proposed for a number of reasons including the need to increase their numbers and to give them some recognition of their work. Leat, however, has pointed out the complex nature of transactions (Leat 1990b). *For Love and Money* discussed the role of payment in encouraging the provision of care (Leat 1990b). While the author found that some carers felt that payment was a recognition of their value, another study found a number of practical and ethical problems (Blacksell and Phillips 1994). The creation of barriers with unpaid volunteers is also possible (NCVO 1996). The lack of insurance cover for some older volunteers was an issue raised by the Carnegie Inquiry (Carnegie Inquiry 1993: 85).

Evaluation: 'There is something almost improper about suggesting that voluntary social work ought to be evaluated. It is rather like proposing to measure the efficiency of concern or goodwill, when the most important thing is that they do or do not exist'. So wrote two researchers who had just completed a study of old people and young volunteers in 1974 (*New Society* 7.11.1974: 356–8). But it is increasingly being argued that there must be evaluation if money and effort are to be put into this form of help for older people. Despite the difficulties, some researchers have attempted to evaluate the work of volunteers and the results are almost entirely favourable, (e.g. Shenfield with Allen 1972, Hadley *et al.* 1975, Holme and Maizels 1978). However, in a study of six residential homes it was found that there was a demand for volunteers but that they did not seem to make much difference to the quality of life of the older people (Power 1986). Leat and Darvill considered that schemes may be evaluated:

'from at least three (sometimes conflicting) viewpoints – elderly people, volunteers and professionals; from each viewpoint it will be possible to specify a number of different criteria of success' (Leat and Darvill 1977: 161).

The volunteer then, like the voluntary body, has a distinctive contribution to make to the care of older people. But, as the Aves Committee declared: 'We wish to make it abundantly clear that nothing we have to say about voluntary workers, their recruitment or their training, is intended to detract from the spontaneous contribution of the neighbour; indeed quite the contrary' (NCSS/NISWT 1969: 19).

Friends and neighbours

Who are they?

When studies of informal networks of caring are undertaken, more often than not the local caring group for an old person turns out to be that person's family. Neighbours, too, although considered as a separate category, may also be relatives. Evidence has already been given (Chapter 10) of the numbers of old people living near their relatives. It is clear from most of the studies that neighbours are not necessarily the people who actually live next door although many of them appear to live quite close. Neighbourly help that is spontaneous and unorganised is easier if people have some sort of link, and physical proximity may be the most important determinant. People who feel that they belong to a physical community may feel a sense of responsibility to one another.

But a community which has physical boundaries may not be the only community network. Friends from many different groups – churches, former workmates, adult classes and clubs of various kinds – form quite a different system from the world of clubs where older people meet only people of their own age. Friends are likely to be of similar age and life stage, and probably educational and social status, and are often a source of reciprocal support (Bulmer 1987). Jerrome's extensive work on intimate relationships shows the importance to older people of friendship (Jerrome 1990). She also shows that whereas men's relationships tend to be sociable rather than intimate and focus on shared activity, women's friendships are characterised by emotional intensity and self-disclosure.

Evidence about help

The 1994 *GHS* asked questions about contact (not help) between people aged 65 and over and neighbours. The overwhelming majority (79 per cent) said that they saw neighbours to talk to at least once a week (OPCS 1996: 182). Only 14 per cent said that they did not see them at all. It is interesting that those living alone were slightly less likely than those living with a spouse to see neighbours at least once a week (78 per cent compared with 83 per cent). But, as noted earlier, those living alone were more likely to see a relative. There was also a steady decline in people seeing a neighbour with advancing age: while 80 per cent of those aged 65–69 saw them at least once a week this dropped to 67 per cent for those aged over 85.

As has been seen, children and spouses are the main source of help by people over the age of 65 for domestic and locomotive/self-care tasks. But in 1994 10 per cent said that a friend or neighbour helped with domestic tasks and 1 per cent with locomotive/self-care tasks. (OPCS 1996: 177 [Document 30]). In the British Gas 1991 study of 764 people over the age of 55, in answer to the question 'If you need extra help, to whom, if anyone, do you turn to' 10 per cent said friends/neighbours (Midwinter 1991: Statistical appendix, Table 33). In the *Eurobarometer Survey* adult children and spouses were mentioned as the main sources of help but 12 per cent mentioned friends and neighbours (Walker 1993: 28).

Wenger's research highlights the importance of family care (as does that of Qureshi and Walker 1989) but her conclusions suggest that when this is not available friends and neighbours help (as Willmott 1986 also found) and 'statutory services fill gaps in the fabric of informal care for a minority' (Wenger 1984: 180).

An analysis of the *British Social Attitudes Survey 1986* suggests that 'the reality of how family and friends provide care and support to older people is more complicated than models have suggested' (Jarvis 1993: 20). Her evidence suggests that: 'People do not turn to others simply because they are related to them, or have no-one to turn to; they turn overwhelmingly to people they live very close to and see regularly, although these people may be friends, neighbours or other relatives, rather than close family relations' (Jarvis 1993: 20). She suggests that it is proximity and intimacy that are important. Heavy reliance on neighbours and friends was found in one study of people who had moved to the seaside (Karn 1977).

Other studies, however, have shown that friends and neighbours, while giving some help, are relatively unimportant as a source of social care, especially tending (e.g Bulmer 1987: 76–7, Allen *et al.* 1992). They may be willing to give some short-term help but often not a long-term commitment. The help may be complementary to kin ties. The danger of overemphasising neighbourly care is well put in the conclusion of Allen *et al.*'s study of older people in the community where just over a quarter had some kind of help: 'there was little indication that this kind of care can be relied on to any extent to help maintain elderly people in the community when they need care of a more intensive nature' (Allen *et al.* 1992: 15).

Formal neighbouring schemes

In some areas there are formal neighbouring schemes which may be a one-to-one relationship of a person helping a neighbour in a completely spontaneous way or a group of people arranging to help individual people – that is, community organised on a regular basis.

DHSS launched an ambitious good neighbour scheme in 1976. A report on some good neighbour schemes, *Limited Liability?*, attempted to look objectively at the evidence and contained some useful case studies (Leat 1979). Some interesting paid good neighbour schemes have developed and have been found to have been successful in helping to keep elderly people in their own homes (Tinker 1984). It is natural that there should be so much more evidence about voluntary organisations and volunteers than about the help given by friends and neighbours. The most extensive study of neighbourhood care in this country is that conducted by Abrams and his colleagues (Abrams *et al.* 1986, 1989). Older people were the largest client group. Although the researchers found it difficult to construct objective measures of success they nevertheless found that the care given did alleviate loneliness and did provide significant social contacts. The Wolfenden Committee suggested that it is so much taken for granted that it is scarcely mentioned in discussion about the provision of social services. These schemes seem very patchy – for example Allen and colleagues found none in their study (Allen *et al.* 1992). This point will be taken up later (Chapter 13) in the discussion about the meaning of community care.

PART THREE

Assessment

CHAPTER 12

The contribution of older people

Introduction

In the last two chapters attention has been focused on the help given to those older people who need some outside support. The main sources of help, apart from the statutory services, were described. In this chapter attention is turned to the help which older people themselves give to others. This is set in the context of theoretical perspectives. The help given by older people, both to their own families and to others, is examined. Then the wider role of older people in policy making is assessed.

Theoretical perspectives

The exchange theory

The exchange relationship can be defined as an encounter in which both giving and receiving takes place. It is nearly always assumed that it is more prestigious to give than to receive and that there is a clear economic and social distinction between the giver and receiver. Often there is stigma attached to receiving and, when older people are in this position, they are usually considered to be in a state of dependency.

One of the most comprehensive analyses of the exchange relationship, as it relates to social policy, is given by Pinker (1971) who also comments on the theories of Titmuss (1968, 1970). This study is not concerned with the wider applications of the theory, but only with those that relate specifically to the social services as a whole as they affect the position of the individual. Whether people do in fact see themselves as involved in this way is, of course, another matter.

There is first the distinction between the exchange relationship in economic matters and that in social matters. Pinker points out that people know where they stand in an economic exchange relationship because money confers a recognised right to buy goods and services (Pinker 1971). In social relationships the rate of exchange is not so clearly agreed.

Second, there is the exchange relationship which applies to all social services. The theory is that people pay a contribution in some way (e.g. taxes, rates, etc.) and therefore should feel as entitled to social services as they do to goods and services in an economic exchange. Pinker claims that this is unrealistic: 'The idea of paying taxes or holding authentic claims by virtue of citizenship remains largely an intellectual conceit of the social scientist ... consequently most applicants for social services remain paupers at heart' (Pinker 1971: 142).

Third, there is the exchange relationship involved in a specific (or particular) service. Forder states that it is, for example, the basis of schemes of national insurance (Forder 1974: 68). People who are currently at work pay into a scheme which supports older people in the expectation that a similar exchange will take place when they themselves reach old age.

Fourth, there is the exchange relationship on an individual basis. Services may be exchanged between individuals or between groups such as families. Recent writers (e.g. Finch 1995) are increasingly drawing attention to this element of reciprocity. Sometimes there will be a real expectation that another service will be conferred in return, while at other times it may be given as a 'gift'. But, as Titmuss points out in *The Gift Relationship*, motives may often be mixed (Titmuss 1970: 210–24).

The position of older people is special because of a number of factors which can make them feel that they receive rather than give. First, for many, there is a sudden ending of employment and of being productive members of the community (Chapter 5). Many older people in pre-industrial society did not retire, but equally many did not survive to old age. Some people, like farmers, are able to 'taper off' in their particular professions, but for the majority the attainment of the age of 60 or 65 means the automatic end to a lifetime as an economic contributor to society. There may, however, be differences between social classes. In some middle-class professions people often do retain some status – the doctor keeps the title on retirement. But the working-class majority hold neither the 'power to strike nor the significant remnants of social acclaim and distinction that accrue to middle-class elderly' (Jones 1976: 93).

Second, there is the current psychological atmosphere in which older people are regarded as being beyond the point when they have anything to contribute. It is part of the false sentimentality about old age where old people are 'frequently required to adopt a somewhat passive role and to express a sense of gratitude for what is provided' (ACE 1972: 49). Another aspect of this is the problem of older people in a youth-centred society.

Third, the emphasis on receiving is underscored because in economic matters most old people are dependent on a state pension for their main source of income. Fourth, Pinker argues that the growth of selective social services differentiates the recipients much more clearly than those social services which are universal and do not single out those who receive (Pinker 1971: 151).

Dependency

All these factors contribute to older people often being looked on as a dependent group, if dependency is defined as being in a subordinate relationship. Whether older people are more or less dependent than in the past is arguable. Some maintain that a state pension lessens their dependence on their families, while others hold the view that they are now more dependent on social services. What seems to be ignored in most discussions about dependency, as Johnson has pointed out, is that we are all to some extent dependent on others (Johnson 1993).

There is no doubt that most older people themselves wish to be independent, although there are many differences in their interpretation of independence. Hunt found that it is often thought of in economic terms (Hunt 1978: 130). For older people who worked it seemed to mean not being dependent on a supplementary pension, while for non-workers it meant being independent of the constraints of employment. For some older people, such as those who lived in granny annexes next to their families, 'independence' meant having one's own front door (Tinker 1976).

Equally important is the feeling of having something useful to do. Age Concern, in *The Attitudes of the Retired and Elderly*, noted that over half felt that no-one relied on them (ACE 1974). It seemed that not being relied on by anyone was part of the poor health–loneliness–social isolation syndrome. Mochansky, a Russian physician, who analysed the emotional effect of the 17-months siege of Leningrad, attributed the lack of breakdowns to the fact that everyone, from the smallest child to the oldest inhabitant, had a job to do (NCSS 1954: 12–13). If people feel that they have no role and they also feel dependent, this may engender a sense of stigma.

Is there any evidence that older people wish to reverse the process of dependency and be more equal contributors to society? The Inquiry on *Ageing* set up by the Church of England invited older people to write in with their views (Board for Social Responsibility 1990). A distressing number of respondents felt patronised or scorned purely on grounds of their age and their letters to the Inquiry made it plain that they felt they had a lot to contribute. Titmuss argues that people have a social and biological need to help (Titmuss 1970). It may therefore be right to take account of the needs of older people to contribute, not only from the point of view of their own welfare, but also of their use to society.

Activity, disengagement and continuity theories

In activity theory the argument is that older people will either continue with activities into old age or will compensate for the loss of traditional roles in their lives by taking on new activities and that this is linked to life satisfaction. In disengagement theory it is argued that people tend to seek voluntary withdrawal from many activities following retirement (see Bond *et al.* 1993, for a discussion of these concepts). In continuity theory it is held that what happens in old age is a development of what people have done before. Davis Smith, in his study of volunteers in the Third Age, suggests that although a longitudinal study would be needed to prove this, what data there is supports this theory (Davis Smith 1992). He says 'the characteristics associated with volunteering amongst younger and middle aged people are the same characteristics associated with volunteering by older people, albeit that older people are less likely than people of middle age to volunteer' (Davis Smith 1992: 48).

Factors affecting the ability of older people to give

Whether older people wish not only to remain independent but to give help to others in some form or other depends on a number of different things. Money and health have been discussed in previous chapters (Chapters 5 and 6). Also of importance are older people's abilities, how they choose to use their time, the opportunities given by society and the general concept of retirement.

Abilities

Some evidence has already been presented in Chapter 6 about the health of older people. Psychological aspects are as important. In an overview of the position, Coleman argues that much research has concentrated on intelligence and that many studies have examined the decline in basic mechanisms (Coleman 1993). He suggests that little attention has been paid to the continued development that is possible. He says 'Cognitive decline is not usually marked before the age of 70 and is primarily determined by processes of physical disease. Decline due to biological ageing *per se* is more limited and mainly affects tasks which have to be performed at high speed. Social and environmental factors also play an important part in encouraging or discouraging older people to maintain high levels of mental functioning ... A culture's expectation of older people's roles within society have a vital role in encouraging or inhibiting personality changes in later life' (Coleman 1993: 96). Twenty years ago Jones was arguing that where opportunities are offered, older people rapidly acquire new knowledge but what prevents many from doing this is limited expectations which they have of themselves and which others have of them (Jones 1976). Many of the submissions to the inquiry on *Ageing* set up by the Church of England emphasised how much enjoyment there is in taking up new activities in later life.

Use of time and leisure activities

In 1995 the most popular use of free time for everyone aged 16 and over was television or radio (19 hours per week) with the highest use by the over-60s (26 hours per week) (CSO 1996: 217). In 1993/4 99 per cent of adults watched television in the four weeks before the interview and this was exactly the same for people aged 60–69; for those aged 70 and over the figure was 97 per cent for men and 98 per cent for women (CSO 1996: 218). The next most popular use of free time for the over-60s was reading (6 hours per week) and then joint second (4 hours per week) visiting friends, talking and socialising and telephoning friends (1996: 216). Retired people, not surprisingly, also had the most free time, both during the week and at the weekend (CSO 1996: 216). People over the age of 70 were much less likely than average to be involved in do-it-yourself activities and listening to records and tapes (1996: 218).

People over the age of 60 in 1993/4 were less likely than younger people to participate in sports and physical activities (CSO 1996: 223). However, encouraging numbers of those aged 60–69 (45 per cent of men and 36 per cent of women) and those over the age of 70 (33 per cent of men and 20 per cent of women) had been involved in walking in the previous four weeks (CSO 1996: 223).

Abrams (1980), however, has shown that averages conceal wide differences and that for both 'passive' (e.g. watching television) and 'active' occupations (e.g. walking) there were sizeable minorities falling into extreme categories. The key to this variety in the use of time and behaviour by those reaching pensionable age lay, he felt, primarily in social class differences (subsequently confirmed in the Carnegie Inquiry, see Schuller and Bostyn 1992), and this was particularly so with men. While the average AB (the highest social classes) man on retirement reduced his paid work time and also reduced the hours he spent on passive leisure activities, the average DE (the lowest social classes) man cut out paid employment almost entirely and increased the time spent on passive leisure activities. The transition for women on reaching old age was less dramatic.

The opportunities given by society

While some older people will wish to relax in their retirement and to remain as uninvolved as they were in their earlier years, others may wish to further their own education, to take up or develop former interests or to contribute to the community. The number of those pursuing educational interests has increased rapidly as opportunities have expanded. Glendenning, writing of lifelong education and the over-60s, stated that only recently have we begun to pay serious attention to the educational needs and potential of the over-60s (Glendenning 1985). The University of the Third Age has been one important development. In 1980 Laslett argued on behalf of older people for the recognition of their cultural and intellectual importance and for their right to a fairer share of the budget, lifelong access to all educational institutions and to national distance learning (Laslett 1980).

Midwinter says that the reluctance of older people to participate in conventional educational activities and their self-perception of what education and learning means, stem alike from deep-set social and cultural factors and from weaknesses in the educational environment rather than, for instance, psychological or intellectual difficulties (Midwinter 1982). Research for the Carnegie Inquiry into the Third Age showed that 'the great majority of those currently in, or just entering, the third age had minimum initial schooling and have had very few opportunities for continuing education. Roughly two out of three of those aged 50 left school at 15 or earlier, and have never obtained any formal qualifications' (Schuller and Bostyn 1992: *vi*). The researchers estimated that about one in ten of those over the age of 50 take part each year in formal learning. They also found that pre-retirement education covered only a small proportion of the population and the potentiality of radio and TV as key vehicles for learning had not been developed.

Others want opportunities for leisure and arts activities (Armstrong *et al.* 1987, Midwinter 1990, 1992a). They look for the chance for really worthwhile things to do in the community, not 'pastimes or diversional therapy to fill in time till death comes' (Stewart 1974: 8).

Retirement and its meaning

When Vic Feather retired as General Secretary of the Trade Union Congress he is reported to have analysed the theme of his retirement cards. The predominant motif was the setting sun closely followed by pictures of 'a decrepit old man sitting in an armchair with, beside him, his faithful hound, its head resting on his knee. From the soulful expression in its eyes the sentiment was clear. If only the dog could speak, it would be saying, "you've had it, chum"' (Pilch 1974: *vii*). This conventional view of retirement is bound up with loss. People tend to retire from something rather than to another phase in life (see Victor 1994: 146–50 and Phillipson 1993: 180–99 for a discussion of the stages of retirement and the implications).

A more positive approach to retirement could be helped by preparation which would start early in life so that people could think about activities and lifestyles well before retirement. Pre-retirement education, while valuable, may be too short and too late for many people. However, new kinds of courses and approaches are developing (Phillipson 1993). In the British Gas Survey people over the age of 55 were asked 'whether they agreed with the statement "People should accept retirement as a new challenge"'. Four in five agreed with this (45 per cent strongly and 35 per cent a little) (Midwinter 1991, Table 20).

Social constraints, including social isolation

Although older people may have both the time and the ability to give help to others, there may be other constraints over the degree to which they are able to do so. There are practical constraints such as whether they can be contacted readily and, in some cases, how mobile they are. One helpful development has been the rise in the numbers of households with someone over the age of 65 with a telephone (now 93 per cent) (see Chapter 8). However, it was also noted in Chapter 8 that only half of older people over the age of 65 had access to a car in 1994 and that older people are less likely to own a car than other households (OPCS 1996: 178). Women and those living alone are particularly disadvantaged.

Social isolation

It is often thought that isolation and loneliness are common problems in old age and that they are both a cause and a result of the lack of a contribution to society by older people. The concept of isolation is by no means straightforward. Shanas *et al.* considered it in four ways:

- by comparison with their contemporaries – peer-contrasted isolation;
- by comparison with younger people – generation-contrasted isolation;
- by comparison with the social relationships and activities enjoyed by [other younger or middle-aged people] – age-related isolation;
- by comparison with the preceding generation of old people – preceding cohort isolation.

(Shanas *et al.* 1968: 260)

Isolation is clearly extremely difficult to measure. It may be objective (e.g. social contacts can be counted) or it can be subjective (people can be asked about their feelings). Most studies of social isolation have been concerned primarily with the first of the four types of isolation just outlined. Measurement usually consists of information about social activities as a way of estimating the number of 'social contacts' (e.g. Townsend 1964, Tunstall 1966, Shanas *et al.* 1968).

Approximately one fifth of those interviewed in these three studies were isolated, or extremely isolated, and the majority were women without children. However, isolation does not necessarily increase with age. The likelihood of going to visit family and friends declines with age but there is little variation in the likelihood of being visited by family and friends (OPCS 1996: 181). Only 3 per cent of people aged 65 and over saw no relatives or friends in 1994.

Loneliness

There is a conceptual distinction between isolation and loneliness. Isolation relates to circumstances (which can usually be measured, however crudely), whereas loneliness relates to feelings (often about these circumstances). Care has to be exercised in measuring loneliness because self-perceptions may be unreliable since there is a stigma attached to the condition (Wenger 1984: 141). One of the most important findings of recent studies of older people has been that loneliness appears to have little relation to lack of contact with relatives, friends, clubs or other social activities. That isolation and loneliness are not synonymous was one of the most important findings in the cross-national survey in 1968 (Shanas *et al.* 1968). Tunstall made important distinctions between living alone, social isolation, loneliness and anomie (a feeling of 'normlessness' or pointlessness) (Tunstall 1966). As Jerrome has pointed out: 'We tend to think of widows, childless people and the never-married and those who live alone, as at risk. In fact the never-married tend to be less vulnerable. One explanation for this is that they have well-developed strategies for establishing and maintaining social contacts' (Jerrome 1993: 252). One of the less obvious groups who experience loneliness are elderly people who live with adult children (Wenger 1984). Widows are also likely to experience loneliness as do others who have been bereaved (Bury and Holme 1991: 107).

Some people seem to enjoy being alone. In Abrams' study of the over-75s he commented: 'Some isolates are happy, satisfied with their lives and feel far from lonely; and at the same time some of those leading highly gregarious lives are not immune from a sense of loneliness and depression' (Abrams 1978: 38). Victor found that of those who were always alone 57 per cent said that they were never lonely and 33 per cent seldom lonely (Victor 1994: 189). In the British Gas survey of people aged 55–69, 20 per cent of people living alone said that they often felt lonely and 40 per cent that they felt lonely occasionally compared with 2 per cent and 13 per cent respectively of couples (Midwinter 1991: Table 46). The prevalence of loneliness does not seem to be higher for older people than for those of younger ages.

Townsend commented on both the isolation and loneliness experienced by a high proportion of older people in residential care: 'The lack of even a single friend; a higher rate of severe or frequent loneliness; the discouragement of spontaneous social activity; the inability of visiting relatives and friends to adopt useful roles; the lack of satisfying, and sociable occupation' (Townsend 1986: 38).

Help given by older people

Evidence has already been presented in Chapters 10 and 11 about the extent of help which older people receive from their families, from their neighbours and from the wider community. But older people also give help to all these groups. In 1991 about a third of people over the age of 65 gave help to someone living outside their own household (Jarvis *et al.* 1996: 62). This declined with age but even so 8 per cent of men and 6 per cent of women over the age of 85 gave such help. There was variation according to gender, age and living arrangements. Men were more likely than women to give help outside their household as were people living with a spouse (39 per cent) compared with those living alone (28 per cent) and those living with others not a spouse (17 per cent) (Jarvis *et al.* 1996: 63). The *Retirement Survey*, which was of people aged 55–69, showed even larger proportions of people helping 'regularly or frequently' than the *GHS* (see Jarvis *et al.* 1996: 63–4).

To families

Because there have been few systematic studies in the past of help given by older people it is impossible to make comparisons. Most current studies only touch on the subject in passing and do not have it as their main focus. Those who look back with nostalgia claim that the old kept a role right to the end; though it is to be hoped that it was not quite such a macabre one as that described by Simmons:

Even with their bent and nearly broken bodies the few surviving old people could be prized for their nimble fingers and ready wits – and above all for their knowledge, skills and experience ...

Old women too feeble to travel stayed indoors, attended household chores, repaired garments, tanned leather ... and shredded with their very worn teeth the sinew of dried caribou and narwhat. While a Chippewa family slept at night with their feet towards the coals, an old man kept watch, smoked and fed fuel to the fire. According to Inca law, elderly persons unfit for work should still serve as scarecrows to frighten birds and rodents from the fields.

(Simmons 1962: 42)

In the 1960s Shanas *et al.* questioned the view that inter-generational contact and mutual exchange of services is less today, even though the standard living pattern is now one of separate households. They said: 'what is found between the generations is "intimacy" at a distance rather than isolation' (Shanas *et al.* 1968: 180).

The British studies of the 1950s and 1960s found that help was still given by older people, though more in areas where they and families live near. Migration of families impedes this flow of services between the generations. Evidence from the 1970s confirmed the extent of help given to families. Hunt found that nearly one third of her sample of older people were able to give help when they visited relatives, but that this declined sharply with age (Hunt 1978: 101).

The 1980s and 1990s have brought fresh evidence of help given by older people to their families. The *GHS* showed that 13 per cent of people over the age of 65 were carers both in 1985 and in 1990 (Green 1988: 8, OPCS 1992: 4). In 1990 30 per cent of carers with a dependant in the same household and 28 per cent of those devoting at least 20 hours per week to caring were over the age of 65 (OPCS 1992: 7). For many this care is likely to be of an older spouse and the extent of this help is shown by the 1994 *GHS* (see also Chapter 10 [and Document 30]). As Wenger demonstrates: 'While older carers appear on average to provide care for shorter periods of time compared with younger carers, the care they do provide is likely to be more intense: in terms of the hours put in; in its intimate nature; and more likely to be done without help, compared with that given by younger carers' (Wenger 1990: 210–11). Arber and Ginn confirm that most time is spent by carers who support an elderly spouse and that this averages 65 hours per week (Arber and Ginn 1991). Some of the problems which spouse carers have are being taken for granted and the assumption by service providers that they find it easy to undertake tasks involving physical intimacy (Atkin 1992).

The *Retirement Survey* of people aged 55–69 showed that 50 per cent of men and 48 per cent of women gave help to their children (Jarvis *et al.* 1996: 65). One of the main ways help is given by older people is with the care of grandchildren. This comes out in all the studies of older people and their families (e.g. Willmott and Young 1960, Shanas *et al.* 1968, Wenger 1984). In a national study, *Women and Employment: A Lifetime Perspective*, it was found that the grandmother was the second most frequent source of child care for women in employment (Martin and Roberts 1984: 39), the most frequent being the husband. For pre-school children, 34 per cent of working mothers used the grandmother and for school-aged children 25 per cent did. In 1990 23 per cent of pre-school children cared for (in the absence of the mother) on domestic premises were cared for by a grandparent compared with 21 per cent by the father (CSO 1995: 47). But Harris has pointed out that the giving and receiving may blur into one: 'Whereas the daughter sees her visits as "keeping an eye on Mum", Mum may see the visits as the daughter turning to her for help and advice' (Harris 1969: 204). He stresses that to be on the receiving end in old age amounts to an abrupt reversal of the parental role.

Until recently grandparenthood has been a neglected area of study (Cunningham-Burley 1986). Academic interest has been much more widespread in the USA (e.g. Bengtson and Robertson 1985). Roles that have been identified are surrogate parent, and formal, authoritarian, fun-seeker and distant figure (Neugarten and Weinsten 1964 – quoted in Victor 1994).

One matter of concern has been the lack of legal rights and obligations that grandparents have in relation to their grandchildren. Until recently grandparents could find after death, divorce or separation had ended the marriage of their son or daughter that there was no way, short of going to the High Court for a wardship order, by which they were legally entitled even to see their grandchildren. The Children Act 1989 has now given legal standing to grandparents in litigation affecting the child (Samuels 1993).

To neighbours

Many older people give help to their neighbours. Sometimes the people helped are other old people. For example in the granny annexe survey there was a good deal of keeping keys for one another, letting in meter readers and so on (Tinker 1976). The reliance of older people in seaside resorts on their neighbours (usually also older) has already been noted in Chapter 11.

Voluntary work

In the 1960s the Aves Committee on volunteers thought that: 'there may be considerable resources among the over 60s of both sexes' (NCSS/NISWT 1969: 120). In a subsequent summary of research on older people as volunteers, it was found that a common objective was for them to feel useful, to meet and relate to other older people and to support each other, rather than to take up issues with outside bodies or general problems (Goldberg and Connelly 1982: 173–4). Marshall has said that many old people can be inhibited through lack of confidence and also that they can be very short of money (Marshall 1990).

In the 1992 *GHS* it was found that 24 per cent of adults aged 16 and over had participated in voluntary work in the year before the interview (Goddard 1994: 6). For those aged 60–69 it was 23 per cent and for those over 70, 15 per cent. These figures are almost identical to 1981. It is interesting that the recently retired participated less than those aged 35–59. One reason could be that help to families and friends was not included in the survey and, as has been seen, older people do give a great deal of help here. Research by the Carnegie Inquiry into Third Age volunteering has already been referred to in Chapter 11 but it is worth noting that they too found relatively high levels of volunteering but that it declined in very old age. Volunteers aged 60 and over were more likely to have visited people in institutions and to have given practical help to an organisation or group than other groups. The most likely activity for third age carers was visiting an elderly or sick person.

Interestingly, older volunteers spent on average more hours on voluntary work compared with younger groups. Volunteers over the age of 70 gave 18.4 hours, those aged 60–69 16 and those aged 35–44 14.4 (Goddard 1994: 15).

One significant development has been along self-help lines. An example of this is the University of the Third Age. Started in France, it now has many branches in the UK and aims to provide educational opportunities for retired people as a group. The tutors are usually retired and groups are managed by retired people too.

Another development is groups such as REACH (Retired Executives Action Clearing House) to encourage the participation of older people in community projects and sometimes offer their services to voluntary organisations. Other schemes include linking older people with children, for example in schools. Some pilot foster grandparents schemes are also starting.

Role in social policy

The challenge to society over older people comes not only through the outward pressure of events such as the rise in numbers of the very old and frail or the increased cost of services; it comes also from within through the growth of an increasingly articulate group of people speaking for themselves. In some cases they may be speaking about their own needs but sometimes more generally.

Social policy for older people

Organisations and individuals concerned about older people are becoming more forceful in putting forward their views. The acceptance of older people speaking for themselves was acknowledged in the DHSS in *A Happier Old Age*, which declared that its policies so far had two main aims but: 'Now we must add a third vital aim. Old people must be able to take their own decisions about their own lives. They must have the fullest possible choice and a major say in decisions that affect them' (DHSS 1978a: 5).

Social policy in general

Older people are reasonably well represented both among MPs and among local councillors. Of those elected to the House of Commons in 1992, 16 per cent (ACE database) (compared with 23 per cent in 1987, 13 per cent in 1974 and 10 per cent in 1977) were over the age of 60, compared with about 20 per cent of that age in the population. There is an above-average representation among local councillors (Table 12.1). Surveys for the Maud Committee on Management of Local Government in 1964 (MHLG 1967), the Robinson Committee of Inquiry on the Remuneration of Councillors in 1976 (DoE 1977a), the Widdicombe Inquiry into the Conduct of Local Authority Business (Secs of St. for the Envir. *et al.* 1986) and research by

Table 12.1 A comparison of the age of councillors in 1964, 1976 and 1985 (percentages in each group)

	1964[1]	1976[2]	1985[3]	1993[4]
55–64	31	30	27	27
65–69	11	12	12	13
70–74	7	7	7	8
75 and over	4	2	3	3
Base (councillors of all ages)	3,970	4,648	1,534	1,612

[1] 1965 MHLG, *Committee on the Management of Local Government* (the Maud Committee), vol. 2, *The Local Government Councillor*, Moss L. and Parker, R. S., HMSO, 1967, Table 1.1, p. 15.

[2] 1976 DoE, *Committee of Inquiry into the System of Remuneration of Members of Local Authorities* (the Robinson Committee), vol II, *The Surveys of Councillors and Local Authorities*, HMSO, 1977, Table 1, p. 8.

[3] 1986 Secretaries of State for the Environment, Scotland and Wales, *The Conduct of Local Authority Business* (the Widdicombe Committee). Research vol. II, *The Local Government Councillor*, HMSO, 1986, Table 2.3, p. 21.

[4] Young, K. and Rao, N. *Coming to Terms with Change?* LGC Communications, 1994, p. 6.

Note:
The Maud Survey covered England and Wales, whereas the Robinson and Widdicombe surveys included Scotland. The 1993 survey covered Great Britain.

The Joseph Rowntree Foundation supported the 1993 project, but the material presented here represents the findings of the authors, not necessarily those of the Foundation.

Young and Rao (1994) showed that there has been little change between 1964, 1985 (both 22 per cent) and 1993 (24 per cent) of councillors aged 65 and over respectively compared with 14 per cent in the population (Secretary of State for the Environment *et al.* 1986: 21, Table 2.31). The Maud Committee saw value in a fairly high proportion of older councillors since they might bring wisdom and experience to local affairs. On the other hand, they declared that they were anxious about the high average age of members and thought that no-one aged 70 or over should be allowed to stand for election.

In *Political Attitudes and Ageing in Britain* the conclusions from a National Opinion Poll survey were that older people were as likely as any other adults to have voted in a general or local election, stood for public office, paid individual membership to a political party and taken an active part in a political campaign (Abrams and O'Brien 1981). They also found that in every general election since 1964, irrespective of which party had an overall victory, support for the Conservatives was highest in the 65 or more age group. Abrams and O'Brien speculate on why older people have not become a powerful pressure group. Among possible explanations are differences between older people (e.g. car owners may oppose free public transport on buses), dislike of being labelled old and an awareness of lack of power (e.g. at being unable to withdraw their labour).

Research in 1987 showed that older voters were as diverse as the rest of the population and they did not necessarily vote out of self-interest (Midwinter and Tester 1987). Another interesting finding was that ageing was not an issue in the 1987 election nor has it been since.

In the United States older people are becoming increasingly involved in lobbying and advocacy and Oriel has speculated about the effect that this growing citizen participation will have on programmes (Oriel 1981). Phillipson argues that older people in this country have been slower to become a political force but claims that there is a gradual emergence of more radical groups of pensioners (Phillipson 1982: 124–5). Whether they will ever attain the power of the American Association of Retired Persons (AARP) is doubtful. Even more questionable is the issue of special political parties formed to further the interests of older people. In the Eurobarometer survey older people were asked whether they would join such a political party. Only a minority (22 per cent on average across the EC) would and the figure was about the same for the UK (Walker 1993: 14). There are however, signs that developments are occurring. In 1992 a European Seniors Parliament met in Luxembourg to discuss issues related to ageing and 518 older people attended (Salvage 1995: 32). In the Netherlands there are two political parties representing older people and they have already won some seats.

Conclusion

Older people can and do give service in various ways. The opportunities in the future may be even greater. For example, the increasing number of mothers who are in paid employment may lead to a demand for more care by grandparents. The increased emphasis on the value of voluntary help in many spheres may also lead to an expansion of help by older people.

On the other hand, there are factors which should not be ignored. The numbers of young older people, who might be expected to contribute through part-time employment or voluntary work, will decline at least in the short term (see Chapter 2). Nor may people want to become involved after a lifetime of work or caring. And society has also to be convinced of the value and usefulness of their contribution. For what everyone is able to contribute to society is determined in part by the social and psychological conditioning to which they are subjected. Those who feel wanted usually find it easier to give help than those who accept a public estimate of their own worthlessness.

What could be the greatest boost for the contribution of older people would be a re-thinking of what people do when they do not work and the whole concept of retirement. If a large proportion of people are going to spend long periods not in paid employment, because they are retired, caring or unemployed, then what they do, or can do, for the community has to be seen as valuable. Contributing in some way to society could give the self-esteem, status and role that many sadly only find now in paid employment. A more assertive attitude by a new generation of older people who refuse to be treated as second-class citizens may make this hope a reality.

CHAPTER 13

Some general problems

Many of the problems encountered in providing for older people are the same as, or similar to, those for other groups. Some old people suffer from physical impairment, and some who are housebound share some of the problems of parents with small children. Those who are deaf, blind or socially isolated present difficulties of communication similar to those experienced by ethnic minorities.

Some of these problems, which will now be discussed, are: differing perspectives of need; the involvement of users; variations in services and the issue of inequalities; take-up of benefits and lack of knowledge of services; the evaluation of services; the meaning of community care; finance and the mixed economy of welfare.

Differing perspectives of need

While social policy theorists have become increasingly concerned with measuring needs there is a danger that those actually providing the service may become less so. If resources continue to be severely limited it is possible that agencies may deal solely with the obvious needs of which they are immediately aware. For example, a local authority with a lengthy waiting list for housing can perhaps be forgiven if it does not go out of its way to uncover any fresh needs. Yet it might be possible for some people on the list to have their needs met in a more appropriate way. Older people on a council list for sheltered housing, for example, may not have considered (or been offered) ways of improving or adapting their home. Similarly, there may be many in need who, for one reason or another, are not on the list. It might, for example, be more economic (and make for greater individual happiness) if some old people in residential homes had their needs examined more closely and, if it were found appropriate, offered an alternative form of housing. A helpful theoretical discussion about needs and welfare outcomes has been provided by Gough and Thomas (1994). One of the most interesting ways of distinguishing types of needs is that developed by Bradshaw (1972). He divided needs into four types: normative, felt, expressed and comparative, and these will be discussed in turn.

Normative

This is need as defined by the experts. Examples of this concept of need, as used for elderly people, are the incapacity scale developed by Townsend (1964) and the measures of social isolation used by Tunstall (1966). Subsequent researchers have constructed similar scales of disability by asking elderly people about their capacity to perform certain tasks. A scale based on questions about disabilities was used in the national disability surveys (Martin *et al.* 1988). In these ways some attempt can be made to measure dependency. A critique of some of these methods has been undertaken by Wilkin and Thompson (1989) and Bowling (1991).

'Experts' may also be used directly to assess needs. But the expert may sometimes conceal needs. For example, old people may not be put on a waiting list for accommodation by their professional advisers – health visitors and social workers – who wish to spare them from disappointment. Another disadvantage of this approach is that the views of experts are likely to be strongly influenced by their own perspectives (Forder 1974: 53–4).

Felt

Bradshaw's second category is felt need. This equates need with wants. Many services are based wholly or partly on this notion of self-referral. The problem here is that what people feel they want is governed very much by their previous experience and their knowledge of what is available. Rising expectations will mean that felt needs will keep on growing. Some older people today do not expect central heating in their homes but the next generation will.

Felt need is probably one of the least satisfactory ways of measuring need. A number of studies have shown that the less people have and the more deprived they are the less likely they are to feel the need for a service. However, subjective views can supplement more quantitative measures. For example, the *Disability Surveys* in 1984–6 asked about people's views on their financial situation, as well as measuring it by level of income (Martin and White 1988).

Expressed

Bradshaw's third category is expressed need. This is when felt needs are turned into action. Need then becomes equated with demand, for it is those who express their need who are said to be 'in need'. But there may be many reasons why people do not demand a service. For example:

- they may not know the service exists;
- they may feel that they do not qualify;
- they may feel that the service is overloaded and they have no chance of obtaining it;
- the service may be very poor;
- there may be stigma attached to the service;
- people may feel it beneath their dignity to apply.

On the other hand, the provision of a service – especially if it is of a high standard – will actually create a demand. The conclusion must be that any assessment of demands is hypothetical until a service is actually provided. When it is provided demand may rocket.

Comparative

The fourth definition Bradshaw used is comparative need. 'A measure of need is found by studying the characteristics of those in receipt of a service. If people with similar characteristics are not in receipt of a service, then they are in need' (Bradshaw 1972: 641). This is the same basis used by Harris in *Social Welfare for the Elderly* (Harris 1968). She examined the records of those getting a service or on live waiting lists. She then asked elderly people for details of the circumstances which led to their being given a particular service. From this she was able to make some assessment of need.

Needs are relative and change over time. With the increased emphasis on the views of the consumers (see next section), it is likely that concepts of need will become more important. All four methods (normative, felt, expressed and comparative) have to be taken into account. It is important to distinguish between individual needs and those of the population (for the assessment of specific needs see Chapter 6 for health, Chapter 7 for housing and Chapter 8 for community care).

The involvement of consumers

It has been seen (especially in Chapter 12) that older people are becoming more overtly involved in social policy but there are many ways in which this could be increased (Midwinter 1992b). There is also increased emphasis on the views of consumers in advice from central government about health and social services (e.g. Secs of St. for Health *et al.* 1989a, 1989b). In health, for example, there is stress on the involvement of users and carers in social services for hospital patients (DoH/SSI 1993c) and in community care (DoH/KPMG Peat Marwick undated). The DoH circular *Community Care Plans, (Consultation) Directions 1993*, (LAC (93)) 4 states that community care plans must be 'marked by collaboration and joint working and by the involvement through consultation with ... service users'. In housing increasing attention is being paid to the views of tenants (e.g. Riseborough 1996a, 1996b).

How far involvement is real is difficult to estimate. Research is increasingly putting this issue in the context of empowerment and advocacy. In order to take part in decisions people need to have power and there are major issues about how this can be done (Osborn 1992, Smale *et al.* 1993, Stevenson and Parsloe 1993, Thornton and Tozer 1994). There are particular problems posed for professionals and these include the need to change the culture of departments, how to deal with ethical issues such as balancing risks, autonomy and protection and communication difficulties (Stevenson and Parsloe 1993).

Sometimes older people will be able to express their needs themselves (self-advocacy) but sometimes this may be through someone else acting on their behalf (citizen advocacy). Research on advocacy (Wertheimer 1993) has been followed by a code of good practice (Dunning 1995).·

Yet another aspect of the involvement of older people is over complaints. In the health service a new procedure was put in place in April 1996. This involves a way of complaining direct to the provider of the service and then a mechanism for an independent review (DoH, press release, 14.3.1996). The Health Service Commissioner (Ombudsman) continues to be at the apex of the complaints procedure. The policy guidance about community care has a detailed section on complaints (DoH 1990a) and an effective process was required to be in position by April 1991 (DoH/SSI Chief Inspector's Report 1994: 72–3). This involves the LA in:

- providing an effective means of allowing service users or their representatives to complain about services;
- ensuring that complaints are acted on;
- aiming to resolve complaints quickly and close to service delivery;
- giving those denied a service a means of challenging the decision made;
- providing for an independent review of a complaint.

A monitoring exercise in 1993 showed that all LAs had complaints procedures in place (DoH/SSI Chief Inspector's Report 1994: 73) but a subsequent review found some areas of concern including 'evidence that procedures were insufficiently advertised, accessible or monitored' (1994: 74). A review in 1996 found some positive findings, such as better information, but some areas of concern such as over half (52 per cent) of complainants being dissatisfied with the outcome of the complaint, the length of time taken to respond and unhelpful staff attitudes (DoH/SSI 1996).

Variations in services and the issue of inequalities

There may be variations (see [Document 31] for a discussion of why the neutral term variations is used by DoH in preference to inequalities) in services and between individuals, between different groups of people and between areas, and there is growing interest in the subject (e.g. Vincent 1995). Numerous examples in welfare services have been documented (e.g. Sinclair *et al.* 1990). Good reasons may well account for this variation. The personal circumstances of people are rarely identical, and neither are local conditions. However, there are signs that the government may be taking the matter of inequalities more seriously, for example in *Variations in Health* (DoH 1995b).

Between individuals

There are numerous examples of inequalities between people in old age. Many, such as those between men and women, between ethnic minorities and the majority population and between rich and poor, existed before retirement. Only a radical change in society and a range of measures is likely to bring greater equality. For some services there is equality, for example, over the amount of the basic old age pension. But for others where there is local discretion there may be considerable differences.

Between groups

The second sort of variation is that which occurs between different groups. Researchers are increasingly looking at inequalities in the health of older people both over general issues (e.g. Henwood 1990, Victor 1991, Royal College of Physicians 1994) and over specific ones such as coronary care (Royal College of Physicians 1994), cancer (Pentiman *et al.* 1990) and resuscitation (Giallombardo and Homer 1994) (see also Chapter 6). Inequalities may exist in treatment but also in preventative measures. For example, women over the age of 65 are not automatically invited for breast screening. Age discrimination also operates over certain benefits. For example to obtain the Disability Living Allowance it is necessary to apply before the age of 66. In the case of older people it is held that not only is there need to improve care, but provision must be made for the continuing increase in the older population. These points are developed further in Chapter 14 under Priority for resources and the intergenerational perspective.

Between areas and local authorities

Variations between areas, such as those noted repeatedly by the Audit Commission (see Chapter 8) occur largely because local authorities are elected bodies with considerable freedom of choice about what they do. For example, some give travel concessions for elderly people. This freedom of choice is given them so that they can take account of local conditions and so that they can experiment and pioneer the services they provide. If successful other authorities may copy.

Other reasons for differences and inequalities between local authorities are the political composition of the council, the demand for the service and the extent of provision in the past (Davies *et al.* 1971, Bebbington and Davies 1982). Wealth came out as important in two studies done for the Royal Commission on Local Government in 1968. The Maud Commission on Management showed the considerable impact of personalities, both elected members and officers (MHLG 1967).

Variations and inequalities have led some to press for more central direction. For example the Griffiths Report called for standards of service delivery to be laid down and for there to be ring-fencing (i.e. a specific grant) for certain services (Griffiths 1988). Local author-ities are subject to considerable central control, not least because most of their income comes from central sources. The controls exercised by central government include loan sanctions, subsidies, confirmation of plans, the right to vet certain key appointments and a whole range of informal advisory roles.

An increase in central control would mean a shift away from the prevailing political attitude of central government in the 1980s and early 1990s which was to encourage local authorities to make their own decisions. However, it is interesting that detailed policy guidance has been laid down following the NHS and Community Care Act 1990 (see Chapter 8).

Variations also occur in health provision (see Chapter 6). The DHSS Report of the Resource Allocation Working Party (RAWP) confirmed the disparities in the way resources had traditionally been allocated to different parts of the country (DHSS 1976b). The report *Variations in Health* gives evidence of geographical variations although it concludes that more research is needed before the problem can be ameliorated (DoH 1995b).

Take-up of benefits and lack of knowledge of services

Access to benefits in the welfare state is one of the most interesting and relevant subjects. A consistent theme running through social surveys is the reluctance of some older people to take up benefits which are theirs by right (e.g. Allen *et al.* 1992). Official statistics, such as those for take-up of various kinds of income support (see Chapter 5) are also an indication of the problem. It is therefore worth exploring some of the reasons for non-take-up.

One reason put forward is that of feeling a sense of stigma (Hill 1976). But stigma is not the only reason why people fail to claim. The attitude of the official to be approached, often referred to as the 'gatekeeper', may be equally important. It is also relevant to consider the expectations of older people. Many have lived through the privations of two World Wars and a depression and are grateful for what they now have. Whether future generations of older people, used to a higher standard of living, will take the same attitude is doubtful.

Lack of knowledge of services can be another reason for non-take-up of services. Research has highlighted lack of information (Tester and Meredith 1987, Tester 1992, Tinker *et al*. 1993). The need for more advice and information services has been made by a long line of government and other committees. One of the main roles of Age Concern is the giving of advice about entitlements and in general about services through their publications and information officers. Without the statutory right to information, such as that in the Disabled Persons (Services, Consultation and Representation) Act 1986, it is doubtful whether people will always know about their entitlements.

The evaluation of services

One of the most difficult tasks in social policy is how to measure the effectiveness of services. A study of research on welfare provision for elderly people concluded that evaluation was lacking in many services (Sinclair *et al*. 1990). In some areas, such as carers, it is virtually non-existent (Twigg *et al*. 1990). But evaluation there must be. In *The Effectiveness of Social Care for the Elderly*, Goldberg and Connelly suggest that as a 'safeguard against the new' (i.e. to assess the usefulness of new schemes which are being pushed but are not tested) and to get public accountability, to ensure that resources are so deployed that they achieve a measure of territorial and social justice, to determine what impact the service has on the well-being of its users, and to assess cost-effectiveness there must be evaluation (Goldberg and Connelly 1982). The complexity of methods used for evaluating health services for older people, where the traditional medical model of the randomised controlled trial may not always be appropriate, have been demonstrated by Hunter (1996). There is no simple way in which evaluation can be done, but some key questions must be asked.

Some questions

What is the total amount of provision? It is possible to measure total provision in a number of ways – amount spent, units provided, numbers of staff or hours allocated – and all these give some indication of the service. But even these figures do not allow for assessment of quality and may mask a poor or unequal service. A large amount of money may be spent but be wastefully used. There may be better, possibly cheaper, ways of providing the service. The amount may not be distributed evenly, either between individuals or between areas, so again the amount spent does not tell the whole story.

What is the range of provision? A wide range gives choice. For example, there are many ways in which food can be provided for older people, but unless all the options, which include meals on wheels, clubs, day centres, allowing home helps to cook meals, having an arrangement with a local café, providing convenience foods possibly with a microwave oven or paying a neighbour, are offered the service is not necessarily an effective one.

What is the quality of the service? Quality is one of the most difficult things to measure. Some would argue that staff who are trained would provide a better quality service, and this was borne out by a study which showed that trained social workers uncovered more of the needs of elderly people than untrained (Goldberg 1970).

Does the service reach the people for whom it is intended? An elaborate, expensive service may be provided but be totally ineffective if it does not reach recipients. If this is because older people do not know about it, the remedy is to find ways of ensuring that they do know. If, however, the older person does not in fact want it, that is a different matter. Older people, as other groups, have the right not to accept a service.

What are the aims and outcomes? Evaluative studies have travelled a long way since it was thought sufficient to ask recipients of services simple questions about satisfaction. More searching questions are now being asked about what are the aims and outcomes of the service. For example, if the aim is to keep people in their own homes, how many go into institutional care, what is the cost and what are the effects on carers?

Some problems

The subjective nature of evaluation: The process of evaluation necessarily entails, as the word suggests, the placing of goods, services or actions in order of values. What these values are and what level of importance is given to them ought always to be openly stated and not, as so often happens, be left as a hidden assumption, since not everyone will necessarily accept the same scale of values. In some research, for example, the assumption is made that keeping older people in their own homes is to some extent a mark of 'success'. This solution may or may not be appropriate.

The views of the present consumers being used as a basis for provision for future generations: Even when it is possible to find out people's views and feelings one has to assess what weight should be given to the views of the present generation when planning for the next, whose expectations may well be different. It would therefore be unwise to plan solely on the basis of what today's older people think. Bedsitters in sheltered housing, for example, might have been acceptable in the past but are less so now.

Comparisons between groups of older people: Another method of evaluation is to compare the information about older people in various studies. Comparisons are an important form of evaluation but there are problems to be faced (see Chapter 2). Problems may arise over different definitions, for example elderly people may be classified as 'elderly' if they are over the age of 60, 65 or of pensionable age. Similarly comparisons of dependency in studies is fraught with difficulties when different measures are used. Cross-national comparisons are even more complex because of the differing variables.

Evaluation still has a long way to go and often seems a relatively esoteric exercise to practitioners. Unless practitioners can become more involved and evaluation is built in as part of their normal work, there is a danger of them ignoring findings. Certainly better dissemination of evaluative studies could go a long way to spread the results, but nothing brings home the value of research more than a small taste of it at first hand. A number of other things, such as replication studies, are needed as well to assess the impact of social intervention. Finally, when evaluations have taken place, it is essential for policy makers and practitioners to be made aware of them. Whether it is good practice resulting in successful outcomes or the reverse, people need to know. They, professionals and older people alike, also have to be prepared to accept changes.

The meaning of community care

The evidence of the previous chapters can now be brought together. The major findings are that some old people need some form of help and that this is substantial in the case of those who are frail. This help comes mainly from the family, but the statutory services, voluntary organisations and friends play an important role. They complement rather than compete. Many older people give help to others and it is suggested that more of them could if given the opportunity.

How do these findings contribute to a theory of community care? If we return to the definition of community care in Chapter 4 it was seen that the meaning is usually polarised between the provision of domiciliary services and a vague idea of caring by the community or society. Caring in this context is usually taken to mean the provision of help, support and protection. But, as a speaker to the Royal Society of Health said in 1972: 'Community care is a treacherous, seductive phrase which creates a warm glow like roses round the cottage door catching the rays of the setting sun'. The reality of care is usually a combination of the two extremes just mentioned. Domiciliary services are important and provide that care which a family is not able to give. But the support of the family is usually of crucial importance.

The concept of community care contains a number of different elements. First there is the public recognition of the importance of the family (usually referred to as informal care but in reality mainly the family). If the family still plays the major role then the aim of the statutory services ought to be to enable them to discharge their task more effectively. At the same time there will always be families who cannot or will not give help, nor is it always the right solution. It would be as foolish to ignore the limitations of the family as to undervalue its potential. Nor is it sensible to ignore the fact that family care, as has been pointed out, has up to now usually been provided by women and that equal opportunities may now mean that men will have to take a greater share in family caring. There are also older people without any relatives and, for them, family support is obviously impossible.

Second it is foolish and shortsighted to see older people (and probably any other group) as being always the recipients of services. The 80-year-old running her son's household after the death of his wife and the 76-year-old disabled man doing his 89-year-old uncle's shopping, found in the granny annexe sample (Tinker 1976), are just as much part of the caring pattern as the family looking after a bedridden grandmother. Unless older people are seen as contributors as well as recipients they are unlikely to be considered equal members of society.

The third element in a social policy based on community care must be the role of neighbours and friends. Little is known about how commitment can be fostered. It is, however, probably unrealistic to expect help from this source to cover long-term care, especially that of a more intimate and personal kind. There is a difference in neighbours getting in shopping for someone and going round to put them on a commode.

A fourth element in community care is the proposition that institutional care can be looked on as a (very necessary) form of community care. Under the NHS and Community Care Act 1990 (Section 46) the definition of community care services includes local authority homes. Where there is an easy exchange between the two, as in respite care schemes, it is easier to see institutions as part of the community. Some argue that when old people live in homes of their own these may become institutional with family members being 'trained up' to give nursing help, administer medicines and so on (Higgins 1989).

Finally there is need to see community care in less narrow terms than the provision of care services and the sole responsibility of social services departments. It needs to be seen in the widest possible context which particularly emphasises housing and income. It also means starting with the needs of the individual old person and building on the person's strengths as well as focusing on crisis points such as bereavement and discharge from hospital.

In conclusion the approaches outlined above are complementary. It is the interleaving of informal, usually family, care with statutory services that is so necessary but so difficult to achieve. What does seem evident is that without good basic statutory services, such as community nursing and help in the home, informal carers will not be able to support older people without cost to their mental and physical health. It is no use paying lip service to support for informal carers if help from professionals is not forthcoming. This may mean a better use of existing resources but it may mean more resources.

Finance

Economic constraints and spending

Economic constraints have dominated social policy in recent years. On the positive side, closer scrutiny of budgets can lead to a radical and valuable reappraisal of policies which might not otherwise have happened. The continued growth in the number of very elderly people has concentrated people's minds because it is usually the care of this group which is the most costly.

What is very difficult to prove is whether public expenditure on social services for elderly people has risen in real terms recently (see also Chapter 8: pp. 169–70). For example a straightforward comparison given by the government shows that net current personal social services expenditure (including special and specific grants) budgeted in 1995/6 was £7,323 million compared with £1,062 million (£3,183 million in real terms) in 1978/9 (DoH/SSI Chief Inspector 1996: 81). What is not apparent is how these figures relate to number of clients/patients. Also part of the increase is accounted for by increases in the salaries of people in the caring professions so there has not necessarily been an improvement in services. More helpful is to relate services to proportions of elderly people in particular age groups. On this basis it is possible to see that while there has been some expansion of services overall for elderly people, for services such as home helps and meals this has not matched the growth in the population aged 75+ and 85+ (Tinker *et al.* 1994: 14). In some services it is easier to see the drop in public provision, as in local authority and housing association housing for elderly people (Chapter 7).

Looking at work force figures it is again difficult to come to firm conclusions about services. For example, between 1981 and 1991 total NHS personnel fell but this was partly a result of competitive tendering when numbers of ancillary staff halved following the privatisation of laundry, catering and domestic services (CSO 1993: 111). Making comparisons with 1994 is difficult because the reduction of the working week of nurses since 1994 distorts the figures (CSO 1996: 146). As was seen in Chapter 8 there has been an increase in numbers of staff in social services except for residential care.

Regardless of economic constraints, it is not always easy to achieve any desired shift in resources. Research may show that it is both possible and cheaper to keep elderly people in their own homes rather than in residential care but it may not be possible to switch buildings and staff at the drop of a hat. The carrot of joint finance has been one way of attempting to bring about this switch.

There have been a number of factors which have contributed to the current interest in costs, such as variations in costs of apparently similar services, the growing interest generally in value for money, and the increasing number of economists and accountants becoming involved in social policy. In government departments, the Audit Commission and bodies connected with local and health authorities, the number of costings studies grew in the 1980s. But the problems should not be minimised. The methodological problems, as DHSS admitted to the House of Commons Social Services Committee in 1980, are difficult (House of Commons Social Services Committee 1980). The Committee recommended that 'high priority' should be given to research on the cost-effectiveness of different packages of care.

Wright's work has contributed much to laying the foundations of a methodology of costings, but he admits that the actual measurement of costs and benefits are 'fiendishly difficult' (Wright 1982). His explanation of the methods of costing is one of the clearest expositions on the subject. He describes two major ways of measuring costs. The simplest is the public expenditures falling on public authorities. The other approach is the opportunity cost which arises from the premise that, as resources are limited, using them in one way means that a benefit is foregone for use for an alternative. Therefore cost is a measure of sacrifice or opportunity lost. The latter approach includes all the resources used in the provision of care, whether or not they belong to public authorities.

While caution should be exercised in any discussion of costs (for example capital costs are often left out of calculations) some comparative costs are significant. A public expenditure costings exercise for DoE, in conjunction with DHSS, which outlined some of the problems, showed that it is possible to cost a package of care for people of similar dependency levels (Tinker 1984, 1989b). This included the capital and revenue costs of particular schemes, such as alarms or very sheltered housing, and all the other public expenditure costs such as pensions and income support. Document 16 shows the relative costs and demonstrates that staying at home options, while not cheap, are very much cheaper than hospital care and cheaper than residential care. Updated costings for staying at home and sheltered housing have been done by DoE [Document 17]. Costs should not be the only factor in decisions. Very few costings studies, for example, take account of informal care (but see McCafferty 1994). It must also be recognised that costs for very dependent people following hospital closures may be more expensive than currently costed packages of care (Glennerster *et al.* 1990).

The important work of the Audit Commission has increasingly included costings for different services and care settings (see Bibliography).

Other work on costings includes the Kent Community Care scheme evaluated by Challis and Davies (1986). This study, which was later replicated, demonstrated the cost-effectiveness of that scheme. The researchers also found that taking account of costs as well as welfare benefits did not distract social workers from their main objectives. Valuable work on costings has also been undertaken by Netten (1993) and Netten and Beecham (1993).

Another area of concern in value for money is over charges. The only free (to the old person) form of housing provision is the hospital; whereas in sheltered housing rent must be paid or the home bought, and for Part III accommodation people may have to sell their home or realise any other capital to pay for their stay (see Chapter 6 for a discussion about continuing care, Chapter 8 for charges for social services and Oldman 1991 for a discussion of personal sources of funding care).

It is interesting that alternative costs are being used to illustrate problems of choice. For example the Health Minister, when talking about the £30 million annual cost of prescription fraud, said that this would 'pay for 7,000 hip replacement operations, or 20,000 cataract operations, or 3,000 heart valve replacements' (DoH press release 12.3.1996). Ham illustrates the effects of medical technology to the NHS where the result could be increased costs (e.g. hip replacements), cost-neutral (e.g. gastric ulcer drugs) and reduced costs (e.g. computerised diagnosis) (Ham 1992: 250).

Lack of information

A prerequisite to any understanding about patterns of expenditure is adequate information. Some of the most interesting evidence on finance in the last few years has come from the House of Commons Social Services Committee. The House of Commons Health Committee has also been a mine of information on public expenditure on health (e.g. House of Commons Health Committee 1991) and community care (e.g. House of Commons Health Committee 1993b).

The mixed economy of welfare

The complexity of the welfare state was demonstrated in Chapter 4. Subsequent chapters have shown the greater emphasis in the 1980s on the independent sector. The growth of private sector pensions, sheltered housing and residential care has been particularly marked. So has the taking over of local authority services, such as day care, by voluntary agencies like Age Concern. Questions need to be asked about the effect on the statutory sector as well as on the private and voluntary.

One positive side to a lack of expansion of the public sector is, in theory anyway, that less taxes will be demanded and therefore people will have more of their own money to spend as they wish and so will have choice. In practice alternative services may not be available, for example the provision of private domiciliary help is very patchy. Also to be taken into account is the likely residualisation of services in the public sector if it increasingly serves only those on low incomes. What public opinion polls have shown is the growing wish of people to spend money on statutory help to obtain better services. In the survey *British Social Attitudes*, the question posed regularly since 1983 has been 'Suppose the Government had to choose between the three options on the card. Which do you think it should choose?' The three options were:

- reduce taxes and spend *less* on health, education and social benefits;
- keep taxes and spending on these services at the *same* level as now;
- increase taxes and spend *more* on health, education and social benefits.

The most popular option in 1994 was the latter – 58 per cent wanted to increase taxes and this compares with 32 per cent in 1983 when the majority (54 per cent) wanted taxes and spending at the same level (Taylor-Gooby 1995: 3). In 1994 88 per cent wanted more spent on health and 78 per cent more on old age pensions (Taylor-Gooby 1995: 4). In 1996 a National Gallup Survey asked, 'If an extra penny was to be put on the pound in income tax which of the following should it be spent on?' (ACE 1996: 7). A clear majority (67 per cent) wanted to see more money spent on an improved health service for all. Pensions was the fourth most popular choice. The order of priorities was the same for the total population as it was for pensioners.

The advantages of non-statutory help include choice, flexibility, and the encouragement of competition. However one essential objective of the private sector is to make a profit, and provision is not primarily a response to need. While the development of private sector provision has gone ahead and opened up more and different services to older people, this has not been without criticism and questioning. Perhaps the most important of these relate to standards of care. Research on private residential homes shows that there are dramatic differences between the standards of the best and the worst. In private sheltered housing older people and their advisers need to look carefully at such things as the service charges. And in many areas of private care such as domiciliary help or chiropody little is known at present about standards. The particular problems in the voluntary sector were identified in Chapter 11. Another problem with a mixed economy of welfare is that planning a coherent social policy may be difficult if those who commission services from outside the state system do not plan and monitor carefully.

These and other issues raised in this chapter need to be considered in the context of groups other than older people and this is one of the purposes of the concluding chapter.

CHAPTER 14

The topic in perspective

The position of older people at the present time, and possible future developments, have been examined. Their needs and who might meet them have been discussed. It is now possible to draw together some of the threads and come to some conclusions. But before doing so it is important to consider older people in relation to the rest of society.

It is easy to be aware that older people are a group which is increasing in size, while other groups, such as children, are at present declining in numbers. But it is not just this demographic fact alone that has caused an upsurge of interest in this group (as witnessed by official pronouncements, academic research, media stories and so on) (Tinker 1990). Although it is difficult to know exactly why this has happened, pressure groups and an increasingly articulate and educated group of older people must have had some impact. Some would argue, however, that this growing interest and public concern is not matched by increased provision of services. Nor is there as much competition for posts in geriatric medicine as in some other fields of medicine or a noticeable queue of people wanting to work in establishments that care for elderly people.

Older people and other groups

The majority of older people continue to live their lives with only marginal state intervention. While nearly all will receive a state pension and some form of state health care, it is only the minority who will receive the many other public services available.

For those who do need help, many of their problems, such as ignorance of benefits and feelings of stigma, will be the same as for other disadvantaged groups. The need for more information about benefits presented in a more lucid form (Tester and Meredith 1987, Tinker et al. 1993) is not peculiar to older people. Similarly, when sources of help are examined a pattern akin to other groups is found. This is particularly noticeable in the extent of family care. For people who have physical disabilities and learning difficulties the bulk of caring is also undertaken by kin (Green 1988, Martin et al. 1988).

The general approach to the delivery of services to older people is also similar in many ways to that being increasingly recommended for other groups such as children, disabled people and the homeless.

All emphasise the importance of community care and joint planning and co-ordination between services.

Older people also share similar experiences with other groups. With the growth of unemployment they are sharing an experience of absence of paid employment. Is it too much to hope that this could bring about a change in the way in which people who are not in paid employment are seen? If more people could find status and satisfaction in their lives through activities other than paid work, then this would be bound to have repercussions on the way in which people see ageing. Instead of old age being the end of 'real life', it could be a more natural continuation of the life they have been living before the age of statutory retirement. Old people also share some of the uncertainties in social policy. What changes, for example, will be required in social policy when there are more people from black and minority ethnic groups? Those who were born abroad may compare the expectation of care that they would have received in their home country, possibly within an extended family system and with enhanced status, with the reality of care in Britain.

Priority for resources and the intergenerational perspective

A question that will be asked increasingly, particularly if resources continue to be limited, is what priority older people should have compared with other groups. In part the question is answered by demographic facts. The large increases in the numbers of very old people (Chapter 2) means, if present trends continue, a greatly increased demand for health and personal social services. Para-doxically, policies of prevention and care are enabling more people to live longer and in better health. But probably in the end there will be a period, perhaps only a short time, when these people are more dependent and will need more services. Those who argue for priority to go to older people also point to the extent of unmet need. But note the large proportion of expenditure which already goes on those over the age of 65. In 1993/4 expenditure on those aged 65 and over was:

- 42 per cent of hospital and community health services;
- 28 per cent of family health services;
- 46 per cent of personal social services (DoH Personal communication July 1996 based on published and non-published figures).

The assumption has often been made that the Welfare State will continue to expand and that the issue is largely about where priority for expansion should take place. Constraints were foreseen in 1975 by Klein, who drew attention to the potential problems of inflation and lack of economic growth (Klein 1975). It is these problems which have caused concern in all the major industrial countries in the last few years. Rising numbers of older people, combined with lack of economic growth, has turned attention to what is usually the largest item in social welfare – pensions. Most state pensions are paid by the taxes of a working generation (known as pay-as-you-go finance) as part of an informal contract. The understanding is that the working generations will have their pensions paid by future generations in paid employment. When the numbers of people in paid employment decline, as will happen in the UK, then the proportion of their income required in taxation will increase to meet the pension costs of the larger number of pensioners (see Chapter 5).

What is happening abroad now, for example in the United States and New Zealand, are some bitter disputes over what has become known as intergenerational justice. This is illustrated in a book *Workers versus Pensioners: Intergenerational Justice in an Ageing World* (Johnson et al. 1989). The authors argue that younger generations see the present group entering old age as having benefited from economic growth, subsidised house purchase, large child benefits and other welfare help that is being increasingly denied to younger people now. In the United States older people have won many advantages in the field of social security and health care at the expense of other social groups (Berliner 1988). It is understandable that younger age groups may feel reluctant to pay for such proportionately large pensions. Some governments are beginning to raise retirement ages, introduce stiffer means testing for benefits and lower the relative level of others so that pensioners will not have the same benefits as previous generations.

While recent research in the United States and New Zealand has suggested that over the last two decades welfare systems have become increasingly generous towards older people and increasingly restrictive towards families with dependent children, this has not been shown to have happened in Britain. Examining direct government expenditure on older people through pensions, health and social services, there is little evidence of any transfer of resources from young to old since the 1960s – any changes in the distribution of welfare payments and services has merely reflected changes in the age structure of the population (Johnson and Falkingham 1988). Both in 1983/4 and in 1993/4 13 per cent of hospital and community health services gross current expenditure (excluding acute services) was spent on elderly people (House of Commons Health Committee 1995a: 26). In some cases, such as total social security benefit expenditure, there has been a decline in the proportion to elderly people. In 1989/90 benefits to older people represented 51 per cent of the total but this had declined to 45 per cent in 1994/5 (DSS 1995b: 10). A National Gallup Survey in 1996 found little evidence of differences between the views of different generations. For example, whereas 12 per cent of those aged 60 and above felt that, where health service resources are limited pensioners should be given a lower priority than younger people, the figure was 8 per cent for those aged 18–39 and 9 per cent for those aged 40–59 (ACE 1996: 11).

It is essential that those who argue for resources to go to one group or another do so on sound evidence. That is not to say that the weight of numbers will always be the most important factor. For example, cases of child abuse in the early 1990s have had an effect on public opinion and concentrated staff resources in this area. What has also to be taken into account is the contribution of older people, including the not insubstantial one of child care (see Chapter 12). Research and discussion is increasingly focusing on what each generation gives to the other. *Uniting Generations: Studies in Conflict and Co-operation* brought together many of the issues and discussed areas of concern in the 'intergenerational contract' (Hobman 1993; see also Walker 1996). In some cases there is concern by both generations, for example when older people have to sell their home to pay for continuing care.

Integration or segregation?

Another basic issue in deciding social policies for older people is that of integration versus segregation. Should older people be (as the dictionary puts it) combined into the whole or should they be set apart? Should they be integrated into society through housing, new forms of employment and social activities, or should they be moved, or encouraged to move, away from the mainstream of life?

There are a number of different theoretical approaches to integration and segregation. First there are those related to historical changes. These assume that while older people used at one time to be integrated into both society and the family, they are now much more likely to be segregated. However, as was pointed out in Chapter 10 when the family was discussed, evidence is lacking to substantiate such theories. What evidence there is does not support the view that the close three-generation family was the norm, and anyway few people actually survived into old age.

Second, there are theories about the advantages and disadvantages accruing to groups when they are singled out for special treatment. The advantages include the value of specialisation and a co-ordinated approach to provision. This has been argued strongly in the case of children. So it was for disabled people, who have had a minister since 1974 to look after their interests. The plea for a Minister for Older People is sometimes put but this could further disadvantage older people by setting them as a race apart. As far as administration is concerned, and particularly over the monitoring of services, it has been suggested that there should be an inspectorate based on client groups rather than on services. However, a service concerned solely with a client group risks the danger of being out of the mainstream of function-based services. This is one of the arguments used against having specialist social workers or geriatric medicine (see Royal College of Physicians 1994: 28–31 for a summary of the advantages and disadvantages of traditional, age-defined and integrated models of acute care for older people). There is also the problem that when a group is chosen for special treatment this can bring stigma. Also, as has been pointed out many times, older people are not a homogeneous group and may not gain from being treated as if they were.

The third approach is concerned with ageing and theories of disengagement. It is held to be normal for older people to disengage and therefore bring about their own segregation from society. The theory is that the individual's activities form a curve during their lifetime and gradually fall away. Preparation for death is made by withdrawing from previous roles and limiting social contacts. There is little evidence to support these theories and some writers suggest that insufficient attention has been paid to forms of compensation, replacement and substitution.

Probably the right basis for assessing the range of views is to note the evidence presented earlier that older people are a varied group. Some want independence with privacy. Others prefer the company of younger people. It seems more sensible to make varied provision in social policy so that, for example, older people can choose to live either in mixed communities or in special schemes for their own age group. The same course should be followed with other provisions such as clubs, since some will want to belong to those for their own age group while others will prefer ones without age restrictions.

Older people in modern society: stresses and compensations

Surveys of old people often concentrate on measurable needs and the extent of services provided. Many show up alleged deficiencies in services or focus on people in particular situations – found dead, suffering from cold, lacking income and so on. A good deal, therefore, is known about the stresses of growing old but much less about its compensations. Nor is there a philosophy of retirement.

There is no doubt from recent evidence that for some old people life does present difficulties. In their own judgement the greatest problems are caused by ill-health, lack of income and loneliness. But for the majority of old people life continues to have a great deal of satisfaction. Hunt commented: 'looking at older people as a whole, it can be said that a great many appear to get a great deal out of life' (Hunt 1978: 31). Abrams found this too when he measured life-satisfaction (Abrams 1978) and so have subsequent surveys (e.g. Wenger 1984, Bury and Holme 1991).

Growing attention has been focused on measuring life-satisfaction and quality of life (Tinker 1983, Hughes 1990). Life-satisfaction is related to the degree to which people feel they achieve their aspirations, morale and happiness. How the quality of life is measured is difficult to decide. Some measures have been documented and criticised (Bowling 1991, 1996). In a useful summary of ways of measuring quality of life Hughes includes:

- individual characteristics of old people such as functional abilities, physical and mental health, dependency, gender, race and class;
- physical environmental factors such as facilities and amenities, standard of housing, control over environment, comfort, security and regime in care settings;
- social environmental factors such as levels of social and recreational activity, family and social networks and contact with organisations;
- socio-economic factors such as income, nutrition, standard of living and socio-economic status;
- personal autonomy factors such as ability to make choices, exercise control and negotiate environment;
- subjective satisfaction: the quality of life as assessed by the old person;
- personality factors such as psychological well-being, morale, life-satisfaction and happiness.

(Hughes 1990: 48)

Some research studies are based on the perceptions of professionals, with questions asked of them rather than of older people themselves. This may save time and achieve answers in a more standard form, but it may be dangerously misleading as a way of finding out how older people themselves really feel. Power, in his study of elderly people in residential care, showed how easy it is to be misled by appearances. Professionals in homes might see elderly people sitting apathetically but when they were interviewed nothing could be further from the truth (Power 1981: 2).

When attempts are made to measure quality of life by asking older people themselves, there are different ways in which this can be done. In some cases direct questions, albeit open ones, are put, but others prefer a less structured biographical approach. Certainly there are some aspects of life which do not come out clearly in a questionnaire. No-one who reads Ronald Blythe's *The View in Winter* can fail to be moved by his chapter on prayer and the importance of a spiritual life to many older people (Blythe 1979). The importance of this aspect of people's lives also came out clearly in the report *Ageing* (Board for Social Responsibility 1990).

Coming to the fore now are other potentially life-enhancing aspects of life which were formerly scarcely touched on. These include sexuality and friendship in later life (e.g. Thienhaus *et al.* 1986, Greengross and Greengross 1989, Jerrome 1993).

What is strikingly apparent is the variety of conditions of older people which give the lie to any attempt to generalise about them. As Brearley has said, each person's attitudes and life are unique and satisfaction for each of us is a highly personal experience (Brearley 1975: 21). Differences between older people of different ages, between men and women, between social classes and between those living alone and those living with others are just four examples.

Of growing interest – and concern – is the first of these and in particular differences between the quality of life of what have been termed the young old and the old old. In a profile of 11 risk groups it was found that the most disadvantaged risk groups were the very old, those who had recently moved or been discharged from hospital and the divorced or separated (Taylor *et al.* 1983). On the other hand, large numbers of very old people, such as those found in a study of the over-90s, said that they were in good health and their morale and well-being was high (Bury and Holme 1991).

Hunt (1976) also made much of the differences between men and women in the quality of their lives as measured by health and access to services. In most cases women came off worse, though one can speculate that some of the disadvantages, such as lower income, were the result of fewer having been in paid employment or employment with equality of pay. Subsequent research, much of it referred to in this book, confirms this disadvantaged position. The study of the over-90s also found that life-satisfaction across the life course was higher for men than for women (Bury and Holme 1991). There is an encouraging growth of interest in gender differences in old age with a focus on women (e.g. Arber and Ginn 1991, Arber and Ginn 1995, Bernard and Meade 1993).

Abrams also considered class differences and found that among very old people those from a professional background led more active lives than those from a manual working-class background (Abrams 1980). But he found no evidence that as a result middle-class old people found their lives more satisfying than working-class people. Where there were differences was in looking back and regretting what they did not do. Working-class people were more prone than middle-class people to look back on a period of frustrated aspirations and disappointed expectations. Different patterns of retirement, often related to the person's previous work or health, have also been noted (Phillipson 1993).

The fourth situation in which there can be differences is in the quality of life of people living alone. Here the evidence is mixed. On the one hand, common sense suggests that older people living alone will have no-one to share their domestic tasks and will have less chance of contacting someone else in an emergency. They are also less likely to have possessions such as a car or washing machine (Jarvis *et al.* 1996). But it is perhaps salutary to remember that Abrams found that satisfaction with particular aspects of their lives (e.g. health, financial position, income) was consistently greater among those living alone than among those living with others. And, in a follow-up study of his sample, he noted that more of those living alone had survived (Abrams 1980). Later evidence shows that those who live alone are more likely to have domestic help and to see relatives or friends every day (Jarvis *et al.* 1996).

Three overlapping problems identified are the restrictions result-ing from poor material conditions and poor health, the effect of combinations of disadvantage (e.g. houses which are difficult to keep warm, frailty and low income) and disability or bereavement which may bring social isolation and which may make old people feel they have little to live for (Sinclair and Williams 1990: 85). Although fears are often expressed about other aspects of life, it is important to remember these three. Some aspects of people's lives, for example as victims of crime, assume more publicity at certain times. Research, however, consistently shows that older people are the least likely to be victims of violent crime.

To allow older people to achieve their potential and to be valued members of society there may be a need for change in the mental picture that people have of old age. Comfort has said that men of his generation knew that their grandmothers dressed in black at 45, and looked like grandmothers, whereas today's grandmothers often wear shorts and play tennis (Comfort 1965: 119). Twelve years later he stated that what was needed was a change of attitude (Comfort 1977: 27). He thought that social gerontology would only have made an impact when an older person came to be seen not as old first and a person second, but as a person who happens to be old (plus experience and minus the consequences of certain physical accidents of time).

Implications for professionals

It is always important for professionals to remember that they will only be in personal contact with a minority of older people. And just as one cannot generalise from a study based on the 3 per cent in residential care, so groups such as social workers should not generalise from those older people who present as clients. For they are bound to be those who have particular difficulties.

What it is hoped that this book has shown is that 95 per cent of old people live out their lives in their own homes supported in the main by their families. But this must not be taken to imply that there is no need to be concerned about them and about those services which they will all have recourse to, such as pensions and health care. There must be constant vigilance that these are adequate and, above all, provided in the most appropriate way with the elderly person having the maximum say in this. What is also crucial is that services for the growing number of frail elderly people should be adequate. These are vital to back up what their families can do and particularly vital for those old people who have no families to turn to.

One of the most encouraging developments is a growing awareness of the needs of older people by professionals. Part of this is a result of a multidisciplinary approach and part is an attempt by professionals to define what it is they are trying to do. And yet evidence continues to be produced about poor standards and a lack of understanding of the needs of older people. Older people have both legal and moral rights and exercising these may lead to voluntary and involuntary risks. Studies such as *Rights and Risks* show the need for a shift 'away from a patronising and paternalistic over-protection from risk and towards acknowledgement of their rights to as much self-determination as is possible for each individual within the limits of the resources available' (Norman 1980: 8).

The issues of rights and risks seem most acute in residential settings where staff may have a powerful influence. It is a problem not only in institutions specifically for old people, such as geriatric hospitals, but for acute hospitals too. The widespread yet unfounded fear amongst the staff of residential and nursing homes that the Coroner's Court may apportion blame following a fatal accident continues to cause many staff to be overprotective, and thus to deprive older people of their liberty, self-responsibility and freedom of movement, claims Norman (1988). Professionals are given little guidance about risk-taking (Wright 1994). The Wagner Committee listed a number of rights which they thought that individuals should have in institutions (Wagner 1988a). These included a trial period, retention of their pension book, a personal key to their room, a clear complaints procedure and also that no-one should have to share a bedroom as a condition of residence (Wagner 1988a: 116). Another important area for professionals is attention to the legal rights of old people (Griffiths *et al.* 1990, Ashton 1994).

This leads on to another point, that while professionals may not consciously opt for working with older people (e.g. medical students who declare adamantly that they wish to work with other age groups), most of them will in fact do so. For example, in 1990/1 46 per cent of acute beds were occupied by people aged 65 and over (Tinker *et al.* 1994: 16) One geriatrician wrote: 'Like Peter Pan, British medicine wishes to stay with the young, dreaming of transplanting this and pioneering that – while avoiding the real health-care needs of our ageing population' (Livesley 1982). And Evans, discussing the case for subsuming geriatric medicine as a speciality into general medicine asks, in view of demographic trends, whether there is a future for general medicine that is not geriatric (Evans 1981).

Some would argue that a fundamental shift in society is needed for older people to have more rights and to be taken more seriously by professionals. Townsend argues that the dependency of older people is being manufactured socially. The major influences, he believes, are the imposition, and acceptance, of earlier retirement, the legitimisation of low income, the denial of rights to self-determination in institutions, and the construction of community services for recipients assumed to be predominantly passive (Townsend 1981). This argument that the experience of old age is determined more by economic and social factors and less by biological or individual ones is stressed by critical gerontologists (e.g. Phillipson and Walker 1986). Wilding also takes a radical approach and suggests that the professions trample on people's rights, help some but disable others, have been guilty of serious failures of responsibilities and are an example of power without accountability (Wilding 1982).

This widespread unease about the present attitude of our society to the care of older people has prompted many calls for more training. More specifically, professional education and training can enhance the understanding of staff who work with older people. Multidisciplinary degrees in gerontology, such as the one pioneered at King's College London, and the growing number of other courses are also helpful in allowing professionals to learn from each other. Reports as diverse as the Wagner one on residential care (Wagner 1988a) and one on training for doctors working in the field of the psychiatry of old age (Royal College of Physicians and the Royal College of Psychiatrists 1989) have stressed the value of training.

Professionals, whether administrators, doctors, social workers, health visitors, nurses or others in the caring professions, must aim to provide the sort of service which they themselves would wish for when they reach retirement. But the well-being of society is not exclusively the concern of the professional. There are many skills and resources available to help in the community, and some indeed are to be found among the users of services. It is the dovetailing of professionals with others that is of importance so that each may contribute to the maximum advantage of society.

The international dimension

Of growing importance in social policy is the impact of events abroad. The effect of European Commission policies, comparative research (see Chapter 3) and the increase in travel by older people and others are beginning to alter policies. Already decisions taken in the European Court of Justice are affecting pensions and the legal position of carers. It is not just care delivery which may be affected, but the possible migration of older people from one country to another, which could have dramatic effects on policies. So could any harmonisation of legal systems where family responsibilities towards relatives vary between countries. It is difficult to assess the effect of events which take place across countries such as the European Year of Older People and Solidarity Between Generations in 1993, but it did lead to a declaration by the Council of Ministers which at least put older people's issues on the political agenda. The constraints of this book mean that it has only been possible to put up a marker about international comparisons.

Conclusion

It is ironic that the carefully measured speech of Prince Charles which stressed the diversity of older people should be headlined

'Prince seeks a dynamic role for the elderly' (*The Times* 16.5.1990). Society swings between highlighting the Third Age type go-getter and the shivering, demented old person living alone. Both, of course, exist. But the majority are at neither of these two extremes. After all the discussion on research and the views of others, perhaps the last word is best left to Mary Stott. In a passionately written book, *Ageing for Beginners*, as she entered her eighth decade, she declared that ageing is not a 'condition' to be treated by doctors or social workers, but a process that brings with it possibilities of new experience and achievement (Stott 1981). The next few years will bring problems, there is no doubt about that, but the most encouraging thing is that older people are more and more taking an active role in saying what sort of society they want. Long may it continue. And may professionals listen to, and learn from, them.

PART FOUR

Documents

List of documents

Document 1
'THE NEW ELDERLY'

In 1975 Dr Mark Abrams prophetically discussed important demographic trends relating to elderly people:

So far and currently, society has the relatively easy task of providing support and care for a population of elderly people who for the most part are comparatively young, mobile, and healthy. From now on the balance of concern will have to shift in favour of the very old, the immobile and the frail.

He went on to say why he thought the focus would change in the future:

Since the 1960s the fortunes of the teenager have been the focus of discussion and research by those interested in age-stratification. He has had his day; from now on the centre of the stage is likely to be occupied by the growing millions who will live well beyond the traditional allotment of three score years and ten.

From: Abrams, M., 'The new elderly', *New Society*, 26.6.75, p. 778

Document 2
MYTHS AND REALITIES OF AGEING

The former Director of Age Concern describes some images of ageing:

The ageing process is deeply enshrined in a range of images leading to stereotypes based on notions of intense wisdom and even God-like proportions at one end of the spectrum, to uselessness and semi-idiocy at the other.

None of these extremes serve the elderly well. They are no more universally wise or nice or kind than they are stupid, but there are a range of half truths and fantasies about age, knowledge and experience which have become enshrined in the folk culture of ageing. Some of them stem from the professionals who practise in care. They also have their root in art and literature.

Perhaps the most important perception to be missing is that of the elderly themselves: People like a 60-year-old woman who wrote about her feelings on having reached the statutory retirement age. She said: 'Pensioners are being got at. We must prepare to do battle to maintain our independence and preserve our attractive personalities ... now I am haunted by the fear that if I cannot dispel the assumption that I am a senior citizen, the following events may reasonably occur. (1) I shall have a gang of young thugs sent to my home to paint my kitchen instead of going to prison; (2) I shall have patients from the local mental hospital drafted to dig my garden; (3) I may be forced to go to suitable entertainments, drink tea and wear a paper hat; (4) I may receive vast boxes of assorted food to which I feel I am not entitled. We pensioners are in a terrifying position. We are *recipients* ... hands off, please. I am in charge of my life.'

This person recognises, but does not accept, one widely held image of ageing full of assumptions and value judgements with its underlying theme of patronising attitudes, setting the elderly as a race apart to be pitied as people who are no longer capable of managing their own lives. It assumes that ageing is synonymous with a changing personality and that the retired adopt common characteristics with an incompetent level of social functioning. It also implies limited intellectual thresholds devoid of critical faculties.

Not only does this image suggest the old are incapable of exercising informed or rational choice and of maintaining a degree of control over their circumstances; but it also implies that they do not have sufficient resources to meet their own needs for recreation, or welfare when, in fact, the young retired now represent a very important resource which could well make a substantial contribution to the health and social well-being of the community as a whole.

From: Hobman, D., 'Myths and realities of ageing', *Social Work Today*, 3.1.78, p. 18

Document 3
**ACTUAL AND PROJECTED POPULATION BY AGE
GROUP, ENGLAND AND WALES, 1951–2034**

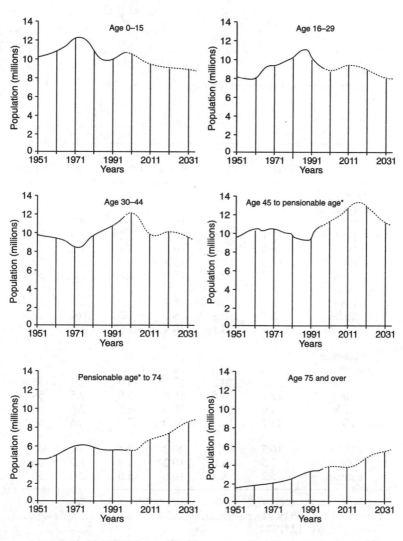

———— Actual population
········· Projected population dependent upon assumptions outlined in the text
    * *Pensionable age of 60 for women, 65 for men*

From: OPCS, Monitor, pp. 2 96/1 *National population projections: 1994-based,*
OPCS 15.2.1996 p. 2 Figure 1.

Document 4
AGE AND SEX STRUCTURE OF THE POPULATION OF
THE UNITED KINGDOM 1951–2025

Census, estimated and projected numbers from 1951–2025.

Millions

	Under 16	16–39	40–64	65–79	80 and over	All ages
Mid-year estimates						
1951[1]			15.9	4.8	0.7	50.3
1961[1]	13.1	16.6	16.9	5.2	1.0	52.8
1971[1]	14.3	17.5	16.7	6.1	1.3	55.9
1981[2]	12.6	19.5	15.8	6.9	1.6	56.4
1986[1]	11.7	20.6	15.8	6.8	1.8	56.8
1991[3]	11.8	20.3	16.7	6.9	2.1	57.8
Males	5.9	10.3	8.1	3.0	0.6	27.9
Females	5.7	10.1	8.4	3.9	1.5	29.35
Mid-year projections[4]						
1996	12.1	20.3	17.2	6.9	2.4	58.9
2001	12.1	19.8	18.4	6.8	2.5	59.6
2006	11.6	19.0	20.0	6.8	2.6	60.0
2011	11.1	18.4	21.0	7.3	2.6	60.4
2025	10.7	17.7	20.2	9.4	3.2	61.2
Males	5.5	9.0	10.2	4.4	1.2	30.3
Females	5.2	8.7	10.0	5.0	2.0	30.9

[1] From: *Social Trends* (No. 22), HMSO, 1992, Table 1.5, p. 27
[2] Government Actuary's Department, *Population Projections 1981–2021*, Series p. 2, No. 12, 1984
[3] Projected figures from Government Actuary's Department, *National Projections 1991 based*, Series p. 2, No. 18, 1993
[4] 1994-based projections. Projected figures from Government Actuary's Department, *Population Projections 1994–2064*, provided on disk

Document 5
GROWING INTEREST IN THE PROBLEMS OF OLD AGE

Two researchers comment on the lack of interest in elderly people in the first half of the twentieth century and a resurgence from the late 1940s.

Between 1901 and 1947 the numbers of persons in Britain who were aged 65 and over grew from under two to five millions. Yet in that period very little information on the problems of the aged living at home or receiving treatment and care in hospitals and other institutions was published. It is an extraordinary fact. At the turn of the century there had been a few studies on pensions and the effect of the Poor Law, three of them by Charles Booth.[1] In 1909 the reports of the Majority and Minority of the Royal Commission on the Poor Laws appeared, and they both contained sections on the aged.[2] In later years there were short passages on the problems of old age in various reports of general surveys.[3] Otherwise there was a dearth of published information and, apparently, of interest too.

Suddenly, in the late forties and fifties, or so it may seem to the historian of the written and spoken word, the problems of old age were discovered. The Nuffield Foundation pioneered the financing of a few studies, including the remarkable work of J. H. Sheldon.[4] The trickle of carefully documented studies became a modest stream, slightly preceding the floodwaters of interest and research in the subject which were released in the United States in the mid-1950s. Among some of the influential studies in Britain have been those of Dr Alex Comfort on the biology of senescence,[5] Dr Alan Welford and his colleagues on psychological adjustment in old age,[6] and Mr F. Le Gros Clark on ageing in industry.[7] There have been many sociological socio-medical and socio-economic surveys which have been based on interviews with samples of the elderly population.

1   Booth, C., *Pauperism: A Picture; and the Endowment of Old Age: An Argument*, London, Macmillan, 1892; *The Aged Poor: Condition*, London, Macmillan, 1894; and *Old Age Pensions and the Aged Poor*, London, Macmillan, 1899.
2   *Report of the Royal Commission on the Poor Laws*, Cmnd 4499, London, HMSO, 1909.
3   See, for example, Caradog-Jones, D., *The Social Survey of Merseyside*, London, Hodder & Stoughton, 1934; Rowntree, B. S., *Poverty and Progress*, London, Longmans, 1941.
4   Sheldon, J. H., *The Social Medicine of Old Age*, Oxford University Press for the Nuffield Foundation, 1948.
5   Comfort, A., *Ageing: The Biology of Senescence*, London, Routledge & Kegan Paul (revised edition), 1964.
6   Welford, A.T., *Ageing and Human Skill*, London, Oxford University Press for the Nuffield Foundation, 1958.
7   For example, Le Gros Clark, F. and Dunne, A. C., *Ageing in Industry*, London, The Nuffield Foundation, 1955.

From: Townsend P. and Wedderburn, D., *The Aged in the Welfare State*, G. Bell & Sons (1965), p. 10

Document 6
TERMS OF REFERENCE OF THE ROWNTREE COMMITTEE

One of the first large-scale social surveys was undertaken in 1944–6 for the Rowntree Committee on the problems of ageing and the care of old people. The terms of reference of the Rowntree Committee, which was appointed by the Nuffield Foundation, were:

TERMS OF REFERENCE

1. The terms of reference under which the Survey Committee were appointed by the trustees of the Nuffield Foundation were:

'To gather as complete information as possible with regard to (i) the various problems – individual, social, and medical – associated with ageing and old age; (ii) the work being done by public authorities and voluntary organisations, and the public and private resources that exist, for the care and comfort of old people in Great Britain; (iii) the provision made for old people in those countries that have given special thought to this matter; (iv) medical research on the causes and results of ageing; and (v) the lines on which action might usefully be taken in the future by public authorities and private organisations, including the Foundation.'

From: Rowntree, B., *Old People. Report of a Survey Committee on the Problems of Ageing and the Care of Old People*, The Nuffield Foundation, Oxford University Press (1947), p. 1

Document 7
SOME CONCLUSIONS OF THE BEVERIDGE COMMITTEE

The Beveridge Committee, in their report on social insurance and allied services, concluded that there were three special problems. One of these was age and they discussed alternative proposals for pensions.

CONCLUSION

254. There is no valid objection, either on the ground of equity or on the ground that a means test may discourage thrift, to postponing introduction of adequate contributory pensions for a substantial period of transition, during which needs are met by pensions subject to means test. As regards equity, the people who reach pensionable age during the transition period will not have paid contributions at the new rates for any substantial time. As regards thrift, only those who are now so old that they may expect to require pensions before the transition period ends can be affected at all, and of these only a small proportion can be affected substantially. The rising scale of contributory pensions will make it possible for everyone except people who are already close to pension age, by a very moderate additional provision of their own, to secure income adequate for subsistence and have no need for any means pension. There is all the difference in the world between a permanent system of pensions subject to means test and a transitional system of supplementation of rising contributory pensions, such as is suggested here. The first must be rejected; the second is not open to serious objection.
255. There is no reason also to doubt the power of large numbers of people to go on working with advantage to the community and happiness to themselves after reaching the minimum pensionable age of 65 for men or 60 for women. The numbers of people past the pensionable age who, at each census, described themselves as still occupied rather than retired is very great. So is the number of those working as exempt persons after this age under the present schemes of health and unemployment insurance. There is no statistical evidence that industrial development is making it harder for people to continue at work later in life than it used to be; such evidence as there is points in the opposite direction. The natural presumption from the increasing length of total life is that the length of years during which working capacity lasts will also rise, as health improves, as by freedom from want in childhood and by freedom from want and idleness in working years the physique and the courage of the citizens are maintained. A people ageing in years need not be old in spirit, and British youth will rise again.

From: Beveridge, Sir W., *Social Insurance and Allied Services* (The Beveridge Report), HMSO (1942), p. 99

Document 8
THE GUIDING PRINCIPLES OF THE BEVERIDGE REPORT

The Beveridge Committee lay down the three guiding principles behind their recommendations for social insurance and allied services.

THREE GUIDING PRINCIPLES OF RECOMMENDATIONS

6. In proceeding from this first comprehensive survey of social insurance to the next task – of making recommendations – three guiding principles may be laid down at the outset.

7. The first principle is that any proposals for the future, while they should use to the full the experience gathered in the past, should not be restricted by consideration of sectional interests established in the obtaining of that experience. Now, when the war is abolishing landmarks of every kind, is the opportunity for using experience in a clear field. A revolutionary moment in the world's history is the time for revolutions, not for patching.

8. The second principle is that organisation of social insurance should be treated as one part only of a comprehensive policy of social progress. Social insurance fully developed may provide income security; it is an attack upon Want. But Want is one only of five giants on the road of reconstruction and in some ways the easiest to attack. The others are Disease, Ignorance, Squalor and Idleness.

9. The third principle is that social security must be achieved by cooperation between the State and the individual. The State should offer security for service and contribution. The State in organising security should not stifle incentive, opportunity, responsibility; in establishing a national minimum, it should leave room and encouragement for voluntary action by each individual to provide more than that minimum for himself and his family.

10. The Plan for Social Security set out in this Report is built upon these principles. It uses experience but is not tied by experience. It is put forward as a limited contribution to a wider social policy, though as something that could be achieved now without waiting for the whole of that policy. It is, first and foremost, a plan of insurance – of giving in return for contributions benefits up to subsistence level, as of right and without means test, so that individuals may build freely upon it.

From: Beveridge, Sir W., *Social Insurance and Allied Services* (The Beveridge Report), HMSO (1942), pp. 6–7

Document 9
THE END OF THE POOR LAW

The National Assistance Act 1948 set up the NAB with a duty to assist persons in need and gave local authorities powers.

An Act to terminate the existing poor law and to provide in lieu thereof for the assistance of persons in need by the National Assistance Board and by local authorities; to make further provisions for the welfare of disabled, sick aged and other persons and for regulating homes for disabled and aged persons and charities for disabled persons; to amend the law relating to non-contributory old age pensions; to make provision as to the burial or cremation of deceased persons; and for purposes connected with the matters aforesaid.

[13th May 1948.]

PART I. INTRODUCTORY

1. The existing poor law shall cease to have effect, and shall be replaced by the provisions of Part II of this Act as to the rendering, out of moneys provided by Parliament, of assistance to persons in need, the provisions of Part III of this Act as to accommodation and other services to be provided by local authorities, and the related provisions of Part IV of this Act.

From: National Assistance Act 1948, p. 1
(See also Document 20)

Document 10
ESTIMATES OF PREVALENCES OF DISABILITY

Figure 3.5   Estimates of prevalence of disability among adults by age and severity category for men and women.

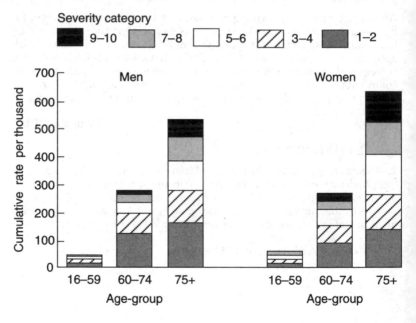

From: Martin, J., Meltzer, H. and Elliot, D., *The Prevalance of Disability Among Adults*, OPCS surveys of disability in Great Britain, No. 1, HMSO, London (1988), Fig 3.5, p. 21

Document 11
VIEWS ABOUT SERVICES FOR ELDERLY PEOPLE FROM THE ROYAL COMMISSION ON THE NATIONAL HEALTH SERVICE

The Royal Commission on the National Health Service felt that the health needs of elderly people were one of the major problems facing the NHS.

6.33. Services for the elderly demonstrate very clearly the requirements for community care already discussed. Everything possible should be done to assist old people to remain independent, healthy and in their own homes. It is important to detect stress and practical problems, and to ward off breakdown, for example by regular visiting of those who are identified through GP case registers as being at risk, by providing physical aids or adapted or sheltered housing, and by assistance from home helps, chiropodists, or meals on wheels. Planned short-term admissions to residential care play an increasing part in helping the elderly remain in their own homes or with relatives. The supporting role of relatives is of great importance and their needs for relief from time to time must be met. Voluntary bodies and volunteers can often help in numerous understanding ways.[1] Where there is illness the full resources of the primary care team have often to be deployed, and a heavy load of work and responsibility falls on the district nurses and the home help services. Day centres are helpful, and day hospitals have been widely developed: their place in a comprehensive service urgently requires critical evaluation and this is being studied by the DHSS. When independence at home is no longer possible, care in a nursing home or local authority residential home may be appropriate.

6.34. Illness in old age commonly has both physical and mental aspects. A deterioration in an old person's faculties may or may not be accompanied by disturbances of behaviour, and may or may not be due to or worsened by physical illness. Detailed assessment is often necessary and the skill of geriatricians, psychiatrists, nurses and social workers may be jointly called upon. We recommend that all professions concerned with the care of the elderly should receive more training in understanding their needs.

6.35. Many elderly patients admitted to district general hospitals do not need the technology which that type of hospital can provide. They frequently remain in hospital long after any investigations or active treatment have been completed because they are not fit to go home and there is nowhere else for them to go. Residential homes cannot care for those who are physically very dependent and need nursing care, or whose behaviour is more than mildly disturbed.

1. Personal Social Services Research Unit, University of Kent, *Kent Community Care Project: an interim report*, 1979.

From: *Royal Commission on the NHS, Report* (the Merrison Committee), Cmnd 7615 (1979), pp. 62–3.

Document 12
HISTORY OF THE PRACTICE TEAM

Before 1948
* General practitioners usually worked singlehandedly

1948–66
* Formation of the College of Practitioners encouraged able thinkers to advocate a team approach in primary care

* The first local authority nursing attachments were made in the 1950s, but many medical officers and general practitioners were wary

1966–90
* The 1966 Family Doctors' Charter enabled employment of practice staff – 70% of the costs were reimbursed

* The role of practice nurses expanded and their number increased

* Practice managers were employed to help with management and administration

* An increasing number of other health care professionals became involved in primary care

1990 onwards
* The workload created by the new general practitioner contract has increased the need for practice nurses and practice managers with proved managerial skills. As their roles expand these members will have a higher profile and may become partners or members of executive boards.

From: Hasler, J. 'The primary health care team: history and contractual forces' in Pringle, M. (ed.), *Change and Teamwork in Primary Care*, BMJ, London (1993), p. 56

Document 13
**A VARIETY OF HOUSING FOR OLD PEOPLE
RECOMMENDED IN 1944**

In 1944 the Ministry of Health, which was responsible for housing, published a *Housing Manual* giving guidance to local authorities on the types of provision that were needed. The section on old people started with some general considerations:

OLD PEOPLE

The type of accommodation required for old people will vary according to their age and disabilities. For the very old who may require a certain amount of care, the accommodation can take the form of small self-contained dwellings grouped together with a common day-room, a room for laundry work, a spare room for visitors, and quarters for a nurse or warden.... Consideration should be given to the possibility of providing hot water to the bathrooms from a common source and a small amount of central heating to give 'background' warmth. [73

For able-bodied old people who can look after themselves, accommodation might be provided in self-contained dwellings, either one or two storey cottages or cottage flats or on the lower floors of blocks of flats. Where there are lifts, the flats could even be on the higher floors. [74

All dwellings for old people should be sited within easy distance of churches and shops and in a position which will give an interesting outlook from the living room window. So far as possible the dwellings should not be segregated, as old people like to have contact with younger generations.... To assist in keeping the dwelling warm a sheltered site should be chosen. [75

From: MOH, *Housing Manual 1944*, HMSO, p. 22

Document 14
CO-ORDINATION OF SERVICES FOR OLD PEOPLE:
ADVICE IN 1961 AND 1992

Advice was given to local authorities in 1961 about services for old people. The need for co-operation was highlighted as is shown below. Later sections dealt with specific services and the role of voluntary organisations.

SERVICES FOR OLD PEOPLE

Co-operation between housing, local health and welfare authorities and voluntary organisations

1. The Minister of Housing and Local Government and the Minister of Health have been considering together how to improve the provisions made for the well-being of old people.
2. Housing, health and welfare authorities are concerned. So are voluntary organisations. All these must work in the closest co-operation if all the varying needs of old people are to be covered. The several services should be regarded as parts of a whole, the authorities and organisations responsible each making their contribution to the whole. This means that all concerned (including in a county borough the different committees) should make it a regular feature of their administration to meet together from time to time to review the provision made in their area, and to decide where and how it needs to be supplemented.
3. It is widely recognised today that old people want to lead an independent life in their own homes for as long as they can, and that to do so gives them the best chance of an active and contented old age. To make this possible, housing authorities must provide, in adequate numbers, a full range of small bungalows, flats and flatlets designed for old people: some in which they can be fully independent (though with neighbours at hand in case help is wanted): others in which some friendly help is available in the person of a warden: others still in which provision can be made for some communal services in addition to a warden. The changes in subsidy proposed in the Housing Bill now before Parliament should enable every housing authority, the less well-off as well as those with adequate resources, to meet, in time, all the demands of their area. With a fully adequate range of housing designed to meet the different tastes and needs of the old, hospital and welfare accommodation can be used by those who really require it.

From: MHLG Circular 10/61; MOH Circular 12/61, *Services for Old People* HMSO, London (1961), p. 1

A joint circular *Housing and Community Care* from the Departments of the Environment and Health included the following sections.

HOUSING STRATEGIES (paras 11–14)

14. It is obviously important that county social services authorities should liaise effectively with district housing authorities and, where social services and housing authorities are part of a unified authority, that discussions should take place with neighbouring or regional bodies in order to establish a strategic pattern of provision wherever this makes sense. Local housing authorities should, similarly, consult social services authorities so that their area strategies can both draw from and contribute to community care planning and assessment. Housing strategies and community care plans should be consistent.

WORKING TOGETHER (para 19)

19. The new proposals will require effective relationships to be established and built upon between all parties involved. The aim should be to provide a seamless service for clients, with a mutual recognition of all authorities' responsibilities. This will require all the relevant agencies, including housing, health and social services authorities, to put an emphasis on discussion, understanding and agreement in the planning of services, rather than unilateral decision making. Joint working will be important to maximise the use of existing resources. Administrative systems will need to be developed, perhaps including existing joint planning structures, in order to monitor and plan the effective use of services. Authorities may wish to set up pilot projects.

From: DoE Circular 10/92; DoH Circular LAC (92/12) *Housing and Community Care*, HMSO, London (1992), pp. 3–5

Document 15
GUIDANCE ON DESIGNING OLD PEOPLE'S HOUSING

A circular in 1969 (usually referred to just as 82/69) gave advice to local authorities on both the principles of housing for elderly people and detailed design guidance which had to be adhered to if a subsidy was required.

APPENDIX VI

This check list is offered as a guide to the special aspects of designing for old people's dwellings.

Introduction to the check list

The mandatory requirements for accommodation specially designed for old people are set out in Appendix I to Circular 82/69 (Welsh Office Circular 84/69), and the yardstick additions in Appendix II to that Circular are based on those standards.

The purpose which underlies the design of housing for the elderly is the provision of accommodation which will enable them to maintain an independent way of life for as long as possible. With improved health services more people may be expected to remain in a home of their own for the rest of their lives. If they are to do this in comfort, they will need housing designed with the special requirements of the elderly in mind, coupled with the availability, as far as possible, of a balanced range of different types of accommodation to meet their varying needs and preferences. It has to be remembered too that most old people for whom housing is being provided will eventually be living alone and all housing for old people needs to be planned for sociability so as to avoid loneliness and isolation. This is particularly desirable where rehousing involves moving to a new area and, though the subject is outside the scope of this circular, good housing management practice can assist by keeping together groups of friends and neighbours as far as practicable.

Of the different types of housing which can be provided for the elderly, bungalows – traditionally regarded by old people themselves as the ideal form of housing – are best suited to couples who are able to maintain a greater degree of independence, who can manage rather more housework and who may want a small garden.

Two storey flats are more economical of land than bungalows, can provide a more compact layout, fit in well with family housing and can be used on infill sites. Many people over the age of 65 can still manage one flight of stairs and an upper flat may be preferred by those who dislike sleeping on the ground floor. Taller blocks with lifts can provide acceptable accommodation for old people, if suitably designed and sited, in those places where the density justifies their use.

For less active old people, often living alone, who need smaller and labour-saving accommodation, grouped flatlets as described in circular 36/67 (Welsh Office Circular 28/67) and the two publications 'Flatlets for

Old People' and 'More Flatlets for Old People' are the most suitable. The tenants of these flatlets will have the services of a warden and also communal facilities such as a common-room and laundry; and possibly a guest room as well. Bathrooms may be shared for one-person flatlets (in a ratio of one bathroom to four flatlets) or private in the case of two-person flatlets but every flatlet will contain a w.c. and hand basin. Additional facilities such as a call-bell system will also be needed.

From: MHLG, *Housing Standards and Costs: accommodation specially designed for old people*, Circular 82/69, HMSO, London (1969), p. 14

Document 16
COMPARATIVE COSTS OF CARE (1)

The table shows the comparative cost of care for an elderly person of high dependency between a hospital, very sheltered housing, sheltered housing or staying at home with an innovatory scheme.

Table 10.4 A comparison of resource costs and transfer payments for a person of high dependency[1] in hospital. Part III, very sheltered housing, sheltered housing and staying at home with an innovatory service.

		£ per person per annum	
1986–87	*Resource costs*	*Resource costs and retirement pension or allowance for personal expenses*	*Resource costs and retirement pension and supplementary pension or allowance for personal expenses*
Hospital:			
Acute	22,014	22,417	22,417
Geriatric	19,525	19,928	19,928
Long-stay	18,649	19,052	19,052
Part III	7,844	8,247	8,247
Very sheltered housing:			
All	4,698	6,710	7,591
All excluding registered residential homes (RRH)	4,137	6,149	7,030
All LA	4,095	6,107	6,988
All HA	5,241	7,253	8,134
All HA excluding RRH	3,811	5,823	6,704
Registered residential homes	7,487	7,958	7,958
1 bed self-contained			
New build	4,842	6,854	7,735
Rehabilitated	3,427	5,429	6,320

Table 10.4 (Cont'd)

1986–87	Resource costs	Resource costs and retirement pension or allowance for personal expenses	Resource costs and retirement pension and supplementary pension or allowance for personal expenses
			£ per person per annum
Bedsitters with shared facilities			
New build (1 scheme)	8,414	8,885	8,885
Rehabilitated	7,030	7,501	7,501
All (those are HC[2] pilots)	7,616	8,087	8,087
Sheltered housing – 1 bed self-contained new-build:			
LA	4,381	6,393	7,274
HA	4,359	6,371	7,252
Innovatory schemes:			
All	3,724	5,736	6,617
Alarms	3,682	5,694	6,575
Care	3,777	5,789	6,670

[1] Leeds scale 8–12.
[2] Housing Corporation.

From: Tinker, A., *An Evaluation of Very Sheltered Housing*, HMSO, London (1989), Table 10.4, p. 114

Document 17
COMPARATIVE COSTS OF CARE (2)

The tables show the comparative costs for an elderly person for various housing and housing with care options.

Average total costs[1] (£ per person p.a.) of subsidised specialised housing for elderly people: category of accommodation by type of provider

Category of accommodation	Local authorities			Housing associations			Abbeyfield Society		Almshouse Societies	
	1	2	2.5	1	2	2.5	2	2.5	1	2
	7,463	9,370	11,673	8,612	9,723	16,359	10,676	20,878	9,243	8,949

Average total costs[1] (£ per person p.a.) for all housing and housing with care options for elderly people by level of dependency

	Average for all levels of dependency				The most dependent[2]			
	Staying at home	Cat. 1	Cat. 2	Cat. 2.5	Staying at home	Cat. 1	Cat. 2	Cat. 2.5
Notional rent	3,512	4,289	4,843	5,379	3,080	4,289	4,843	5,379
Revenue costs	598	709	1,023	5,237	536	709	1,023	5,237
Health and social care	297	431	735	1,014	813	842	1,511	1,948
Gross revenue costs	4,407	5,429	6,601	11,630	4,429	5,840	7,377	12,564
Informal care	4,324	0	0	0	5,500	0	0	0
State benefits	2,946	3,007	3,077	3,195	3,461	3,697	3,657	3,814
Total costs	11,677	8,436	9,618	14,825	13,390	9,537	11,034	16,378

[1] This includes the gross resource costs ie. notional rent, revenue costs and health and social care costs together with state benefits
[2] Clackmannan Group G

From: McCaffrey, P., *Living Independently*, HMSO, London (1992), p. 78, Table 3.16 and p. 167, Table 3.14

Document 18
POWERS TO PROVIDE HOME HELPS AND OTHER SERVICES

Under the National Health Service Act 1946 local authorities were given powers to provide home helps and certain preventive services.

PREVENTION OF ILLNESS, CARE AND AFTER-CARE

28.–(1) A local health authority may, with the approval of the Minister, and to such extent as the Minister may direct, shall make arrangements for the purpose of the prevention of illness, the care of persons suffering from illness or mental defectiveness, or the after-care of such persons, but no such arrangements shall provide for the payment of money to such persons, except in so far as they may provide for the remuneration of such persons engaged in suitable work in accordance with the arrangements.

(2) A local health authority may, with the approval of the Minister, recover from persons availing themselves of the services provided under this section such charges (if any) as the authority consider reasonable, having regard to the means of those persons.

(3) A local health authority may, with the approval of the Minister, contribute to any voluntary organisation formed for any such purpose as aforesaid.

DOMESTIC HELP

29.–(1) A local health authority may make such arrangements as the Minister may approve for providing domestic help for households where such help is required owing to the presence of any person who is ill, lying-in, an expectant mother, mentally defective, aged, or a child not over compulsory school age within the meaning of the Education Act, 1944.

(2) A local health authority may, with the approval of the Minister, recover from persons availing themselves of the domestic help so provided such charges (if any) as the authority consider reasonable, having regard to the means of those persons.

From: National Health Service Act 1946, paras 28–9

Document 19
POWERS TO PROMOTE WELFARE

Under the National Assistance Act 1948 local authorities were empowered to promote the welfare of certain disadvantaged groups. Elderly people who came into any of these categories benefited from this legislation.

WELFARE SERVICES

29.–(1) A local authority shall have power to make arrangements for promoting the welfare of persons to whom this section applies, that is to say persons who are blind, deaf or dumb, and other persons who are substantially and permanently handicapped by illness, injury, or congenital deformity or such other disabilities as may be prescribed by the Minister.

(2) In relation to persons ordinarily resident in the area of a local authority the authority shall, to such extent as the Minister may direct, be under a duty to exercise their powers under this section.

Local authorities were also empowered to make contributions to voluntary organisations.

31. A local authority may make contributions to the funds of any voluntary organisation whose activities consist in or include the provision of recreation or meals for old people.

From: National Assistance Act 1948, Section 29 (1), (2) and 31

Note: Consolidating legislation relating to the provision of meals and recreation for old people was given in the Health and Social Services and Social Security Adjudications Act 1983.

Document 20
A DUTY TO PROVIDE RESIDENTIAL ACCOMMODATION

The National Assistance Act 1948 laid a duty on local authorities to provide residential accommodation for needy old people.

LOCAL AUTHORITY SERVICES

Provision of accommodation

21.–(1) It shall be the duty of every local authority, subject to and in accordance with the provisions of this Part of this Act, to provide –

(*a*)   residential accommodation for persons who by reason of age, infirmity or any other circumstances are in need of care and attention which is not otherwise available to them;

(*b*)   temporary accommodation for persons who are in urgent need thereof, being need arising in circumstances which could not reasonably have been foreseen or in such other circumstances as the authority may in any particular case determine.

(2) In the exercise of their said duty a local authority shall have regard to the welfare of all persons for whom accommodation is provided, and in particular to the need for providing accommodation of different descriptions suited to different descriptions of such persons as are mentioned in the last foregoing subsection.

From: National Assistance Act 1948, Part III, Section 21 (1) and (2)
(See also Document 9)

Document 21
POWER TO PROVIDE WELFARE SERVICES FOR OLD PEOPLE

The general power for a local authority to provide welfare services for old people, either itself or through a voluntary organisation, was given in the Health Services and Public Health Act 1968.

PROMOTION BY LOCAL AUTHORITIES OF THE WELFARE OF OLD PEOPLE

45.–(1) A local authority may with the approval of the Minister of Health, and to such extent as he may direct shall, make arrangements for promoting the welfare of old people.

(2) A local authority may recover from persons availing themselves of any service provided in pursuance of arrangements made under this section such charges (if any) as, having regard to the cost of the service, the authority may determine, whether generally or in the circumstances of any particular case.

(3) A local authority may employ as their agent for the purposes of this section any voluntary organisation having for its sole or principal object, or among its principal objects, the promotion of the welfare of old people.

From: The Health Services and Public Health Act 1968, Section 45 (1), (2) and (3)

Under the National Health Service and Community Care Act 1990, Part III, para. 42 (7) for the words 'any voluntary organisation' onwards there was substituted 'any voluntary organisation or any person carrying on, professionally or by way of trade or business, activities which consist of or include the provision of services for old people, being an organisation or person appearing to the authorities to be capable of promoting the welfare of old people'.

Document 22
THE SEEBOHM COMMITTEE AND OLD PEOPLE

The Committee on *Local Authority and Allied Personal Social Services* (the Seebohm Report) 1968 recommended the creation of a new social service department which would have a co-ordinated approach to people's problems. Comments were made about the need for the development of domiciliary services, as well as a comprehensive approach, for old people.

THE DEVELOPMENT OF THE DOMICILIARY SERVICES

309. Although for many years it has been part of national policy to enable as many old people as possible to stay in their own homes, the development of the domiciliary services which are necessary if this is to be achieved has been slow. There are certain services of home care, such as home nursing and domestic help, which are provided by all local authorities. Neither service is specially for the old though both are used largely by them. There is also a wide variety of other help for old people, like meals on wheels, chiropody, and laundry services, which is provided by local authorities or voluntary committees or sometimes jointly, but the extent of their cover differs considerably from place to place and nowhere do they assist more than a very small proportion of the old. Furthermore it appears that individual services have been started without sufficient thought for priorities or evidence of need over the whole area to be served. This piecemeal and haphazard development is unlikely to use scarce resources to the best advantage even though some assistance may be given to a fortunate few.
310. A unified social service department will be able to take a more comprehensive view of the development of such services, but to do so it will have to know the extent and pattern of need in its area and be aware of all the local resources likely to be available. It will have to discover from local voluntary organisations what part they can play in providing a comprehensive service to the maximum number of old people. It will have to investigate fully the contribution which relatives, neighbours and the wider community can make and how the social service department can best enable such potential assistance to be realised. In this sense a considerable development of community care for the old may be achieved, even in the near future, by enlisting such help.
311. In particular, of course, services for old people in their own homes will not be adequately developed unless greater attention is paid to supporting their families who in turn support them. The problems of old people living alone have attracted much attention, but many of those who are most dependent live with younger relatives who often are themselves getting on in years. Just as we emphasised the need for shared responsibility between the family and the personal social services where there were problems in the social care of children so we wish to stress it in the case of the old. If old people are to remain in the community, support and assistance must often be directed to the whole family of which they are members. This is one of the

reasons which convinced us that services for the elderly should become an integral part of the social services department.

From: Home Office *et al.*, *Local Authority and Allied Personal Social Services* (the Seebohm Committee), HMSO, London (1968), p. 96

Document 23
PROBLEMS OF COMMUNITY CARE

2. FUNDAMENTAL UNDERLYING PROBLEMS

49. There are a number of factors causing difficulties with the introduction of community care. Some result from the greater complexity of organising care in the community and from the difficulties of managing change. These are unavoidable and are an inherent aspect of the implementation process. However, there are also difficulties which should be avoidable.

50. One reason that is frequently advanced to explain the slow progress is a lack of finance. However, a much wider range of community based services could be provided within present levels of funding – although, as with all health and personal social services, more money can always be put to good use. Increased funding is, at best, only part of the answer to the problems described in the previous chapter. At worst, it could mask, temporarily at least, the need for some basic changes in the way that care for mentally ill, mentally handicapped, physically handicapped and elderly people is provided and paid for. The Commission has concluded that the slow and uneven progress towards community care is due to some fundamental underlying problems which need to be tackled directly:

(i)   Although out of the total amounts of money being spent (some £6 billion a year) there should be enough to provide at least a much improved level of community-based services, the methods for distributing the available finance do not match the requirements of community care policies.

(ii) Additional short-term bridging finance is required to fund the transition to community care.

(iii) Social security policies are undermining any switch from residential to community care.

(iv) A fragmented organisation structure causes delays and difficulties; and there has been a failure to adapt systems and structures to accommodate the shift in policy.

(v)   Staffing arrangements are inadequate, with a failure to provide sufficient re-training for existing staff in hospitals and to recruit the additional staff required in the community.

From: Audit Commission, *Making a Reality of Community Care*, HMSO, London (1986), p. 29

Document 24
THE BRITISH ASSOCIATION OF SOCIAL WORKERS LAYS DOWN GUIDELINES FOR SOCIAL WORK WITH ELDERLY PEOPLE

In 1977 BASW pointed out that many agencies seemed to give work with elderly people a low priority and often workers with little experience or training were expected to undertake all, or a large proportion of, the work with this group. They suggested certain guidelines which they summarised as:

1. These guidelines have illustrated the same need for expertise in social work with the elderly as with other vulnerable groups. Those who are most vulnerable amongst the elderly are those whose identity is damaged by retirement, those who are bereaved and who suffer loss of any kind and the mentally and physically frail, many of whom will be over 75.
2. Many agencies seem to give work with the elderly a low priority and often workers with little experience or training are expected to undertake all, or a large proportion of, work with this group. The enormous contribution made by volunteers, social work assistants, relatives, neighbours and *all* others concerned with the social and emotional care of the elderly is neither denied nor minimised by emphasising those areas which are seen to be most appropriately dealt with by the qualified social worker. These can be summarised as follows:
   (*a*) Assessing need in deciding the help required and by whom it should be given. This should, where possible, be multidisciplinary in nature, the social worker operating as a member of a caring team.
   (*b*) Providing skilled social work help with problems of relationship, problems arising from crises, loss, change or other social, emotional or medical condition. The complex nature of many problems in old age arising from medical, social or psychological sources should be continuously borne in mind.
   (*c*) Providing the skill in helping to overcome psychological problems related to receiving practical, financial and advocatory help. More skill is required to enable to elderly to make the best use of the practical resources than is often appreciated.
   (*d*) Providing group and community work, where the social worker has received training in appropriate skills. Group work with the elderly offers a further dimension to social work with the elderly. Both the elderly and their relatives gain mutual strength and ability to cope with other problems through group discussions.
   (*e*) Understanding and accepting the degree of risk which the client is prepared to take, and balancing this with the sometimes over-anxious reaction of society. Enabling relatives and neighbours to tolerate these dilemmas.
   (*f*) Enabling and supporting others in caring, such as relatives, 'good neighbours' and volunteers.

(*g*) Participating in planning and policymaking related to elderly people. This is not the exclusive terrain of the qualified social worker, though her knowledge of areas of social need will give her an important role in this process.

3. Another conclusion which must be drawn from these guidelines is that social work courses should include more teaching on the process of ageing and work with the elderly, and more placements for students in this field.

4. Social work with elderly people is as demanding and rewarding as work with any other client group. It can succeed in making life positive and meaningful for those with whom we have been most concerned in these guidelines.

From: *Social Work Today*, 12.4.77, p. 1

Document 25

NURSING, RESIDENTIAL AND LONG-STAY HOSPITAL CARE OF ELDERLY, CHRONICALLY ILL AND YOUNG PHYSICALLY DISABLED PEOPLE, PLACES BY SECTOR, UK 1970–95

1 Apr	Residential homes places[1]			Nursing home places[2]			Long-stay geriatric places	Long-stay psycho-geriatric places	Long-stay YPD places[3]	Total places
	LA	Private	Voluntary	Priv/Vol			NHS	NHS	NHS	
1970	108,700	23,700	40,100	20,300			52,000	23,000	2,500	270,300
1975	128,300	25,800	41,000	24,000			49,000			
1980	134,500	37,400	42,600	26,900			46,100			
1985	137,100	85,300	45,100	38,000			46,300			
				Priv	Vol					
1987	135,500	114,600	42,200	52,000	8,300		43,000			
1988	133,500	127,900	43,000	68,700	9,600		51,400[4]	29,300	2,500	465,800
1990	125,600	155,600	40,000	112,600	10,500		47,200[5]	27,000	2,500	521,000
1993	95,000	165,400	51,000	168,200	15,000		37,800[5]	22,300	2,200	556,900
1994	86,400	167,500	50,700	178,800	16,000		34,600[5]	20,200	2,100	556,300
1995	80,800	167,500	52,800	191,000	17,000		33,200	18,500	1,900	563,000

[1] Includes residential places in dual registration homes

[2] Includes nursing places in dual registration homes

[3] Younger physically disabled

[4] The increase in 1988 is an artefact caused by reclassification of hospital types when Korner aggregates were introduced

[5] NHS long-stay geriatric beds estimated since 1988 on the assumption that acute/rehabilitation geriatric beds in England have remained constant and all the decline in beds in the speciality of geriatrics overall is attributable to loss of long-stay beds.

From: Laing and Buisson, *Care of Elderly People Market Survey*, Laing and Buisson (1996), p. 18, Table 2.2

Document 26
THE PRINCIPLES BEHIND A MOVE TO RESIDENTIAL CARE

PRINCIPLES

People who move into a residential establishment should do so by positive choice. A distinction should be made between the need for accommodation and need for services. No one should be required to change their permanent accommodation in order to receive services which could be made available to them in their own homes.

Living in a residential establishment should be a positive experience ensuring a better quality of life than the resident could enjoy in any other setting.

Local authorities should make efforts, as a matter of urgency, to meet the special needs of people from ethnic minority communities for residential and other services.

Every person who moves into a residential establishment retains their rights as a citizen. Measures need to be taken to ensure that individuals can exercise their rights. Safeguards should be applied when rights are curtailed.

People who move into a residential establishment should continue to have access to the full range of community support services.

Residents should have access to leisure, educational and other facilities offered by the local community and the right to invite and receive relatives and friends as they choose.

Residential staff are the major resource and should be valued as such. The importance of their contribution needs to be recognised and enhanced.

From: Wagner Report, *Residential Care: a positive choice*, HMSO, London (1988), p. 114

Document 27
THE LAST REFUGE

In a survey of residential institutions and homes for elderly people Peter Townsend presented disquieting evidence about their conditions:

So far as it is possible to express in a few words the general conclusion of this book it is that communal Homes of the kind which exist in England and Wales today do not adequately meet the physical, psychological and social needs of the elderly people living in them, and that alternative services and living arrangements should quickly take their place.

and about the lack of alternative accommodation:

In investigating the physical and mental capacities of elderly residents, the events and circumstances leading to their admission and the life they follow in Homes, we reached certain important conclusions. The majority are not so handicapped by infirmity that they could not, given a small amount of support from the domiciliary social services, live in homes of their own in an ordinary community. A large number enter Homes for reasons of poverty, lack of housing, social isolation and absence of secondary sources of help among relatives and friends, and they do so unwillingly. Few of them take the initiative themselves and rarely are they offered practicable alternatives – such as housing, emergency grants and services or permanent help from the domiciliary services. Nearly all, once admitted, are expected to stay permanently, although the great majority, so it seems, would prefer not to do so.

From: Townsend, P., *The Last Refuge*, Routledge & Kegan Paul, London (1964), pp. 222, 226

Document 28
ELDERLY MENTALLY HANDICAPPED PEOPLE IN
INSTITUTIONAL CARE

In a report of the Secretary of State for Social Services by the National Development Group for the Mentally Handicapped entitled *Helping Mentally Handicapped People in Hospital* special recommendations were made about elderly people.

6.7 ELDERLY RESIDENTS

6.7.1. Most elderly hospital residents are only mildly intellectually handicapped. Many of them were admitted over 20 years ago, and some have even lived in hospital since early childhood, having been admitted under Poor Laws and similar legislation at a time when society relied on mental handicap hospitals to provide care and shelter for people who would under no circumstances be admitted today.

6.7.2. For this group more than for any other the mental handicap hospital is their home. They have not known any other home, and may not wish to be 'rehabilitated'. On the other hand, they should not have decisions on such matters made for them by others who take it on themselves to announce that it would be 'cruel' or 'unkind' for them to live outside hospital. Many of them are quite capable of thinking for themselves, and should be given the opportunity to consider alternatives to hospital if these can be made available.

6.7.3. A number of authorities have followed a policy of opening old people's homes specifically for people who have lived in hospitals for many years. These homes enable friends to stay together and to use the home as a base from which to use local facilities. A few live in ordinary old people's homes, and others, while remaining in hospital, live in accommodation very like an old people's home – sometimes a converted nursing home or a large house formerly belonging to the medical superintendent. Hospital authorities have also purchased or made use of larger houses in the community for elderly mentally handicapped people.

6.7.4. Particular care must always be taken in moving any elderly person from one environment to another. The transition should be very carefully planned and should be effected very slowly and by small degrees. The resident should be able to change his mind if he decides that he would rather stay in hospital after all, and should be allowed to return to hospital if his new life in a hostel or an old people's home does not suit him. Every effort must be made to involve the resident himself in the determination of his needs and, like all residents, the elderly should be individually reviewed as part of the process of assessment and meeting of needs . . .

6.7.5. The BGS/RCN [British Geriatrics Society/Royal College of Nursing] Report identified four main categories of problems as regards the care of the elderly:

i.   The lack of consideration of feelings and of maintenance of dignity, privacy and personal identity.

ii.   Failure to maintain independence and mobility.
iii. Shortcomings related to personal hygiene and physiological needs.
iv.   Lack of social, remedial and recreational stimulation.

These problems apply just as forcefully to the elderly residents of mental handicap hospitals.

From: DHSS, The National Development Group for the Mentally Handicapped, *Helping Mentally Handicapped People in Hospital*, HMSO, London (1978), pp. 67–8

Document 29
FAMILY OBLIGATIONS

FAMILY OBLIGATIONS IN THE PUBLIC DOMAIN

I have placed the emphasis so far on the personal and negotiated elements in both family support and the morality of obligation which underscores it. But it is plain that such negotiations do not take place in a social vacuum. Indeed, governments' attempts to encourage people to develop a sense of responsibility towards their relatives place these arrangements firmly in the public domain, and imply that apparently private arrangements are open to pressure – even manipulation from outside.

I have emphasized in early chapters that social and economic circumstances in general do have an important bearing upon the structures of support which are developed in families. The economic climate, as it affects individuals and their relatives, creates the conditions under which some people have need for support and others have the capacity to provide it. The demographic structure of the population at any given point in time affects the shape of individual kin groups, and therefore the range of options for giving, receiving and sharing assistance. Most dramatically at the present time, demographic change has created much larger numbers of very elderly people than ever had to be supported by previous generations, at a time when the numbers of people born in succeeding generations has shrunk.

If we take a fairly long historical perspective, we can see that people in the present are not necessarily any more or less willing to support their relatives than in the past; but the circumstances under which they have to work out these commitments themselves have changed and created new problems to be solved. External conditions of this kind do not straight forwardly determine what any of us does for our relatives, but they do form part of the materials out of which we have to create our own commitments. They affect the nature of the choices which present themselves. For example (to stay with the question of the care of elderly people), a decision about whether you should take an elderly father to live with you looks very different if you are an only child, than it would have done under the demographic conditions of early generations, when you could expect to have several siblings. It looks different again if economic circumstances have worked in your favour, so that you can afford to pay a professional nurse to look after him, by comparison with someone for whom the choice about co-residence also entails using their own labour to provide nursing care.

In this complex equation we also have to insert the action of governments who, through the law and through their policies, modify the external circumstances under which commitments to relatives are negotiated. How important a factor is this? Can governments make us do more for our kin, or even alter the morality of family obligations, to fit their own policy preferences? If government keeps up the pressure, will we find in the future that the family becomes the first, rather than the last, port of call when any of us needs assistance?

We move into the realms of speculation here, but that speculation can be informed by looking at what has happened in similar circumstances in the past. There have been several times during the last two centuries when governments have tightened the screws, to try to ensure that people relied on their families rather than on the state for financial assistance: the creation of the New Poor Law in 1834; the tightening of Poor Law regulations in the late nineteenth century; the creation of the household means test for unemployed people in the 1930s. The historical evidence suggests that on each occasion the measures were less successful than their hard-line advocates would have wished. On each occasion when government was attempting to impose a version of family responsibilities which people regarded as unreasonable, many responded by developing avoidance strategies: moving to another household, losing touch with their relatives, cheating the system. If anything it has been the state's assuming some responsibility for individuals – such as the granting of old age pensions – which has freed people to develop closer and more supportive relationships with their kin. It seems that it is not in the power of governments straightforwardly to manipulate what we do for our relatives, let alone what we believe to be proper.

Of course we cannot tell precisely what governments will try to do in the future, nor what the consequences will be. But the lesson of our past is that governments are quite capable of promoting a view of family obligations which is out of step with what most people regard as proper or reasonable, and with the commitments people have arrived at themselves, through the delicate processes of negotiation described above. Undoubtedly that situation creates great difficulties for some people, who feel that they are under sustained and unreasonable pressure, and eventually some will give in. But on the evidence of the past, many will not. Governments in this situation may try to ensure that their own views prevail, but their chances of success are probably partial at best. Happily, I should like to add.

From: Finch, J., *Family Obligations and Social Change*, Polity Press, (1989), pp. 242–3

Document 30
SOURCES OF HELP FOR THOSE ABLE TO DO VARIOUS TASKS ONLY WITH HELP

The table shows the usual source of help for those unable to carry out tasks by themselves.

Usual source of help for those able to do various tasks only with help by household type

Persons aged 65 or over   Great Britain 1994

Household type and usual source of help	Locomotion and self-care[1]	Cutting toenails	Bathing, showering, washing all over	Domestic tasks[2] (including cooking)	Going out & walking down the road	Using public transport
All household types	%	%	%	%	%	%
Spouse or partner	66	12	41	52	39	48
Other household member	20	3	10	13	17	10
Non-household relative	7	5	21	28	29	21
Friend/neighbour	1	1	2	10	11	15
Voluntary worker	0	0	0	1	0	0
NHS or personal social services	11	2	22	8	3	1
Paid help	0	0	1	12	0	0
Chiropodist	0	77	0	0	0	0
Other	0	0	2	1	1	5
Base = 100%[3]	119	1064	255	2176	190	111

[1] Locomotion and self-care includes: getting around the house, getting to the toilet, getting in and out of bed, dressing and undressing, and feeding.

[2] Domestic tasks includes shopping, dealing with personal affairs, washing dishes, cleaning windows, using a vacuum cleaner, doing jobs involving climbing, laundry, opening screw tops, cooking a meal, preparing a snack and making a cup of tea.

[3] Some elderly people are helped by more than one helper and therefore the percentages may add to more than 100.

From: OPCS, *Living in Britain: Results from the 1994 General Household Survey*, HMSO, London (1996), p. 177, Table 6.35

Document 31
THE CHIEF MEDICAL OFFICER OF HEALTH,
DEPARTMENT OF HEALTH, DISTINGUISHES BETWEEN
EQUITY AND INEQUALITY

EQUITY AND EQUALITY

There is increasing interest in variations in health and health care and the inequities and inequalities which can occur. Over the past year a number of reports have highlighted these variations, which are well recognised and have been for a long time. The accurate recording of information on health, begun in the early 19th century, made such differences apparent – and they still exist.

Health is determined by a number of factors including biological and genetic factors, lifestyle and behaviour, the environment (including communicable diseases), social and economic factors, and health services. In all of these, the concepts of equity and equality are important and the variations in health and health care which exist may be related to any of them – either alone or, more frequently, in combination. The term 'variations' is essentially neutral and is used to describe factual information about health and health care. However, the words 'equity' and 'equality' are often used interchangeably despite important distinctions between them. Equity is about fairness and justice, and implies that everyone should have an opportunity to attain their full potential for health. Equality, on the other hand, is about comparisons between the level of health, or ability to obtain access to health care, of individuals and communities. Some inequalities may be unavoidable, and therefore generally not considered unfair, while others might be avoided and so considered inequitable. Natural, biological and genetic variations may have unavoidable (though very important) health inequalities related to them. Lifestyle and behaviour patterns chosen by individuals can also result in inequalities in health – for example, cigarette smoking. In some instances health promotion activities, if selectively taken up, may even increase the inequalities – but again this might not be considered inequitable as they are the result of personal choice. However, lifestyle and behaviour that is not freely chosen, and which results in poorer health, might be considered as avoidable and thus inequitable. Health inequalities arising from the level of resources, housing conditions, dangerous working conditions, or exposure to environmental hazards, and which lead to health inequalities, would be examples of these. Inadequate access to health care or other public services might also be inequitable if the cause was avoidable and the result was inequality: such factors might include transport, lack of information, or inaccessibility of information as a result of language difficulties.

The NHS is strongly committed to the concept of equity, which is one of its key principles. Action to tackle some of the inequalities by the NHS is a continuous process. The report of the Variations in Health Sub-group concentrates specifically on action by the NHS that will assist progress in the Health of the Nation key areas. In relation to other determinants of health there will need to be further discussion on the physical environment, a greater understanding of the blocks to taking up healthier lifestyles, and more research on the social and economic factors which underpin such issues. The targeting of resources to those most in need, information provision and personal choice are complementary aspects of improving health.

It is hoped that this brief discussion of the distinction between equity and equality will assist in targeting particularly those inequalities which are avoidable. Dealing with issues of inequality is complex and there are no simple solutions. We need more locally based research projects in this area to help to provide some solutions, and the evaluation of such work needs to be as rigorous as in other branches of health service research.

From: Department of Health Annual Report of the Chief Medical Officer *On the State of the Public Health 1994*, IIMSO, London (1995), pp. 7–8

Bibliography

Please see list of abbreviations on p. xiii)

Abel-Smith, B. (1978) *The National Health Service*, HMSO, London.
Abel-Smith, B. and Townsend, P. (1965) *The Poor and the Poorest*, G. Bell and Sons, London.
Abrams, M. (1975) 'The New Elderly', *New Society*, 26.6.75, p. 778.
Abrams, M. (1978) *Beyond Three Score and Ten*, First Report, Age Concern England (ACE), London.
Abrams, M. (1980) *Beyond Three Score and Ten*, Second Report, ACE, London.
Abrams, P., Abrams, S., Humphrey, R. and Snaith, R. (1986) in Leat, D. (ed.), *Creating Care in the Neighbourhood*, Advance, London.
Abrams, P., Abrams, S., Humphrey, R. and Snaith, R. (1989) *Neighbourhood Care and Social Policy*, HMSO, London.
Abrams, M. and O'Brien, J. (1981) *Political Attitudes and Ageing in Britain*, ACE, London.
Achenbaum, W. A. (1995) *Crossing Frontiers: gerontology emerges as a science*, Cambridge University Press, Cambridge.
Action on Elder Abuse (1995) *Everybody's Business: taking action on elder abuse*, Action on Elder Abuse, London.
Agate, J. and Meacher, M. (1969) *The Care of the Old*, Fabian Society, London.
Age Concern England (ACE) (1972) *Easing the Restrictions on Ageing*, ACE, London.
ACE (1974) *The Attitudes of the Retired and Elderly*, ACE, London.
ACE (1975) *Manifesto on the Place of the Retired and the Elderly in Modern Society*, ACE, London.
ACE (1986) *The Law and Vulnerable Elderly People*, ACE, London.
ACE (1990a) *Transport and Older People* (ACE Briefings), ACE, London.
ACE (1990b) *The Impact of Technology, The Economic Equation, The Lifelong Environment, The Human Factor, Rights and Choices* (Resource Papers), ACE, London.
ACE (1992) *The Coming of Age in Europe*, ACE, London.
ACE (1994) *On the Move: transport, mobility and older people*, ACE, London.
ACE (1995) *Charging for Non-residential Services*, ACE, London.
ACE (1996) *Age Matters: report on a national Gallup survey*, ACE, London.
Age Concern England and Help The Aged Housing Trust (1984) *Housing for Ethnic Elders*, ACE/Help the Aged Housing Trust, London.
Age Concern England and National Housing And Town Planning Council (1995) *A Buyer's Guide to Retirement Housing*, ACE and National

Housing and Town Planning Council, London.

Ahmad-Aziz, A., Froggatt, A., Richardson, I., Whittaker, T. and Leung, T. (1992) *Improving Practice with Elders*, Central Council for Education and Training in Social Work, London.

Aiken, Lewis R. (1995) *Aging: an introduction to gerontology,* Sage, London.

Alcock, P. (1987) *Poverty and State Support*, Longman, London.

Allen, D. (1987) 'Performance Indicators in the Health Service', *Social Policy and Administration*, 21(1), pp. 70–84.

Allen, I. (1983) *Short-Stay Residential Care for the Elderly*, Policy Studies Institute (PSI), London.

Allen, I. (ed.) (1989) *Social Services Departments as Managing Agencies*, PSI, London.

Allen, I., Hogg, D. and Peace, S. (1992) *Elderly People: choice, participation and satisfaction*, PSI, London.

Allsop, J. (1995) *Health Policy and the NHS: towards 2000*, Longman, London.

Anderson, W. F. and Judge, T. (1974) *Geriatric Medicine*, Academic Press, London.

Andrews, G. (1990) 'Role of Primary Health Care' in Kane, R. C. *et al.* (eds), *Improving the Health of Older People*, Oxford University Press/ WHO, Oxford, pp. 346–61.

Appleton, N. (1996) *The Value of Handyperson's Schemes for Older People*, JRF Findings Housing Research 179, JRF, York.

Arber, S. and Evandrou, M. (eds) (1993) *Ageing, Independence and the Life Course*, Jessica Kingsley, London.

Arber, S., Gilbert, N. and Evandrou, M. (1988) 'Gender, Household Composition and Receipt of Domiciliary Services by the Elderly Disabled', *Journal of Social Policy*, 17(2), pp. 153–76.

Arber, S. and Ginn, J. (1991) *Gender and Later Life: a sociological analysis of resources and constraints*, Sage, London.

Arber, S. and Ginn, J. (1995) *Connecting Gender and Ageing*, Open University Press, Buckingham.

Arblaster, L., Conway, J., Foreman, A. and Hawtin, M. (1996) *Inter-agency Working for Housing, Health and Social Care Needs of People in General Needs Housing*, JRF Findings Housing Research 183, JRF, York.

Arie, T. (ed.) (1981) *Health Care of the Elderly*, Croom Helm, London.

Arie, T. (ed.) (1985) *Recent Advances in Psychogeriatrics 1*, Churchill Livingstone, London.

Arie, T. (1986) 'Management of Dementia: a review', *British Medical Bulletin* 42(1), pp. 91–6.

Arie, T. (1988) 'Questions in the Psychiatry of Old Age', in Evered, D. and Whelan, J. (eds), *Research and the Ageing Population*, Wiley, Chichester, pp. 86–105.

Arie, T. (ed.) (1992) *Recent Advances in Psychogeriatrics 2*, Churchill Livingstone, London.

Armstrong, J., Midwinter, E. and Wynne-Harley, D. (1987) *Retired Leisure: four ventures in post-work activity*, CPA, London.

Ashton, G. (1994) *The Elderly Client Handbook*, The Law Society, London.

Askham, J. (1989) 'The Need for Support', in Warnes, A. M. (ed.), *Human Ageing and Later Life*, Edward Arnold, London, pp. 107–18.

Askham, J. (1992) 'The Problems and Rewards of Caring in the Third Age', in Askham, J., Grundy, E., Tinker, A. with Hancock, R., McCreadie, C., Whyley, C. and Wright, F. *Caring: the importance of Third Age carers*, Carnegie UK Trust, Dunfermline, pp. 18–32.

Askham, J., Glucksman, E., Owens, P., Swift, C., Tinker, A. and Yu, G. (1990) *A Review of Research on Falls Among Elderly People*, Department of Trade and Industry, London.

Askham, J., Hancock, R. and Hills, J. (1995), *Opinions on Pensions: older people's attitudes to incomes, taxes and benefits*, ACIOG, London.

Askham, J., Henshaw, L. and Tarpey, M. (1995) *Social and Health Authority Services for Black and Minority Ethnic Communities*, HMSO, London.

Askham, J. and Thompson, C. (1990) *Dementia and Home Care*, ACE, London.

Association of Community Health Councils (1994) *Community Health Services*, ACHC, London.

Association for Continence Advice (1993) *Guidelines for Continence Care*, Association for Continence Advice, London.

Association of Retirement Housing Managers (1996) *Private Sheltered Housing: code of practice*, Association of Retirement Housing Managers, Rochester, Kent.

Atkin, K. (1992) 'Similarities and Differences between Informal Carers', in Twigg, J. (ed.) *Carers: research and practice*, HMSO, London, pp. 30–58.

Atkinson, A. B. (1991) *The Development of State Pensions in the United Kingdom*, Suntory-Toyota International Centre for Economics and Related Disciplines, London School of Economics, London.

Atkinson, A. B. (1994), *State Pensions Today and Tomorrow*, ACIOG, London.

Attenburrow, J. (1976) *Grouped Housing for the Elderly*, Department of the Environment, Building Research Establishment, London.

Audit Commission (1985) *Managing Social Services for the Elderly More Effectively*, HMSO, London.

Audit Commission (1986) *Making a Reality of Community Care*, HMSO, London.

Audit Commission (1989) *Housing the Homeless: the local authority role*, HMSO, London.

Audit Commission (1992a) *Homeward Bound: a new course for community health*, HMSO, London.

Audit Commission (1992b) *Lying in Wait: the use of medical beds in acute hospitals*, HMSO, London.

Audit Commission (1992c) *Community Care: managing the cascade of change*, HMSO, London.

Audit Commission (1992d) *The Community Revolution: personal social services and community care*, HMSO, London.

Audit Commission (1993a) *Their Health, Your Business: the new role of the District Health Authority*, HMSO, London.

Audit Commission (1993b) *Taking Care: progress with care in the community*, HMSO, London.

Audit Commission (1994a) *Finding a Place: a review of mental health services for adults*, HMSO, London.

Audit Commission (1994b) *Taking Stock: progress with community care*, HMSO, London.

Audit Commission (1995) *United They Stand*, HMSO, London.

Audit Commission (1996a) *Balancing the Care Equation: progress with community care*, HMSO, London.

Audit Commission (1996b) *What the Doctor Ordered: a study of GP fundholders in England and Wales*, HMSO, London.

Audit Commission/DoH/SSI (1996) *Reviewing Social Services*, DoH, London.

Baker, S. and Parry, M. (1983) *Housing for Sale to the Elderly*, Housing Research Foundation, University of Surrey, Guildford.

Baker, S. and Parry, M. (1984) *Housing for Sale to the Elderly* (Second Report), Housing Research Foundation, University of Surrey, Guildford.

Baker, S. and Parry, M. (1986) *Housing for Sale to the Elderly* (Third Report), Housing Research Foundation, University of Surrey, Guildford.

Baldwin, S. and Falkingham, J. (eds) (1994) *Social Security and Social Change: new challenges to the Beveridge model*, Harvester Wheatsheaf, London.

Baldwin, S., Godfrey, C. and Propper, C. (eds) (1990) *Quality of Life: perspectives and policies*, Routledge, London.

Baldwin, S. and Lunt, N. (1996) *Charging Ahead: local authority charging policies for community care*, The Policy Press, Bristol.

Barelli, J. (1992) *Underoccupation in Local Authority and Housing Association Housing*, HMSO, London.

Barker, C., Watchman, P. and Robinson, J. (1990) 'Social Security Abuse', *Social Policy and Administration* 24(7), pp. 104–19.

Barker, J. (1983) *Black and Asian Old People in Britain*, ACE, London.

Bebbington, A. and Davies, B. (1982) 'Patterns of Social Service Provision for the Elderly' in Warnes, A. M. (ed.) *Geographical Perspectives on the Elderly*, Wiley, Chichester, pp. 355–74.

Bell, L. and How, L. (1996) *Home Care: the business of caring*, ACE, London.

Bellairs, C. (1968) *Old People: cash and care*, Conservative Political Centre, London.

Bengtson, V. and Robertson, J. (eds) (1985) *Grandparenthood*, California Sage Publications, Beverly Hills, California.

Bengtson, V., Rosenthal, C. and Burton, L. (1990) 'Families and Ageing: diversity and heterogeneity', in Binstock, R. and George, L. (eds) *Handbook of Aging and the Social Sciences*, Academic Press, London, pp. 263–87.

Bennett, G. J. and Ebrahim, S. (1992) *Health Care of the Elderly*, Edward Arnold, London.

Bennett, G. and Kingston, P. (1993) *Elder Abuse: concepts, theories and interventions*, Chapman and Hall, London.

Benzeval, M., Judge, M. and Whitehead, M. (1995) *Tackling Inequalities in Health: an agenda for action*, King's Fund, London.

Bergmann, K. and Jacoby, R. with collaboration from Coleman, P., Jolley, D. and Levin, E. (1983) 'The Limitations and Possibilities of Community Care for the Elderly Demented', in DHSS *Elderly People in the Community: their service needs*, HMSO, London.

Berliner, H. (1988) 'Old but Cold', *The Health Service Journal*, 4.8.88, p. 885.

Bernard, M. and Meade, K. (eds) (1993) *Older Women Come of Age*, Edward Arnold, London.

Beveridge, W. (1942) *Social Insurance and Allied Services*, HMSO, London.

Beyer, G. and Nierztrasz, F. (1967) *Housing the Aged in Western Countries*, Elsevier, Amsterdam, New York.

Bhalla, A. and Blakemore, K. (1981) *Elders of the Ethnic Minority Groups*, All Faiths for One Race, Birmingham.

Binstock, R. and George, L. (eds) (1990) *Handbook of Aging and the Social Sciences*, Academic Press Ltd, London.

Birren, J. E. and Schaie, K. W. (1990) *Handbook of the Psychology of Ageing* (3rd edn), Van Nostrand Reinhold, New York.

Blacksell, S. and Phillips, D. (1994) *Paid to Volunteer: the extent of paying volunteers in the 1990s*, The Volunteer Centre, London.

Blakemore, K. (1985) 'The State, the Voluntary Sector and New Developments in Provision for the Aid of Minority Social Groups', *Ageing and Society*, 5(2), pp. 175–90.

Blakemore, K. and Boneham, M. (1994) *Age, Race and Ethnicity*, Open University Press, Buckingham.

Bland, R., Bland, R., Cheetham, J., Lapsley, I. and Llewellyn, S. (1992) *Residential Homes for the Elderly: their costs and quality*, The Scottish Office, Edinburgh.

Blythe, R. (1979) *The View in Winter*, Penguin, London.

Board For Social Responsibility, Church Of England General Synod (1990) *Ageing*, Church House Publishing, London.

Boldy, D., Abel, P. and Carter, K. (1973) *The Elderly in Grouped Dwellings – a profile*, University of Exeter, Exeter.

Bond, J., Bond, S., Donaldson, C., Gregson, B. and Atkinson, A. (1989) *A Summary Report of an Evaluation of Continuing-Care Accommodation for Elderly People*, Health Care Research Unit, University of Newcastle upon Tyne, Newcastle.

Bond, J., Coleman, P. and Peace, S. (eds) (1993) *Ageing in Society: an introduction to social gerontology*, Sage, London.

Bone, M. (1996) *Trends in Dependency Among Older People in England*, OPCS, London.

Bone, M., Gregory, J., Gill, B. and Lader, D. (1992), *Retirement and Retirement Plans*, OPCS, HMSO, London.

Bonnett, D. (1996) *Incorporating Lifetime Homes Standards into Modernisation Programmes*, Joseph Rowntree Foundation Findings Housing Research 174, York.

Bookbinder, D. (1991) *Housing Options for Older People*, ACE, London.

Bosanquet, N. (1975) *New Deal for the Elderly*, Fabian Society, London.

Bowl, R. (1986) 'Social Work with Old People' in Phillipson, C. and Walker, A. (eds), *Ageing and Social Policy: a critical assessment*, Gower, Aldershot, pp. 128–45.

Bowling, A. (1991) *Measuring Health: a review of quality of life measurement scales*, Open University Press, Buckingham.

Bowling, A. (1995) *Measuring Disease*, Open University Press, Buckingham.

Bowling, A. (1996) 'Quality of Life' in Ebrahim, S. and Kalache, A. (eds), *Epidemiology in Old Age*, BMJ, London, pp. 221–27.

Bowling, A. and Cartwright, A. (1982) *Life after a Death*, Tavistock, London.

Bowling, B. (1990) *Elderly People from Ethnic Minorities: a report on four projects*, ACIOG, London.

Bradshaw, J. (1972) 'The Concept of Social Need'. *New Society*, 3.3.72, pp. 640–43.

Bradshaw, J. (1988) 'Financing Private Care for the Elderly' in Baldwin, S. *et al.* (eds), *Social Security and Community Care*, Avebury, Aldershot, pp. 175–90.

Brandon, R. (1972) *Seventy Plus: easier living for the elderly*, British Broadcasting Corporation, London.

Brearley, P. (1975) *Social Work, Ageing and Society*, Routledge and Kegan Paul, London.

Brearley, P. and Mandelstam, M. (1992) *A Review of the Literature 1986–91 on Day Care Services for Adults*, HMSO, London.

Briggs, A. and Oliver, J. (eds) (1985) *Caring: experiences of looking after disabled relatives*, Routledge and Kegan Paul, London.

British Medical Journal (1992) *The Future of General Practice*, BMJ, London.

Brockington, F. and Lempert, S. (1966) *The Social Needs of the Over Eighties*, Manchester University Press, Manchester.

Brocklehurst, J., Tallis, R. C. and Fillit, H. M. (1992) *Textbook of Geriatric Medicine and Gerontology* (4th edn), Churchill Livingstone, London.

Bromley, D. B. (ed.) (1984) *Gerontology: social and behavioural perspectives*, Croom Helm, London.

Bromley, D. B. (1990) *Behavioural Gerontology: central issues in the psychology of ageing*, Wiley, Chichester.

Brown, J. (1990) *Social Security for Retirement*, Joseph Rowntree Foundation, York.

Buckle, J. (1971) *Work and Housing of Impaired Persons in Great Britain*, HMSO, London.

Bull, J. and Poole, L. (1989) *Not Rich Not Poor*, Shelter Housing Advice Centre/Anchor Housing Trust, London.

Bulmer, M. (1987) *The Social Basis of Community Care*, Allen and Unwin, London.

Bulusu, L. and Alderson, M. (1984) 'Suicides 1950–82', *Population Trends*, 35, pp. 11–17.

Burns, A. (ed.) (1993) *Ageing and Dementia*, Edward Arnold, London.

Bury, M. and Holme, A. (1991) *Life after Ninety*, Routledge, London.

Butler, A. (ed.) (1985) *Ageing: recent advances and creative responses*, Croom Helm, London.

Butler, A., Oldman, C. and Greve, J. (1983) *Sheltered Housing for the Elderly: policy, practice and the consumer*, Allen and Unwin, London.

Butler, J. and Madeley, P. (1995) 'Depression in Carers' in *Geriatric Medicine*, Feb., pp. 41–3.

Bytheway, W. (1995) *Ageism*, Open University Press, Buckingham.

Bytheway, W. and James, L. (1978) *The Allocation of Sheltered Housing*, Medical Sociology Research Centre, University College of Swansea, Swansea.

Bytheway, W. and Johnson, J. (eds) (1990) *Welfare and the Ageing Experience*, Avebury, Aldershot, Hants.

Calling for Help Group (1994) *Community Alarms Services: a national survey*, Anchor, Help the Aged, National Housing and Town Planning Council, Research Institute for Consumer Affairs, London.

Cambridge, P. and Knapp, M. (eds) (1988) *Demonstrating Successful Care in the Community*, Personal Social Services Research Unit, University of Kent, Canterbury, Kent.

Carey, S. (1995) *Private Renting in England 1993/94*, HMSO, London.

Carnegie Inquiry Into The Third Age (1993), *Life, Work and Livelihood in the Third Age,* Carnegie UK Trust, Dunfermline, Scotland.

Carpenter, I. (1996) 'Value of Screening in Later Life', in Ebrahim, S. and Kalache, A. (eds) *Epidemiology in Old Age,* BMJ, London, pp. 136–44.

Carter, J. (1981) *Day Services for Adults: somewhere to go,* Allen and Unwin, London.

Cartwright, A. (1996) 'Dying', in Ebrahim, S. and Kalache, A. (eds) *Epidemiology in Old Age,* BMJ, London, pp. 408–16.

Cartwright, A. and Henderson, G. (1986) *More Trouble with Feet,* HMSO, London.

Cartwright, A., Hockey, L. and Anderson, J. (1973) *Life Before Death,* Routledge and Kegan Paul, London.

Central Statistical Office (1983) *Social Trends 13,* HMSO, London.

Central Statistical Office (1990) *Social Trends 20,* HMSO, London.

Central Statistical Office (1991) *Social Trends 21,* HMSO, London.

Central Statistical Office (1992) *Social Trends 22,* HMSO, London.

Central Statistical Office (1993) *Social Trends 23,* HMSO, London.

Central Statistical Office (1994) *Social Trends 24,* HMSO, London.

Central Statistical Office (1995) *Social Trends 25,* HMSO, London.

Central Statistical Office (1996) *Social Trends 26,* HMSO, London.

Centre For Policy On Ageing (CPA) (1982) *Out of Sight – Out of Mind,* CPA, London.

CPA (1984) *Home Life: a code of practice for residential care,* CPA, London.

CPA (1989) *World Directory of Older Age,* CPA, London.

CPA (1996) *A Better Home Life: a code of practice for residential care,* CPA, London.

Challis, D. and Davies, B. (1986) *Case Management in Community Care,* Gower, Aldershot, Hants.

Challis, D. and Ferlie, E. (1988) 'The Myth of General Practice: specialization in social work', *Journal of Social Policy,* 17(1), pp. 1–22.

Chancellor of The Exchequer (1954) *Report of the Committee on the Economic and Financial Problems of the Provision for Old Age* (Phillips Report), HMSO, London.

Chancellor of the Exchequer, The Secretary of State for Social Security, The President of the Board of Trade, The Secretary of State for Health, The Secretary of State for Northern Ireland, The Secretary of State for Scotland and The Secretary of State for Wales (1996) *New Partnerships for Care in Old Age: a consultation paper,* HMSO, London.

Charities Aid Foundation (1996) *Dimensions of the Voluntary Sector,* Charities Aid Foundation, London.

Charity Commission (1994) *Charities and Local Authorities,* HMSO, London.

Charlesworth, A., Wilkin, D. and Durie, A. (1984) *A Comparison of Men and Women Caring for Dependent Elderly People,* Equal Opportunities Commission, Manchester.

Chew, C., Wilkin, D. and Glendinning, C. (1994a) 'Annual Assessments of Patients Aged 75 Years and Over: general practitioners and practice nurses' views and experiences' *British Journal of General Practice,* (44), pp. 263–7

Chew, C., Wilkin, D. and Glendinning, C. (1994b) 'Annual Assessment of Patients Aged 75 and Over: views and experiences of elderly people' *British Journal of General Practice,* (44), pp. 567–70.

Clapham, D. and Franklin, B. (1995) *Housing Management, Community*

Care and Compulsory Competitive Tendering, Joseph Rowntree Foundation Findings Housing Research 135, York.

Clapham, D., Means, R. and Munro, M. (1993) 'Housing, the Life Course and Older People', in Arber, S. and Evandrou, M. (eds), *Ageing, Independence and the Life Course*, Jessica Kingsley, London, pp. 132–48.

Clapham, D. and Munro, M. (1990) 'Ambiguities and Contradictions in the Provision of Sheltered Housing for Older People', *Journal of Social Policy*, 19(1), pp. 27–46.

Clapham, D. and Munro, M. with Macdonald, J. and Roberts, M. (1988) *A Comparison of Sheltered and Amenity Housing for Older People*, Centre for Housing Research, University of Glasgow, Glasgow.

Clarke, L. (1995) 'Family Care and Changing Family Structure: bad news for the elderly?' in Allen, I. and Perkins, E. (eds) *The Future of Family Care for Older People*, HMSO, London, pp. 19–50.

Clarke, M. and Stewart, J. (1990) 'The Future of Local Government: issues for discussion', *Public Administration*, 68(2), pp. 249–58.

Clegg, J. (1971) *Dictionary of Social Services*, Bedford Square Press, London.

Cole, D. and Utting, J. (1962) *The Economic Circumstances of Old People*, Codicote Press, Welwyn, Herts.

Coleman, D. and Salt, J. (1992) *The British Population: patterns, trends and processes*, Oxford University Press, Oxford.

Coleman, P. (1993) 'Psychological Ageing' in Bond *et al.* (eds) *Ageing in Society: an introduction to social gerontology*, Sage, London, pp. 68–96.

Colledge, N. R. and Ford, M. J. (1994) 'Hospital Readmission and the Elderly', *Reviews in Clinical Gerontology*, 4, pp. 359–64.

Collins, K. (1989) 'Hypothermia and Seasonal Mortality in the Elderly', *Care of the Elderly* 1(6), pp. 257–59.

Colvez, A. (1996) 'Disability Free Life Expectancy', in Ebrahim, S. and Kalache, A. (eds) *Epidemiology in Old Age*, BMJ, London, pp. 41–8.

Comfort, A. (1965) *The Process of Ageing*, Weidenfeld and Nicolson, London.

Comfort, A. (1977) *A Good Age*, Mitchell Beazley, London.

Commission on Social Justice (1994) *Social Justice: strategies for renewal*, the Report of the Committee on Social Justice, Institute for Public Policy Research, London.

Consumers Association (1986) 'Sounding the Alarm', *Which?*, July 1986, pp. 318–21.

Counsel and Care (1991) *Not Such Private Places*, Counsel and Care, London.

Counsel and Care (1992) *From Home to a Home*, Counsel and Care, London.

Council of Europe Study Group on Violence Against Elderly People (1993), *Report*, Council of Europe, Strasbourg.

Cox, B. D., Blaxter, M., Buckle, A., Fenner, H., Golding, J., Gore, M., Huppert, F., Hickson, J., Roth, M., Stark, J., Wadsworth, M. and Whichelow, M. (1987) *The Health and Lifestyle Survey*, The Health Promotion Research Trust, London.

Craig, G. (1992) *The Social Fund: reform or replacement?* Social Policy Research Unit, University of York, York.

Crane, M. (1990) *Elderly Homeless People in Central London*, ACE and Age Concern Greater London, London.

Crane, M. (1993) *Elderly Homeless People Sleeping on the Streets in Inner*

London: an exploratory study, ACIOG, London.

Crosby, G. (ed.) (1993) *The European Directory of Older Age*, CPA, London.

Cullingworth, B. (1960) *Housing Needs and Planning Policy*, Routledge and Kegan Paul, London.

Cumberlege Report, (1986) *Neighbourhood Nursing – a focus for care*, Report of the Community Nursing Review, HMSO, London.

Cunningham-Burley, S. (1986) 'Becoming a Grandparent'. *Ageing and Society*, 6(4), pp. 453–70.

Daatland, S. O. (1990) 'What are Families For?: on family solidarity and preference for help', *Ageing and Society*, 10(1), pp. 1–16.

Davey, J. (1995) *Living With a Home Income Plan: the users experience of equity release*, Hutton and Wild Ltd, Surbiton, Surrey.

Davies, B., Barton, A., McMillan, I. and Williamson, V. (1971) *Variations in Services for the Aged*, G. Bell and Sons, London.

Davies, B. and Challis, D. (1986) *Matching Resources to Needs in Community Care*, Gower, Aldershot, Hants.

Davies, L. (1981) *Three Score Years ... and Then?*, Heinemann Medical Books, London.

Davis Smith, J. (1991) *The 1991 National Survey of Voluntary Activity*, The Volunteer Centre, London.

Davis Smith, J. (1992) *Volunteering: widening horizons in the Third Age*, Carnegie UK Trust, Dunfermline, Scotland.

Davis Smith, J. (1996) 'Volunteering in Europe', in Charities Aid Foundation, *Dimensions of the Voluntary Sector*, CAF, London, pp. 180–9.

Dawson, A. and Evans, G. (1987) 'Pensioners' Incomes and Expenditure 1970–85', *Employment Gazette*, May, pp. 243–52.

Day, P. and Klein, R. (1987) 'The Business of Welfare', *New Society*, 19.6.87, pp. 11–13.

Deakin, N. (1996) 'Editorial', in Charities Aid Foundation, *Dimensions of the Voluntary Sector*, CAF, London, pp. 7–8.

Decalmer, P. and Glendenning, F. (eds) (1993) *The Mistreatment of Elderly People*, Sage, London.

Department of the Environment (DoE) (1976) *Housing for Old People: a consultation paper*, DoE/DHSS/WO, London.

DoE (1977a) *Committee of Inquiry into the System of Remuneration of Members of Local Authorities* (the Robinson Committee), HMSO, London.

DoE (1977b) *Housing Policy: a consultative document*, HMSO, London.

DoE (1978) *Organising a Comprehensive Housing Service*, DoE, London.

DoE (1985) *Home Improvement: a new approach*, HMSO, London.

DoE (1987) *Housing: the government's proposals*, HMSO, London.

DoE (1989) *The Government's Review of the Homelessness Legislation*, DoE, London.

DoE (1993) *English House Condition Survey 1991*, HMSO, London.

DoE (1995a) *A National and Regional Survey of Elderly People in the Community*, Report No. 7, DoE, London.

DoE (1995b) *A National and Regional Survey of Elderly People in Specialised Housing*, Report No. 8, DoE, London.

DoE Housing Services Advisory Group (1977) *The Assessment of Housing Requirements*, DoE, London.

DoE Housing Services Advisory Group (1978) *Allocation of Council Housing*, DoE, London.

Department of The Environment (DoE) and Welsh Office (WO) (1973a) *Widening the Choice: the next steps in housing*, HMSO, London.

DoE and WO (1973b) *Better Homes: the next priorities*, HMSO, London.

Department of Health (DoH) (1989) *Personal Social Services, Local Authority Statistics, Residential Accommodation for Elderly and for Younger Physically Handicapped People: all residents in local authority voluntary and private homes*, year ending 31.3.89, RA/89/2, and year ending 31.3.94, DoH, London.

DoH (1990a) *Community Care in the Next Decade and Beyond: policy guidance*, HMSO, London.

DoH (1990b) *On the State of the Public Health for the Year 1989*, HMSO, London.

DoH (1991a) *The Health of the Nation: a consultative document for health in England*, HMSO, London.

DoH (1991b) *The Patients Charter*, DoH, London.

DoH (1992a) *The Health of the Nation: a strategy for health in England*, HMSO, London.

DoH (1992b) *On The State of The Public Health 1991*, HMSO, London.

DoH (1993a) *The Health of the Nation: one year on*, DoH, London.

DoH (1993b) *The Health of the Nation, Key Area Handbook: accidents*, DoH, London.

DoH (1993c) *Caring for People: information pack for the voluntary and private sectors*, DoH, London.

DoH (1993d) *Training for the Future*, DoH, London.

DoH (1994) *Hospital Discharge Workbook*, DoH, London.

DoH (1995a) *Fit for the Future: second progress report on the health of the nation*, DoH, London.

DoH (1995b) *Variations in Health: what can the Department of Health and the NHS do?*, DoH, London.

DoH Central Health Monitoring Unit (1992) *The Health of Elderly People: an epidemiological review*, Companion Papers, HMSO, London.

DoH Central Health Monitoring Unit (1996) *Health Related Behaviour: an epidemiological overview*, HMSO, London.

DoH/Chief Medical Officer (1995) Annual Report *On the State of the Public Health 1994*, HMSO, London.

DoH/KPMG Peat Marwick (undated) *Informing Users and Carers*, DoH, London.

DoH/NHS Executive (1994) *Feet First*, DoH, London.

Department of Health/Social Services Inspectorate (DoH/SSI) (1989) *Homes are for Living In*, HMSO, London.

DoH/SSI (1990) *Caring for Quality: guidance of standards for residential homes for elderly people*, HMSO, London.

DoH/SSI (1992a) *Confronting Elder Abuse*, HMSO, London.

DoH/SSI (1992b) *Caring for Quality in Day Services*, HMSO, London.

DoH/SSI (1993a) *The Health of the Nation. Key Area Handbook: mental illness*, DoH, London.

DoH/SSI (1993b) *No Longer Afraid: the safeguards of older people in domestic settings*, HMSO, London.

DoH/SSI (1993c) *Social Services for Hospital Patients III: users and carers perspective*, DoH, London.

DoH/SSI (1993d) *Developing Quality Standards for Home Support Services*, HMSO, London.

322   Bibliography

DoH/SSI (1993e) *Training for the Future*, HMSO, London.

DoH/SSI (1994a) *Abuse of Older People in Domestic Settings*, DoH, London.

DoH/SSI (1994b) *Second Overview Report of the Complaints Procedure in Local Authority Social Services Departments*, DoH, London.

DoH/SSI (1994c) *Inspection of Assessment and Care Management Arrangements in Social Services Departments, Second Overview Report*, DoH, London.

DoH/SSI (1995a) *Building Community Services: the mental illness specific grant. a review of the first four years 1991–1994*, HMSO, London.

DoH/SSI (1995b) *Responding to Residents*, DoH, London.

DoH/SSI (1995c) *Training Support Programme: a report on targets and achievements in 1993/94*, DoH/SSI, London.

DoH/SSI (1995d) *What Next for Carers: findings from an SSI project*, DoH, London.

DoH/SSI (1995e) *Caring Today: national inspection of local authority support to carers*, DoH, London.

DoH/SSI (1996) *SSI Inspection of Complaints Procedures in Local Authority Social Services Departments – Third Overview Report*, DoH, London.

DoH/SSI/NHS Executive (1994a) *Care Management*, DoH, London.

DoH/SSI/NHS Executive (1994b) *Community Care Packages for Older People*, DoH, London.

DoH/SSI/NHS Executive (1994c) *The F Factor: reasons why some older people choose residential care*, DoH/SSI/NHS Executive, London.

DoH/SSI/NHS Executive (1995) *Community Care Monitoring Report 1994*, DoH, London.

DoH/SSI/The Chief Inspector Social Services Inspectorate (1992) *Concern for Quality. The First Annual Report of the Chief Inspector 1991/1992*, HMSO, London.

DoH/SSI/The Chief Inspector Social Services Inspectorate (1993) *Raising the Standard. The Second Annual Report of the Chief Inspector 1992/1993*, HMSO, London.

DoH/SSI/The Chief Inspector Social Services Inspectorate (1994) *Putting People First. The Third Annual Report of the Chief Inspector 1993/94*, HMSO, London.

DoH/SSI/The Chief Inspector Social Services Inspectorate (1995) *Partners in Caring: The Fourth Annual Report of the Chief Inspector (1994/1995)*, HMSO, London.

DoH/SSI/The Chief Inspector Social Services Inspectorate (1996) *Progress Through Change: The Fifth Annual Report of the Chief Inspector 1995/96*, HMSO, London.

Department Of Health and Social Security (DHSS) (1971) *Better Services for the Mentally Handicapped*, HMSO, London.

DHSS (1972) *A Nutrition Survey of the Elderly*, HMSO, London.

DHSS (1973) *Report of the Committee on Abuse of Social Security Benefits* (The Fisher Report), HMSO, London.

DHSS (1975) *Better Services for the Mentally Ill*, HMSO, London.

DHSS (1976a) *The Elderly and the Personal Social Services*, DHSS, London.

DHSS (1976b) *Sharing Resources for Health in England*, HMSO, London.

DHSS (1976c) *Prevention and Health: everybody's business*, HMSO, London.

DHSS (1976d) *A Lifestyle for the Elderly*, DHSS, London.
DHSS (1976e) *Priorities for Health and Personal Social Services in England. A consultative document*, HMSO, London.
DHSS (1977) *Priorities in the Health and Social Services: the way forward*, HMSO, London.
DHSS (1978a) *A Happier Old Age. A discussion document*, HMSO, London.
DHSS (1978b) *Collaboration in Community Care. A discussion document*, HMSO, London.
DHSS (1979) *Nutrition and Health in Old Age*, HMSO, London.
DHSS (1981a) *Care in Action*, HMSO, London.
DHSS (1981b) *Report of a Study on Community Care*, DHSS, London.
DHSS (1981c) *Care in the Community*, DHSS, London.
DHSS (1981d) *Growing Older*, HMSO, London.
DHSS (1981e) *The Report of a Study on the Acute Hospital Sector*, HMSO, London.
DHSS (1981f) *The Respective Roles of the General Acute and Geriatric Sectors in the Care of the Elderly Hospital Patient*, DHSS, London.
DHSS (1982a) *Ageing in the United Kingdom*, DHSS, London.
DHSS (1982b) *Public Expenditure on the Social Services. Reply by the Government to the Second Report from the Select Committee on Social Services, Sessions 1981–82*, HMSO, London.
DHSS (1983a) *Elderly People in the Community: their service needs*, HMSO, London.
DHSS (1983b) *Explanatory Notes on Care in the Community*, DHSS, London.
DHSS (1985) *Progress in Partnership. Report of the Working Group on Joint Planning*, DHSS, London.
DHSS Joint Central And Local Government Working Party (1985) *Supplementary Benefit and Residential Care*, DHSS, London.
DHSS Joint Central And Local Government Working Party (1987) *Public Support for Residential Care* (The Firth Report), DHSS, London.
Department of Health and Social Security/Social Services Inspectorate (DHSS/SSI) (1987) *From Home Help to Home Care: an analysis of policy, resourcing and service management*, DHSS, London.
DHSS/SSI (1988a) *Managing Policy Change in Home Help Services*, DHSS, London.
DHSS/SSI (1988b) *Conference on Services for Black Elders*, DHSS, London.
DHSS Social Work Service Development Group (1984) *Supporting the Informal Carers: 'fifty styles of caring'*, DHSS, London.
Department of Social Security (DSS) (1991) *Options for Equality in State Pension Age*, HMSO, London.
DSS (1994) *Security, Equality and Choice: the future for pensions*, HMSO, London.
DSS (1995a) *The Pensioners' Incomes Series 1993*, HMSO, London.
DSS (1995b) *The Government's Expenditure Plans 1995/96 to 1997/98*, HMSO, London.
DTI (Department of Trade and Industry) Consumer Safety Unit (1995) *Home Accident Surveillance System: report on 1993 accident data and safety research*, DTI, London.
Department of Transport (1991) *The Older Road User*, DTI, London.
Dibden, J. and Hibbett, A. (1993) 'Older Workers – an overview of recent

research', *Employment Gazette*, June, pp. 238–50.

Dickenson, D. and Johnson, M. (eds) (1993) *Death, Dying and Bereavement*, Sage, London.

di Gregorio, S. (ed.), (1987) *Social Gerontology: new directions*, Croom Helm, London.

Disability Unit DSS (1994) *Summary of a Consultation on Government Measures to Tackle Discrimination Against Disabled People*, Disability Unit, London.

Donaldson, C., Atkinson, A., Bond, J. and Wright, K. (1988) 'QALYs and Long-term Care for Elderly People in the UK: scales for assessment of quality of life', *Age and Ageing* 17(6), pp. 379–87.

Donaldson, L. (1986) 'Health and Social Status of Elderly Asians: a community survey', *British Medical Journal*, 293, 25.10.86, pp. 1079–81.

Dooghe, G. and Vanden Boer, L. (eds) (1993) *Sheltered Accommodation for Elderly People in an International Perspective*, Swets and Zeitlinger, Amsterdam.

Dorrell, S. (June 1996) *Primary Care: the future*, NHS Executive, London.

Drake, M., O'Brien, M. and Biebuyck, T. (1981) *Single and Homeless*, HMSO, London.

Drury, E. (1990) *Social Developments Affecting Elderly People in the European Commission Member States*, Eurolink Age, London.

Duncan, S., Downey, P. and Finch, H. (1983) *A Home of Their Own*, DoE, London.

Dunn, D. (1987) *Food, Glorious Food: a review of meals services for older people*, CPA, London.

Dunning, A. (1995) *Citizen Advocacy with Older People: a code of good practice*, CPA, London.

Eastman, M. (1994) *Old Age Abuse: a new perspective*, Chapman and Hall, London.

Ebrahim, S. (1996) 'Migration and Ethnicity', in Ebrahim, S. and Kalache, A. (eds), *Epidemiology in Old Age*, BMJ, London, pp. 201–9.

Ebrahim, S., and Kalache, A. (eds) (1996) *Epidemiology in Old Age*, BMJ, London.

Elder, G. (1977) *The Alienated*, Writers and Readers Publishing Co-operative, London.

Elford, J. (ed.) (1987) *Medical Ethics and Elderly People*, Churchill Livingstone, London.

Elkan, R. and Kelly, D. (1991) *A Window in Homes: links between residential care homes and the community – a literature review*, Social Care Association, Surbiton, Surrey.

Equal Opportunities Commission (1980) *The Experience of Caring for Elderly Handicapped Dependents*, Equal Opportunities Commission, Manchester.

Equal Opportunities Commission (1982) *Caring for the Elderly and Handicapped: community care policies and women's lives*, Equal Opportunities Commission, Manchester.

Ermisch, J. (1990) *Fewer Babies, Longer Lives*, Joseph Rowntree Foundation, York.

Evandrou, M. (1987) *The Use of Domiciliary Services by the Elderly: a survey*, Suntory-Toyota International Centre for Economics and Related Disciplines, London School of Economics, London.

Evans, A. and Duncan, S. (1988) *Responding to Homelessness: local authority policy and practice*, HMSO, London.

Evans, J. G. (1981) 'Institutional Care', in Arie, T. (ed.), *Health Care of the Elderly*, Croom Helm, London, pp. 176–93.

Evans, J. G. (1988) 'Ageing in disease', in Evered, D. and Whelan, J. (eds), *Research and the Ageing Population*, Wiley, Chichester, pp. 38–57.

Evans, J. G. (ed.) (1993a) *Oxford Textbook of Geriatric Medicine*, Oxford University Press, Oxford.

Evans, J. G. (1993b) 'Hypothesis: healthy active life expectancy (HALE) as an index of effectiveness of health and social services for elderly people' *Age and Ageing*, 22(4), pp. 297–301.

Evans, J. G. (1994) 'Can we live to be a healthy hundred?', in MRC News, Autumn, p. 64.

Evans, J. G., Goldacre, M., Hodkinson, M., Lamb, S. and Savory, M. (1992) *Health: abilities and wellbeing in the Third Age*, The Carnegie UK Trust, Dunfermline, Scotland.

Eyden, J. (1971) *The Welfare Society*, Bedford Square Press, London.

Falkingham, J. and Gordon, C. (1988) *Fifty Years On: the income and household composition of the elderly in Britain*, Suntory-Toyota International Centre for Economics and Related Disciplines, London School of Economics, London.

Falkingham, J. and Victor, C. (1991) *The Myth of the Woopie?: incomes, the elderly, and targetting welfare*, Suntory-Toyota International Centre for Economics and Related Disciplines, London School of Economics, London.

Featherstone, M. and Hepworth, M. (1993) 'Images of Ageing' in Bond, J. et al., (eds), *Ageing in Society*, Sage, London, pp. 304–32.

Featherstone, M. and Wernick, A. (eds) (1995) *Images of Ageing*, Routledge, London.

Fennell, G. (1986) *Anchor's Older People: what do they think?*, Anchor Housing Association, Oxford.

Fennell, G. (1987) *A Place of My Own*, Bield Housing Association, Edinburgh.

Fennell, G., Phillipson, C. and Evers, H. (1988) *The Sociology of Old Age*, Open University Press, Buckingham.

Ferlie, E., Challis, D. and Davies, B. (1989) *Efficiency – improving innovation in social care of the elderly*, Gower, Aldershot, Hants.

Fiegehen, G. (1986) 'Income after Retirement', in CSO *Social Trends* 16, HMSO, London, pp. 13–18.

Fielder, S., McIntosh, A. and Tremlett, N. (1994) *Review of the Home Improvement Agency Grant Programme*, DoE, London.

Finch, J. (1989) *Family Obligations and Social Change*, Polity Press, Blackwell, Oxford.

Finch, J. (1995) 'Responsibilities, Obligations and Commitments', in Allen, I. and Perkins, E. (eds), *The Future of Family Care for Older People*, HMSO, London, pp. 51–64.

Finch, J. and Groves, D. (1980) 'Community Care and the Family: a case for equal opportunities?', *Journal of Social Policy*, 9(4), pp. 487–514.

Finch, J. and Groves, D. (eds), (1983) *A Labour of Love: women, work and caring*, Routledge and Kegan Paul, London.

Finch, J. and Mason, J. (1993) *Negotiating Family Responsibilities*, Routledge, London.

Fleiss, A. (1985) *Home Ownership Alternatives for the Elderly*, HMSO, London.

Fletcher, P. (1991) *The Future of Sheltered Housing – Who Cares? Policy Report*, NFHA, London.

Fletcher, P. and Gillie, D. (1991) *The Future of Sheltered Housing – Who Cares? Practice Guide*, NFHA, London.

Fletcher, R. (1966) *The Family and Marriage in Britain*, Penguin, London.

Fogarty, M. (1987) *Meeting the Needs of the Elderly*, The European Foundation for the Improvement of Living and Working Conditions, Dublin.

Forder, A. (1974) *Concepts in Social Administration*, Routledge and Kegan Paul, London.

Foster, P. (1983) *Access to Welfare*, Macmillan, London.

Fowkes, A., Oxley, P. and Heiser, B. (undated) *Cross-Sector Benefits of Accessible Public Transport*, Cranfield University School of Management, Cranfield.

Franklin, B. and Clapham, D. (1995) *Housing Management, Community Care and Compulsory Competitive Tendering*, JRF Findings Housing Research 135, York.

Freer, C. (1988) 'Old Myths: frequent misconceptions about the elderly', in Wells, H. and Freer, C. (eds), *The Ageing Population: burden or challenge?*, Macmillan, London, pp. 3–16.

Froggatt, A. (1990) *Family Work with Elderly People*, Macmillan, London.

Gaffin, J. (1996) 'Services for People who are Terminally Ill', in National Association of Health Authorities and Trusts (NAHAT) *NAHAT 1996/97 NHS Handbook*, NAHAT, London, pp. 221–3.

General Household Surveys – see OPCS.

Giallombardo, E. and Homer, A. (1994) 'Resuscitation: a survey of policies', *Journal of British Society of Gerontology*, 3, 4, pp. 5–7.

Gilmore, A. and Gilmore, S. (eds) (1988) *A Safer Death*, Plenum Press, New York.

Glendinning, C. and McLaughlin, E. (1993) *Paying for Care: lessons from Europe*, HMSO, London.

Glendenning, F. (ed.) (1985) *Educational Gerontology: international perspectives*, Croom Helm, London.

Glennerster, H. (1992) *Paying for Welfare: the 1990s*, Harvester Wheatsheaf, Hemel Hempstead, Herts.

Glennerster, H., Falkingham, J. and Evandrou, M. (1990) 'How Much do we Care?' *Social Policy and Administration* 24(2), pp. 93–103.

Glennerster, H., Matsaganis, M. and Owens, P. with Hancock, S. (1994) *Implementing GP Fundholding*, Open University Press, Buckingham.

Goddard, E. (1994) *1992 General Household Survey: voluntary work*, HMSO, London.

Goldberg, E. M. (1970) *Helping the Aged: a field experiment in social work*, Allen and Unwin, London.

Goldberg, E. M. and Connelly, N. (1982) *The Effectiveness of Social Care for the Elderly*, Heinemann, London.

Goldsmith, S. (1974) *Mobility Housing*, DoE, Housing Development Directorate, London.

Goldsmith, S. (1975) *Wheelchair Housing*, DoE, Housing Development Directorate, London.

Goode, R. (1993) *Pension Law Reform* (Report of the Pension Law Reform Committee), HMSO, London.

Goodman, A. (1976) *Charity Law and Voluntary Organisations*, Bedford Square Press, London.

Gough, I. with Thomas, T. (1994) 'Need, Satisfaction and Welfare Out-comes: theory and explanations, *Social Policy and Administration*, 28(1), pp. 33–56.

Gould, A. (1993) *Capitalist Welfare Systems*, Longman, London.

Government Actuaries Department (1996) *Population Projections 1994–2064 mid-1994 based*, provided on disk.

Government Statistical Service (1995a) *Community Care: detailed statistics on local authority personal social services for adults, England*, DoH, London.

Government Statistical Service (1995b) DoH Personal Social Services Local Authority Statistics *Residential Accommodation for Elderly People and People with Physical and/or Sensory Disabilities. All Residents in Local Authority Voluntary and Private Homes Year Ending 31.1.1994*, DoH, London.

Government Statistical Service (1995c) DoH Personal Social Services Local Authority Statistics *Residential Accommodation for All Client Groups: admission to local authority, voluntary and private homes 1994 England*, DoH, London.

Government Statistical Service (1996a) DoH Statistical Bulletin *Community Care Statistics 1995: Personal Social Services: day and domiciliary services for adults England*, DoH, London.

Government Statistical Service (1996b) *Key Indicators of Local Authority Social Services*, DoH, London.

Government Statistical Service (1996c) DoH Personal Social Services Local Authority Statistics S/F 95/1 *Staff of Local Authority Social Services Departments at 30.9.95*, DoH, London.

Gray, J. A. M. (1996) 'Preventive Medicine' in Ebrahim, S. and Kalache, A. (eds), *Epidemiology in Old Age*, BMJ, London, pp. 145–52.

Gray, J. A. M. (1987) 'Preventive Care for Elderly People', *The Practitioner*, 231, pp. 829–30.

Green, H. (1988) *Informal Carers*, HMSO, London.

Green, H. and Hansbro, J. (1995) *Housing in England 1993/94*, HMSO, London.

Greengross, W. and Greengross, S. (1989) *Living, Loving and Ageing*, ACE, London.

Griffin, J. and Dean, C. (1975) *Housing for the Elderly: the size of grouped schemes*, HMSO, London.

Griffiths, A., Grimes, R. and Roberts, G. (1990) *The Law and Elderly People*, Routledge, London.

Griffiths, R. (1983) *NHS Management Inquiry*, HMSO, London.

Griffiths, R. (1988) *Community Care: agenda for action*, A Report to the Secretary of State for Social Services, HMSO, London.

Grundy, E. (1983) 'Demography and Old Age', *Journal of the American Geriatrics Society*, 31, pp. 799–802.

Grundy, E. (1987) 'Retirement migration and its consequences in England and Wales', *Ageing and Society*, 7, pp. 57–82.

Grundy, E. (1989) 'Longitudinal Perspectives on the Living Arrangements of the Elderly', in Jefferys, M. (ed.), *Growing Old in the Twentieth Century*, Routledge, London, pp. 128–47.

Grundy, E. (1991a) 'Women and Ageing: demographic aspects' in George, S. and Ebrahim, S. (eds), *Health Care for Older Women*, Oxford University Press, Oxford, pp. 1–15.

Grundy, E. (1991b) 'Age-related Change in Later Life', in Hobcraft, J. and

Murphy, M. (eds), *Population Research in Britain, Supplement to Population Studies* 45, pp. 133–56.

Grundy, E. (1992) 'The Living Arrangements of Elderly People', *Reviews in Clinical Gerontology*, 2, pp. 253–361.

Grundy, E. (1995a) 'Demographic Influences on the Future of Family Care', in Allen, I. and Perkins, E. (eds), *The Future of Family Care for Older People*, HMSO, London, pp. 1–18.

Grundy, E. (1995b) 'Intergenerational Transfers and Pressures on Those in Late Middle Age', in House of Commons Health Committee, *Long-Term Care*, Minutes of Evidence, 7.12.95, pp. 90–3.

Grundy, E. (1996a) 'Population Review: (5) the population aged 60 and over', *Population Trends*, 84, pp. 14–20.

Grundy, E. (1996b) 'Social Networks and Support', in Ebrahim, S. and Kalache, A. (eds), *Epidemiology in Old Age*, BMJ, London, pp. 236–41.

Grundy, E. and Arie, T. (1982) 'Falling Rates of Provision of Residential Care for the Elderly', *British Medical Journal*, 284, pp. 799–802.

Gurney, C. and Means, R. (1993) 'The Meaning of Home in Later Life', in Arber, S. and Evandrou, M. (eds), *Ageing, Independence, and the Life Course*, Jessica Kingsley, London, pp. 119–31.

Hadley, R., Webb, A. and Farrell, C. (1975) *Across the Generations: old people and young volunteers*, Allen and Unwin, London.

Haffenden, S. (1991) *Getting it Right for Carers*, HMSO, London.

Ham, C. (1992) *Health Policy in Britain*, Macmillan, London.

Hancock, R. (1994) 'Assessing Population Needs and Costing Options', in McCreadie (ed.), *Planning and Updating Community Care Plans*, ACIOG, London, pp. 22–32.

Hancock, R. and Jarvis, C. (1994) *The Long Term Effects of Being a Carer*, HMSO, London.

Hancock, R., Jarvis, C. and Mueller, G. (1995) *The Outlook for Incomes in Retirement: social trends and attitudes*, ACIOG, London.

Hancock, R. and Weir, P. (1994) *More Ways than Means: a guide to pensioners' incomes in Great Britain during the 1980s*, ACIOG, London.

Handy, C. (1983) *Taking Stock: being fifty in the eighties*, BBC, London.

Hannah, L. (1986) *Inventing Retirement: the development of occupational pensions in Britain*, Cambridge University Press, Cambridge.

Harding, T. (1990) 'Opportunities and Pitfalls: a voluntary sector view of the legislation', in Morton, J. (ed.), *Packages of Care for Elderly People: how can the voluntary sector contribute?* ACIOG, London, pp. 27–31.

Harris, A. (1968) *Social Welfare for the Elderly*, HMSO, London.

Harris, A. (1971) *Handicapped and Impaired in Great Britain*, HMSO, London.

Harris, C. (1969) *The Family*, Allen and Unwin, London.

Harris, D. (1990) *Sociology of Aging*, Harper and Row, New York.

Harrop, A. (1990) *The Employment Position of Older Women in Europe*, ACIOG, London.

Harrop, A. and Grundy, E. (1991) 'Geographic Variations in Moves into Institutions among the Elderly in England and Wales', *Urban Studies*, 28, pp. 65–86.

Hart, D. and Chalmers, K. (1990) *The Housing Needs of Elderly People in Scotland*, The Central Research Unit, Scottish Office, Edinburgh.

Haskey, J. (1989) 'Families and Households of the Ethnic Minority and White Populations of Great Britain', *Population Trends*, 57, pp. 8–19.

Health Advisory Service, (1982) *The Rising Tide: developing services for mental illness in old age*, National Health Service, Health Advisory Service, London.

Hedges, B. and Clemens, S. (1994) *Housing Attitudes Survey*, HMSO, London.

Hedley, R. and Norman, A. (1982) *Home Help: key issues in service provision*, CPA, London.

Hems, L. (1996) 'The Dimensions of the Voluntary Sector in the UK', in Charities Aid Foundation, *Dimensions of the Voluntary Sector*, CAF, London, pp. 14–18.

Hendricks, J. and Hendricks, D. (1986) *Ageing in the Mass Society – myths and realities*, Little, Brown and Co., Boston and Toronto.

Henwood, M. (1990) *Community Care and Elderly People*, Family Policy Studies Centre, London.

Henwood, M. (1995) *Making a Difference? Implementation of the community care reforms two years on*, Nuffield Institute for Health/King's Fund Centre, London.

Henwood, M. and Wistow, G. (1994) *Monitoring Community Care: a review*, Nuffield Institute for Health, Leeds.

Heumann, L. and Boldy, D.P. (1993) *Ageing in Place with Dignity*, Praeger, Connecticut.

Heywood, F. (1994) *Adaptations: finding ways to say yes*, School for Advanced Urban Studies, Bristol.

Hicks, C. (1988) *Who Cares?: looking after people at home*, Virago, London.

Higgins, J. (1989) 'Defining Community Care'. *Social Policy and Administration*, 23(1), pp. 3–16.

Higgs, P. and Victor, C. (1993) 'Institutional Care and the Lifecourse', in Arber, S. and Evandrou, M. (eds), *Ageing, Independence and the Life Course*, Jessica Kingsley, London, pp. 186–200.

Hill, M. (1976) *The State, Administration and the Individual*, Fontana, London.

Hill, M. (1993) *The Welfare State in Britain: a political history since 1945*, Edward Elgar, Aldershot, Hants.

Hills, D. (1991) *Carer Support in the Community*, DoH Social Services Inspectorate, London.

Hills, J. (1993) *The Future of Welfare: a guide to the debate*, Joseph Rowntree Foundation, York.

Hills, J., Glennerster, H. and Le Grand, J. (1993) *Investigating Welfare: final report of the ESRC Welfare Research Programme*, STICERD/LSE, London.

Hinton, C. (1995) *Using Your Home as Capital*, ACE, London.

Hinton, J. (1972) *Dying*, Penguin, London.

Hobman, D. (ed.) (1993) *Uniting Generations: studies in conflict and co-operation*, ACE, London.

Hodkinson, H. (1975) *An Outline of Geriatrics*, Academic Press, London.

Hole, W. and Pountney, M. (1971) *Trends in Population, Housing and Occupancy Rates 1861–1961*, HMSO, London.

Hollingbery, R. (1993) 'Gerocomist: a new trans-disciplinary profession', Paper presented to the British Society of Gerontology Conference, Norwich, September.

Holly, K. (1996) 'NHS Charitable Trust Funds', in Charities Aid Foundation, *Dimensions of the Voluntary Sector*, CAF, London, pp. 96–110.

Holmans, A. (1995a) *Housing Demand and Need in England 1991–2011*, Joseph Rowntree Foundation, York.

Holmans, A. (1995b) 'The Rising Number of Households Requiring Homes – the national and regional picture', in Wilcox, S. (ed.), *Housing Finance Review 1995/96*, Joseph Rowntree Foundation, York, pp. 16–24.

Holme, A. and Maizels, J. (1978) *Social Workers and Volunteers*, Allen and Unwin, London.

Home Office (1992) *The Individual and the Community: the role of the voluntary sector*, Home Office, London.

Home Office (1995) *Make a Difference: an outline volunteering strategy for the UK*, Home Office, London.

Home Office, Department of Education and Science, Ministry of Housing and Local Government and Ministry of Health (1968) *Report of the Committee on Local Authority and Allied Personal Social Services* (Seebohm Report), HMSO, London.

House Builders Federation (1990) *Guidance Note on Management and Services*, House Builders Federation/National Housing and Town Planning Council, London.

House Builders Federation and National Housing And Town Planning Council (1988) *Sheltered Housing For Sale*, An Advice Note, HBF and NHTPC, London.

House of Commons Employment Committee (1989) *Second Report. The Employment Patterns of the Over-50s*, Vol. 1, HMSO, London.

House of Commons Health Committee (1991) *Public Expenditure Health Matters*, HMSO, London.

House of Commons Health Committee (1993a) *Community Care: the way forward*, HMSO, London.

House of Commons Health Committee (1993b) *Community Care: funding from April 1993*, HMSO, London.

House of Commons Health Committee (1994) *Better off in the Community? The care of people who are seriously mentally ill*, HMSO, London.

House of Commons Health Committee (1995a) *Public Expenditure on Health and Personal Social Services*, HMSO, London.

House of Commons Health Committee (1995b) *Long-term Care: NHS responsibilities for meeting continuing health care needs, Volume 1 Report*, HMSO, London.

House of Commons Health Committee (1996) *Long-term Care: future provision and funding*, HMSO, London.

House of Commons Social Services Committee (1980) *The Government's White Papers on Public Expenditure: the social services*, Vol. 1, HMSO, London.

House of Commons Social Services Committee (1981) *Public Expenditure on the Social Services*, HMSO, London.

House of Commons Social Services Committee (1982) *Session 1981–82. 1982 White Paper: public expenditure on the social services*, Vol. 1, HMSO, London.

House of Commons Social Services Committee (1985) *Second Report Session 1984–85. Community Care: with special reference to adult mentally ill and mentally handicapped people*, Vol. 1, HMSO, London.

House of Commons Social Services Committee (1990a) *Fifth Report. Community Care: carers*, HMSO, London.

House of Commons Social Services Committee (1990b) *Eleventh Report. Community Care: services for people with a mental handicap and people with a mental illness*, HMSO, London.

Housing Corporation (1996) *Housing for Older People*, Housing Corporation, London.

Howe Report (1992) *The Quality of Care: report of the residential staff inquiry* (Chaired by Lady Howe), Local Government Management Board, London.

Hughes, B. (1990) 'Quality of Life', in Peace, S. (ed.), *Researching Social Gerontology*, Sage, London, pp. 46–58.

Hugman, R. (1994) *Ageing and the Care of Older People in Europe*, Macmillan, London.

Hunt, A. (1978) *The Elderly at Home*, Office of Population Censuses and Surveys, Social Survey Division, HMSO, London.

Hunter, D. (1996) 'Evaluation of Health Services', in Ebrahim, S. and Kalache, A. (eds) *Epidemiology in Old Age*, BMJ, London, pp. 85–95.

Hunter, D. Burley, L., Headland, L. and Killeen, J. (eds) (1987) *Dementia: developing innovative services in the community*, Scottish Action on Dementia, Edinburgh.

Institute Of Personnel Management (IPM) (1993) *Age and Employment: policies, attitudes and practice*, IPM, London.

Isaacs, B. and Evers, H. (1984) *Innovations in the Care of the Elderly*, Croom Helm, London.

Isaacs, B., Livingstone, M. and Neville, Y. (1972) *Survival of the Unfittest*, Routledge and Kegan Paul, London.

Itzin, C. and Phillipson, C. (1993) *Age Barriers at Work*, Metropolitan Authorities Recruitment Agency, Solihull, Warwickshire.

Jacoby, R. and Oppenheimer, C. (eds) (1991), *Psychiatry in the Elderly*, Oxford University Press, Oxford.

Jamieson, A. and Illsley, R. (eds) (1990) *Contrasting European Policies for the Care of Older People*, Avebury, Aldershot, Hants.

Jarvis, C. (1993) *Family and Friends in Old Age and the Implications for Informal Support: evidence from the British Social Attitudes Survey*, ACIOG, London.

Jarvis, C., Hancock, R., Askham, J. and Tinker, A. (1996) *Getting Around After 60: a profile of Britain's older population*, HMSO, London.

Jeffery, J. and Seager, R. (1993) *Housing Black and Minority Ethnic Elders*, Federation of Black Housing Organisations, London.

Jegede, F. (1993) *Transport for Elderly Persons*, University of Derby, Derby.

Jerrome, D. (ed.) (1983) *Ageing in Modern Society*, Croom Helm, London.

Jerrome, D. (1990) 'Intimate Relationships', in Bond, J. and Coleman, P. (eds), *Ageing in Society*, Sage, London, pp. 181–208.

Jerrome, D. (1993) 'Intimate Relationships', in Bond *et al.* (eds), *Ageing in Society*, Sage, London, pp. 226–54.

Johnson, M. (1972) 'Self-perception of Need Among the Elderly', *Sociological Review*, 20(4), pp. 521–31.

Johnson, M. (1993) 'Dependency and Interdependency', in Bond *et al.* (eds), *Ageing in Society*, Sage, London, pp. 255–79.

Johnson, P., Conrad, C. and Thomson, D. (eds) (1989) *Workers Versus Pensioners: intergenerational justice in an ageing world*, Manchester University Press, Manchester.

Johnson, P. with Dilnot, A., Disney, P. and Whitehouse, E. (1992) *Income: pensions, earnings and savings in the Third Age*, The Carnegie UK Trust, Dunfermline, Scotland.

Johnson, P., Disney, R. and Stears, G. (1996) *Pensions: 2000 and Beyond*, Vol. 2, The Retirement Income Inquiry, London.

Johnson, P. and Falkingham, J. (1988) 'Intergenerational Transfers and Public Expenditure on the Elderly in Modern Britain', *Ageing and Society*, 8(2), pp. 1129–46.

Johnson, P. and Falkingham, J. (1992) *Ageing and Economic Welfare*, Sage, London.

Jolly, J., Creigh, S. and Mingay, A. (1980) *Age as a Factor in Employment*, Department of Employment, London.

Jones, A. (1994) *The Numbers Game: black and minority ethnic elders and sheltered accommodation*, Anchor Housing Trust, Oxford.

Jones, C. (1985) *Patterns of Social Policy*, Tavistock, London.

Jones, S. (ed.) (1976) *The Liberation of the Elders*, Beth Foundation Publications and Department of Adult Education, University of Keele, Keele.

Joseph Rowntree Foundation (1991) *Inquiry into British Housing: second report*, Joseph Rowntree Foundation, York.

Joseph Rowntree Foundation (1995) *Joseph Rowntree Foundation Inquiry into Income and Wealth*, JRF, York.

Joseph Rowntree Foundation (1996) *Meeting the Costs of Continuing Care: recommendations of the inquiry*, JRF, York.

Joshi, H. (ed.) (1989) *The Changing Population of Britain*, Blackwell, Oxford.

Joshi, H. (1995) 'The Labour Market and Unpaid Caring: conflict and compromise', in Allen, I. and Perkins, E. (eds), *The Future of Family Care for Older People*, HMSO, London, pp. 93–118.

Kafetz, K. (1987) 'Hypothermia and Elderly People', *The Practitioner*, 231, pp. 864–7.

Kalache, A. (1996) 'Health Promotion', in Ebrahim, S. and Kalache, A. (eds), *Epidemiology in Old Age*, BMJ, London, pp. 153–61.

Kalache, A., Warnes, A. and Hunter, D. (1988) *Promoting Health Among Elderly People*, King's Fund, London.

Karn, V. (1977) *Retiring to the Seaside*, Routledge and Kegan Paul, London.

Kaye, L. W. and Monk, A. (eds) (1991) *Congregate Housing for the Elderly: theoretical, policy and programmatic perspectives*, The Howarth Press, New York.

Keddie, K. (1978) *Action with the Elderly*, Pergamon, London.

Kellaher, L. (1986) 'Determinants of Quality of Life in Residential Settings for Old People', in Judge, K. and Sinclair, I. (eds), *Residential Care for Elderly People*, HMSO, London, pp. 127–38.

Kelling, K. (1991) *Older Homeless People in London*, Age Concern Greater London, London.

Kendall, J. and Knapp, M. (1996) *The Voluntary Sector in the UK*, Oxford University Press, Oxford.

Kennedy, I. (Chairman) (1988) *The Living Will: a working party report*, Age Concern Institute of Gerontology and Centre of Medical Law and Ethics, King's College London, Edward Arnold.

Kennedy, J. and Stewart, J. (1994) 'Planning and Updating Community Care Plans: background information on policy and practice', in McCreadie (ed.), *Planning and Updating Community Care Plans*, ACIOG, London, pp. 3–16.

Kennie, D. (1993) *Preventive Care for Elderly People*, Cambridge University Press, Cambridge.

Khaw, K. T. (1996) 'Nutritional Status', in Ebrahim, S. and Kalache, A. (eds), *Epidemiology in Old Age*, BMJ, London, pp. 171–83.

King Edward's Hospital Fund and National Association of Health Authorities, (1987) *Care of the Dying: a guide for health authorities*, King Edward's Hospital Fund, London.

Kingston, P. and Penhale, B. (eds) (1995) *Family Violence and the Caring Professions*, Macmillan, London.

Kinsella, K. (1996) 'Demographic Aspects', in Ebrahim, S. and Kalache, A. (eds), *Epidemiology in Old Age*, BMJ, London, pp. 32–40.

Klein, R. (1975) *Inflation and Priorities*, Centre for Studies in Social Policy, University of Bath, Bath.

Knapp, M. and Davis Smith, J. (1995) *Who Volunteers and Why? The key factors which determine volunteering*, The Volunteer Centre, London.

Kroll, U. (1988) *Growing Older*, Collins, London.

Kubler-Ross, E. (1970) *Death and Dying*, Tavistock, London.

Laczko, F. (1990) 'New Poverty and the Old Poor: pensioners' incomes in the European Community', *Ageing and Society*, 10(3), pp. 261–78.

Laczko, F. and Phillipson, C. (1990) 'Defending the Right to Work: age discrimination in employment', in McEwen (ed.), *Age: the unrecognised discrimination*, ACE, London, pp. 84–96.

Laczko, F. and Victor, C. (eds) (1992) *Social Policy and Elderly People*, Avebury, Aldershot, Hants.

Laing and Buisson (1996) *Care of Elderly People Market Survey 1996*, Laing and Buisson, London.

Langan, J. and Means, R. (1995) *Personal Finances, Elderly People with Dementia and the 'New' Community Care*, Anchor Housing Association, Oxford.

Laslett, P. (1980) *The Education of the Elderly in Britain*, Unpublished (personal communication).

Laslett, P. (1989) *A Fresh Map of Life: the emergence of the Third Age*, Weidenfeld and Nicolson, London.

Law, C. M. and Warnes, A. M. (1982) 'The Destination Decision in Retirement Migration', in Warnes, A. M. (ed.), *Geographical Perspectives on the Elderly*, Wiley, Chichester, pp. 53–82.

Law Commission (1995) *Mental Incapacity*, HMSO, London.

Lazarowich, N. M. (ed.) (1991) *Granny Flats as Housing for the Elderly: international perspectives*, The Haworth Press, New York.

Le Gros Clark, F. (1966) *Work, Age and Leisure*, Joseph, London.

Leat, D. (1979) *Limited Liability?*, The Volunteer Centre, London.

Leat, D. (1990a) 'Care and the Voluntary Sector', in Sinclair *et al.* (eds), *The Kaleidoscope of Care*, NISW, HMSO, London, pp. 227–90.

Leat, D. (1990b) *For Love and Money*, Joseph Rowntree Foundation, York.

Leat, D. and Darvill, G. (1977) *Voluntary Visiting of the Elderly*, The Volunteer Centre, London.

Leat, D. and Gay, P. (1987) *Paying for Care*, Policy Studies Institute, London.

Leathard, A. (1990) *Health Care Provision: past, present and future*, Chapman and Hall, London.

Leather, P. and Mackintosh, S. (1990) *Monitoring Assisted Agency Services. Part 1: home improvement agencies – an evaluation of performance*, HMSO, London.

Leather, P. and Wheeler, R. (1988) *Making Use of Home Equity in Old Age*, Building Societies Association, London.

Levin, E., Sinclair, I. and Gorbach, P. (1989) *Families, Services and Confusion in Old Age*, Gower, Aldershot, Hants.

Lewis, J. (1993) 'Developing the Mixed Economy of Care – emerging issues', *Journal of Social Policy*, 4(93), pp. 173–92.

Lewis, J. and Meredith, B. (1988) *Daughters who Care*, Routledge, London.

Lilley, J. M., Arie, T. and Chilvers, C. (1995) 'Special Review: accidents involving older people: a review of the literature', *Age and Ageing*, 24(4), pp. 346–65.

Lindesay, J. (1996) 'Health Service Use in Mental Illness', in Ebrahim, S. and Kalache, A. (eds) *Epidemiology in Old Age*, BMJ, London, pp. 96–105.

Livesley, B. (1982) 'Silent Epidemic', *The Health Services*, 24, p. 14.

Local Government Management Board (1995) *Employment of Older Workers and Age Auditing*, The Local Government Management Board, London.

Local Government Management Board and Association of Directors of Social Services (1995) *Social Services Workforce Analysis. Main report*, The Local Government Management Board, London.

Lowry, S. (1991), *Housing and Health*, BMJ, London.

McCafferty, P. (1994) *Living Independently: a study of the housing needs of elderly and disabled people*, HMSO, London.

McCormick, A., Fleming, D. and Charlton, J. (1995) *Morbidity Statistics from General Practice: fourth national study 1991–1992*, HMSO, London.

McCreadie, C. (1991) *Elder Abuse: an exploratory study*, ACIOG, London.

McCreadie, C. (ed.) (1994) *Planning and Updating Community Care Plans: the needs of older people and their carers*, ACIOG, London.

McCreadie, C. (1996) *Elder Abuse: update on research*, ACIOG, London.

McEwen, E. (1990) *Age: the unrecognised discrimination*, ACE, London.

McGlone, F. and Cronin, N. (1994) *A Crisis in Care: the future of family and state care for older people in the European Union*, Family Policy Studies Centre, London.

McGrother, C. and Clarke, M. (1996) 'Incontinence', in Ebrahim, S. and Kalache, A. (eds), *Epidemiology in Old Age*, BMJ, London, pp. 353–60.

McKay, S. (1992) *Pensioners' Assets*, Policy Studies Institute, London.

Mack, J. and Lansley, S. (1985) *Poor Britain*, Allen and Unwin, London.

Mackintosh, S. and Leather, P. (1993) *The Performance of Home Improvement Agencies in 1990*, HMSO, London.

Mackintosh, S., Leather, P. and McCafferty, P. (1993) *The Role of Housing Agency Services in Helping Disabled People*, HMSO, London.

Maclennan, D., Gibb, K. and More, A. (1990) *Paying for Britain's Housing*, National Federation of Housing Associations, London.

Maclennan, W. (1986) 'Subnutrition in the Elderly', *British Medical Journal*, 293, pp. 1189–90.

McManus, L. (1985) *Hypothermia: the facts*, ACE, London.

Maggi, S. (1996) 'Osteoporosis', in Ebrahim, S. and Kalache, A. (eds), *Epidemiology in Old Age*, BMJ, London, pp. 290–99.

Marks, L. (1991) *Home and Hospital Care: redrawing the boundaries*, King's Fund Institute, London.

Marsh, A. and Riseborough, M. (1995) *Making Ends Meet: older people, housing association costs and the affordability of rented housing*, Centre for Urban and Regional Studies, University of Birmingham, NFHA, London.

Marshall, M. (1990) *Social Work with Old People*, Macmillan, London.
Martin, B. (1990) 'The Cultural Construction of Ageing: or how long can the summer wine really last?', in Bury, M. and MacNicol, J. (eds), *Aspects of Ageing*, Royal Holloway and Bedford New College, Egham, Surrey, pp. 53–81.
Martin, J., Meltzer, H. and Elliot, D. (1988) *The Prevalence of Disability Among Adults*, OPCS surveys of disability in Great Britain, Report 1, HMSO, London.
Martin, J. and Roberts, J. (1984) *Women and Employment: a lifetime perspective*, HMSO, London.
Martin, J. and White, A. (1988) *The Financial Circumstances of Disabled Adults Living in Private Households*, OPCS surveys of disability in Great Britain, Report 2, HMSO, London.
Martin, J., White, A. and Meltzer, H. (1989) *Disabled Adults: services, transport and employment*, OPCS surveys of disability in Great Britain, Report 4, HMSO, London.
Meacher, M. (1972) *Taken for a Ride*, Longman, London.
Medical Research Council (1994a) *The Health of the UK's Elderly People*, MRC, London.
Medical Research Council (1994b) *MRC News*, Autumn 1994, 64. MRC, London.
Medical Research Council (1995) *Suicide and Parasuicide*, MRC, London.
Meredith, B. (1994) *The Next Steps: lessons for the future of community care*, ACE, London.
Meredith, B. (1995) *The Community Care Handbook*, ACE, London.
Midwinter, E. (1982) *Age is Opportunity: education and older people*, CPA, 1982, London.
Midwinter, E. (1985) *The Wage of Retirement: the case for a new pensions policy*, CPA, London.
Midwinter, E. (1990) *Creating Chances: arts by older people*, CPA, London.
Midwinter, E. (1991) *The British Gas Report on Attitudes to Ageing 1991*, British Gas, London.
Midwinter, E. (1992a) *Leisure: new opportunities in the Third Age*, The Carnegie UK Trust, Dunfermline, Scotland.
Midwinter, E. (1992b) *Citizenship: from ageism to participation*, Carnegie UK Trust, Dunfermline, Scotland.
Midwinter, E. and Tester, S. (1987) *Polls Apart?: older voters and the 1987 General Election*, CPA, London.
Ministry of Health (MoH), (1956) *Report of the Committee of Enquiry into the Cost of the National Health Service* (The Guillebaud Committee), HMSO, London.
MoH (1957) *Survey of Services Available to the Chronic Sick and Elderly 1954–55*, Summary report prepared by Boucher, C.A., HMSO, London.
MoH (1962) *Hospital Plan*, HMSO, London.
MoH (1963) *Health and Welfare: the development of community care*, HMSO, London.
MoH (1965) *Care of the Elderly in Hospitals and Residential Homes*, MoH, London.
MoH (1966) *Health and Welfare: the development of community care*, HMSO, London.
Ministry of Health and Department of Health for Scotland (1959) *Report of the Working Party on Social Workers in Local Authority Health and Welfare Services* (The Younghusband Report), HMSO, London.

Ministry of Housing (1958) *Flatlets for Old People*, HMSO, London.
Ministry of Housing (1960) *More Flatlets for Old People*, HMSO, London.
Ministry of Housing and Local Government (MHLG) (1962a) *Some Aspects of Designing for Old People*, HMSO, London.
MHLG (1962b) *Grouped Flatlets for Old People*, HMSO, London.
MHLG (1963) *Housing*, HMSO, London.
MHLG (1966) *Old People's Flatlets in Stevenage*, HMSO, London.
MHLG (1967) *Management of Local Government* (The Maud Report), Vol. 1, Report of the Committee, HMSO, London.
MHLG (1969) *Council Housing Purposes, Procedures and Priorities* (The Cullingworth Report), HMSO, London.
MHLG/Welsh Office (1965) *The Housing Programme 1965 to 1970*, HMSO, London.
Ministry of Pensions and National Insurance (1954) *Reasons Given for Retiring or Continuing at Work*, HMSO, London.
Ministry of Pensions and National Insurance (1966) *Financial and Other Circumstances of Retirement Pensioners*, HMSO, London.
Molnar, B. and Davies, C. (1993) *All Our Tomorrows: housing and older people*, National Housing Forum, London.
Moore, J., Tilson, B. and Whiting, G. (1994) *An International Overview of Employment Policies and Practices Towards Older Workers*, Department of Employment, London.
Morgan, K. (ed.) (1992) *Gerontology: responding to an ageing society*, Jessica Kingsley, London.
Morley, D. (1974) *Day Care and Leisure Provision for the Elderly*, ACE, London.
Moroney, R. (1976) *The Family and the State*, Longman, London.
Morris, J. (1995) *Housing and Floating Support: Review*, York Publishing Services, York.
Morton, J. (1982) *Ferndale: a caring repair service for elderly home owners*, Shelter/Help the Aged, London.
Morton, J. (ed.) (1989a) *Enabling Elderly People with Dementia to Live in the Community*, ACIOG, London.
Morton, J. (ed.) (1989b) *Achieving Change in Home Care Services*, ACIOG, London.
Morton, J. (ed.) (1989c) *New Approaches to Day Care for Elderly People*, ACIOG, London.
Morton, J. (ed.) (1990a) *Packages of Care for Elderly People: how can the voluntary sector contribute?*, ACIOG, London.
Morton, J. (ed.) (1990b) *Packages of Care for Elderly People: how can the private sector contribute?*, ACIOG, London.
Morton, J. (ed.) (1991) *Very Sheltered Housing*, ACIOG, London.
Mullings, B. and Hamnett, C. (1992) 'Equity Release Schemes and Equity Extraction by Elderly Households in Britain', *Age and Society*, 12, pp. 413–42.
Murphy, E. (1986) 'Social Factors in Late Life Depression', in Murphy, E. (ed.), *Affective Disorders in the Elderly*, Churchill Livingstone, London, pp. 79–96.
National Assistance Board (1966) *Homeless Single Persons*, HMSO, London.
National Association of Health Authorities (1988) *Actions Not Words: a strategy to improve health services for black and minority ethnic groups*, NAHA, Birmingham.

National Audit Office (1987) *Community Care Developments*, HMSO, London.

National Audit Office (1991) *The Social Fund*, HMSO, London.

National Audit Office (1994) *General Practitioner Fundholding in England*, HMSO, London.

National Consumer Council (1990) *Consulting Consumers in the NHS: a guideline study*, NCC, London.

National Consumer Council (1995), *Charging Consumers for Social Services: local authority policy and practice*, NCC, London.

National Council of Social Service (1954) *Living Longer*, NCSS, London.

National Council of Social Service (1967) *Caring for People: staffing residential homes* (The Williams Report), Allen and Unwin, London.

National Council of Social Service and National Institute for Social Work Training (1969) *The Voluntary Worker in the Social Services* (The Aves Report), Bedford Square Press and Allen and Unwin, London.

National Council of Voluntary Organisations (1996) *Meeting the Challenge of Change: voluntary action into the 21st century*, NCVO, London.

National Economic Development Office (1989) *Defusing the Demographic Time Bomb*, NEDO, London.

National Federation of Housing Associations (NFHA) (1985) *Report of the Inquiry into British Housing: chaired by HRH The Duke of Edinburgh*, NFHA, London.

National Federation of Housing Associations/MIND (1989) *Housing: the foundation of community care*, NFHA, London.

National Federation of Housing Associations and Special Needs Housing Advisory Service (1987) *A Guide to the Registered Homes Act*, NFHA, London.

National Federation of Housing Association Statistics (1995) *Housing Associations Weekly*, December, pp. 23–6.

National Federation of Housing Authorities (1993) *Rented Housing for Older People: implementing a new framework*, Policy White Paper, NFHA, London.

National House Building Council (NHBC) (1990) *The NHBC Sheltered Housing Code of Practice*, NHBC, London.

National Institute for Social Work (1982) *Social Workers: their role and tasks* (The Barclay Report), Bedford Square Press, London.

Neill, J., Sinclair, I., Gorbach, P. and Williams, J. (1988) *A Need for Care? Elderly applicants for local authority homes*, Avebury, Aldershot, Hants.

Neill, J. and Williams, J. (1992) *Leaving Hospital: elderly people and their discharge to community care*, HMSO, London.

Netten, A. (1993) 'Costing Informal Care', in Netten, A. and Beecham, J. (eds), *Costing Community Care*, Ashgate, Aldershot, pp. 43–60.

Netten, A. and Beecham, J. (1993) *Costing Community Care: theory and practice*, Ashgate, Aldershot, Hants.

Neuberger, J. (1987) *Caring for Dying People of Different Faiths*, Austen Cornish, London.

Niner, P. (1989) *Housing Needs in the 1990s: an interim assessment*, National Housing Forum, London.

Niner, P., Mullins, D. with Marsh, A. and Walker, B. (1996) *Evaluation of the 1991 Homelessness Code of Guidance*, HMSO, London.

Noffsinger, D., Martin, J. P. and Lewis, S. H. (1990) 'Hearing Disorders of Ageing: identification and management', in Kane *et al.* (eds), *Improving*

the Health of Older People, OUP/WHO, Oxford, pp. 237–61.
Nolan, M. (1994) 'Geriatric Nursing: an idea whose time has gone? A polemic', *Journal of Advanced Nursing*, 20, pp. 989–96.
Norman, A. (1980) *Rights and Risk*, National Corporation for the Care of Old People, London.
Norman, A. (1985) *Triple Jeopardy: growing old in a second homeland*, CPA, London.
Norman, A. (1988) *Rights and Risk: a discussion document on civil liberty in old age*, CPA, London.
Norman, I. and Redfern, S. (eds) (1997) *Mental Health Care of Elderly People*, Churchill Livingstone, London.
Norton, C. (1989) 'Continence: a real case for team work', *Social Work Today*, 24.4.89, pp. 23–5.
Nuffield Foundation (1986) *The Nuffield Inquiry into Pharmacy*, Nuffield Foundation, London.
Nuttall, S. R., Blackwood, R., Bussell, B. *et al.* (1993) *Financing Long-Term Care in Great Britain*, Institute of Actuaries, London.
O'Callaghan, B., Dominian, L. with Evans, A., Dix, J., Smith, R., Williams, P. and Zimmeck, M. (1996) *Study of Homeless Applicants*, HMSO, London.
Office Of Population Censuses And Surveys (OPCS) (1982) *General Household Survey 1980*, HMSO, London.
OPCS (1989) *General Household Survey 1986*, (including a chapter on *GHS* 1985), HMSO, London.
OPCS (1992) *General Household Survey: carers in 1990*, OPCS Monitor SS92/2, OPCS, London.
OPCS (1993) *Great Britain 1991 Census: communal establishments*, HMSO, London.
OPCS (1994a) *1991 General Household Survey: people aged 65 and over*, HMSO, London.
OPCS (1994b) *1992 General Household Survey*, HMSO, London.
OPCS (1995) *General Household Survey, 1993*, HMSO, London.
OPCS (1996) *Living in Britain: results from the 1994 General Household Survey*, HMSO, London.
OPCS and Government Actuary's Department, 'Centenarians: 1991 estimates', *Population Trends* No. 75, Spring 1994, pp. 30–2.
OPCS Topic Monitor (1993 February) *1991 Census: sex, age and marital status, GB*, OPCS, London.
OPCS Topic Monitor (1993 July) *1991 Census: persons aged 60 and over in GB*, OPCS, London.
OPCS Topic Monitor (1993 December a) *1991 Census: communal establishments GB*, OPCS, London.
OPCS Topic Monitor (1993 December b) *1991 Household Composition GB*, OPCS, London.
Oldman, C. (1990) *Moving in Old Age: new directions in housing policies*, HMSO, London.
Oldman, C. (1991) *Paying for Care: personal sources of funding care*, Joseph Rowntree Foundation, York.
Oppenheim, C. (1993) *Poverty: the facts*, Child Poverty Action Group, London.
Organisation for Economic Co-operation and Development (OECD)(1988) *Ageing Populations: the social policy implications*, OECD, Paris.
OECD (1994) *Caring for Frail Elderly People: new directions in care*, OECD, Paris.

Oriel, W. (1981) 'Ageing as a political force', in Hobman, D. (ed.), *Uniting Generations*, ACE, London, pp. 33–52.

Osborn, A. (1988) *Developing Local Services and Action for Dementia Sufferers and their Carers*, Age Concern Scotland, Edinburgh.

Osborn, A. (1992) *Taking Part in Community Care Planning*, The Nuffield Institute for Health Services Studies, University of Leeds/Age Concern Scotland, Leeds.

Osborne, S. P. (1994) *The Role of Voluntary Organisations in Innovation in Social Welfare Services*, Joseph Rowntree Foundation Findings No. 46, February, York.

Page, D. (1995) 'Social Housing in a Changing World', in Smith, M. (ed.), *Housing Today and Tomorrow*, 2nd Supplement to the Guide to Housing, 3rd edn., Housing Centre Trust, London, pp. 1–14.

Page, D. and Muir, T. (1971) *New Housing for the Elderly*, Bedford Square Press, London.

Pahl, J. (1988) *Day Services for Elderly People in the Medway Health District*, Health Services Research Unit, University of Kent, Canterbury, Kent.

Parker, G. (1992) 'Counting Care: numbers and types of informal carers', in Twigg, J. (ed.), *Carers: research and practice*, HMSO, London, pp. 6–29.

Parker, G. (1994) *Where Next for Research on Carers?*, Nuffield Community Care Studies Unit, University of Leicester, Leicester.

Parker, G. and Lawton, D. (1994) *Different Types of Care, Different Types of Carer*, HMSO, London.

Parker, H. (ed.) (1995) *Modest but Adequate? Modest but adequate budgets for four pensioner households*, The Family Budget Unit/ACE, London.

Parker, R. (1981) 'Tending and Social Policy', in Goldberg, E. and Hatch, S. (eds), *A New Look at the Personal Social Services*, Policy Studies Institute, London, pp. 17–32.

Parker, R. (1990) 'The Role of the Private Sector in the Care of the Elderly', in Morton, J. (ed.), *Packages of Care for Elderly People: how can the private sector contribute?*, ACIOG, London, pp. 3–9.

Parkes, C. (1975) *Bereavement: studies of grief in adult life*, Penguin, London.

Pathy, M. (ed.) (1991) *Principles and Practice of Geriatric Medicine*, John Wiley and Sons, Chichester.

Peace, S. (ed.) (1990) *Researching Social Gerontology*, Sage, London.

Peace, S., Kellaher, L. and Willcocks, D. (1982) *A Balanced Life. A consumer study of residential life in one hundred local authority old people's homes*, Research Report No. 14, Survey Research Unit, School of Applied Social Studies and Sociology, Polytechnic of North London, London.

Peaker, C. (1988) *Who Pays? Who Cares?*, National Council for Voluntary Organisations, London.

Pentiman, I. S. *et al.* (1990) 'Cancer in the Elderly: why so badly treated?' *The Lancet*, April 28, pp. 1020–2.

Pharoah, C. (1995) *Primary Health Care for Elderly People from Black and White Minority Ethnic Communities*, HMSO, London.

Pharoah, T. and Warnes, A. (1992) 'Personal Travel and Transport', in Warnes, A. (ed.), *Homes and Travel: local life in the Third Age*, Carnegie UK Trust, Dunfermline, pp. 52–61.

Phillipson, C. (1982) *Capitalism and the Construction of Old Age*, Macmillan, London.

Phillipson, C. (1993) 'The Sociology of Retirement', in Bond, J. *et al.* (eds), *Ageing in Society*, Sage, London, pp. 180–99.

Phillipson, C., Bernard, M. and Strang, P. (eds) (1986) *Dependency and Interdependency in Old Age: theoretical perspectives and policy alternatives*, Croom Helm, London.

Phillipson, C. and Walker, A. (eds) (1986) *Ageing and Social Policy: a critical assessment*, Gower, Aldershot, Hants.

Pilch, M. (1974) *The Retirement Book*, Hamish Hamilton, London.

Pincus, L. (1974) *Death and the Family*, Faber, London.

Pinker, R. (1971) *Social Theory and Social Policy*, Heinemann, London.

Pinker, R. (1992) 'Making Sense of the Mixed Economy of Welfare', *Social Policy and Administration*, 26, (4), pp. 273–84.

Plank, D. (1977) *Caring for the Elderly. A report of a study of various means of caring for dependent elderly people in eight London boroughs*, Greater London Council Research Memorandum, GLC, London.

Power, M. (1981) *Volunteer Support for Very Elderly People Living in Residential Homes*, Report to Department of Health and Social Security, London.

Power, M. (1986) 'Volunteer Support to Residential Homes', in Judge, K. and Sinclair, I. (eds), *Residential Care for Elderly People*, HMSO, London, pp. 151–8.

Pratt, M. and Norris, J. (1994) *The Social Psychology of Aging*, Blackwell, Oxford.

Prescott-Clarke, C., Clemens, S. and Park, A. (1994) *Routes into Local Authority Housing*, HMSO, London.

Prescott-Clarke, P., Allen, P. and Morrissey, C. (1988) *Queuing for Housing: a study of council housing waiting lists*, HMSO, London.

Pringle, M. (ed.) (1993) *Change and Teamwork in Primary Care*, BMJ, London.

Pritchard, J. (1992) *The Abuse of Elderly People*, Jessica Kingsley, London.

Pruner, M. (1974) *To the Good Long Life*, Universe Books, New York.

Qureshi, H. and Walker, A. (1989) *The Caring Relationship*, Macmillan, London.

Raphael, B. (1984) *The Anatomy of Bereavement*, Hutchinson, London.

Rattee, A. (1977) *A Study on Boarding Out of the Elderly*, Brunel University, Uxbridge, Middlesex.

Rauta, I. (1986) *Who Would Prefer Separate Accommodation?*, HMSO, London.

Redfern, S. (1989) 'Key Issues in Nursing Elderly People', in Warnes, A. (ed.), *Human Ageing and Later Life*, Edward Arnold, London, pp. 146–60.

Research Institute For Consumer Affairs (RICA) (1986) *Dispersed Alarms. A guide for organisations installing systems*, RICA, London.

Retirement Income Inquiry (1996) *Pensions: 2000 and Beyond*, Vol. 1, The Retirement Income Inquiry, London.

Riggs, L. and Melton, L. (1988) 'Osteoporosis and Age-related Fracture Syndromes', in Evered, D. and Whelan, J. (eds), *Research and the Ageing Population*, Wiley, Chichester, pp. 129–42.

Riseborough, M. (ed.) (1995) *Opening up the Resources of Sheltered Housing to the Wider Community*, Anchor Housing Association, Oxford.

Riseborough, M. (1996a) *Listening to and Involving Older Tenants: Part One*, Anchor Trust, Oxford.

Riseborough, M. (1996b) *Listening to and Involving Older Tenants: Part Two*, Anchor Trust, Oxford.

Riseborough, M. and Niner, P. (1994) *I Didn't Know You Cared!*, Anchor Housing Trust, Oxford.

Robb, B. (1967) *Sans Everything*, Nelson, London.

Robbins, D. (ed.) (1993) *Community Care: findings from DoH funded research 1988–92*, HMSO, London.

Roberts, N. (1970) *Our Future Selves: care of the elderly*, Allen and Unwin, London.

Robins, A. and Wittenberg, R. (1992) 'The Health of Elderly People: economic aspects', in DoH, Central Health Monitoring Unit, *The Health of Elderly People: an epidemiological review*, Companion Papers, HMSO, London, pp. 10–19.

Rolfe, S., Mackintosh, S. and Leather, P. (1993) *Age File '93*, Anchor Housing Trust, Oxford.

Rolfe, S., Mackintosh, S. and Leather, P. (1995) *Retirement Housing: ownership and independence*, Anchor Housing Association, Oxford.

Roose, T. (1994) *Maximising the Use of Sheltered Housing: discussion document*, NFHA, London.

Rowlings, C. (1981) *Social Work with Elderly People*, Allen and Unwin, London.

Rowntree, B. Seebohm (1947) *Old People. Report of a survey committee on the problems of ageing and the care of old people*, The Nuffield Foundation, Oxford University Press, Oxford.

Royal College of Nursing (1992) *A Scandal Waiting to Happen?*, Royal College of Nursing, London.

Royal College of Physicians (1991) *Preventive Medicine*, Royal College of Physicians, London.

Royal College of Physicians (1992) *High Quality Long-Term Care for Elderly People: guidelines and audit measures*, Royal College of Physicians, London.

Royal College of Physicians (1994) *Ensuring Equity and Quality of Care for Elderly People*, Royal College of Physicians, London.

Royal College of Physicians (1995) *Incontinence: causes, management and provision of services*, Royal College of Physicians, London.

Royal College of Physicians and Royal College of Psychiatrists (Joint Report) (1989) *Care of Elderly People with Mental Illness: specialist services and medical training*, Royal College of Physicians and Royal College of Psychiatrists, London.

Royal Commission on The National Health Service (1979) *Report* (The Merrison Committee), HMSO, London.

Royal Pharmaceutical Society (1992) *Pharmaceutical Care: the future for community pharmacy*, Royal Pharmaceutical Society, London.

Russell, L., Scott, D. and Wilding, P. (1996) 'The Funding of Voluntary Action – the contribution of local studies', in Charities Aid Foundation, *Dimensions of the Voluntary Sector*, CAF, London, pp. 150–2.

Sainsbury, R. (1996) 'Rooting out Fraud – innocent until proven fraudulent', *Poverty*, 93, pp. 17–20.

Salvage, A. (1993) *Cold Comfort*, ACE, London.

Salvage, A. (1995) *Who Will Care? Future prospects for family care of older people in the European Union*, European Foundation for the

Improvement of Living and Working Conditions, Dublin.

Samuels, A. (1993) 'Grandparents and the Grandchild: the legal position', *Eagle*, Oct/Nov., pp. 14–16.

Saunders, C. (1978) *The Management of Terminal Disease*, Edward Arnold, London.

Schuller, T. and Bostyn, A. M. (1992) *Learning: education, training and information in the Third Age*, The Carnegie UK Trust, Dunfermline, Scotland.

Scrutton, S. (1989) *Counselling Older People – a creative response to ageing*, Edward Arnold, London.

Scrutton, S. (1995) *Bereavement and Grief – supporting older people through loss*, Edward Arnold, London.

Seale, C. (1989) 'What Happens in Hospices: a review of research evidence', *Social Science and Medicine*, 28, pp. 551–9.

Seale, C. and Cartwright, A. (1994) *The Year Before Death*, Avebury, Aldershot, Hants.

Secretaries of State for the Environment and Wales (1995a) *Our Future Homes: opportunity, choice, responsibility*, HMSO, London.

Secretaries of State for the Environment and Wales (1995b) *More Choice in the Social Rented Sector*, HMSO, London.

Secretaries of State for the Environment, Scotland and Wales (1986) *The Local Government Councillor* (The Widdicombe Committee), HMSO, London.

Secretary of State for Health (1991) *The Health of the Nation: a consultative document for health in England*, HMSO, London.

Secretaries of State for Health for Wales, Northern Ireland and Scotland (1989a) *Working for Patients*, HMSO, London.

Secretaries of State for Health, Social Security for Wales and Scotland (1989b) *Caring for People: community care in the next decade and beyond*, HMSO, London.

Secretaries of State for Social Services for Wales, Northern Ireland and Scotland (1986) *Primary Health Care: an agenda for discussion*, HMSO, London.

Secretaries of State for Social Services for Wales, Northern Ireland and Scotland (1987) *Promoting Better Health: the government's programme for improving primary health care*, HMSO, London.

Secretary of State for Social Security (1996) *The Government's Expenditure Plans 1996–97 to 1998–99*, HMSO, London.

Secretary of State for Social Services (1985a) *Reform of Social Security* Vol. 1, HMSO, London.

Secretary of State for Social Services (1985b) *Reform of Social Security: programme for action*, HMSO, London.

Shanas, E., Townsend, P., Wedderburn, D., Henning, F., Milhof, P. and Stehouwer, J. (1968) *Old People in Three Industrial Societies*, Routledge and Kegan Paul, London.

Sheldon, J. (1948) *The Social Medicine of Old Age*, Nuffield Foundation, London.

Shenfield, B. (1957) *Social Policies for Old Age*, Routledge and Kegan Paul, London.

Shenfield, B. with Allen, I. (1972) *The Organisation of Voluntary Services*, Political and Economic Planning, London.

Simmons, L. (1962) 'Ageing in Primitive Society', *Law and Contemporary Problems*, Winter, p. 42.

Sinclair, I. (1988) 'The Client Reviews: elderly', in Wagner Report *Residential Care: the research reviewed*, HMSO, London, pp. 241–92.

Sinclair, I., Crosbie, D., O'Connor, P., Stanforth, L. and Vickery, A. (1989) *Bridging Two Worlds: social work and the elderly living alone*, Avebury, Aldershot, Hants.

Sinclair, I., Parker, R., Leat, D. and Williams, J. (1990) *The Kaleidoscope of Care: a review of research on welfare provision for elderly people*, National Institute for Social Work, HMSO, London.

Sinclair, I. and Williams, J. (1990) 'Elderly People: coping and quality of life', in Sinclair, I. *et al.* (eds), *The Kaleidoscope of Care*, NISW, HMSO, London, pp. 67–86.

Sixsmith, A. (1990) *The Meaning and Experience of 'Home' in Later Life*, in Bytheway, W. and Johnson, J. (eds), *Welfare and the Ageing Experience*, Avebury, Aldershot, pp. 172–92.

Smale, G. and Tuson, G. with Biehal, N. and Marsh, P. (1993) *Empowerment, Assessment, Case Management and the Skilled Worker*, HMSO, London.

Smeaton, D. and Hancock, R. (1995) *Pensioners' Expenditure: an assessment of changes in living standards, 1979–1991*, ACIOG, London.

Smith, K. (1986) *I'm Not Complaining*, Kensington and Chelsea Staying Put for the Elderly Ltd in association with Shelter Housing Advice Centre, London.

Social And Community Planning Research (1990) *On Volunteering: a qualitative research study of images, motivations and experiences*, The Volunteer Centre, UK, London.

Social Security Advisory Committee (1982) *First Report 1981*, HMSO, London.

Social Security Advisory Committee (1988) *Sixth Report 1988*, HMSO, London.

Social Security Consortium (1986) *Of Little Benefit: a critical guide to the Social Security Act 1986*, Social Security Consortium, HMSO, London.

Spencer, J. and Edwards, C. (1992) 'Pharmacy Beyond the Dispensary: general practitioners' views', *BMJ*, 304, pp. 1670–2.

Squires, A. and Livesley, B. (1993) 'The Future of Physiotherapy with Older People: demographic, epidemiological and political influences', *Physiotherapy*, 79 (12), pp. 850–7.

Squires, A. (ed.) (1991) *Multicultural Health Care and Rehabilitation of Older People*, Edward Arnold, London.

Stacey, M. (1969) *Comparability in Social Research*, Heinemann, London.

Standing Conference Of Ethnic Minority Senior Citizens (1986) *Ethnic Minority Senior Citizens – The question of policy*, Standing Conference of Ethnic Minority Citizens, London.

Statham, R., Korczak, J. and Monaghan, P. (1988) *House Adaptations for People with Physical Disabilities: A guidance manual for practitioners*, HMSO, London.

Stevenson, O. and Parsloe, P. (eds) (1978) *Social Service Teams: the practitioner's view*, HMSO, London.

Stevenson, O. and Parsloe, P. (1993) *Community Care and Empowerment*, Joseph Rowntree Foundation, York.

Stewart, E. and Askham, J. (1995) *Breaking the Silence*, ACE, London.

Stewart, M. (1974) *Social Rehabilitation of the Elderly*, ACE, London.

Stilwell, B. (1986) 'Nurses as Co-practitioners: threat or promise?' *The Practitioner*, 230, pp. 501–2.

Stokes, G. (1992) *On Being Old: the psychology of later life*, The Palmer Press, London.

Stott, M. (1981) *Ageing for Beginners*, Blackwell, Oxford.

Straka, G. (1990) 'Training Older Workers for and in the Years after 2000', *Journal of Educational Gerontology*, 5(2), pp. 68–78.

Stuart-Hamilton, I. (1991) *The Psychology of Ageing: an introduction*, Jessica Kingsley, London.

Sundström, G. (1994) 'Care by Families: an overview of trends', in OECD *Caring for Frail Elderly People*, OECD, Paris, pp. 15–56.

Swain, J., Finkelstein, V., French, S. and Oliver, M. (eds) (1993) *Disabling Barriers: enabling environments*, Sage, London.

Swift, C. (1996) 'Iatrogenesis', in Ebrahim, S. and Kalache, A. (eds), *Epidemiology in Old Age*, BMJ, London, pp. 398–407.

Tait, E. (1983) *Report of the Findings of a Questionnaire Conducted among Local Authorities in England of Adult Boarding Out Schemes*, London Borough of Brent, London.

Taylor, H. (1983) *The Hospice Movement in Britain: its role and its future*, CPA, London.

Taylor, J. and Taylor, D. (1989) *Mental Health in the 1990s: from custody to care?*, Office of Health Economics, London.

Taylor, P. and Walker, A. (1995) 'Utilising Older Workers', *Employment Gazette*, April, pp. 141–5.

Taylor, R., Ford, G. and Barber, H. (1983) *The Elderly at Risk*, ACE, London.

Taylor-Gooby, P. (1995) 'Comfortable, Marginal and Excluded', in Jowell, R., Curtice, J., Park, A., Brook, L. and Ahrendt, D. (eds) *British Social Attitudes – the twelfth report*, Dartmouth Publishing Co., Aldershot, Hants, pp. 1–17.

Tester, S. (1989) *Caring By Day: a study of day care services for older people*, CPA, London.

Tester, S. (1992) *Common Knowledge: a co-ordinated approach to information-giving*, CPA, London.

Tester, S. and Meredith, B. (1987) *Ill-informed? A study of information and support for elderly people in the inner city*, Policy Studies Institute, London.

Thane, P. (1982) *The Foundations of the Welfare State*, Longman, London.

Thienhaus, O., Conter, E. and Bossman, B. (1986) 'Sexuality and Ageing', *Ageing and Society*, 6(1), pp. 39–54.

Thomas, A. (1981) *Agency Services: their role in house improvement*, Centre for Urban and Regional Studies, University of Birmingham, Birmingham.

Thompson, P., Itzin, C. and Abendstern, M. (1990) *I Don't Feel Old: the experience of later life*, Oxford University Press, Oxford.

Thornton, P. (1989) *Creating a Break*, ACE, London.

Thornton, P. and Moore, J. (1980) *The Placement of Elderly People in Private Households*, Department of Social Policy Research Monograph, University of Leeds, Leeds.

Thornton, P. with Mountain, G. (1992) *A Positive Response: developing community alarm services for older people*, Joseph Rowntree Foundation, York.

Thornton, P. and Tozer, R. (1994) *Involving Older People in Planning and Evaluating Community Care: a review of initiatives*, Social Policy Research Unit, University of York, York.

Thorpe, G. (1993) 'Enabling more Dying People to Remain at Home', *British Medical Journal*, 307, pp. 915–8.

Tierney, A. and Worth, A. (1995) 'Review: readmission of elderly patients to hospital', *Age and Ageing*, 24, pp. 163–6.

Tillsley, C. (1995) 'Older Workers: findings from the 1994 Labour Force Survey', *Employment Gazette*, April, pp. 133–40.

Tinker, A. (1976) *Housing the Elderly: how successful are granny annexes?*, Department of the Environment, Housing Development Directorate 1976 (reprinted HMSO, 1980), London.

Tinker, A. (1980a) *The Elderly in Modern Society*, Longman, London.

Tinker, A. (1980b) *Housing the Elderly near Relatives: moving and other options*, HMSO, London.

Tinker, A. (1983) 'Improving the Quality of Life and Promoting Independence of Elderly People', in DHSS, *Elderly People in the Community: their service needs*, HMSO, London, pp. 47–68.

Tinker, A. (1984) *Staying at Home: helping elderly people*, HMSO, London.

Tinker, A. (1989a) *The Telecommunications Needs of Disabled and Elderly People*, Office of Telecommunications, London.

Tinker, A. (1989b) *An Evaluation of Very Sheltered Housing*, HMSO, London.

Tinker, A. (1990) *Why the Sudden Interest in Ageing?*, Inaugural Lecture, 13.11.89, King's College London.

Tinker, A. (1994) 'The Role of Housing Policies in the Care of Elderly People', in OECD *Caring for Frail Elderly People*, OECD, Paris, pp. 57–82.

Tinker, A. (1995) 'Some Implications for Policy of Likely Demographic Trends and the Provision of Long-term Care', in House of Commons Health Committee, *Long-term Care: future provision and funding*, Minutes of Evidence 7.12.95, pp. 93–102.

Tinker, A. (in press) 'Housing, Environment and Health in Old Age', in Pathy, J. (ed.), *Principles and Practice of Geriatric Medicine*, 3rd edn, John Wiley, Chichester.

Tinker, A. (1997) 'The Development of Service Provision', in Norman, I. and Redfern, S. (eds), *Mental Health Care of Elderly People*, Churchill Livingstone, London, pp. 441–57.

Tinker, A., McCreadie, C., and Hancock, R. (1992) 'The Financial Costs of Caring', in Askham, J., Grundy, E. and Tinker, A. with Hancock, R., McCreadie, C., Whyley, C. and Wright, F. *Caring: the importance of Third Age carers*, Carnegie UK Trust, Dunfermline, pp. 33–94.

Tinker, A., McCreadie, C., and Salvage, A. (1993) *The Information Needs of Elderly People – An exploratory study*, ACIOG, London.

Tinker, A., McCreadie, C., Wright, F. and Salvage, A. (1994) *The Care of Frail Elderly People in the United Kingdom*, HMSO, London.

Tinker, A., Wright, F. and Zeilig, H. (1995) *Difficult to Let Sheltered Housing*, HMSO, London.

Titmuss, R. (1968) *Commitment to Welfare*, Unwin, London.

Titmuss, R. (1970) *The Gift Relationship*, Allen and Unwin, London.

Tobin, G. (1987) 'Incontinence in the Elderly', *The Practitioner*, 231, pp. 843–7.

Tobin, G. (1992) *Incontinence in the Elderly*, Edward Arnold, London.

Tompkins, P. (1989) *Flexibility and Fairness*, Lane, Clark and Peacock, London.

Townsend, P. (1957) *The Family Life of Old People*, Routledge and Kegan Paul, London.

Townsend, P. (1964) *The Last Refuge*, Routledge and Kegan Paul, London.

Townsend, P. (1979) *Poverty in the United Kingdom*, Penguin, London.

Townsend, P. (1981) 'The Structured Dependency of the Elderly: creation of social policy in the twentieth century', *Ageing and Society*, 1(1), pp. 5–28.

Townsend, P. (1986) 'Ageism and Social Policy', in Phillipson, C. and Walker, A. (eds), *Ageing and Social Policy*, Gower, Aldershot, pp. 15–44.

Townsend, P. and Davidson, N. (1982) *Inequalities in Health*, Penguin, London.

Townsend, P. and Wedderburn, D. (1965) *The Aged in the Welfare State*, G. Bell and Sons, London.

Trinder, C., Hulme, G. and McCarthy, U. (1992) *Employment: the role of work in the Third Age*, The Carnegie Inquiry into the Third Age, The Carnegie UK Trust, Dunfermline.

Tunstall, J. (1966) *Old and Alone*, Routledge and Kegan Paul, London.

Twigg, J. (ed.) (1992) *Carers: research and practice,* HMSO, London.

Twigg, J. and Atkin, K. (1994) *Carers Perceived: policy and practice in informal care*, Open University Press, Buckingham.

Twigg, J., Atkin, K. and Perring, C. (1990) *Carers and Services: a review of research*, HMSO, London.

Ungerson, C. (1987) *Policy is Personal: sex, gender and informal care*, Tavistock, London.

Utting, D. (1994) 'Where Should Charity Begin Now?' *Search*, 2, pp. 4–7.

Victor, C. (1987) *Old Age in Modern Society*, Croom Helm, London.

Victor, C. (1990) 'A Survey of the Delayed Discharge of Elderly People from Hospitals in an Inner City Health District', in Bytheway, W. and Johnson, J. (eds), *Welfare and the Ageing Experience*, Avebury, Aldershot, pp. 69–80.

Victor, C. (1991) *Health and Health Care in Later Life*, Open University Press, Buckingham.

Victor, C. (1994) *Old Age in Modern Society*, Chapman and Hall, London.

Vincent, J. (1995) *Inequality and Old Age*, University College London Press, London.

Wade, B., Sawyer, L. and Bell, J. (1983) *Dependency with Dignity: different care provision for the elderly*, Bedford Square Press, London.

Wager, R. (1972) *Care of the Elderly: an exercise in cost benefit analysis*, Institute of Municipal Treasurers and Accountants, London.

Wagner Report (1988a) *Residential Care: a positive choice*, HMSO, London.

Wagner Report (1988b) *Residential Care: the research reviewed*, HMSO, London.

Wagstaff, P. and Coakley, D. (1988) *Physiotherapy and the Elderly Patient*, Croom Helm, London.

Walker, A. (1990) 'The Benefits of Old Age?', in McEwen, E. (ed.), *Age: the unrecognised discrimination*, ACE, London, pp. 58–70.

Walker, A. (1992) 'Pensions and the Living Standards of Pensioners in the EC', in ACE, *The Coming of Age in Europe*, ACE, London, pp. 161–80.

Walker, A. (1993) *Age and Attitudes: main results from a Eurobarometer survey*, Commission of the European Communities, Brussels.

Walker, A. (1994) *Half a Century of Promises*, Counsel and Care, London.

Walker, A. (ed.) (1996) *The New Generational Contract*, University College London Press, London.

Walker, K. (1952) *Commentary on Age*, Jonathan Cape, London.

Warburton, R.W. (1994) *Home and Away: a review of recent evidence to explain why some elderly people enter residential care homes while others stay at home*, DoH, London.

Warner, N. (1994) *Community Care: just a fairy tale?*, The Carers National Association, London.

Warnes, A. (ed.) (1982) *Geographical Perspectives on the Elderly*, Wiley and Sons Ltd, Chichester.

Warnes, A. (1987) 'Geographical Locations and Social Relationships among the Elderly', in Pacione, M. (ed.), *Social Geography: progress and prospect*, Croom Helm, London, pp. 253–93.

Warnes, A. (ed.) (1989) *Human Ageing and Later Life*, Edward Arnold, London.

Warnes, A. (1990) 'Geographical Questions in Gerontology: needed directions for research', *Progress in Human Geography* 14(1), pp. 24–56.

Warnes, A. and Ford, R. (1995) 'Migration and Family Care', in Allen, I. and Perkins, E. (eds) *The Future of Family Care for Older People*, HMSO, London, pp. 65–92.

Weale, R. (1989) 'Eyes and Age', in Warnes, A. (ed.), *Human Ageing and Later Life*, Edward Arnold, London, pp. 38–46.

Webb, A. and Wistow, G. (1987) *Social Work, Social Care and Social Planning: the personal social services since Seebohm*, Longman, London.

Wenger, C. (1984) *The Supportive Network: coping with old age*, Allen and Unwin, London.

Wenger, C. (1990) 'Elderly Carers: the need for appropriate intervention', *Ageing and Society*, 10(2), pp. 197–220.

Wenger, C. (1992) *Help in Old Age – Facing up to change*, Liverpool University Press, Liverpool.

Wertheimer, A. (1993) *Speaking Out: citizen advocacy and older people*, CPA, London.

West, S. (1994) *The Pensions Debate*, ACE, London.

Westland, P. (1986) 'Joint Planning – the last chance?', in Chant, J. (ed.), *Health and Social Services: collaboration or conflict?*, Policy Studies Institute, London, pp. 63–9.

Weston, T. and Ashworth, P. (1963) *Old People in Britain*, Bow Group, London.

Wheeler, R. (1985) *Don't Move: we've got you covered*, Institute of Housing, London.

Whiteford, P. and Kennedy, S. (1995) *Incomes and Living Standards of Older People*, SPRU, York.

Whitehead, C. (1989) *Housing Finance in the UK in the 1980s*, Suntory-Toyota International Centre for Economics and Related Disciplines, London School of Economics, London.

Whitting, G., Moore, J. and Tilson, B. (1995) 'Employment Policies and Practices Towards Older Workers: an international overview', *Employment Gazette*, April, pp. 147–52.

Wicks, M. (1978) *Old and Cold*, Heinemann, London.

Wilcox, S. (1995) *Housing Finance Review 1995/96*, Joseph Rowntree Foundation, York.

Wilding, P. (1982) *Professional Power and Social Welfare*, Routledge and Kegan Paul, London.

Wilkin, D. and Thompson, C. (1989) *Users Guide to Dependency Measures for Elderly People*, Joint Unit for Social Services Research, University of Sheffield, Sheffield.

Willcocks, D., Peace, S. and Kellaher, L. (1986) *Private Lives in Public Places*, Tavistock, London.

Williams, E. I. and Wallace, P. (1993) *Health Checks for People Aged 75 and Over*, The Royal College of General Practitioners, London.

Williams, F. (1989) *Social Policy: a critical introduction*, Blackwell, Oxford.

Williams, G. (1990) *The Experience of Housing in Retirement*, Gower, Aldershot, Hants.

Williams, J. (1990) 'Elders from black and ethnic minority communities', in Sinclair *et al.* (eds), *The Kaleidoscope of Care*, NISW, HMSO, London, pp. 107–36.

Willmott, P. (1963) *The Evolution of a Community*, Routledge and Kegan Paul, London.

Willmott, P. (1986) *Social Networks, Informal Care and Public Policy*, Policy Studies Institute, London.

Willmott, P. and Young, M. (1960) *Family and Class in a London Suburb*, Routledge and Kegan Paul, London.

Wilson, D., Aspinall, P. and Murie, A. (1995) *Factors Influencing Housing Satisfaction Among Older People*, Centre for Urban and Regional Studies, University of Birmingham, Birmingham.

Winner, M. (1992) *Quality Work with Older People: developing models of good practice*, Central Council for Education and Training in Social Work, London.

Wirz, H. (1982) *Sheltered Housing in Scotland – A research report*, Scottish Office, Edinburgh.

Wistow, G. and Hardy, B. (1994) 'Community Care Planning: learning from experience', in McCreadie (ed.), *Planning and Updating Community Care Plans*, ACIOG, London, pp. 41–9.

Wistow, G., Knapp, M., Hardy, B., Forder, J., Manning, R. and Kendall, J. (1994) *Social Care Markets: progress and markets executive summary*, DoH, London.

Wolfenden, L. (1978) *The Future of Voluntary Organisations* (The Wolfenden Committee), Croom Helm, London.

Wright, F. (1992) *Fee Shortfalls in Residential and Nursing Homes: the impact on the voluntary sector*, ACIOG, London.

Wright, F. (1994) *Accident Prevention and Risk-taking by Elderly People: the need for advice*, ACIOG, London.

Wright, F. (1996) *Opening Doors: a case study of multi-purpose residential homes*, HMSO, London.

Wright, F. and Randall, F. (1970) *Basic Sociology*, Macdonald and Evans, Plymouth.

Wright, K. (1982) 'The Economics of Community Care', in Walker, A. (ed.), *Community Care: the family, the state and social policy*, Blackwell, Oxford, pp. 161–78.

Wright, K., Cairns, J. and Snell, M. (1981) *Costing Care*, Joint Unit for Social Services Research, University of Sheffield, Sheffield.

Youll, P. and McCourt-Perring, C. (1993) *Raising Voices: ensuring quality in residential care*, HMSO, London.

Young, K. and Rao, N. (1994) *Coming to Terms with Change? The local government councillor in 1993*, LGC Communications, London.

Young, M. and Willmott, P. (1957) *Family and Kinship in East London*, Penguin, London.

Young, P. (1988) *The Provision of Care in Supported Lodgings and Unregistered Homes*, HMSO, London.

Zarb, G. and Oliver, M. (1993) *Ageing with a Disability*, University of Greenwich, London.

INDEX

Abbeyfield Society, 127
Abel-Smith, B., 87
Abel-Smith, B. and Townsend, P.,
    47, 51, 52
Abrams, M., 7, 9, 21–2, 201, 229,
    232, 259, 261, doc 1
Abrams, M. and O'Brien, J., 237
Abrams, P. *et al.*, 222
abuse, 61, *see also* elder abuse
accidents, 76–7, 83, 93, 109, 165
Achenbaum, W. A., 24
Action on Elder Abuse, 188
acute sickness, 73
activity theory, 227–8
adaptations, *see* housing;
    adaptations
advocacy, 212, 217, 238, 243
Agate, J. and Meacher, M., 26
Age Concern England (ACE) 25–8,
    33, 66, 126, 135, 167, 170–1,
    191, 208–9, 211, 214, 226–7,
    236, 246, 253, 257
    publications, 25, 27–8, 53, 66,
    126, 165, 167, 170–1, 173, 191
Age Concern Institute of
    Gerontology, King's College
    London, 24, 27, 212, 264
Age Concern – local organisations,
    38, 211, 253
ageing, 3–4, 8–10, 22–7, 32, 65,
    121, 128, 138, 238, 256–7, doc
    5
    images of, perceptions, 9–10, 65,
    70, 256, 262, doc 2
    inquiry on, 227–8, 260
    medical and psychological
    aspects, 20, 23, 65
ageism, age barriers, 9, 218
Ahmad-Aziz, A. *et al.*, 153
Aiken, L., 24
AIMS (Advice, Information and
    Mediation Service for

Retirement Housing), 126
Alcock, P., 52
Allen, D., 86
Allen, I., 110, 163, 174
Allen, I. *et al.*, 145–6, 160, 168,
    205, 221–2, 245
Allsop, J., 23, 69, 91, 93
almshouses, 33, 38, 208
Alzheimer's disease, *see also*
    dementia, 149, 178
amenities – housing, 115–6
American Association of Retired
    Persons (AARP), 238
Anchor Housing Association, 123,
    125, 134
Anderson, W. F. and Judge, T., 23
Andrews, G., 94
anthropology, 25
Appleton, N., 134
Arber, S. and Evandrou, M., 24
Arber, S. and Ginn, J., 25, 197, 234,
    261
Arber, S. *et al.*, 203
Arblaster, L. *et al.*, 137
Arie, T., 23, 182
Armstrong, J. *et al.*, 230
Ashton, G., 263
Askham, J., 196, 203
Askham, J. and Thompson, C., 182,
    184, 205
Askham, J., Hancock, R. and Hills,
    J., 53–4, 56, 60
Askham, J., Henshaw, L. and
    Tarpey, M., 25, 192
Askham, J. *et al.*, 71, 76
Association for Continence Advice,
    79
Association of Retirement Housing
    Managers (ARHM), 126
Atkin, K., 203, 234
Atkinson, A. B., 53, 55
Attenburrow, J., 122